Windows on the World Economy

AN INTRODUCTION TO INTERNATIONAL ECONOMICS

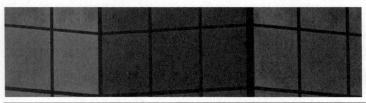

Kenneth A. Reinert
School of Public Policy
George Mason University

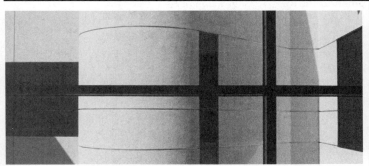

THOMSON
™
SOUTH-WESTERN

Australia · Canada · Mexico · Singapore · Spain · United Kingdom · United States

Windows on the World Economy:
An Introduction to International Economics
Kenneth A Reinert

VP/Editorial Director:
Jack W. Calhoun

VP/Editor-in-Chief:
Michael P. Roche

Publisher:
Michael B. Mercier

Acquisitions Editor:
Michael W. Worls

Developmental Editor:
Andrew McGuire

Executive Marketing Manager:
Janet Hennies

Production Editor:
Starratt E. Alexander

Manufacturing Coordinator:
Sandee Milewski

Media Developmental Editor:
Peggy Buskey

Media Production Editor:
Pam Wallace

Production House:
Rebecca Gray Design

Cover and Internal Designer:
Justin Klefeker

Cover Images:
© Corbis and © Digital Stock

Printer:
Phoenix Color
Book Technology Park

ISBN: 0-030-31399-6
Book only: 0-324-29018-7

Library of Congress Control
Number: 2003114662

For permission to use material from
this text or product, contact us by
Tel (800) 730-2214
Fax (800) 730-2215
http://www.thomsonrights.com

For more information
contact South-Western,
5191 Natorp Boulevard,
Mason, Ohio, 45040.
Or you can visit our Internet site at:
http://www.swlearning.com

To Gelaye and Oda Telila

About the Author

Ken Reinert is an Associate Professor in the School of Public Policy at George Mason University, where he won the Distinguished Teaching Award in 2003. He is also a Research Fellow with the Rural Development Research Consortium at the University of California, Berkeley. He held previous positions at Kalamazoo College and the U.S. International Trade Commission. He has published widely in the areas of trade policy and development policy and co-edited *Applied Methods for Trade Policy Analysis: A Handbook*, published by Cambridge University Press. With undergraduate and graduate degrees in Geography, Prof. Reinert later completed a Ph.D. in Economics in order to better understand aspects of the world economy that were beyond the realm of Geography. He has written this book to help other students and professionals make similar transitions in their own understanding.

Brief Contents

Contents

Preface to the Student or Professional

This book grew out of a realization I had a number of years ago. Many of my students had a keen interest in the world economy that grew out of their language classes, study abroad, business classes, or international studies classes. However, this interest in the world economy was not always accompanied by an interest in economics *per se*. At first, this was something of a rude shock for me. Over time, however, I wondered if it might be possible to explain the basics of the world economy to students and professionals with only an introductory background in economics. From there, I wondered if it might even be possible to do this for students who have taken only introductory microeconomics. This was the challenge I set for myself, and this book is my attempt to meet this challenge. I hope that I have been at least partly successful.

I imagine that you are a student majoring in business, languages, the social sciences, or public policy who desires to broaden your understanding of the world economy. Or perhaps you are a professional working in the business or public policy realm, and you need to increase your understanding of the global economic environment in which you work. This book has been written for you. It will introduce you to the basic concepts of international trade, international production, international finance, and international development that are essential for operating in the modern, global economy. I have chosen the concepts covered in the book not just based on my experience as an economics professor. My choice of concepts also reflects my experience as a professional international economist working outside of academia and as a consultant to international economic organizations. I hope you can trust that the concepts covered in this book are the very ones you need to be exposed to.

So how will we proceed? In Chapter 1, I will introduce you to some broad trends of the world economy. Here, we will try to give some content to the loosely-defined notion of "globalization." In doing so, you will be introduced to the four "windows on the world economy" that will structure the remainder of the book. These are international trade, international production, international finance, and international development.

In Part 1, you will be introduced to the first window on the world economy, *international trade*. You will learn about the theory of international trade, trade policy analysis, and the institutional features of international trade. You will understand how trade arises, why there are potential gains from trade, why some groups oppose increased trade, the effects of government interventions in "free" trade, how the World Trade Organization functions, and the role of regional trade agreements in the world trading system.

As many business students know, international trade is only one possible mode of foreign market entry. A major alternative to trade is foreign investment or *international production*. This is the subject we take up in Part 2. Here, you will learn about the foreign market entry process, theories of international competitiveness, and contemporary thinking on international management. Much of Part 2 is absent from other texts on international economics. Having read and thought about this material, however, I think you will agree that it is important.

As the recent crises in Asia, Russia, Brazil, and Argentina testify, we ignore international financial realities at our peril. Consequently, we turn to a serious consideration of *international finance* in Part 3. You will first learn about macroeconomic accounting relationships and the balance of payments. Then you will be introduced to basic exchange rate definitions, flexible and fixed exchange rate regimes, the International Monetary Fund, financial crises, and monetary unions such as the European Monetary Union. My hope is that you finish this section of the book with a respect for the power of international finance and a critical understanding of the imperfections of existing international financial arrangements.

The final section of the book, Part 4, addresses the field of *international development*. Our task here will be to understand some of the ways that the previous parts of the book have special relevance to the developing countries of the world. As we will see, there are some extraordinary disparities in levels of per capita income and other measures of economic development among the countries of the world economy. Understanding how international trade, international production, and international finance can influence these disparities is one of the most important tasks of international economics. We will begin this section of the book by introducing you to alternative conceptions and measures of economic development. You will then learn about the relationships among growth, trade, and development. Finally, you will become familiar with the World Bank and the controversial subject of structural adjustment.

As with any field, international economics has its own vocabulary. To help you absorb this new vocabulary, I have included a glossary at the end of the book. Please do not forget to use it! It will help you progress with more ease through the material. As a new term is introduced, it will be in boldface, and the glossary definition will be nearby in the margin. This means that its definition can always be found in the glossary. For curious and investigative readers, I have also included suggestions for further readings and have listed Web-based resources at the end of each chapter.

Finally, this book has its own Web site. You can access it at **http://reinert. swlearning.com**. Check here for updates on various time-sensitive issues raised in the text.

Preface to the Instructor

Many students and professionals have developed a keen interest in the world economy that is not always accompanied by an interest in economics *per se*. This book is written for such a person. *Windows on the World Economy* will introduce the student or professional reader to the basic concepts of international trade, international production, international finance, and international development. However, its only prerequisite is an introductory-level understanding of microeconomics. The book draws upon principles-level concepts such as the circular flow diagram, the supply and demand model, the production possibilities frontier, and the value chain, each of which is developed using real-world examples. These basic concepts should be familiar to nearly all readers.

Windows on the World Economy is designed primarily for a one-semester, introductory course in international economics. Despite this narrow scope, the book is broad enough to satisfy the interests of a range of academic programs, including economics, business, international studies, public policy, and development studies. Also, despite its introductory-level nature, *Windows on the World Economy* covers some often-neglected, but important topics in international economics. These include intra-industry trade, intra-firm trade, foreign market entry, competitive advantage, and structural adjustment. The book also covers the major institutions of the world economy in an historical perspective. These include the World Trade Organization, the International Monetary Fund, and the World Bank, each of which is of some interest to almost all students.

Coverage

Chapter 1 introduces the student to some basic characteristics of the modern, world economy, providing some much-needed content to students' concerns with "globalization." It sets up the framework of the four "windows on the world economy," namely, trade, production, finance, and development. Its conversational tone should put the student at ease.

Part 1 takes up the field of *international trade*. Chapter 2 starts on familiar ground, utilizing the supply and demand framework to analyze absolute advantage, and an appendix reviews the concepts of consumer and producer surplus. Chapter 3 utilizes the production possibilities frontier to analyze comparative advantage, and an appendix is included for students who have forgotten the PPF diagram. Chapter 4 is devoted to intra-industry trade, with an appendix on the Grubel-Lloyd index for more advanced students. The politics of trade (including the Stolper-Samuelson theorem) are discussed in Chapter 5, and this leads into an analysis of trade policies in Chapter 6. The latter chapter contains an analysis of a tariff rate quota in an appendix for more advanced students. Chapter 7 covers

the basic institutional detail of the WTO. Finally, Chapter 8 addresses regional trade agreements and includes the EU, NAFTA, Mercosur, and the FTAA as examples. Here, the instructor might want to include an additional RTA in class lecture, based on his or her own regional interests and expertise.

Part 2 addresses *international production* and will be of special interest to business students. As many business students know, international trade is only one possible mode of foreign market entry. This market entry concept, the motivation for international production, and the historical rise of multinational enterprises are all addressed in Chapter 9. Chapter 10 introduces the student to value chains, intangible assets, and internalization. The value chain concept is used to motivate the FDI strategy of market entry, as well as the well-known OLI framework. Finally, Chapter 11 takes up the contemporary issues of international competitiveness and management. Here the student will be introduced to the Porter diamond and the related issue of spatial clusters. Bartlett and Ghoshal's framework for international management is then introduced, and cultural aspects of international management are briefly discussed. None of these issues are taken up in standard international economics texts, and I hope their inclusion here will be helpful to instructors in business programs.

Part 3 takes up the field of *international finance*. I first introduce the student to macroeconomic and balance of payments accounts in Chapter 12, using the circular flow diagram as a point of departure. For the advanced student, the appendices to this chapter covers the subject of accounting matrices as well as a simple, open-economy macroeconomic model. Chapter 13 introduces the student to both the nominal and real exchange rate, as well as the purchasing power parity approach to long-run exchange rate determination and forward markets. Chapters 14 and 15 develop a model of exchange rates in the context of flexible and fixed regimes, respectively. The primary model is a simple version of the assets approach to exchange rate determination, developed in terms of basic macroeconomics aggregates. Monetary policies are discussed in the appendices to each chapter and can be used if the students are capable of understanding this material. Chapter 15 also introduces the student to the "policy trilemma" idea.

Chapters 16, 17, and 18 cover the International Monetary Fund, recent financial crises, and monetary unions, respectively. These three chapters will give the student a basic understanding of the history and institutional structure of international finance. Given the very rapid pace of financial events, some of this material will date quickly. For this reason, the instructor will need to be prepared to comment on more recent developments. Additionally, some topics will be updated quarterly on the book's Web site.

The final section of the book, Part 4, addresses the field of *international development*. This will be of particular interest to programs in development and regional studies, although not exclusively. Chapter 19 introduces the student to both the per capita income and human development approaches to economic development, highlighting their strengths and weaknesses. Chapter 20 takes up the issue of growth theory, both in its "old" and "new" variants. The latter, endogenous growth theory, is linked to human development, and then to issues of trade, education, health, and population. The presentation of growth theory is almost entirely graphical, with a few algebraic manipulations presented in the appendix.

Issues surrounding the hosting of multinational enterprises are presented in Chapter 21, which adopts a broad, benefits, and costs approach. Alternative policy stances, the promotion of backward linkages to domestic suppliers, transfer pricing, and institutional considerations (e.g., the Multilateral Agreement on Investment) are all covered here. Chapters 22 and 23 take up the World Bank and structural adjustment, respectively. The World Bank is described historically, in all of its lending phases. Structural adjustment is carefully analyzed using the production possibilities frontier and the notions of internal and external balance. Structuralist views, as well as the order of economic liberalization are both explained in some detail. Very few of these issues are taken up in standard international economics texts, and I hope their inclusion here will be helpful to instructors in development studies programs.

Finally, I have included an epilogue on "connecting windows." This attempts to integrate lessons learned throughout the text and to raise a preliminary set of future challenges for the world economy. These are meant to be suggestive rather than conclusive and to be used as a point of departure for end-of-semester review.

Text Features

The text employs a number of stylistic components to facilitate the reader's absorption of the material. These are as follows:

Definitions When a new term is introduced, it is presented in boldface. Each term so identified is included in the glossary at the end of the book. In my experience, some students tend to underutilize glossaries. A mid-semester reminder of its existence can be helpful.

Boxes Boxes are used for both key results and for separating some applications and cases from the main text.

Chapter Summaries Each chapter ends with a summary of major concepts and results.

Review Exercises Following chapter summaries, a set of review exercises is available for student use or for classroom discussion.

Further Reading and Web Resources Each chapter also includes a section directing the student to sources for further reading. These have been chosen with the student perspective in mind. Additionally, key Web sites are described. Both of these can be utilized in writing assignments.

Interviews Each of the four parts of the book concludes with an interview with a well-known international economist. These can be used for classroom discussion.

Supplements

The following supplements to the text are meant to assist both you and your students in the teaching/learning process.

Web Site The book is supported by a Web site, the primary purpose is to provide updates to events in a number of areas. These areas are indicated in the text. See **http://reinert.swlearning.com**.

South-Western's Economic Applications (**http://econapps.swlearning.com**)
This site includes dynamic Web features: EconNews Online, EconDebate Online, and EconData Online. Organized by pertinent economic topics, and searchable by topic or feature, these features are easy to integrate into the classroom. EconNews, EconDebate and EconData all deepen your understanding of theoretical concepts through hands-on exploration and analysis for the latest economic news stories, policy debates, and data. These features are updated on a regular basis. The Economic Applications Web site is complimentary to every new book buyer via an access card that's packaged with the books. Used book buyers can purchase access to the site at http://econapps.swlearning.com.

Instructor's Manual and Test Bank To assist you in your teaching, please consult K.A. Reinert and A. Wallace, *Instructor's Manual and Test Bank for Windows on the World Economy: An Introduction to International Economics*, available from your South-Western/Thomson Learning representative. This supplement contains answers to end-of-chapter questions, teaching tips, and test questions.

ExamView – Computerized Testing Software This software contains all of the questions in the printed test bank. This program is an easy-to-use test creation software compatible with Microsoft Windows®. Instructors can add or edit questions, instructions, and answers, and select questions by previewing them on the screen, selecting them randomly, or selecting them by number. Instructors can also create and administer quizzes online, whether over the Internet, a local area network (LAN), or a wide area network (WAN). Contact your South-Western/Thomson Learning sales representative for ordering information.

PowerPoint® Lecture Slides PowerPoint slides are available for use by students as an aid to note-taking, and by instructors for enhancing their lectures. Pamela Hall of Western Washington University has created these slides, and they contain bullet point outlines of the chapters in addition to key graphs and tables from the text.

Suggested Use

The following table shows suggested approaches for using the book.

Suggested Chapter Use by Program

Chapter	Economics	Business	International Studies	Development Studies
1 Windows on the World Economy	X	X	X	X
Part 1 International Trade				
2 Absolute Advantage	X	X	X	X
3 Comparative Advantage	X	X	X	X
4 Intra-Industry Trade	X	X		
5 The Politics of Trade	X	X	X	X
6 Trade Policy Analysis	X	X	X	X
7 The World Trade Organization	X		X	X
8 Regional Trade Agreements	X	X	X	X

Suggested Chapter Use by Program *(continued)*

Chapter	Economics	Business	International Studies	Development Studies
Part 2 International Production				
9 Foreign Market Entry and International Production		X		
10 Foreign Direct Investment and Intra-Firm Trade		X		
11 International Competition and Management		X		
Part 3 International Finance				
12 Accounting Frameworks	X	X	X	X
13 Exchange Rates and Purchasing Power Parity	X	X	X	X
14 Flexible Exchange Rates	X	X	X	X
15 Fixed Exchange Rates	X	X	X	X
16 The International Monetary Fund	X		X	X
17 Crises and Responses	X	X	X	X
18 Monetary Unions	X		X	
Part 4 International Economic Development				
19 Development Concepts	X		X	X
20 Growth, Trade, and Development	X		X	X
21 Hosting Multinational Enterprises		X		X
22 The World Bank			X	X
23 Structural Adjustment				X
Epilogue: Connecting the Windows	X	X	X	X

Acknowledgements

My primary debt incurred while writing this book is to Gelaye Debebe for her unflinching support over many years, even while completing her own Ph.D. dissertation. I also need to thank my students at Kalamazoo College and the School of Public Policy at George Mason University for their patience with many drafts of the book. Andy McGuire and Mike Mercier of South-Western/Thomson Learning provided excellent guidance in the development and revision process. Starratt Alexander of South-Western/Thomson Learning and Rebecca Gray of Rebecca Gray Design skillfully guided me through the production process. Finally, I would like to thank a number of international economists who have influenced my thinking on the subjects covered in this book: Christopher Clague, Alan Deardorff, Joseph Francois, Sanjaya Lall, Michael Lipton, Li-Gang Liu, James Markusen, Keith Maskus, Arvind Panagariya, Chris Rodrigo, David Roland-Holst, and Clinton Shiells.

The following individuals have provided comments on at least some part of the book, and I would like to express my gratitude to each of them.

Sisay Asefa, *Western Michigan University*

Barbara Craig, *Oberlin College*

Gelaye Debebe, *George Washington University*

Desmond Dinan, *School of Public Policy, George Mason University*

Gerald Epstein, *University of Massachusetts*

Diane Flaherty, *University of Massachusetts*

Jon Nadenichek, *California State University, Northridge*

Chris Rodrigo, *School of Public Policy, George Mason University*

Wendy Takacs, *University of Maryland, Baltimore County*

Dominique van der Mensbrugghe, *World Bank*

Tony Wallace, *School of Public Policy, George Mason University*

Kenneth A. Reinert

Windows on the World Economy

In the mid-1990s, I met an anthropology student who had just returned from a year in Senegal. As soon as she learned that I was an international economist, she asked, "Can you tell me about the CFA franc devaluation? Why was it necessary? It has made life very difficult in Senegal." Sometime later, I met a religion student who had just returned from a semester spent in Haiti working in a health clinic. As soon as he learned that I was an international economist, he asked, "Can you tell me about structural adjustment programs? I have some serious concerns about how they are being applied to Haiti."

These are not rare incidents. I receive such questions on a routine basis. Increasingly, it seems, more and more of us need to know something about the world economy—anthropology and religion students, as well as economics and business students. Why is this? Put simply, the world economy has increasingly significant impacts on us. It is becoming very difficult to take shelter in our respective majors and professions without being knowledgeable about the fundamentals of international economics. Increasingly, trade flows, exchange rates, and multinational enterprises matter to us all, even if we would prefer that they did not.

Students also have significant concerns about globalization. Shortly before the Seattle Ministerial Meeting of the World Trade Organization (WTO) in December 1999, I received a phone call from a former student. She was about to travel from Kentucky to Seattle to join in the protests against the WTO. She knew that I had spent a brief amount of time at the WTO, and before she traveled to Seattle, she wanted to raise her concerns with me about globalization and the impact it was having on the rural economy of Kentucky. The Seattle Ministerial was not successful, in part due to the efforts of my former student and her fellow protesters.

Were my student's concerns well placed? Is globalization the evil that some contend it is? Or is it the unmitigated good that others contend it is? Most likely, the actualities of globalization are more variegated than the good/evil dichotomy that is often invoked. Discovering the nuances of globalization is the task we take up in this book. We will try to explore the world economy and globalization in as balanced a manner as possible. This will help us develop informed views and opinions, whatever they might be.

Developing informed views and opinions about globalization and the world economy requires a serious study of international economics. This field of study is typically divided into two parts: international trade and international finance. Indeed, these two parts often constitute the only two courses in a standard "core-course" series. In this book, however, we are going to approach things a bit differently. Acknowledging the diverse interests of readers, as well as the diverse aspects of the world economy, we are going to explore four different *windows* on the modern world economy. These are international trade, international production, international finance, and international development. The following four sections of this chapter will briefly introduce you to each of these realms.

International Trade

International trade
The exchange of merchandise and services among the countries of the world economy.

Our first window on the world economy is **international trade**.[1] International trade refers to the exchange of merchandise *and* services among the countries of the world. In the previous sentence, the "and" is important. It is typically the case that when we picture international trade, we imagine trade in *merchandise*. Perhaps we consider international trade in steel, automobiles, wine, or bananas. However, this view is very incomplete. It is important to acknowledge that a significant portion of world trade is composed of trade in *services*. Financial services, architectural services, and engineering services are all traded internationally. In fact, trade in services is about one-fourth the magnitude of trade in merchandise.[2]

As it turns out, international trade is playing an increasing role in the world economy. Consider the data presented in Figure 1.1. This figure plots two series of data for the years 1980 to 1999. The first series, represented

Figure 1.1 Industrial Production and Exports in the World Economy (1980–100)

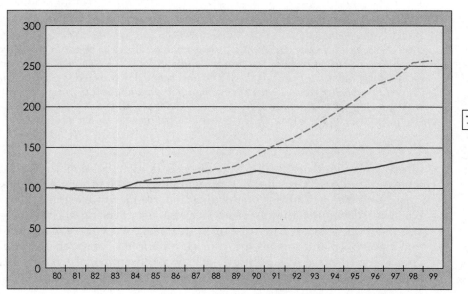

Source: Based on data in *International Financial Statistics Yearbook*, published by the International Monetary Fund in various years.

---

[1] Every time you encounter a term in boldface in this book, you can find its definition in the glossary.
[2] It is sometimes said that "merchandise" refers to things you can drop on your toe. Therefore, "services" refers to things you *cannot* drop on your toe!

by a solid line, is industrial production in industrial countries as reported by the International Monetary Fund. It has been normalized so that the value in 1980 is 100, and the values for each other year are measured relative to 1980. The second series, represented by a dashed line, is real (price-adjusted) world exports calculated from International Monetary Fund data.[3] This series has been normalized in the same way as the production series. Between 1980 and 1983, exports more or less track production, both series dipping downward in the 1982 world recession. From that point on, however, world exports increased faster than world production until 1999. Especially after slowing in the recession of the early 1990s, export growth was particularly strong. Figure 1.1 makes it clear that trade activities tend to increase faster than production activities in the world economy. This is one of the main features of globalization.

You will begin to understand the major factors behind international trade in Part 1 of the book. You will also be introduced to a set of key policy issues surrounding the management of international trade, including issues pertaining to the World Trade Organization and regional trade agreements such as the North American Free Trade Agreement (NAFTA). Part 1 will allow you to understand why the world economy exhibits the trend illustrated in Figure 1.1.

International Production

Our second window on the world economy is **international production**. Production patterns in the modern world economy can be relatively complex. For example, when my son was a toddler, his favorite book was *Bear's Busy Family*, published by Barefoot Books. Barefoot Books is a company run by Tessa Strickland and Nancy Traversy from their homes in the United Kingdom, but it also has an office in New York City. The color separation for *Bear's Busy Family* was done in Italy, and the actual printing took place in Malaysia. So the book my son held with such interest was a result of a production process that took place in (at least) four countries. Production of a product in multiple countries is what we mean by international production.[4]

International production can take place through contracts (international licensing and franchising) such as is used by McDonald's, or it can take place through a process known as **foreign direct investment (FDI)** undertaken by **multinational enterprises (MNEs)**. FDI involves firms based in one country owning at least a controlling interest in firms producing in another country. MNEs are now a major component of the world economy. To see this, consider the following facts:

1. *MNEs account for approximately one-fourth of world* **gross domestic product (GDP)** *or aggregate output.*
2. *The sales of foreign affiliates of MNEs now exceed the volume of world trade.*

International production
A production of a good or service with processes located in more than one country.

Foreign direct investment (FDI)
Occurs when a firm acquires shares in a foreign-based enterprise that exceed a threshold of between 10 to 20 percent, implying managerial control over the foreign enterprise. Contrasts with portfolio investment. FDI may be horizontal, backward vertical, or forward vertical.

Multinational enterprise (MNE)
Also known as the multinational corporation or the transnational corporation. A firm operating production, sales, and service operations in more than one country.

Gross domestic product (GDP)
The value of all final goods and services produced within a country's borders during a year.

---

[3] Note that world imports track world exports very closely, so we can use the level of exports as a proxy for the overall level of world trade.
[4] International production is one part of the production featured in Figure 1.1. The other is domestic production.

3. *MNEs are involved in approximately three-fourths of all world trade.*
4. *Approximately one-third of world trade takes place within MNEs.*
5. *MNEs account for approximately three-fourths of worldwide civilian research and development.*

As these facts indicate, the operation of MNEs is another main feature of globalization. You will gain an understanding of MNEs and their role in international production in Part 2 of the book. This will include an appreciation of the relatively complex decisions facing global firms, and the management issues that arise when firms are spread across international borders. Part 2 will help you understand the processes behind facts 1 through 5.

International Finance

International finance
The exchange of assets among the countries of the world economy.

Assets
Financial objects characterized by a monetary value that can change over time and make up individuals' and firms' wealth portfolios.

Our third window on the world economy is **international finance**. Whereas international trade refers to the exchange of merchandise and services among the countries of the world, international finance refers to the exchange of **assets** among the countries of the world. Assets are financial objects characterized by a monetary value that can change over time. They make up individuals' and firms' wealth portfolios. For example, individuals and firms around the world conduct international transactions in currencies, equities, government bonds, corporate bonds (commercial paper), and even real estate as part of their management of portfolios. The way in which the prices of these assets change in response to these international transactions impacts the countries of the world in important ways. Additionally, as we will see, these transactions can provide a source of savings to countries over and above the domestic savings of their households and firms.

International finance is playing an increasingly important role in the world economy. Consider the perspective of foreign exchange transactions, one type of asset. Foreign exchange transactions are much larger than trade transactions. Figure 1.2 plots two variables for 3-year intervals between 1989 and 2001. The first variable, plotted as the darker vertical bars, is *total annual exports*. Given what we saw in Figure 1.1, it comes as no surprise that these values increased over the 1989 to 2001 time period.[5] The second variable, plotted as the lighter vertical bars, is the *total daily foreign exchange turnover* as measured by the Bank for International Settlements (BIS) in its triennial April survey.[6] The important message of Figure 1.2 is that *daily* turnover in foreign exchange is a significant fraction of *annual* exports. This fraction began at approximately 20 percent in 1989, rose to 27 percent in 1998, and fell back to approximately 20 percent in 2001. This makes it strikingly clear that, on an annual basis, global transactions in foreign exchange dwarf global trade transactions. For example, in 1998, *global foreign exchange transactions were nearly 100 times the value of exports*. In other words, international finance matters.

---

[5] Be careful if you compare the export data in Figures 1.1 and 1.2. The data in Figure 1.1 are price adjusted; those in Figure 1.2 are not.

[6] The Bank of International Settlements defines exchange rate turnover as the gross value of all new deals entered into in the month of the survey.

Figure 1.2 Annual Exports and Daily Foreign Exchange Market Turnover (billions of U.S. dollars)

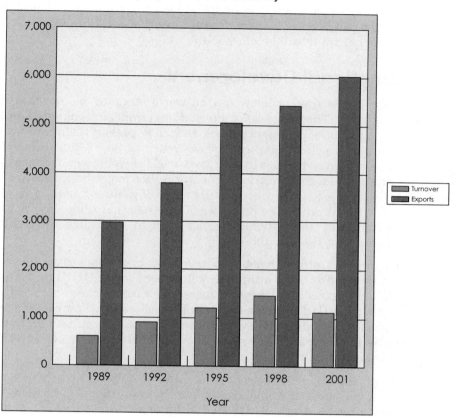

Sources: Based on data in *International Financial Statistics Yearbook*, published by the International Monetary Fund in various years and in the *Triennial Central Bank Survey*, published by the Bank for International Settlements in various years.

The importance of international finance, seen in Figure 1.2, became very evident in the latter part of the 1990s. Investors quickly sold assets in Mexico, Thailand, Indonesia, the Philippines, Russia, and Brazil, causing **balance of payments** crises and financial crises. This was a process known as **capital flight**. Capital flight involves investors selling a country's assets and reallocating their portfolios to other countries' assets. The effects of some of these crises were quite dramatic. For example, the number of people below the poverty line in Thailand, Indonesia, and the Philippines as a group increased by 50 percent. All three of these countries, as well as Russia, have not yet recovered from the capital flight of these years.[7]

As we have seen, then, international finance is a realm of increasing importance in the modern world economy, and this is an additional main

Balance of payments
A detailed set of economic accounts focusing on the transactions between a country and the rest of the world. Two important subaccounts are the current account and the capital account.

Capital flight
A situation in which investors sell a country's assets and reallocate their portfolios towards other countries' assets. It tends to cause a capital account deficit for the country in question.

[7] Such events are precipitated by what Friedman (2000) calls the *electronic herd*, "anonymous stock, bond and currency traders and multinational investors, connected by screens and networks" (p. 113).

feature of globalization. You will enter into this realm in Part 3 of the book. You will learn about exchange rate determination, the international monetary system, and the financial crises of the 1990s. Throughout Part 3, the asset considerations that set international finance apart from international trade will be paramount.

International Development

International development
A concept with many meanings, including increases in per capita incomes, improvements in health and education, structural change toward manufacturing and services production, and institutional "modernization."

The fourth and final window on the world economy is **international development**. The processes of international trade, international production, and international finance reflect the many goals of their participants. From a public policy perspective, however, it is hoped that these three processes would contribute to improved levels of welfare and standards of living throughout the countries of the world. Two major issues are involved here. The first is how we conceptualize levels of welfare or standards of living. The second is how the processes of international trade, international production, and international finance help to determine international development (or the lack thereof).

Human development index (HDI)
A conception of economic development introduced by the United Nations Development Program that stresses health and education levels along with per capita income. The human development index is reported in the annual *Human Development Report*.

One inclusive, although not uncontroversial, measure of these differences in living standards is the **human development index (HDI)** measured by the United Nations Development Program. For our purposes here, suffice it to say that the HDI reflects per capita income (adjusted for cost of living), average life expectancy, and average levels of education. Some data on these measures for the year 2000, as well as on the HDI itself, are presented for a small sample of countries in Table 1.1.

As we can see from the data presented in Table 1.1, there is a wide range in measures of well-being among the countries of the world. GDP per capita ranges from only US$660 in Ethiopia to over US$34,000 in the

Table 1.1 Measures of Living Standards, 2000

Country	Per Capita Income (PPP U.S. dollars)	Life Expectancy at Birth (years)	Adult Literacy Rate (percent)	Human Development Index (max. 1.0)
Ethiopia	660	44	39	0.327
India	2,390	63	57	0.577
China	3,940	71	84	0.726
Costa Rica	8,250	76	96	0.820
South Korea	17,340	75	98	0.882
United States	34,260	77	99	0.939

Sources: The *World Development Report*, published by the World Bank in 2002 and the *Human Development Report*, published by the United Nations Development Program in 2002.

United States.[8] Life expectancies range from 44 years in Ethiopia to 77 years in the United States.[9] Literacy rates range from approximately 40 percent of the population in Ethiopia to near universal literacy in other countries. When combined into the single measure of the HDI, we see a wide variance as well. The HDI ranges from approximately 0.33 to 0.94. In sum, levels of development vary widely among the countries of the world.

You will begin to understand how the activities of international trade, production, and finance affect international development in Part 4 of the book. Here, we will consider alternative concepts of development, the way trade can contribute to economic growth, the process of hosting MNEs, and the role of the World Bank and structural adjustment in developing countries.

Connecting Windows

I was once talking to a soon-to-graduate student about her educational experience. During our conversation, she said to me, "There are many windows on the world. Each offers a view, and each has a frame." This powerful insight applies to our four windows on the world economy: international trade, international production, international finance, and international development. Each offers a view, but each has a frame. That is, each offers some insight into the world economy, an insight that needs to be supplemented by one or more of the other windows. It is important for you to remember this as you continue with your exploration of international economics.

Let me give you an example. In 1991, I was working for the U.S. International Trade Commission (USITC) in Washington, DC. At that time, most of my efforts were dedicated to analyzing the *trade* effects of the North American Free Trade Agreement (NAFTA). Based on the narrow trade window, I was excited about Mexico's prospects. One day, the USITC was receiving a delegation from Mexico, and I had an hour-long appointment with the Mexican economist accompanying the delegation. As it turned out, he was as worried about Mexico's prospects as I was excited. During our conversation, he said, "I am very worried about the future. All of the excitement over NAFTA is causing an inflow of portfolio investment. It is very short term, and it is financing a large trade deficit. It could turn around in a day! And then where will we be?"

As it turned out, this Mexican economist was right, and I was wrong. The portfolio investment did turn around and caused a crisis in late 1994 and early 1995. My window on the Mexican economy was insufficient to allow me (and many other trade economists) to appreciate where Mexico was heading. The Mexican economist was more attuned to the realities of the Mexican economy because he was viewing it through more than one window. He was using the window of international finance as well.

Take another example. In the previous section, we mentioned the international financial crises of the late 1990s. These crises generated a great

---

[8] The per capita income measures are purchasing power parity measures, which adjust for differences in costs of living among countries (see Chapter 19).
[9] Some countries (e.g., Canada) have life expectancies higher than those in the United States.

deal of argument and debate about international financial institutions, debates that took place almost exclusively within the window of international finance. In October 1998, however, World Bank president James Wolfensohn presented a speech to the World Bank Board of Governors entitled "The Other Crisis." In this speech, he stated:[10]

> Today, while we talk of financial crisis—17 million Indonesians have fallen back into poverty, and across the region a million children will now not return to school. Today, while we talk of financial crisis—an estimated 40 percent of the Russian population now lives in poverty. Today, while we talk of financial crisis—across the world, 1.3 billion people live on less than $1 a day; 3 billion live on under $2 a day; 1.3 billion have no access to clean water; 3 billion have no access to sanitation; 2 billion have no access to power.

What Wolfensohn did in this speech was to remind the global policy community that the international finance window needs to be supplemented by the international development window. Again, a single-window view is incomplete.

I want to suggest that you take the integrated view illustrated in Figure 1.3. Here, the four windows of our book are represented with four boxes. More importantly, there are six connections between the windows, represented by double-headed arrows. These are the connections among our four windows that we must keep in mind. NAFTA was an agreement for liberalizing trade and investment among the countries of North America, but its effects went beyond the trade and production windows to the finance window. The crises of the 1990s took place in the realm of international finance, but the effects were strongly transmitted to the realm of international development. So as you proceed through the remainder of this book, it will be important for you to identify connections among our four windows.

Although Figure 1.3 helps us to be cognizant of the connections among the four aspects of international economics that you will explore in this book, there are additional realms that we must keep in mind that affect the way in which the world economy evolves over time. These are *technology*,

Figure 1.3 Connecting Windows

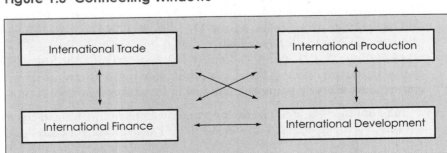

---

[10]Recently, Sala-i-Martin (2002) has questioned the poverty figures used by Wolfensohn (and others).

Technological Change in the World Economy

We mentioned that the connected realms of international trade, international production, international finance, and international development are embedded in the larger technological, political, cultural, and environmental contexts of the world economy. As a dynamic, driving force for global economic change, however, technology has recently been key. Indeed, a large part of the globalization process can be attributed to revolutions in two areas: telecommunications and information technology. Advances in telecommunications and information technology, in turn, have been dependent on digitization.

Digitization is the process through which sounds, images, and alphanumeric characters are reduced to codes consisting of 0's and 1's. This reduction makes transmission of sounds, images, and characters across great distances easy. It is digitization that allows an employee of Philips, the Dutch consumer-electronics firm, to use the Internet in order to adjust a television assembly line process in the Flextronics factory in Guadalajara, Mexico. It is digitization that allows a fund manager in London to quickly buy or sell equities on the Johannesburg stock exchange. Digitization sets the modern era off from most of the postwar twentieth century.

If there is one of our four windows in which technological change has had the most profound impact, it is international production. Importantly, and seemingly ironically, this impact is in two opposing directions: toward greater global integration and toward selective disintegration of production systems.

Communication and coordination costs of multinational production have long been a deterrent to FDI, requiring that MNEs possess offsetting advantages before engaging in successful foreign production. Advances in telecommunications and information technology have lowered these costs, contributing to increased integration of global production systems. Swissair, for example, has set up an accounting subsidiary in Mumbai (Bombay) India. Since close-of-business in Switzerland corresponds to morning in Mumbai, this accounting work is done on an overnight basis from the Swiss standpoint. This is an example of services being globalized but remaining *internal* to the firm.

At the same time, however, a second process has been at work. Improvements in telecommunications and information technology have resulted in firms contracting out on a global basis functions that they used to carry out in-house. For example, many U.S. firms now contract their software development to Indian firms, notably to Tata Consultancy Services and Tata Unysys Ltd. Also, a number of hospitals in the United States now contract with Indian firms for medical transcription services, making use of satellite technology. These are examples of services being globalized while being *external* to the firm.

Both of these scenarios, FDI and contracting out, are made possible by information technology and telecommunications advances that have only occurred in the last decade. These advances are causing a global reconfiguration of the way work is done. In fact, the motto of the Indian National Association of Software and Services Companies is "Move work to India."

Sources: Dicken, (1998); *The Economist* (2000); and Friedman (2000).

politics, culture, and the *environment.* At various points in the book, we will discuss how these factors play important roles. It is fair to say that the boxes and arrows of Figure 1.3 should be thought of as being strongly influenced by technological, political, cultural, and environmental factors.[11]

By all accounts, technological change in the world economy is a key driver of events. The accompanying box takes up this issue in some detail.

---

[11] These other factors are discussed at length in Friedman (2000).

The environmental issue can be easily illustrated with reference, once again, to NAFTA. As I mentioned earlier, I was analyzing the trade effects of NAFTA for the USITC during the early 1990s. Along with not being aware enough of the international finance issues surrounding NAFTA, I (and many other trade economists) did not fully appreciate the role of environmental considerations in the ensuing debate. Consequently, there was little empirical evidence on the environmental impacts of NAFTA to guide the debate in the early 1990s. It was only years later, in 2000, that a conference on the subject was organized by the North American Commission for Environmental Cooperation (NACEC), and a significant amount of empirical evidence was gathered together.[12] This conference showed how public gatherings can be structured to link narrow realms of international economics to broader concerns of the environment to better inform public policy. Given the unrelenting nature of globalization and the concomitant concerns of broad parts of the public all over the world about the nature of the globalization process, we should hope that many more such gatherings will occur so that we can all better understand and participate in the evolution of the world economy.[13]

---

[12]See the NACEC Web site at http://www.cec.org.

[13]The World Trade Organization addressed the links between trade and the environment in Nordström and Vaughan (1999). Students interested in cultural issues should consult Adler (2001).

Conclusion

It is becoming increasingly difficult for us to ignore the important realities of the world economy. Students and professionals of many types are finding that a basic understanding of international economics is necessary for them to operate successfully in the world. Perhaps you have had the same experience. A thorough understanding of the world economy involves the study of four realms of international economics: international trade, international production, international finance, and international development. These are the four windows on the world economy that we explore in this book.

International trade is increasing faster than global production. International production, meanwhile, is taking on more and more complex forms, involving both contractual arrangements and foreign direct investment. FDI is undertaken by multinational enterprises, and these now play a critical role in the world economy, one that cannot be ignored. However, as we have seen, viewing the world through trade and production windows is also incomplete. The realm of international finance is paramount, with foreign exchange transactions dwarfing trade transactions.

It is hoped that international trade, international production, and international finance will contribute positively to international development, improving welfare and living standards. Understanding how this occurs (or does not occur) provides an important fourth window on the world economy.

These four windows—trade, production, finance, and development—must be seen as being connected. Further, these four windows are strongly affected by the realms of technology, politics, culture, and the environment. The task of understanding how our four windows and the four larger realms evolve over time in a system of globalization is not, to say the least, an easy one. Indeed, it takes us far beyond the scope of this book. However, with persistence and some patience, you will begin to build an intellectual foundation for understanding this system in the remaining chapters.

Review Exercises

1. Why are you interested in international economics? What is motivating you? How are your interests, major, or profession affected by the world economy?

2. What are the four windows on the world economy?

3. What is the difference between trade in merchandise and trade in services?

4. What is the difference between international trade and foreign direct investment?

5. What is the difference between international trade and international finance?

6. Identify one way in which the activities of international trade, finance, and production could *positively* contribute to international development. Identify one way in which these activities could *negatively* contribute to international development. How could you demonstrate that the activities have either a positive or negative impact on development?

Further Reading and Web Resources

The reader with a broad interest in the process of globalization can begin his or her exploration by reading Rodrik's *Has Globalization Gone Too Far?* (1997) and Friedman's *The Lexus and the Olive Tree* (2000). Economics majors should take a look at Eichengreen's *Globalizing Capital* (1996). Business majors would do well by consulting Meier's *The International Environment of Business* (1998), and social science students can read Dicken's *Global Shift* (1998). Public policy students should consult *Global Public Goods*, edited by Kaul, Grunberg, and Stern (1999), and development studies students should see Rodrik's *The New Global Economy and Developing Countries* (1999) and the volume edited by Meier and Stiglitz (2001), *Frontiers of Development Economics*. Finally, those with an interest in the role of technology in the world economy should see Rycroft and Kash, *The Complexity Challenge* (1999).

The Institute for International Economics in Washington, DC, provides timely and readable analyses of many issues in international economics. Its Web site is **http://www.iie.com**. Two quality sources on international economic developments are *The Economist* and *The Financial Times*. Their Web sites are **http://www.economist.com** and **http://www.ft.com**. PBS maintains an interesting Web site on the subject of globalization and human rights at **http://www.pbs.org/globalization/home.html**. You can view the entire Wolfensohn speech, "The Other Crisis," at **http://www.worldbank.org/html/extdr/am98/jdw-sp/am98-en.htm**. You can visit the Indian National Association of Software and Service Companies (NASSCOM) at **http://www.nasscom.org**.

For occasional updates to the data presented in Chapter 1, visit **http://reinert.swlearning.com**.

References

Adler, N.J. (2001) *Boston to Beijing: Managing with a Worldview*, South-Western, Cincinnati.

Dicken, P. (1998) *Global Shift: Transforming the World Economy*, Guilford, New York.

The Economist (2000) "Have Factory, Will Travel," February 12, 61–62.

Eichengreen, B. (1996) *Globalizing Capital: A History of the International Monetary System*, Princeton University Press, Princeton.

Friedman, T.L. (2000) *The Lexus and the Olive Tree: Understanding Globalization*, Random House, New York.

Kaul, I., I. Grunberg, and M.A. Stern (1999) *Global Public Goods: International Cooperation in the 21st Century*, Oxford University Press, Oxford.

Meier, G.M. (1998) *The International Environment of Business: Competition and Governance in the Global Economy*, Oxford University Press, Oxford.

Meier, G.M., and J.E. Stiglitz (2001) *Frontiers of Development Economics: The Future in Perspective*, Oxford University Press, Oxford.

Nordström, H., and S. Vaughan (1999) *Trade and the Environment*, World Trade Organization, Geneva.

Rodrik, D. (1999) *The New Global Economy and Developing Countries: Making Openness Work*, Overseas Development Center, Washington, DC.

Rodrik, D. (1997) *Has Globalization Gone Too Far?* Institute for International Economics, Washington, DC.

Rycroft, R.W., and D.E. Kash (1999) *The Complexity Challenge: Technological Innovation in the 21st Century*, Pinter, London.

Sala-i-Martin, X. (2002) *The Disturbing "Rise" of Global Income Inequality*, National Bureau of Economic Research Working Paper 8904, Cambridge, Massachusetts.

Part 1

Windows on the World Economy:
International Trade

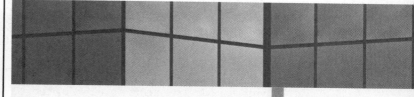

2

Absolute Advantage

Throughout most of the 1980s, Vietnam imported rice. In 1989, however, Vietnam exported more than 1 million tons of rice. In the 1990s, its annual rice exports increased to more than 3 million tons, and these may reach 4 million tons in the first decade of the twenty-first century. This increase in rice exports represents one important aspect of Vietnam's entry into the world economy through the process of trade expansion, which we discussed in Chapter 1.

Why does a country export a particular good? Why does it import a particular good? What forces are behind the expansion of world trade? This chapter takes a first step in helping you to answer these questions by utilizing a framework that should be familiar to you from your introductory economics class: the supply and demand diagram.[1] We are going to use the supply and demand diagram to illustrate an important concept in international economics, that of absolute advantage. Absolute advantage refers to the possibility that, due to differences in supply conditions, one country can produce a product at a lower price than another country. In this chapter, we will consider the product rice and the fact that Vietnam can produce rice more cheaply than Japan. This situation will cause rice to be exported from Vietnam to Japan. It will also involve what international economists call the gains from trade, which benefits *both* Vietnam and Japan. These gains are what motivate countries to take part in trading relationships.

Supply and Demand in a Domestic Market

Throughout the world, rice is exchanged in markets. Although these markets are international, let's assume for a moment that we can analyze a single domestic market in isolation. This will help orient you to the supply and demand model that we will use in this and other chapters. Figure 2.1 illustrates such a market. The diagram has two axes. The horizontal axis plots the quantity (Q) of rice in tons. The vertical axis plots the price (P) of rice per ton. There are two curves in the diagram, identified by the symbols S and D. S is the supply curve and represents the behavior of domestic rice-producing firms. D is the demand curve and represents the behavior of domestic consumers of rice, both firms and households.[2]

---

[1] Do you need to remind yourself of the main features of the supply and demand diagram? Then please see Chapter 4 of Mankiw (2004).
[2] Firms consuming rice use it as an intermediate product to produce a final product such as rice flour or a restaurant meal.

Figure 2.1 A Domestic Rice Market

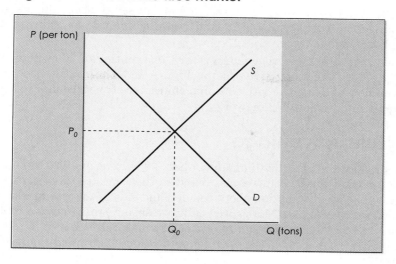

There are a number of properties of the supply and demand curves in Figure 2.1 that are important to understand. Let's take the supply curve first. It is upward sloping, and this indicates that firms supply more rice to the market as the price increases. Consequently, changes in price are represented in the diagram by *movements along* the supply curve. These movements are known as **changes in quantity supplied**. There are two additional supply-side factors relevant to the supply curve. These are input prices and technology. Reductions in input prices and improvements in technology shift the supply curve to the right. This means that producers supply more rice than before at every price. Increases in input prices and technology setbacks shift the supply curve to the left. This means that producers supply less rice than before at every price. We can see that changes in input prices and technology are represented by *shifts of* the supply curve. These shifts are known as **changes in supply**.

Now let's take a look at the rice demand curve. It is downward sloping, and this indicates that consumers demand less rice from the market as the price increases. Consequently, changes in price are represented in the diagram by *movements along* the demand curve. These movements are known as **changes in quantity demanded**. There are a number of additional demand-side factors relevant to the demand curve. Two important ones are incomes and preferences. Increases in incomes and increased preference for rice consumption shift the demand curve to the right. This means that consumers demand more rice than before at every price. Decreases in incomes and decreased preference for rice consumption shift the demand curve to the left. This means that consumers demand less rice than before at every price. Consequently, changes in incomes and preferences are represented by *shifts of* the demand curve. These shifts are known as **changes in demand**.

Finally, the intersection of the supply and demand curves in Figure 2.1 determines the equilibrium in the domestic rice market. The equilibrium price is P_0, and the equilibrium quantity is Q_0. Given what we have just

Change in quantity supplied
A movement along a supply curve due to a change in the price of the good.

Change in supply
A shift of the supply curve due to a change in technology or input prices.

Change in quantity demanded
A movement along a demand curve due to a change in the price of a good.

Change in demand
A shift of a demand curve due to a change in income, wealth, preferences, expectations, and prices of related goods.

stated about the role of input prices, technology, incomes, and preferences in shifting the two curves in Figure 2.1, you can see that any such shifts will change the equilibrium price and quantity for rice by shifting the demand or supply curves.

As we stated earlier, rice markets are international. Therefore, we cannot analyze them effectively using Figure 2.1. The next section will show you how to bring the international character of the rice market into the supply and demand framework.

Absolute Advantage

Rice is produced in both Vietnam and Japan. To help us analyze the international market for rice that arises between these two countries, we are going to make an assumption about the demand side of the rice market in both Vietnam and Japan. More specifically, we assume that *demand conditions are exactly the same in both countries*. That is, there are no differences in preferences, incomes, or the way demand responds to price changes in Vietnam and Japan. This implies that the demand curves for rice in the two countries are exactly the same. This is illustrated in Figure 2.2.

Trade often arises due to differences in supply conditions. Therefore, we will allow supply conditions for rice to differ between Vietnam and Japan. In particular, we will assume that the supply curve for Vietnam is farther to the right than the supply curve for Japan, which means that at every price Vietnam supplies more rice than Japan. Why might this be? One possibility is that Vietnam produces rice using *technology* superior to Japan so that labor productivity in rice production in Vietnam is higher than in Japan. This possibility, however, is not relevant to rice production in these two countries.[3] Another possibility is that the prices for *inputs* used in rice production are lower in Vietnam than in Japan. This, in turn, could reflect the fact that Vietnam is more abundantly endowed with rice production factors (available land and agricultural labor) than Japan. It is this latter factor that is relevant in the current case.

Autarky
A situation of national self-sufficiency in which a country does not import or export.

Absolute advantage
The possibility that, due to differences in supply conditions, one country can produce a product at a lower price than another country.

This situation is depicted in Figure 2.3. The upward-sloping supply curves reflect the positive relationship between price and quantity supplied. The difference in supply conditions positions Vietnam's supply curve farther to the right than Japan's supply curve. The intersections of the supply and demand curves determine the equilibrium prices of rice in the two markets. The two prices are recorded as P^V and P^J in the figure. Because no trade is involved, these two prices are known in international economics as **autarky** prices. Autarky is a situation in which a country has no economic relationships with other countries.

Figure 2.3 depicts a situation in which the autarky price of rice is lower in Vietnam than in Japan. That is

$$P^V < P^J \tag{2.1}$$

In international trade theory, this situation is interpreted as Vietnam having an **absolute advantage** in the production of rice vis-à-vis Japan.

---

[3] For a case where technology is relevant, see the box on Japan's advantage in industrial robots.

Figure 2.2 Demand for Rice in Vietnam and Japan

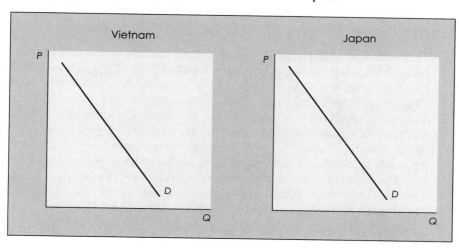

Figure 2.3 Absolute Advantage in the Rice Market

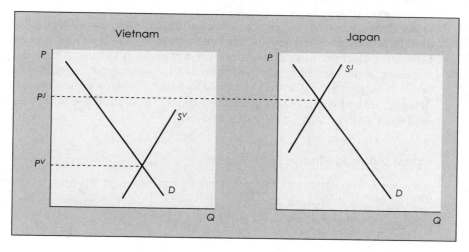

This absolute advantage reflects the differences in supply conditions in the two countries. The presence of absolute advantage makes international trade a possibility. This we consider in the following section.

International Trade

The idea of absolute advantage was first stated in Adam Smith's *The Wealth of Nations*, published in 1776. Adam Smith stated the following: "If a foreign country can supply us with a commodity cheaper than we ourselves can make it, better buy it of them with some part of the produce of our own industry, employed in a way in which we have some advantage" (1937, p. 424). In other words, a pattern of absolute advantage implies a potential pattern of trade. How does this apply to our example? If the two countries forgo autarky and begin to trade, the world price of rice will lie somewhere between the two autarky prices:

$$P^V < P^W < P^J \qquad\qquad \textbf{(2.2)}$$

This situation is depicted in Figure 2.4. In the movement from autarky to trade, Vietnam experiences an increase in the price of rice to the world level. Quantity supplied will increase, while quantity demanded will decrease. The amount by which quantity supplied exceeds quantity demanded in Vietnam constitutes its *exports* of rice, E^V. Japan experiences a decrease in the price of rice to the world level. Here, quantity supplied will decrease, while quantity demanded will increase. The amount by which quantity demanded exceeds quantity supplied in Japan constitutes its *imports* of rice, Z^J.[4] The country that has an absolute advantage (Vietnam) expands its quantity supplied and exports the good in question, while its trading partner (Japan) contracts its quantity supplied and imports the good.

The associations you should have in your mind from the preceding discussion are presented in Figure 2.5 on page 20. The starting points are comparative levels of technological proficiency and endowments of factors used in the production of the sector's product. The latter affects the relevant input prices for a sector in a country. Vietnam, for example, has lower domestic prices for rice-growing land and labor. These technological and factor characteristics determine a pattern of absolute advantage between two countries. This pattern of absolute advantage, in turn, can generate a pattern of trade. Vietnam tends to export rice, while Japan tends to import rice. Another example in which Japan's technological proficiency in the production of industrial robots is given in the following box on Japan's advantage in industrial robots.

Figure 2.4 Trade in the Rice Market

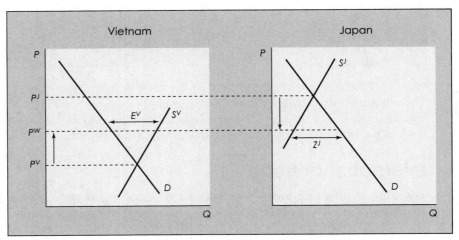

---

[4] We use a *Z* to denote imports throughout this book. Why *Z*? As we will see, *I* is used in economics to denote investment, and *M* is used to denote money. Therefore, we cannot use the first two letters of the word "imports."

Japan's Advantage in Industrial Robots

The world's leading exporter of industrial robots is Japan. However, the world's first industrial robot was built in the United States in 1961 by the industrialist Joseph Engelberger. Engelberger had a moment of fame in 1966 when a robot he built appeared on Johnny Carson's *Tonight Show*. The robot opened a can of beer and poured it for Johnny Carson. In 1967, Engelberger was invited to Japan and addressed 600 Japanese scientists and business executives. As a result, Japan imported its first industrial robots from the United States. In 1969, robot production began in Japan under a licensing agreement with Engelberger's firm, Unimation. In 1972, the Japanese Industrial Robotics Association was founded. Thus began Japan's involvement with what has been called "the most important manufacturing innovations of recent times" (Mansfield, 1989, p. 19).

Japan's first exports of industrial robots began in 1975. Thereafter, exports grew slowly but steadily. By the end of the 1980s, Japan became the leader in most areas of the robotics industry such as numerical controllers, machine tools, motors, and optical sensors. It accounted for one-half of the world production of industrial robots. The technological nature of Japan's advantage in robot production has been captured by Porter (1990): "The pace of innovation and new product introduction among the Japanese firms was feverish. Product innovations were soon imitated or upstaged by other producers. For example, the American firm Adept Technology introduced the world's first commercially successful direct-drive robot near the end of 1984. Less than a year later, seven Japanese firms, including Yamaha, Matsushita, and FANUC, introduced direct drive robots" (p. 235). Along with faster innovation times, Japanese firms benefited from lower innovation costs. There is some evidence that Japan's faster innovation times and lower innovation costs were due to a greater emphasis on manufacturing over marketing in the innovation process in comparison with the United States.

Accompanying and contributing to Japan's technological lead in industrial robots was the degree of competition in the Japanese industrial robots industry. With fewer than 10 firms in 1968, the industry expanded to nearly 300 firms by 1987. Another important factor has been *intrafirm diffusion*, where firms requiring the use of robots (such as the electronic equipment industry) begin producing robots for their own use. A final factor pushing the use of robots in Japan is the presence of significant labor shortages in many areas; robots replaced humans where these shortages appear. As of 1997, Japan used one robot for every 36 manufacturing employees; the United States used only one robot for every 250 manufacturing employees. Currently, one-half of the world's industrial robots are installed in Japan.

Sources: *The Economist* (1980); Horiuchi (1989); Mansfield (1989); Porter (1990); and Tanzer and Simon (1990).

It is important to stress here that Figure 2.5 is only a *preliminary* look at international trade. In the real world, international trade is actually determined by *comparative advantage* rather than absolute advantage. This is why we use the word "tendency" in the far right-hand boxes of the figure. Consequently, you will not have a full appreciation of how international trade is determined until you complete Chapter 3. Nevertheless, our discussion in this chapter is useful in order to understand how the traditional demand and supply framework must be modified to account for trading relations and to understand the gains from trade.

Figure 2.5 A Schematic View of Absolute Advantage

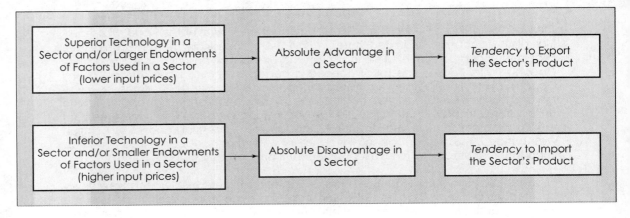

A question that often arises in students' minds is: What ensures that the amount exported by Vietnam is the same as the amount imported by Japan? If E^V were smaller than Z^J, there would be excess demand or a shortage in the world market for rice. As we know from introductory microeconomics, excess demand causes the price to rise. As P^W rose, exports of Vietnam would expand and imports of Japan would contract until the excess demand in the world market disappeared. Similarly, if E^V were larger than Z^J, P^W would fall to bring the world market back into equilibrium.

Before we discuss the gains from trade, another key concept in international economics, let's summarize what we have learned thus far:

> **Differences in supply conditions among the countries of the world give rise to complementary patterns of absolute advantage. These patterns of absolute advantage, in turn, make possible complementary patterns of international trade.**

Gains from Trade

Consumer surplus
The benefit accruing to consumers from the fact that, in equilibrium, the consumers receive a price lower than their willingness to pay for lesser quantities.

Producer surplus
The benefit accruing to producers from the fact that, in equilibrium, the producers receive a price higher than their willingness to accept for lesser quantities.

To this point, we have seen that, given a pattern of absolute advantage, it is possible for a country to give up autarky in favor of importing or exporting. Japan can import rice, and Vietnam can export rice. But *should* a country actually do this? We can answer this question by examining Figure 2.4 from the point of view of **consumer surplus** and **producer surplus**. This is done in Figure 2.6. If for any reason, you do not recall these two concepts from your introductory microeconomics course, please consult the appendix to this chapter.

Let us first consider Vietnam. In its movement from autarky to exporting in the rice market, producers experience both an increase in price and an increase in quantity supplied along the supply curve. This should be good for producers, and you can see in Figure 2.6 that there has been an increase in producer surplus of area $A + B$ as a result of the movement from autarky to trade. Consumers, on the other hand, experience an

Figure 2.6 Gains from Trade in the Rice Market

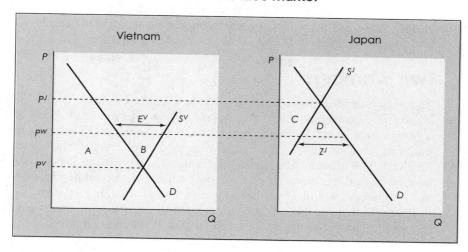

increase in price and a decrease in quantity demanded along the demand curve. This should harm consumers, and you can see in Figure 2.6 that there has been an decrease in consumer surplus of area A.

What do these effects mean for Vietnam? Producers have gained area $A + B$, while consumers have lost area A. The gain to producers exceeds the loss to consumers. For the economy as a whole, then, there is a net welfare increase of area B. Vietnam gains from its entry into the world economy as an exporter.

Next, consider Japan. In its movement from autarky to importing in the rice market, producers experience a decrease in price and a decrease in quantity supplied along the supply curve. This should harm these producers. You can see in Figure 2.6 that there has been a decrease in producer surplus of area C. Consumers, on the other hand, experience a decrease in price and an increase in quantity demanded. These contribute to an increase in consumer surplus of area $C + D$.

What do these effects mean for Japan? Consumers have gained $C + D$, while producers have lost area C. The gain to consumers exceeds the loss to producers. For the economy as a whole, then, there is a net welfare increase of area D. Japan gains from its entry into the world economy as an importer.

You can see from these examples that moving from autarky to either importing or exporting involves a net increase in welfare for the country involved. This net increase in welfare is known as the **gains from trade**. Not only is it possible for a country to give up autarky in favor of importing or exporting, but it also makes sense to do so from the standpoint of overall welfare.

The gains from trade is an important concept. To judge from the tone and content of many popular writings on the world economy, trade relationships are a win–lose proposition for the countries involved. To export is to win; to import is to lose. The gains from trade idea, however, tells us that trade can

Gains from trade Advantages that accrue to a country from engaging in importing and exporting relationships. In an absolute advantage framework, gains from trade are identified as a net gain between consumer and producer surplus effects. In a comparative advantage framework, gains from trade are identified as an increase in consumption of all goods.

be *mutually* beneficial to the countries involved. For this reason, you need to be cautious in your assessment of some popular writing of the win–lose variety. Although there are specific instances in which trade can be a win-lose proposition, this is not the case for trade in general.[5]

Two Warnings

The notion of absolute advantage, first suggested by Adam Smith in *The Wealth of Nations*, is useful to understanding international trade in the context of the familiar supply and demand framework. It is also useful to understand that trade can improve overall welfare for the countries involved. The concept has its limits, though. In particular, it suggests the possibility that a country could not have an absolute advantage in *anything* and, therefore, would have nothing to export at all. This, it turns out, is unlikely. To understand why, we must turn to a more sophisticated notion of trade, comparative advantage. We do this in the next chapter.

The notion of the gains from trade also has its limits. It suggests that countries *as a whole* mutually gain from trade. It does not suggest, however, that *everyone within* a country will gain from trade. In the examples in this chapter, producers of rice in Japan lose from trade, and consumers of rice in Vietnam lose from trade. We will take up the subject of the winners and losers from trade in earnest in Chapter 5.

---

[5] This point has been emphasized by Krugman (1996).

Conclusion

Autarky refers to a situation in which a country does not engage in either imports or exports. It is a rare situation. More commonly, countries engage in both importing and exporting relationships with other countries of the world economy. It this chapter, you begin to understand why. Absolute advantage reflects differences between countries in technology or factor conditions. A country with better technology and larger endowments of the factors necessary to produce an item is more likely to have absolute advantage in the production of that item. It is also more likely to export that item. Patterns of absolute advantage in the world economy also make possible mutual gains from trade in which the overall welfare of the countries involved increase.

The notion of absolute advantage has its limits. First, it suggests that a country might not have anything to export at all. This, as we will see in the next chapter, is an unlikely outcome. Second, it does not suggest that all persons in a country will gain from trade. Within any country, there can be both winners and losers from international trade. We take up this issue in Chapter 5.

Review Exercises

1. Use Figure 2.1 to consider the following changes: a fall in incomes due to a recession; an increased preference for rice consumption; an increase in input prices for rice production; and an improvement in rice production technology. Use diagrams to analyze the effects of these changes on equilibrium price and quantity.

2. Create an example of an absolute advantage model by choosing two countries and a single product.
   a. Draw a diagram describing *autarky* and a *pattern of absolute advantage* for your example.
   b. Show the transition from autarky to trade in your diagram, label the trade flows, and demonstrate the *gains from trade*.
   c. In a new diagram, and starting from a trading equilibrium, show what would happen to the world price if *income increased* by exactly the same, small amount in both countries.

3. Can you recall from introductory microeconomics the notions of the price elasticity of demand and price elasticity of supply? If so, can you say what would happen to the gains from trade as supply *and* demand in Vietnam *and* Japan become more and more *inelastic*?

Further Reading and Web Resources

The idea of absolute advantage was first discussed in Chapter II, Book IV of Smith (1937). This book is available in the nonfiction section at **http://www.bibliomania.com**. The supply and demand diagram is considered in Chapter 4 of Mankiw (2004). The use of the supply and demand diagram to consider international trade is covered in Chapter 9 of Mankiw (2004) and in Chapter 1 of Walther (1997).

An analysis of international trade in rice in the Asia–Pacific region can be found at **http://www.agribusiness.asn.au/review/Perspectives/asia_pacific_rice.htm**. Trading and foreign direct investment relationships between Vietnam and the United States can be followed at **http://www.usvietnam.com**.

References

The Economist (1980) "Robots," October 17, 116.

Horiuchi, T. (1989) "Development Process of Robot Industries in Japan," *Rivista Internazionale di Scienze Economiche e Commerciali*, 36:12, 1089–1108.

Krugman, P. (1996) "The Illusion of Conflict in International Trade," *Pop Internationalism*, MIT Press, Cambridge, 69–84.

Mankiw, N.G. (2004) *Principles of Economics*, South-Western/Thomson Learning, Mason, Ohio.

Mansfield, E. (1989) "Technological Change in Robotics: Japan and the United States," *Managerial and Decision Economics*, Special Issue, 19–25.

Porter, M.E. (1990) *The Competitive Advantage of Nations*, The Free Press, New York.

Smith, A. (1937) *The Wealth of Nations*, Modern Library, New York (first published in 1776).

Tanzer, A., and R. Simon (1990) "Why Japan Loves Robots and We Don't," *Forbes*, 145:8, April 16, 148–153.

Walther, T. (1997) *The World Economy*, John Wiley, New York.

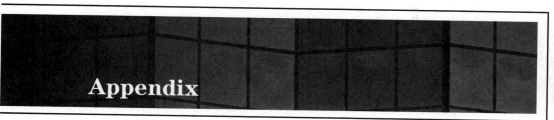

Appendix

Consumer and Producer Surplus

Our discussion of the gains from trade in this chapter utilized the notions of consumer surplus and producer surplus. These concepts are illustrated in Figure 2A.1.[6] This figure considers equilibrium in a single market. The equilibrium price is P_0, and the equilibrium quantity is Q_0. The height of the demand curve shows consumers' *willingness to pay* for the good in question. For quantities between zero and Q_0, however, the willingness to pay is *greater than* what consumers actually pay. That is, the height of the demand curve is greater than the market price. This gives the consumers a premium on each unit up to Q_0, and the sum of the consumer premia is the upper triangle in the figure, consumer surplus.

Figure 2A.1 Consumer and Producer Surplus

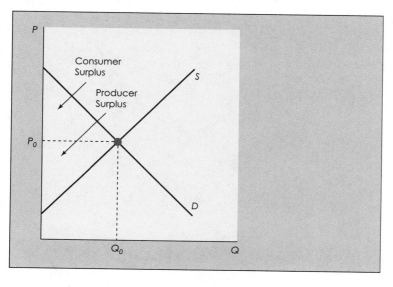

---

[6] See also Chapter 7 of Mankiw (2004).

The height of the supply curve shows the producers' *willingness to accept* for the good in question. For quantities between zero and Q_0, however, the willingness to accept is *less than* what the producers actually receive. That is, the height of the supply curve is less than the market price. Producers too, then, receive a premium on each unit up to Q_0. The sum of the producer premia is the lower triangle in the figure, producer surplus.

In demonstrating the gains from trade in this chapter, we considered the changes in consumer and producer surplus that result from the price changes brought on by the move from autarky to trade.

Comparative Advantage

3

In Chapter 2, we used the concept of absolute advantage to examine trade in rice between Vietnam and Japan. For Vietnam, rice is a significant component of the country's total production and an important component of domestic consumption. As incomes increase in Vietnam, however, there is another product that many Vietnamese begin to think about buying. That product is a motorcycle. Motorcycles in general, and the Honda Dream motorcycle in particular, are all the rage in Vietnam. Hundreds of new motorcycles are registered daily in the city of Hanoi alone, and tourists visiting this city report being overwhelmed by the chaos of motorcycle traffic, reminiscent of Italian driving styles in Rome.

In this chapter, we will place motorcycles alongside rice so that you can begin to understand the powerful concept of comparative advantage and its role in generating patterns of trade among the countries of the world. This, in turn, requires that we utilize the concept of a production possibilities frontier (PPF). The PPF should be familiar to you from an introductory microeconomics course. If it is not, please see the appendix to this chapter.[1]

Autarky and Comparative Advantage

Consider again our two countries, Vietnam and Japan. Both of these countries produce two goods, rice and motorcycles. To help us in our analysis of comparative advantage, we will assume that demand for rice and motorcycles in both Vietnam and Japan is such that these two goods are consumed in the *same, fixed proportions*.[2] This assumption is depicted in Figure 3.1. In the diagrams for Vietnam and Japan, the quantity of rice (Q_R) is measured on the horizontal axes, and the quantity of motorcycles (Q_M) is measured on the vertical axes. Because demand for these two goods is in the same, fixed proportions, we can represent it by diagonal lines from the origins. We label both of these lines *DD* for "demand diagonal." Any change in preferences for the two products would rotate these diagonal demand lines either up or down, maintaining the intercept at the origin. Changes in income would move a country up and down a given demand diagonal.[3]

---

[1] See also Chapter 2 of Mankiw (2004).
[2] We use this assumption to simplify the presentation of comparative advantage for the introductory student. However, this assumption can be relaxed without changing any of the results of this chapter. Indeed, this is exactly what is done in more advanced texts.
[3] Some caution is necessary here. The *DD* lines in Figure 3.1 are *not* demand curves. Demand curves show a relationship between price and quantity demanded, but no price appears in Figure 3.1. Furthermore, demand curves are downward sloping, not upward sloping as the *DD* curves are in Figure 3.1.

Figure 3.1 Demand Diagonals in Vietnam and Japan

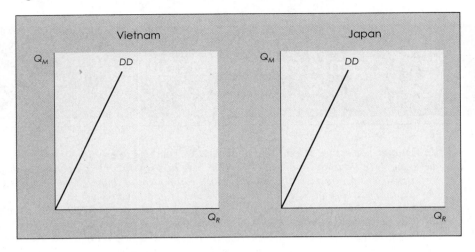

Production possibilities frontier (PPF)
A diagram that illustrates the constraints on production in general equilibrium imposed by scarce resources and technology. It shows all the combinations of two goods that a country can produce given its resources and technology.

As we saw in Chapter 2, trade often arises due to differences in supply conditions. Therefore, we once again allow supply conditions to differ between Vietnam and Japan. In particular, we assume that resource or technology conditions in Vietnam give it a **production possibilities frontier (PPF)** that is biased towards rice, while resource or technology conditions in Japan give it a PPF that is biased towards motorcycles. Why might this pattern arise? Vietnam might have superior technology in rice production, and Japan might have superior technology in motorcycle production. Alternatively, Vietnam might be better endowed in rice production factors (land and labor), and Japan might be better endowed in motorcycles production factors (physical capital). Whatever the reason, the PPFs take on complementary shapes as depicted in Figure 3.2. We label the intersection of the PPFs with our demand lines with the letter *A*.

In our discussion of absolute advantage in Chapter 2, we were able to determine the price of rice by the intersections of supply and demand curves in Vietnam and Japan. What do we do when we have two goods as in Figures 3.1 and 3.2? The *DD* lines represent the demand sides of the two economies, and the PPFs represent the supply sides of the two economies. How do we determine prices, though? The slope of the PPFs shows how many motorcycles must be given up to produce additional rice. Recall from introductory microeconomics that this slope measures the **opportunity cost** of producing the item on the horizontal axis, rice, expressed in terms of how many units of the item on the vertical axis, motorcycles, must be given up, that is, not produced because resources have switched to rice.

Opportunity cost
What has to be given up to gain something. Along a production possibilities frontier, there is an opportunity cost of increasing the output of one good in the form of less production of another good.

In a system of freely operating markets and full employment of production factors, opportunity costs are fully reflected in *relative* prices. Therefore, the slope of a PPF where the demand diagonal crosses it is the relative price of rice, (P_R/P_M). We represent this in Figure 3.3 by drawing in the *tangent* lines to the PPFs at the point where the demand lines cross

Figure 3.2 Demand and Production Possibility Frontiers in Vietnam and Japan

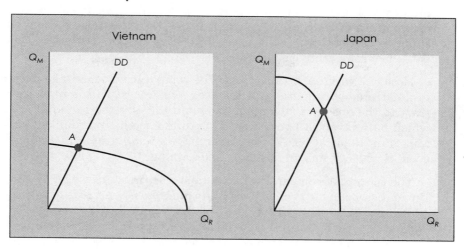

Figure 3.3 Relative Prices in Vietnam and Japan Under Autarky

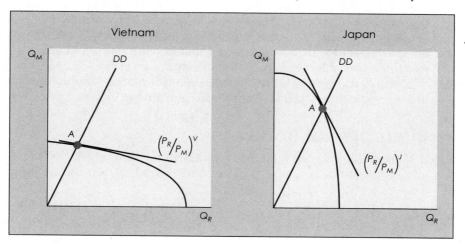

them, points A.[4] Points A in the two PPFs of Figure 3.2 represent the two countries under autarky.

Looking at points A in Figure 3.3, you can see that the tangency line giving relative prices is flatter in Vietnam than in Japan. That is, the opportunity cost of rice is lower in Vietnam than in Japan. In other words, under autarky:

$$\left(\frac{P_R}{P_M}\right)^V < \left(\frac{P_R}{P_M}\right)^J \qquad\qquad (3.1)$$

[4] We discuss this further in the appendix to this chapter.

This equation says that the relative price of rice is lower in Vietnam than in Japan. Because Vietnam is the country that has a supply advantage in producing rice, Equation 3.1 makes sense. This inequality is an expression of a pattern of **comparative advantage**. Differences in economy-wide supply conditions cause differences in relative autarky prices and hence a pattern of comparative advantage.

Comparative advantage
A situation where a country's relative autarkic price ratio of one good in terms of another is lower than that of other countries in the world economy.

Note one very important thing. The comparative advantage inequality illustrated by Equation 3.1 involves *four prices*. This is in sharp contrast to the absolute advantage inequality illustrated by Equation 2.1, which only involved two prices. This difference has an immediate and important implication: A country can have a *comparative advantage* in a good in which it has an *absolute disadvantage*.[5]

The concept of comparative advantage was first introduced in 1817 by David Ricardo in his *Principles of Political Economy and Taxation* (Ricardo, 1951). In a footnote in Chapter 7 of that book, Ricardo stated: "It will appear . . . that a country possessing very considerable advantages in machinery and skill, and which may therefore be enabled to manufacture commodities with much less labour than her neighbors, may, in return for such commodities, import a portion of its corn required for its consumption, even if its land were more fertile, and corn could be grown with less labour than in the country from which it was imported." This country, in our example, is Japan, whose endowments of "machinery and skill" perhaps give it an absolute advantage in producing motorcycles. Corn in Ricardo's time was the word for "grain," and in our example, this is rice. Ricardo therefore suggests that Japan can import rice, even if it has an absolute advantage in rice production, given its comparative advantage in motorcycles.

International Trade

If Vietnam and Japan abandon autarky in favor of trade, the world relative price of rice $(P_R/P_M)^W$ will lie somewhere between the two autarky price ratios:

$$\left(\frac{P_R}{P_M}\right)^V < \left(\frac{P_R}{P_M}\right)^W < \left(\frac{P_R}{P_M}\right)^J \tag{3.2}$$

This situation is depicted in Figure 3.4. The world price ratio here is depicted with dashed lines that have the slope $(P_R/P_M)^W$. These lines are steeper than the autarky price line in Vietnam and flatter than the autarky price line in Japan, as is indicated in Equation 3.2. The tangencies of these world price lines with the PPFs determine the new production points in Vietnam and Japan. These points are labeled B. In Vietnam, the movement along the PPF from A to B involves an increase in the production of rice; in Japan, this movement involves an increase in the production of motorcycles. The important lesson you should understand here is that moving from autarky to trade restructures an economy's production

---

[5] The reader who is not convinced of this can work with the following example: $P_R^V = 2$, $P_R^J = 1$, $P_M^V = 4$, $P_M^J = 1$. Here, you will see that Japan has an *absolute* advantage in producing both goods ($P_R^J < P_R^V$ and $P_M^J < P_M^V$), but Vietnam has a *comparative* advantage in producing rice.

towards the good in which the country has a comparative advantage. This is one reason why opening economies up to trading relations with the rest of the world can be difficult for the countries involved. Workers and other resources must be moved from one sector of the economy to another in the process.[6]

Consumption points for Vietnam and Japan must be along our diagonal demand lines. These points, labeled C in Figure 3.4, occur where the dashed world price lines intersect the demand lines. Why is this? Both consumption and production must respect world prices. That is, *both* points B and C must be on the world price lines. In contrast to autarky, consumption and production points are now different. How can this be so? Through trade. Look ahead to Figure 3.5, which removes the autarky points and autarky price lines.

Figure 3.4 Autarky and Comparative Advantage in Vietnam and Japan

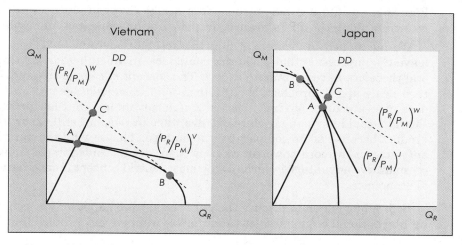

Figure 3.5 Trade Between Vietnam and Japan

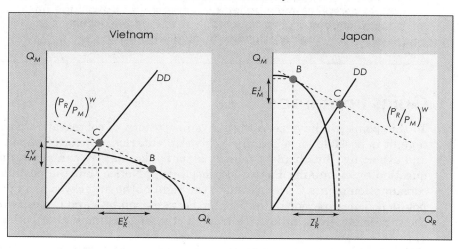

---

[6] We take up the political implications of these resource movements in Chapter 5.

In Vietnam, production of rice exceeds consumption of rice, and the difference is exported (E_R^V). Production of motorcycles, however, falls short of consumption of motorcycles, and this shortfall is imported (Z_M^V).[7] In Japan, production of motorcycles exceeds consumption of motorcycles, and the difference is exported (E_M^J). Production of rice, however, falls short of production, and this shortfall is imported (Z_R^J). What we see in Figure 3.5 is that a pattern of comparative advantage, based on differences in supply conditions between two countries, gives rise to a complementary pattern of trade.

What ensures that the quantities imported and exported in Figure 3.5 balance? Suppose that E_R^V were smaller than Z_R^J. If this were the case, there would be excess demand for (or a shortage of) rice in the world market. As we saw in our absolute advantage model of Chapter 2, excess demand for rice would cause P_R^W to rise. Therefore, the $\left(P_R/P_M\right)^W$ lines in Figure 3.5 would become steeper. This would direct production in both countries along the PPFs toward rice, alleviating the excess demand.

We mentioned in Chapter 2 that the absolute advantage concept can leave the impression that a country could lack an advantage in anything, and therefore have nothing to export. The concept of comparative advantage clears up this problem. Having an *absolute* disadvantage in a product does not preclude having a *comparative* advantage in that product. Vietnam could have an absolute disadvantage in rice, but still export this product because of its comparative advantage. This is why comparative advantage is a more powerful concept than absolute advantage. Indeed, comparative advantage is perhaps the most central concept in international economics.

Before moving on to discuss the gains from trade, another key concept in international economics, let's summarize what we have shown this far:

> **Differences in supply conditions among the countries of the world give rise to complementary patterns of comparative advantage. These patterns of comparative advantage, in turn, make possible complementary patterns of international trade.**

Gains from Trade

To this point, we have seen that, given a pattern of comparative advantage, it is possible for a country to give up autarky in favor of importing and exporting. But should a country actually do this? We can answer this question by examining Figure 3.4 once again. Notice that the post-trade consumption points C are up and to the right of the autarky consumption points A. This directional relationship between points A and C means that the movement from autarky to trade increases consumption of both rice

---

[7] As in Chapter 2, we use Z to denote imports, because the symbols I and M are taken up by investment and money, respectively.

Comparative Advantage and the Environment

An increasing amount of attention is being given to the environmental impacts of trade, and trade between developed and developing countries has received particular scrutiny in this regard. Hiro Lee and David Roland-Holst have examined trade between Japan and Indonesia during the years 1965 to 1990. Lee and Roland-Holst introduce a concept they call *embodied effluent trade (EET)* "to capture the idea that traded commodities embody an environmental service: the amount of pollution emitted domestically when goods are produced for export" (p. 523). They find that, with respect to the bilateral trade between these two countries, Indonesia has developed a comparative advantage in pollution-intensive industries relative to Japan. More specifically, they conclude that "Indonesia's net embodied effluents per unit exported to Japan are over six times the reverse flow and 29 percent higher than for its exports to the rest of the world. For Japan's part, imports from Indonesia have about twice the embodied effluent content per unit of its imports from elsewhere. This trend has remained relatively stable over the 1965–90 period, and the result is a sustained and significant transfer of environmental costs between the two countries" (p. 523). Indonesia is experiencing the bulk of environmental damage in its trading relationship with Japan.

Lee and Roland-Holst do not conclude that Indonesia should move away from its trading relationship with Japan. Instead, they recommend the use of *effluent taxes* as a way of reducing the environmental consequences of trade and specialization. In their words, "it is possible to abate industrial pollution while maintaining or even increasing real output when . . . (effluent) taxation is combined with trade" (p. 542). Thus, the environmental impacts of trade require intelligent policy responses.

Source: Lee and Roland-Holst (1997).

and motorcycles. Increased consumption of both goods, in turn, implies that economic welfare has increased. Vietnam and Japan have experienced mutual **gains from trade** based on comparative advantage.[8]

A few caveats are in order. First, the gains from trade occur for the country as a whole. The fact that a country as a whole benefits in the aggregate from trade does not mean that every individual or group within the country benefits. Indeed, as you will see in Chapter 5, there are good reasons to expect that there will be groups that lose from increased trade. These groups will oppose increased trade despite the overall gains to their country. For example, rice producers in Japan have a long history of opposing imports of rice.

Second, in recent years, there has been a great deal of discussion of the impacts of trade based on comparative advantage on the environment. It is sometimes alleged that international trade is almost always detrimental to the environment.[9] However, the situation is not always this straightforward. Both theoretical and empirical results demonstrate that increased trade can be either good or bad for the environment, and that we need to

Gains from trade
Advantages that accrue to a country from engaging in importing and exporting relationships. In an absolute advantage framework, gains from trade are identified as a net gain between consumer and producer surplus effects. In a comparative advantage framework, gains from trade are identified as an increase in consumption of all goods.

---

[8] Our implicit assumption here is the standard one in economics, namely that welfare is determined by consumption levels. For a challenge to this assumption, see Sen (1989).
[9] See, for example, Daly (1993).

approach the trade and environment issue on a case-by-case basis.[10] A case in which trade based on comparative advantage has detrimental environmental impacts on a country is given in the box.[11]

Third, some goods are traded that do not contribute to increased welfare. Land mines, heroin, and prostitution services are all traded internationally, but their consumption significantly reduces welfare rather than increases it. For this reason, you need to be careful not to generalize the gains from trade concept too far.[12]

---

[10]See, for example, Runge's *Freer Trade, Protected Environment* (1994), as well as the article by Beghin and Potier (1997).
[11]We return to the issue of trade and the environment in the context of the World Trade Organization in Chapter 7.
[12]See, for example, Flowers (2001).

Conclusion

Differences in technology and/or factor endowments among the countries of the world can generate patterns of comparative advantage. Although patterns of comparative advantage are *influenced* by patterns of absolute advantage, they are not *determined* by patterns of absolute advantage. Indeed, a country can have a comparative advantage in a good in which it has an absolute disadvantage. Patterns of comparative advantage determine patterns of trade in the world economy and generate mutual gains from trade.

As with our analysis of absolute advantage in Chapter 2, it is important to remember that the gains from trade arising from comparative advantage are for countries as a whole, and not for all individuals and groups within a country. Within any country, there can be both winners and losers from international trade.

Review Exercises

1. What is the difference between *absolute* and *comparative* advantage?

2. Create an example of a comparative advantage model by choosing two countries and two products.
   a. Draw a diagram describing *autarky* and a *pattern of comparative advantage* for your example.
   b. Show the transition from autarky to trade in your diagram, label the trade flows, and demonstrate the *gains from trade*.

3. Can you think of any patterns of comparative advantage and trade in the world economy that might have some significant environmental impacts? What are they?

Further Reading and Web Resources

A relatively accessible discussion of some of the material of this chapter can be found in Chapter 2 of Williamson and Milner (1991). A more advanced treatment can be found in Chapter 5 of Markusen et al. (1995). MIT economist Paul Krugman has written an interesting essay on comparative advantage entitled "Ricardo's Difficult Idea." This essay can be found on his Web site at **http://web.mit.edu/krugman/www/ricardo.htm**. Business students will find a relevant discussion of dynamic comparative advantage in Chapter 2 of Meier (1998).

If this chapter has inspired you to travel in Vietnam on a motorcycle, you should first consult Peter M. Geiser's Asian travel guide. Its Web site address is **http://www.pmgeiser.ch/vietnam/transport/motorcycle.htm**. A cautionary view of the role of motorcycles in Vietnam's urban development is found on the International Institute for Sustainable Development's Web site at **http://iisd1.iisd.ca/didigest/special/urban.htm**. IISD also has an interesting statement on the trade and environment issue that can be found at **http://iisd1.iisd.ca/trade/statement.htm**.

References

Beghin, J., and M. Potier (1997) "Effects of Trade Liberalisation on the Environment in the Manufacturing Sector," *The World Economy*, 20:4, 435–456.

Daly, H. (1993) "The Perils of Free Trade," *Scientific American*, November, 50–57.

Flowers, R.B. (2001) "The Sex Trade Industry's Worldwide Exploitation of Children," *Annals of the American Academy of Political and Social Science*, 575, 147–157.

Lee, H., and D.W. Roland-Holst (1997) "Trade and the Environment," in J.F. Francois and K.A. Reinert (eds.), *Applied Methods for Trade Policy Analysis: A Handbook*, Cambridge University Press, Cambridge, 517–550.

Mankiw, N.G. (2004) *Principles of Economics*, South-Western/Thomson Learning, Mason, Ohio.

Markusen, J.R., J.R. Melvin, W.H. Kaempfer, and K.E. Maskus (1995) *International Trade: Theory and Evidence*, McGraw-Hill, New York.

Meier, G.M. (1998) *The International Environment of Business*, Oxford University Press, Oxford.

Ricardo, D. (1951) *On the Principles of Political Economy and Taxation*, Cambridge University Press, Cambridge (first published in 1817).

Runge, C.F. (1994) *Freer Trade, Protected Environment*, Council on Foreign Relations, New York.

Sen, A. (1989) "Development as Capability Expansion," *Journal of Development Planning*, 19, 41–58.

Williamson, J., and C. Milner (1991) *The World Economy*, New York University Press, New York.

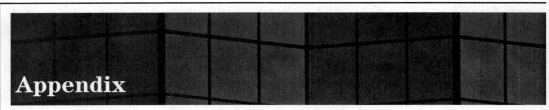

Appendix

The Production Possibilities Frontier

Consider an economy that produces two goods, rice and motorcycles. The quantities in these two sectors we will call Q_R and Q_M, respectively. We will depict the supply side of this economy using a production possibilities frontier (PPF) diagram. The PPF depicts the combinations of output of rice and motorcycles that the economy can produce given its available resources and technology. The PPF is depicted in Figure 3.A1. The PPF is depicted as the *concave* line in this figure. Given the available resources and technology, the economy can produce anywhere on or inside the PPF. Point A, on the PPF itself, is one such point. If the economy were at point A on the PPF, it would be producing Q_{RA} of rice and Q_{MA} of motorcycles. If the economy were to move from point A to point B, the output of rice would increase from Q_{RA} to Q_{RB}. However, the output of motorcycles would *fall* from Q_{MA} to Q_{MB}. The fall in motorcycle output is an example of a very general and very important concept in economics: *opportunity cost*. Opportunity cost is what must be forgone when a particular decision is made. If this economy choos-

Figure 3.A1 The Production Possibilities Frontier

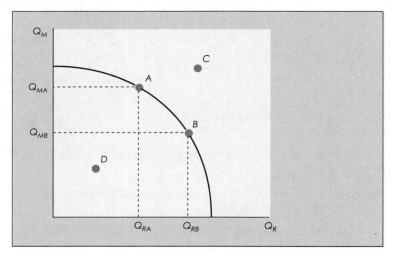

es to move from point A to point B, the decreased production of motorcycles is the opportunity cost of the increased production of rice.

Point C is another production point in Figure 3.A1. It is more desirable than either points A or B, since point C provides more of both rice and motorcycles compared to A and B. Point C, however, is infeasible given the resources and technology of the economy. Point D, inside the PPF, is feasible. However, in comparison to points A and B, it offers less of both rice and motorcycles. Points A and B are said to be *efficient* in that at these points the economy is getting all it can from its scarce resources. This is not true at point D, and consequently, point D is *inefficient*.

How are the relative prices we use in this chapter determined in a PPF? We consider this in Figure 3.A2, using the following steps:

Step 1. The slope of the PPF $\left(\Delta Q_M / \Delta Q_R\right)$ is the opportunity cost of the good on the horizontal axis, rice. It indicates how many motorcycles must be given up to produce an additional unit of rice.

Step 2. In a perfectly competitive market system, when resources are fully employed, the opportunity costs are fully reflected in relative prices. The relative price of rice, the good on the horizontal axis, is $\left(P_R / P_M\right)$.

Step 3. A tangent line to the PPF shares the same slope of the PPF, namely $\left(\Delta Q_M / \Delta Q_R\right)$.

Step 4. Given Steps 1, 2, and 3, we can see that a tangent line to the PPF has a slope equal to the relative price of the good on the horizontal axis, $\left(P_R / P_M\right)$.

This is the result we use in this chapter and indicated in Figure 3.A2.

Does the result of step 4 that the slope of a tangent line represents the relative price of rice, the good on the horizontal axis, make any sense? Let's

Figure 3.A2 Relative Prices and the Production Possibilities Frontier

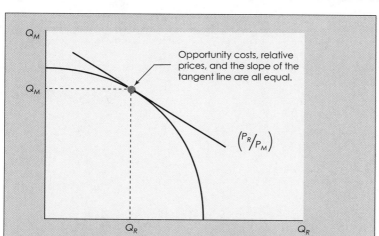

look at this a bit further in Figure 3.A3. Suppose that, from point A, we want to *increase* the output of rice from Q_{RA} to Q_{RB}. Because there are opportunity costs of production represented by the PPF, this implies a *decrease* in the output of motorcycles from Q_{MA} to Q_{MB}. As production moves from point A to point B, the slope of the PPF increases, reflecting increasing opportunity costs of rice production. To offset these increasing opportunity costs, the relative price of rice must rise. Therefore, increasing the output of rice requires increasing its relative price from $(P_R/P_M)_A$ to the steeper $(P_R/P_M)_B$. This supply relationship, equivalent to the upward-sloping rice supply curve of Chapter 2, indeed makes economic sense.

Figure 3.A3 An Increase in Rice Output

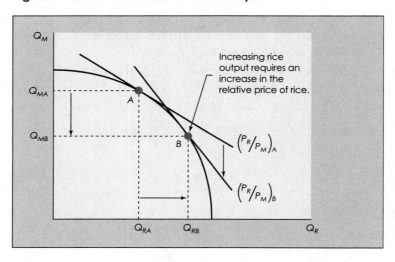

Intra-Industry Trade

Once, while visiting the World Trade Organization in Geneva, I took a 3-day side trip to Cleremont-Ferrand, France, in order to visit some students who were on study abroad in that beautiful city. At my first buffet breakfast in the hotel, I noticed an exceptional-looking blue cheese. It was as exceptional to eat as to look at, and upon my inquiry, I learned that this was the famed blue d'Auvergne *from the surrounding region.[1] I ate as much of it as I could during my short trip and, upon my return to the United States, began to purchase it whenever possible. In this way, I began to contribute to the total volume of cheese imports of the United States. It turns out, however, that the United States also exports cheese, especially what is known as "food-service" cheese (admittedly less exceptional than the* blue d'Auvergne*). Thus, the United States both imports and exports cheese, a phenomenon known as* intra-industry trade.*

In this chapter, you will begin to appreciate this important type of trade. You will also understand how it differs from inter-industry trade, why it occurs, and its role in the world economy.

Intra-Industry Versus Inter-Industry Trade

In Chapter 3, we discussed the important concept of comparative advantage. In our example in that chapter, we saw that Japan imported rice and exported motorcycles, while Vietnam exported rice and imported motorcycles. This is an example of how comparative advantage is associated with **inter-industry trade**. In inter-industry trade, a country *either* imports *or* exports a given product. Our example of U.S. cheese trade is quite different. The United States *both* imports *and* exports cheese. As is indicated in Table 4.1, you should have the following associations in mind when distinguishing **intra-industry trade** from inter-industry trade:

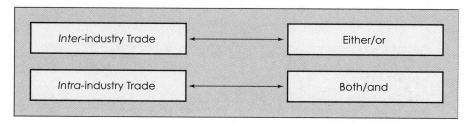

| *Inter*-industry Trade | ⟷ | Either/or |
| *Intra*-industry Trade | ⟷ | Both/and |

Inter-industry trade
A pattern of trade in which a country either imports or exports in a given sector.

Intra-industry trade
A pattern of trade in which a country both imports and exports in a given sector.

---

[1] The term *blue d'Auvergne* is one example of what is known as a *regional indicator* in international trade law. We will encounter regional indicators in our discussion of intellectual property in Chapter 7.

Table 4.1 Two Types of Trade

Type of Trade	Phrase	Meaning	Source
Inter-industry	Either/or	Either imports or exports in a given sector of the economy	Comparative advantage
Intra-industry	Both/and	Both imports and exports in a given sector of the economy	Product differentiation

As we mentioned earlier, and as indicated in Table 4.1, inter-industry trade has its source in comparative advantage, in the differences in technology and factor endowments of countries. Intra-industry trade is different. Its source lies in *product differentiation.*[2] The United States both imports and exports cheese because the cheese it imports is different from the cheese it exports. *Blue d'Auvergne* is not the same kind of product as food-service cheese or Wisconsin cheddar. Similarly, a Ford Escort is not exactly the same kind of product as a Honda Civic. These differences within product categories are what contribute to the phenomenon of intra-industry trade.[3]

Many textbooks in international economics pay little attention to intra-industry trade. This is unfortunate, because a very large proportion of world trade takes place as intra-industry trade. Although estimates vary, approximately one-fourth of world trade is of an intra-industry nature.[4] However, intra-industry trade is especially prominent in the trade of manufactured goods among the developed or high-income countries of the world, where it probably accounts for up to 70 percent of trade. Globally, intra-industry trade is becoming more important over time. We will have more to say about patterns of intra-industry trade in the world economy later in this chapter. Next, let's see how and why this type of trade occurs.

An Explanation of Intra-Industry Trade

We are now going to develop an explanation of intra-industry trade using the example of U.S. trade in cheese. In order to do this, we are going to have to allow for product differentiation among types of cheese. To keep things simple, we will restrict ourselves to two types of cheese: blue cheese (denoted by B) and food-service cheese (denoted by F). Because

[2] As stated by van Marrewijk (2002), "A satisfactory theoretical explanation (of intra-industry trade) should . . . be able to distinguish between goods and services which are close, but imperfect substitutes" (p. 183).
[3] Some caution is necessary here. Due to a lack of disaggregation, comparative advantage can work beneath what appears to be intra-industry trade. Suppose the United States exports computer chips to Mexico; these chips are then assembled into an actual computer. Next, the computer is exported back to the United States. This appears to be intra-industry trade in "computers and related devices." However, as noted by Krugman and Obstfeld (2000, p. 138n), it is really "pseudo-intra-industry trade" based on inexpensive labor in Mexico, giving Mexico a comparative advantage in labor-intensive goods such as computer assembly. See, however, footnote 9.
[4] See Krugman and Obstfeld (2000, p. 138).

there are two distinct products, there are two distinct markets, each with it own price and quantity. This situation is represented in Figure 4.1.

Figure 4.1 depicts the two cheese markets from the perspective of the United States. There are two sets of axes, one for each type of cheese, with prices (P_B and P_F) on the vertical axes and quantities (Q_B and Q_F) on the horizontal axes. U.S. households consume both types of cheese, and U.S. firms produce both types of cheese. U.S. demand curves for the two types of cheese are denoted D_B and D_F, and these are downward sloping. U.S. supply curves for the two types of cheese are denoted S_B and S_F, and these are upward sloping. The U.S. supply curve for food-service cheese is farther to the right than its supply curve for blue cheese. This reflects the presence of more firms producing food-service cheese than blue cheese.

The trade implications of these supply and demand relationships are illustrated in Figure 4.2. To simplify the situation, we are going to assume that the United States cannot influence the world price of either type of

Figure 4.1 Markets for Blue and Food-Service Cheese

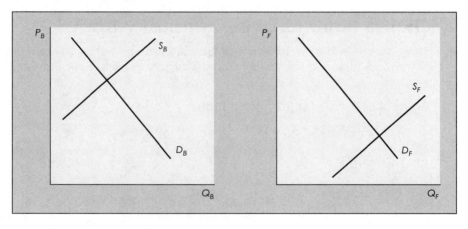

Figure 4.2 U.S. Intra-Industry Trade in Cheese

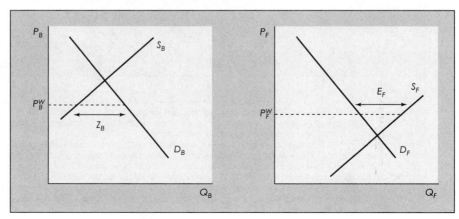

cheese.[5] Thus, in Figure 4.2, the United States cannot affect the values of either P_B^W or P_F^W along the vertical axes. Therefore, even with quality differences implying that the world price of food-service cheese is below the world price of blue cheese ($P_F^W < P_B^W$), the United States exports E_F of food-service cheese and imports Z_B of blue cheese. In this way, the United States engages in intra-industry trade in cheese, both importing and exporting cheese.

Does intra-industry trade in cheese benefit the United States, or is it unnecessary and wasteful? Some observers would argue the latter, claiming that it would be better if each country produced and consumed a single variety of a product.[6] We take up this issue in Figure 4.3. This figure is the same as Figure 4.2, but it includes autarky prices for the United States (P_B^{US} and P_F^{US}). Take first the blue cheese market. You can see that, as the United States moves from autarky to trade, the gain in U.S. consumer surplus ($A + B$) exceeds the loss in U.S. producer surplus (A) by area B.[7] Next take the food-service cheese market. You can see that, as the United States moves from autarky to trade, the gain in U.S. producer surplus ($C + D$) exceeds the loss in U.S. consumer surplus (C) by area D. Therefore, the movement from autarky to intra-industry trade entails a total gain of areas B and D. There are gains from intra-industry trade as well as from inter-industry trade.

Global Patterns of Intra-Industry Trade

As we stated in the introduction to this chapter, approximately one-fourth of world trade is intra-industry trade. This increases to approximately 70

Figure 4.3 The Gains from Intra-Industry Trade

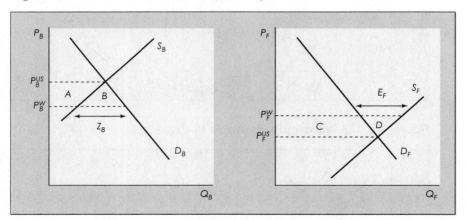

[5] This comprises what international economists call the "small country assumption." For the case of the United States in world cheese markets, this might not always be a good assumption. We use it here, however, to simplify our analysis of intra-industry trade.

[6] For example, Daly (1993) states: "Contrary to the implications of comparative advantage, more than half of all international trade involves the simultaneous import and export of essentially the same goods. For example, Americans import Danish sugar cookies, and Danes import American sugar cookies. Exchanging recipes would surely be more efficient" (p. 51). Daly's estimate of the extent of intra-industry trade exceeds the estimate of Krugman and Obstfeld (2000) cited in our introduction.

[7] Recall that there is an appendix to Chapter 2 reviewing the consumer surplus and producer surplus ideas. Please refer to it if you need to refresh your memory.

percent if we consider only trade among the high-income countries of the world. Indeed, intra-industry trade was first analyzed in the context of trade among the countries of Western Europe, as well as trade between the United States and Europe. The early study by Grubel and Lloyd (1975) focused on intra-industry trade among 10 countries of the Organization for Economic Cooperation and Development (OECD), an organization consisting of mostly high-income countries. These 10 countries were Australia, Belgium, Canada, France, Italy, Japan, the Netherlands, the United Kingdom, the United States, and West Germany. These authors developed an index used to measure the degree of intra-industry trade that is explained in the appendix to this chapter. Using this index, they noted an increase in intra-industry trade among these 10 countries during the 1960s. Subsequent studies found that this trend continued into the 1970s and beyond.

It turns out, however, that it is a mistake to envision intra-industry trade as taking place exclusively among high-income countries. I mentioned in Chapter 1 that I spent the early years of the 1990s analyzing NAFTA for the U.S. International Trade Commission. As part of this analysis, I had to develop a database of trade among the countries of North America: Canada, Mexico, and the United States. My first such database was for the year 1988. The trade flows from this database are presented in Table 4.2. What struck me at the time was the decidedly intra-industry character of these trade flows. With the few exceptions of petroleum, non-metallic minerals, and nonelectrical machinery, trade between these two countries was very balanced. I realized at that time that intra-industry trade could take place between low- and high-income countries as well as between high-income countries.[8] Shortly thereafter, Globerman (1992) published results indicating substantial increases in intra-industry trade between the U.S. and Mexico between 1980 and 1988. Ruffin (1999) analyzed trade between Mexico and the United States for 1998, a decade later than the year of my database. His conclusion was that "about 80 percent of U.S. trade with Mexico is intra-industry" (p. 8).[9]

More recently, evidence of increases in intra-industry trade in Asia has surfaced. As indicated in the box, intra-industry trade in Asia appears to be most important among the newly industrialized countries (Singapore, Hong Kong, and South Korea) and the newly exporting countries (Malaysia, Thailand, the Philippines, and Indonesia). However, evidence also exists of increasing intra-industry trade between Japan and other Asian countries (e.g., Wakasugi, 1997), as well as in the trade of China and

---

[8] Thus, the following statement from Grimwade (1989) is not always an accurate guide: "When any two countries are at different stages of economic development, inter-industry trade is likely to be relatively more important than intra-industry trade" (p. 128). That said, however, the U.S.–Mexico case could be special due to their common border, as Grimwade acknowledges: "Intra-industry trade is greatest between countries which either share a common border or are in close geographic proximity" (p. 132).

[9] For reasons we discussed in footnote 3, some of what appears to be intra-industry trade in Table 4.2 might actually be "psuedo-intra-industry trade," reflecting the labor-abundant nature of Mexico. It would be wrong, however, to conclude that *all* of the intra-industry trade in this table is of this nature. See Ruffin (1999) who notes that "The United States exports automobile parts to Mexico, where the cars are assembled, and some are shipped back. But the flow of automobile parts is actually heavier from Mexico to the United States" (p. 8).

Table 4.2 Trade Between the United States and Mexico, 1988 (millions of U.S. dollars)

Sector	U.S. Imports from Mexico	Mexico's Imports from U.S.
Agriculture	1,145	1507
Mining	129	126
Petroleum	4,179	467
Food processing	922	823
Textiles	154	376
Clothing	546	336
Leather	218	215
Paper	443	967
Chemicals	1,173	1,328
Rubber	438	1,167
Nonmetalic minerals	9	130
Metals	1,059	906
Wood and metal products	1,271	927
Nonelectrical machinery	724	3,836
Electrical machinery	6,599	5,061
Transportation equipment	3,499	2,224
Other manufacturing	1,018	240

Source: Reinert, K.A., Roland-Holst, D.W., and Sheills, C.R. (1993). "Social Accounts and the Structure of the North American Economy." *Economics System Research* 5 (3): 295-326. Used with permission of Taylor & Francis Journals, http://www.tandf.co.uk.

her major trading partners (e.g., Hu and Ma, 1999). Hence, we can view intra-industry trade as a global process that is increasing over time.[10]

The increasing extent of intra-industry trade in the world trading system has some important implications for the adjustment of economies to increasing trade. Recall from Chapters 2 and 3 that increases in inter-industry trade based on absolute or comparative advantage involve import sectors contracting and export sectors expanding. This, in turn, requires that productive resources, most notably workers, shift from contracting to expand-

[10]Some results from the China study are presented in the appendix to this chapter.

Intra-Industry Trade in Asia

The phenomenon of intra-industry trade was first noticed in the expansion of trade among the countries of Western Europe and between Western Europe and the United States that occurred after World War II. Lately, however, researchers have recognized its importance for the countries of Asia. For example, Lisbeth Hellvin classified ten Asian countries into three groups: newly industrialized countries or NICs (Singapore, Hong Kong, Republic of Korea); newly exporting countries or NECs (Malaysia, Thailand, the Philippines, and Indonesia); and less developed countries or LDCs (India, Sri Lanka, and Pakistan). Hellvin's results on the percent of trade that is intra-industry in nature among these Asian countries was as follows:

Trade Between	Percentage
NICs–NICs	23.4
NICs–NECs	29.0
NECs–NECs	21.1
LDCs–LDCs	1.1
NICs–LDCs	6.2
NECs–LDCs	0.7

As can be seen from these results, the Asian LDCs are *much* less involved in intra-industry trade than the Asian NECs and NICs. This reflects the importance of manufactured goods in intra-industry trade. The trade of Asian LDCs is much more focused on primary products where product differentiation, and hence intra-industry trade, is less likely.

Source: Table 1 in Hellvin, L. (1994). "Intra-Industry Trade in Asia." *International Economic Journal*, 8 (4): 29.

ing sectors in order to avoid unemployment. Workers in Vietnam must shift from the motorcycle sector to the rice sector. Workers in Japan must shift from the rice sector to the motorcycle sector. This is not always an easy process and, as we will discuss in Chapter 5, it often gives rise to calls for protection.

The adjustment process in the case of intra-industry trade is very different. A given sector experiences increases in imports and exports simultaneously. Therefore, workers are less likely to need to shift between sectors. Workers in the U.S. cheese sector can adjust to the expansion of imports of cheese by expanding exports of a different variety. Consequently, demands for protection from increased imports are less likely.[11]

In my experience, both international economists and the general public resist these insights with regard to intra-industry trade. For this reason, I am going to take the liberty of quoting from two sources on the matter to further emphasize the point:

---

[11]Empirical evidence of intra-industry trade reducing demand for trade protection was first given in Marvel and Ray (1987).

(I)ntra-industry specialization is likely to give rise to fewer adjustment problems than inter-industry specialization. This is because it necessitates a movement of resources within rather than between industries. Inter-industry specialization necessitates a movement of resources from import-competing to export-expanding industries. Adjustment problems can arise where resources, especially labor, are geographically and occupationally immobile in the short run. Large-scale structural employment might result. To a large extent, intra-industry specialization is achieved without the necessity for workers to leave a particular industry or region. The risk of structural unemployment is reduced (Grimwade, 1989, p. 139).

One of the great benefits of intra-industry trade is that international trade need not cause the dislocations associated with inter-industry trade (Ruffin, 1999, p. 7).

To appreciate these insights, let's briefly apply them to the trade history of the United States. The expansion of trade that took place between the United States and Europe after World War II was primarily based on intra-industry trade in manufactured products. It therefore developed with relatively little political difficulty. On the contrary, the expansion of trade that took place between the United States and the developing world was less smooth. The United Sates resisted accepting imports of agricultural goods and clothing from the developing world because these tended to reflect patterns of inter-industry trade. Indeed, as we will see in Chapter 7, trade in these sectors was largely outside of the General Agreements on Tariffs and Trade (GATT).

Conclusion

In Chapters 2 and 3, we considered models of inter-industry trade. However, approximately one-fourth of world trade consists of intra-industry trade. Consequently, in this chapter, we have used the supply and demand diagram to develop a simple analysis of this second kind of trade. If, as you proceed through this book, you have trouble distinguishing the two kinds of trade, refer to Table 4.1, which summarizes the difference. Our model of intra-industry trade allows for product differentiation. The result is that there can be *both* imports *and* exports in a given sector. This kind of trade can be politically more palatable than inter-industry trade because it requires less adjustment in industry structure and employment.

Review Exercises

1. In your own words, explain the difference between inter-industry and intra-industry trade.

2. How is the phenomenon of intra-industry trade related to product diversification?

3. Create your own example of an intra-industry trade model by choosing a country and a product. Draw a diagram equivalent to Figure 4.2 describing intra-industry trade for your example. Next, draw a diagram equivalent to Figure 4.3 describing the gains from intra-industry trade.

4. Explain why the adjustment process stemming from intra-industry trade is easier for a country to accommodate than the adjustment process stemming from inter-industry trade.

Further Reading and Web Resources

The original work on intra-industry trade was by Grubel and Lloyd (1975). Overviews of intra-industry trade can be found in Bergstrand (1982), Chapter 3 of Grimwade (1989), Greenaway and Torstensson (1997), Ruffin (1999), and in Chapter 6 of Krugman and Obstfeld (2000). Francois and Reinert (1997, Section I.3) discuss different approaches to product differentiation in intra-industry trade models, and a concise review of the intra-industry trade literature is given in Chapter 10 of van Marrewijk (2002).

The excellent Ruffin article on intra-industry trade can also be found online at **http://www.dallasfed.org/htm/pubs/pdfs/efr/efr9904a.pdf**. The U.S. Dairy Export Council maintains a Web site at **http://www. usdec.org**.

References

Bergstrand, J.H. (1982) "The Scope, Growth, and Causes of Intra-Industry International Trade," *New England Economic Review*, September–October 1982, 45–61.

Daly, H.E. (1993) "The Perils of Free Trade," *Scientific American*, November, 50–57.

Francois, J.F., and K.A. Reinert (1997) "Applied Methods for Trade Policy Analysis: An Overview," in J.F. Francois and K.A. Reinert (eds.), *Applied Methods for Trade Policy Analysis: A Handbook*, Cambridge University Press, Cambridge, 3–24.

Globerman, S. (1992) "North American Trade Liberalization and Intra-Industry Trade," *Weltwirtschaftliches Archiv*, 128:3, 487–497.

Greenaway, D., and J. Torstensson (1997) "Back to the Future: Taking Stock on Intra-Industry Trade," *Weltwirtschaftliches Archiv*, 133:2, 249–269.

Grimwade, N. (1989) *International Trade: New Patterns of Trade, Production, and Investment*, Routledge, London.

Grubel, H.G., and P.J. Loyd (1975) *Intra-Industry Trade: The Theory and Measurement of International Trade in Differentiated Products*, John Wiley, New York.

Hellvin, L. (1994) "Intra-Industry Trade in Asia," *International Economic Journal*, 8:4, 27–40.

Hu, X., and Y. Ma (1999) "International Intra-Industry Trade of China," *Weltwirtschaftliches Archiv*, 135:1, 82–101.

Krugman, P.R., and M. Obstfeld (2000) *International Economics: Theory and Policy*, Addison-Wesley, Reading, Massachusetts.

Marvel, H.P., and E.J. Ray (1987) "Intraindustry Trade: Sources and Effects on Production," *Journal of Political Economy*, 95:6, 1278–1291.

Reinert, K.A., D.W. Roland-Holst, and C.R. Shiells (1993) "Social Accounts and the Structure of the North American Economy," *Economic Systems Research*, 5:3, 295–326.

Ruffin, R.J. (1999) "The Nature and Significance of Intra-Industry Trade," *Federal Reserve Bank of Dallas Economic and Financial Review*, 4th Quarter, 2–9.

van Marrewijk, C. (2002) *International Trade and the World Economy*, Oxford University Press, Oxford.

Wakasugi, R. (1997) "Missing Factors of Intra-Industry Trade: Some Empirical Evidence Based on Japan," *Japan and the World Economy*, 9:3, 353–362.

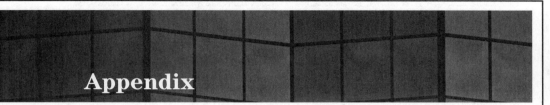

Appendix

The Grubel-Lloyd Index

We mentioned in this chapter that Grubel and Lloyd (1975) completed the first important study of intra-industry trade. In this study, these authors developed what is now a well-known index for measuring the degree of intra-industry trade. This measure is called the **Grubel-Lloyd index**. This appendix introduces you to this index and provides a brief example of its application to China.

The Grubel-Lloyd index looks at a given product category denoted by the letter i. The index of intra-industry trade in this product category is usually denoted by B_i. B_i is calculated based on the level of imports of product i (denoted Z_i) and the level of exports of product i (denoted E_i). The Grubel-Lloyd index is calculated as

$$B_i = \left[1 - \frac{|E_i - Z_i|}{(E_i + Z_i)} \right] \times 100$$

Recall that $|E_i - Z_i|$ refers to the *absolute value* of the difference between exports and imports of product i. This value is always positive. The best way to make sense of the Grubal-Lloyd index is to consider the case where intra-industry trade is at its maximum. That is where exports and imports of product i are exactly equal to one another. In this case, $|E_i - Z_i| = 0$ and $B_i = (1 - 0) \times 100 = 100$. Therefore, the Grubal-Lloyd index ranges from 0 to 100. As the index increases from 0 to 100, the amount of intra-industry trade in product category i increases.

Table 4.A1 reports a few measures of intra-industry trade for China calculated by Hu and Ma (1999) using the Grubal-Lloyd index. As you can see from this table, and as noted by Hu and Ma, the level of intra-industry trade in China varies greatly among industries.

Grubel-Lloyd index
An index of the degree of intra-industry trade that varies between 0 and 100.

Table 4.A1 China's Intra-Industry Trade in 1995

Sector	Grubel-Lloyd Index
Organic chemicals	0.02
Toys and sporting goods	14.9
Aircraft	18.9
Iron, steel, plate, sheet	41.4
Aluminum	58.8
Cotton fabrics, woven	61.3
Telecom equipment	73.9
Organic-inorganic compounds, etc.	85.4
Nitrogen-function compounds	90.6
Knitted fabrics, etc.	96.4

Source: Hu, X. and Y. Ma (1999). "International Intra-Industry Trade of China." *Weltwirtschaftliches Archiv*, 135 (1): 32-101. Copyright © 1999 by Springer-Verlag.

The Politics of Trade

5

In Chapter 3, you learned that it was possible for countries to move from autarky to inter-industry trading relationships based on patterns of comparative advantage. So, for example, Japan could export motorcycles to Vietnam while importing rice from Vietnam. You also learned that such movements from autarky to trade involved improvements in welfare for the countries involved. In other words, both Japan and Vietnam experienced gains from trade. In point of fact, however, Japan has a long history of preventing the importation of rice. This reluctance to import rice has been explained by the consulate general of Japan in San Francisco:

> *Rice has been the staple of the Japanese for over 200 years and can be considered the most important element in the evolution of the Japanese culture and social structure. Therefore, a significant segment of the Japanese population express cultural concerns over rice imports. In addition, many Japanese rice producers have historically been strongly opposed to accepting rice imports for both economic security and cultural reasons.*

Indeed, during the Uruguay Round of multilateral trade negotiations, the Japanese Diet (parliament) passed three resolutions opposing the proposed partial liberalization of the Japanese rice market. At the very end of the Uruguay Round negotiations (in 1994), Japan was given "special treatment" to continue to restrict rice imports.[1]

Welcome to the politics of international trade. In Chapters 2 and 3, we were careful to mention that the improvement in overall welfare in a country that occurs due to the gains from trade does not necessarily imply an improvement in welfare for *every* individual and group in that country. In this chapter, you will learn that it is both possible and likely that, in countries moving from autarky to trade, certain groups actually *lose* from this change. Japanese rice producers are one such politically powerful group. The fact that there are both winners and losers from international trade gives rise to the politics of trade. This is a realm where the theory of international trade begins to merge somewhat into political science, a very exciting prospect for many scholars and practitioners.

We will begin in this chapter by revisiting the model of comparative advantage we developed in Chapter 3. This will be the initial framework in which we examine the politics of trade. We will then consider the role of factors of production in comparative advantage as described by the Heckscher-Ohlin model of trade. Next, we will take up a famous result

---

[1] More recently, in early 2001, Japan began to investigate the possibility of restricting imports of *shiitake* mushrooms from China. Again, "economic security and cultural reasons" were involved.

in the politics of trade known as the Stolper-Samuelson theorem. We will examine the application of this theorem to the topic of North–South trade. Finally, we will consider the role of specific factors in the politics of trade.

Comparative Advantage Revisited

In order to begin talking more specifically about the politics of trade, it is useful to revisit the model of comparative advantage we developed in Chapter 3. Figure 5.1 reproduces Figure 3.4 from that chapter. Recall that Vietnam has a comparative advantage in the production of rice (denoted R) and Japan has a comparative advantage in the production of motorcycles (denoted M). As these two economies move from autarky to trade, production in each country expands in the direction of the sector in which it has comparative advantage. In the movement from points A to B along the production possibility frontiers in Figure 5.1, rice production expands in Vietnam, and motorcycle production expands in Japan. At an elementary level, then, we can say that trade in this case is "good" for the rice sector in Vietnam and for the motorcycle sector in Japan. However, trade is "harmful" to the motorcycle sector in Vietnam and to the rice sector in Japan, both of which experience a decline in output. The purpose of this chapter is to analyze these simple statements more carefully.

What determines the pattern of comparative advantage illustrated in Figure 5.1? Recall from Chapters 2 and 3 that there are two broad determinants: technology and factors of production. An analysis of the politics of trade takes up the latter determinant and examines the implications of the movement from points A to B in Figure 5.1 for factors of production in Vietnam and Japan. We begin this inquiry in the following section.

Figure 5.1 Autarky and Comparative Advantage in Vietnam and Japan

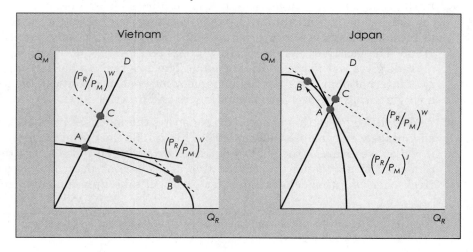

Trade and Factors of Production

Suppose that the pattern of comparative advantage illustrated in Figure 5.1 is based on different *endowments* of factors of production. More specifically, suppose that Vietnam's comparative advantage in rice reflects the fact that it has a relatively large endowment of land. In the language of international trade theory, Vietnam is relatively *land abundant*. By this, we mean that the ratio of land to physical capital is larger in Vietnam than in Japan. This relative abundance of land gives Vietnam a comparative advantage in producing the land-intensive good, rice. Similarly, suppose that Japan's comparative advantage in motorcycles reflects the fact that it has a relatively large endowment of physical capital. In the language of international trade theory, Japan is relatively *capital abundant*. By this, we mean that the ratio of physical capital to land is larger in Japan than in Vietnam. This relative abundance of capital gives Japan a comparative advantage in producing the capital-intensive good, motorcycles.[2]

We must pause here for a moment. In the previous paragraph, we associated the term "endowments" with countries (Vietnam, Japan) and the term "intensities" with sectors or goods (rice, motorcycles). It is very easy forget these associations, so we must keep them firmly in mind. Here is something you can write down on a piece of paper to refer to as you read the remainder of this section:

Factor endowments ⟷ Countries
Factor intensities ⟷ Sectors or goods

The explanation of comparative advantage in terms of factor endowments is associated with the **Heckscher-Ohlin model** of international trade.[3] This model is one of the most famous models in trade theory. The logic of Heckscher-Ohlin model is illustrated in the top six boxes of Figure 5.2. The top two boxes of this figure concern factor endowments. Vietnam is relatively land abundant, and Japan is relatively capital abundant. The next two boxes concern the pattern of comparative advantage. Vietnam has a comparative advantage in rice (land intensive), and Japan has a comparative advantage in motorcycles (capital intensive). The third level of boxes in Figure 5.2 concerns trade flows. In accordance with the pattern of comparative advantage, Vietnam exports rice to Japan, and Japan exports motorcycles to Vietnam.

More generally, the Heckscher-Ohlin model of international trade gives the following result with regard to trade:

Heckscher-Ohlin model
A model of international trade based on differences in factor endowments among the countries of the world.

> **A country exports the good whose production is intensive in its abundant factor. It imports the good whose production is intensive in its scarce factor.**

---

[2] You need to interpret these statements with care. We are saying that Vietnam is relatively land abundant in comparison to Japan. In comparison to its own population, land is indeed scarce in Vietnam. See *The Economist* (2002b).

[3] This model originated in the work of Heckscher (1949) and Ohlin (1933). A more modern description can be found in Chapter 8 of Markusen et al. (1995).

Figure 5.2 The Heckscher-Ohlin Model and the Stolper-Samuelson Theorem

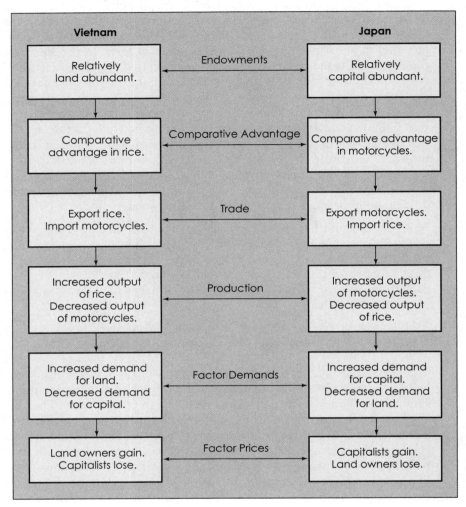

The implication of Figure 5.2 for the politics of trade is addressed in the bottom six boxes. In Vietnam, the comparative advantage in rice causes an increase in the output of rice at the expense of motorcycles. Consequently, there is an increase in demand for land and a decrease in demand for physical capital. These factor demand changes have the result that Vietnamese land owners gain from trade, while Vietnamese capital owners (capitalists) lose from trade.[4]

In Japan, the comparative advantage in motorcycles causes an increase in the output of motorcycles at the expense of rice. Consequently, there is an increase in demand for physical capital and a

---

[4] Given that Vietnam is a socialist country, we need to be careful here. Institutions of ownership can be very different than in fully market-oriented countries.

decrease in demand for land. These changes cause Japanese capital owners to gain from trade and Japanese land owners to lose from trade.

Given the results of Figure 5.2, we would expect that land owners in Vietnam and capital owners in Japan would support trade. Political opposition to trade would come from capital owners in Vietnam and land owners in Japan. Thus, we can see why the strong and persistent opposition to rice imports in Japan discussed in the introduction to this chapter arises and persists. It is due, at least in part, to the political clout of Japanese land owners. The reason, however, is not "economic security and culture." Rather, it is income loss.

Let's summarize these results in more general terms. In both Vietnam and Japan, the sector intensive in the country's abundant factor expands, while the sector intensive in the country's scarce factor contracts. This, in turn, causes an increase in the demand for the abundant factor in each country and a decrease in demand for the scarce factor in each country. These changes in demand, in turn, have implications for the returns to or incomes of the factors in question.

The Heckscher-Ohlin model thus has an important implication for the politics of trade, and these implications are summarized in a central result of international trade theory, the **Stolper-Samuelson theorem**.[5] In general terms, this theorem can be stated as follows:

> **As a country moves from autarky to trade, the country's abundant factor of production (used intensively in the export sector) gains, while the country's scarce factor of production (used intensively in the import sector) loses.**

Stolper-Samuelson theorem
A result of international trade theory concerning the politics of trade. It states that an increase in the relative price of a commodity (e.g., as a result of trade) raises the return to the factor used intensively in the production of that good and lowers the return to the other factor.

The Stolper-Samuelson theorem cannot be applied blindly. It applies only to trade based on different endowments in factors of production. Trade based on differences in technology can mitigate the effects described by the theorem. Technological considerations arise in the application of the theorem to the issue of North–South trade and wages.

North–South Trade and Wages

There is an application of the Stolper-Samuelson theorem that has generated a great deal of recent interest and controversy. This is the question of North–South trade and wages. The term "North" refers to the high-income or "developed" countries of the world; the term "South" refers to the low-income or "developing" countries of the world. High-income countries tend to be relatively capital abundant; low-income countries tend to be relatively labor abundant. The implications of these relative factor

---

[5] This theorem originated in a famous article by Wolfang Stolper and Paul Samuelson (1941). In the words of Deardorff (1998), "One might have thought and hoped that the broader gains from trade . . . might have allowed both abundant and scarce factors to gain from trade. . . . But alas no, Stolper and Samuelson showed this is not the case" (p. 364). Students and professionals struggling to publish their own work can take some comfort from the fact that the Stolper-Samuelson article was *rejected* by the first journal to which it was submitted.

endowments are illustrated in Figure 5.3. The Heckscher-Ohlin model of trade would suggest that the North has a comparative advantage in capital-intensive goods (CIGs) and that the South has a comparative advantage in labor-intensive goods (LIGs). This is illustrated in the top six boxes of Figure 5.3. Furthermore, the Stolper-Samuelson theorem would suggest that labor in the North would *lose* as a result of trade. This is illustrated in the bottom six boxes of Figure 5.3. The possibility of Northern labor losing as a result of trade has led labor interests in the North to be, in many instances, opposed to increased trade. For example, the U.S. labor movement opposed both the North American Free Trade Agreement (NAFTA) and the formation of the World Trade Organization (WTO).[6]

Figure 5.3   The Stolper-Samuelson Theorem and North–South Trade (LIGs—labor-intensive goods; CIGs—capital-intensive goods)

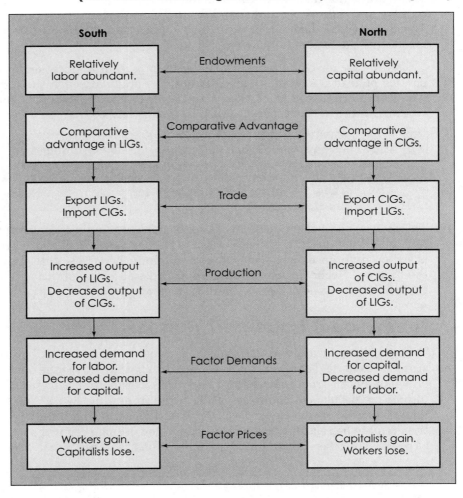

---

[6] In general, the labor movement in the European Union has a more nuanced approach to trade matters. I once met a German labor union representative who expressed trepidation about meeting with her U.S.–based colleagues to discuss trade matters. She considered them to be "too protectionist."

Trade and Wages in Latin America

We have suggested that developing countries in the South have a comparative advantage in *unskilled* labor-intensive goods. As suggested by the Heckscher-Ohlin model, this is a result of these countries being abundant in unskilled labor. If this is the case, then according to the Stolper-Samuelson theorem, increased trade would benefit unskilled labor in developing countries, relative to skilled labor. It turns out, however, that in some Latin American countries, the opposite appears to have been the case. For example, Tim Gindling and Donald Robbins have shown that trade liberalization in Chile and Costa Rica has been accompanied by decreases in the relative wages of unskilled workers. Why would the Stolper-Samuelson theorem be wrong?

One reason is trade in physical capital. As Chile and Costa Rica liberalized their trading regimes, firms imported more physical capital (machines) in order to remain competitive. Embodied in these machines was a newer technology level that demanded relatively more skilled workers than the old technology that had been in use. Consequently, as trade was liberalized, the technology effects overpowered the Stolper-Samuelson effects, and the net result was that unskilled workers lost relative to skilled workers as a result of trade.

Here, then, is another important case of the politics of trade. Given that the majority of workers in Latin America are unskilled and Latin American counties already have severe inequality problems, these results are of some cause for concern. They indicate that trade can, in some instances, exacerbate existing inequalities and, thereby, contribute to political tensions.

Sources: Robbins and Gindling (1999) and Gindling and Robbins (2001).

Although the possibility of Northern labor as a whole losing as a result of increased international trade with the South is in itself of some interest, there is a more subtle issue in the ongoing debate concerning North–South trade and wages that is very much worth emphasizing here. There is evidence that developing countries in the South have comparative advantage in *unskilled* labor-intensive goods (ULIGs) and that developed countries in the North have comparative advantage in *skilled* labor-intensive goods (SLIGs). If this is indeed true, then according to the Stolper-Samuelson theorem, the Northern workers who lose as a result of increased North–South trade are actually *unskilled* workers. This possibility is of a great deal of interest and concern. For example, since the early 1980s in the United States, unskilled workers have seen their wages decline relative to skilled workers, with negative impacts for the overall income distribution. Perhaps increased North–South trade has caused this relative wage decline.[7]

Since the early 1990s, these concerns have prompted ongoing empirical investigation into the effects of trade on Northern wages (see the box for the case of Southern wages). The number of studies is too large, and the technical issues too detailed, for a review here.[8] However, we can

---

[7] In the case of the United States, the concern has been summarized by Krugman and Lawrence (1996) as follows: "The conventional wisdom holds that foreign competition has eroded the U.S. manufacturing base, washing out the high-paying jobs that a strong manufacturing sector provides. . . . And because imports increasingly come from Third World countries with their huge reserves of unskilled labor, the heaviest burden of this foreign competition has ostensibly fallen on less educated American workers" (p. 35).

[8] For reviews, see Freeman (1995), Richardson (1995), and Deardorff (1998).

note the important empirical result that there are two (not one) main causes for the decline in relative wages of Northern unskilled workers: trade and technology.

The trade impacts are those suggested by the Stolper-Samuelson theorem, namely, that Northern unskilled workers lose because the North has a comparative advantage in skilled labor-intensive goods. These effects, however, tend to be smaller than the Stolper-Samuelson theorem would suggest. Why is this? First, there is some evidence that export-oriented industries in the United States pay higher wages than other industries. Consequently, the labor reallocations caused by increased trade tend to boost average wages.[9] Second, some North–South trade is based on higher labor productivity (better technology) in the North rather than differences in factor endowments. For these reasons, although important, trade is a less significant factor than technology for the decline in relative wages of Northern unskilled workers.

Let's turn to the technology effects of North–South trade on Northern unskilled workers. There appears to be an ongoing process of technological change in the North that increases demand for skilled workers and makes these workers more productive, relative to unskilled workers.[10] This is the process we mentioned in Chapter 1 in the box entitled "Technological Change in the World Economy." Deardorff (1998) aptly summarizes the relevance of this process to wage changes:

> *The computer revolution has made it possible for highly skilled workers, manipulating their environments with electronic devices, to produce far more than equally skilled workers could have previously, also replacing to a large extent the unskilled workers whose tasks are taken over increasingly by intelligent machines. As a result, the productivity and wages of skilled workers rise, while those of unskilled workers do not (p. 368).*

There are policy analysts in the North, with well-grounded concerns about the plight of unskilled Northern workers, who call for trade restrictions to address the effects of North–South trade on unskilled wages in the North. For a number of reasons, this is probably not the best policy approach. First, technology appears to be a more important factor than trade, and few policy analysts call for limiting technological change. Second, trade restrictions will suppress overall gains from trade in both the North and South. Third, such restrictions could violate multilateral commitments made in the WTO (see Chapter 7). Fourth, trade restrictions might harm unskilled workers in the South who are in more dire straits than their Northern counterparts. A more long-term and productive policy approach would be to offer other forms of support to unskilled Northern workers. These could be income supports (including trade adjustment assistance) or, perhaps more importantly, support to increase human capital assets (education, training). If there is one factor contributing to wage and income inequality in the North, it is the failure

---

[9] See Bernard and Jensen (1995).
[10] This appears to be part of the shift toward flexible manufacturing systems and has had the effect of suppressing blue-collar wages. We will discuss flexible manufacturing systems in Chapter 9.

to complete secondary (high school) education. Remedying educational failures is an important, and neglected, policy imperative in Northern countries as well as in Southern countries.

The Role of Specific Factors

There is a central assumption that is part of the Heckscher-Ohlin model and its Stolper-Samuelson theorem. This is that resources or factors of production such as labor, physical capital, and land can move effortlessly among different sectors of trading economies. So, for example, Japanese resources are assumed to be able to shift back and forth between rice and motorcycle production. The same is assumed to be true for Vietnam. For some types of analysis, particularly that applying to the long run, this "perfect factor mobility" assumption is reasonable. In other instances, the assumption can be at odds with reality. Instead, factors of production can be sector specific. These types of factors are known in trade theory as **specific factors**. Specific factors are those that cannot move easily from one sector to another, and they can play an important role in the politics of trade.[11]

Specific factors
Factors of production that cannot move easily from one sector to another.

The presence of specific factors requires a modification of the Stolper-Samuelson theorem. To see this, let's consider the example of steel production in the United States. The United States is, without a doubt, relatively abundant in physical capital. The Stolper-Samuelson theorem would therefore suggest that capital owners in the United States would *gain* as a result of increased trade. But here is a puzzle. In its 2000 annual report, the U.S.–based Weirton Steel Corporation drew attention to what it called an "import crisis" and pledged to fight the "import war." It said it planned to "aggressively seek changes in Washington (DC) to stop the devastation caused by unfair trade." This hardly sounds like capitalists gaining from trade.

Why would capitalists in a capital abundant country oppose increased trade in violation of the Stolper-Samuelson theorem? As it turns out, the notion of specific factors helps us to address this puzzle. Weirton Steel Corporation, and many other U.S. steel firms, are owners of large amounts of specific factors in the form of steel mills, some of them very large, integrated facilities. These facilities cannot move into the production of other products such as semiconductors. They are *specific* to the production of steel.

A modification of the Stolper-Samuelson theorem in the face of such specific factors is important to understanding the U.S. steel case. This modification is as follows:

> **Factors of production that are specific to import sectors tend to lose as a result of trade, while factors of production specific to export sectors tend to gain as a result of trade.**

---

[11]Jones (1971) first emphasized the role of specific factors in models of international trade.

U.S. Steel Protection

In September 1998, twelve U.S. steel companies, including Weirton Steel, filed cases with the U.S. government alleging that the hot-rolled steel exports of Russia, Japan, and Brazil had been unfairly "dumped" or sold at "less than fair value" in U.S. markets. The U.S. International Trade Commission (USITC) found in favor of the U.S. steel industry, and protection to offset the dumping was applied. In June 1999, seven U.S. steel companies, again including Weirton Steel, filed follow-up cases involving cold-rolled steel exports of China, South Africa, Turkey, Brazil, Argentina, Thailand, Russia, Venezuela, Japan, Indonesia, Slovakia, and Taiwan. The USITC found in favor of the U.S. steel industry in the cases of Indonesia, Slovakia, and Taiwan. Next, in October 1999, Weirton steel filed an antidumping case against Japan's exports of tin mill products, and the USITC found in Weirton's favor.

Despite these results, capping two decades of special protection, the U.S. steel industry felt that a more comprehensive solution was required to support the incomes of its sector-specific factors. Under the banner "Stand Up for Steel," the U.S. steel industry pressed on with a campaign for further protection. This campaign, in which Weirton played a leading role, included petitions, lobbying, and even motorcycle rallies ("Ride for Steel"). The efforts were most well-organized in Weirton's home state, West Virginia, a state that helped secure George W. Bush's position as President through switches in party loyalties.

In June 2001, President Bush's administration instructed the USITC to undertake a *global safeguard investigation* of U.S. steel imports. Such an investigation does not require a finding of "unfair" trade or "dumping," nor is it targeted to specific countries. In December 2001, the USITC found that the U.S. steel industry had been subject to injury as a result of imports and recommended certain remedies. In March 2002, the Bush administration imposed a number of protection measures, including tariffs of up to 30 percent, on US$30 billion worth of steel imports. The European Union and Japan, both of whom were targets in the protection, vowed to appeal to the World Trade Organization in Geneva.

Sources: *The Economist* (2002a) and Weirton Steel Corporation.

Thus, Weirton Steel's actions are not difficult to understand. It is a company in an import sector that is characterized by sector-specific physical capital (and perhaps even labor). The owners of Weirton Steel therefore stand to lose as a result of increased trade. Consequently, as described in the box, the firm entered the "import war" to attempt to reduce imports and protect the incomes of its specific factors.

It is not always easy to keep the difference between specific and mobile factors in mind when assessing the politics of trade. For this reason, we need a box to help us.

Mobile factors of production: **The Stolper-Samuelson theorem applies. The abundant factor of production (used intensively in the export sector) gains, while the scarce factor of production (used intensively in the import sector) loses.**

Specific factors of production: **The Stolper-Samuelson theorem does *not* apply. The factor of production specific to the export sector gains, while the factor of production specific to the import sector loses. The fate of mobile factors is uncertain.**

When you come upon a politics of trade issue, in any country of the trading world, it will be very helpful to your understanding if you first pause for a moment and try to identify the mobile or specific factors of production involved. Then glance at the previous box. The politics of trade issue should be very much clarified by this process. If not, it is probably the case that technology, not factors of production, drives the trade involved.

Conclusion

In this chapter, we have seen that the movement from autarky to trade in any country can hurt some groups of people in that country. According to the Stolper-Samuelson theorem of the Heckscher-Ohlin model, this can be as a result of owning a factor of production that is scarce in their country. Alternatively, it can also be a result of owning a factor specific to an import sector. Suppose that these losing groups become unhappy with the level of trade in their country. What might they do? It is possible that they would lobby their government to intervene in the trade relationship as we saw in the case of the U.S. steel industry. It turns out that such trade policy interventions are common. Despite the gains from trade described in Chapters 2, 3, and 4, governments usually intervene in free trade in some way in response to political pressures from constituencies. The purpose of our next chapter is to analyze these trade policy interventions.

Review Exercises

1. Consider the trade between Germany and the Dominican Republic. Germany is a capital abundant country, and the Dominican Republic is a labor abundant country. There are two goods, a capital-intensive good chemicals and a labor-intensive good clothing.
   a. Draw a comparative advantage diagram such as Figure 5.1 for trade between Germany and the Dominican Republic, labeling the trade flows along the axes of your diagrams.
   b. Using the Stolper-Samuelson theorem, describe who will support and who will oppose trade in these two countries. Use a flow chart diagram like that of Figure 5.2 to help you in your description.

2. In the early 1800s in England, a debate arose in Parliament over the Corn Laws, restrictions on imports of grain into the country. David Ricardo, the father of the comparative advantage concept, favored the repeal of these import restrictions. Consider the two relevant political groups in England at that time: land owners and capital owners. Who do you think agreed with Ricardo? Why?

3. Use daily papers to identify a politics of trade issue. Can you also identify the factors of production involved in this issue? Are they mobile factors as in the Heckscher-Ohlin model, or are they specific factors? Alternatively, are there any elements of technology involved?

Further Reading and Web Resources

A very useful starting point for the reader interested in the politics of trade is Baldwin (1989). A more technical approach can be found in Chapter 19 of Markusen et al. (1995). A volume dedicated to the Stolper-Samuelson theorem has been edited by Deardorff and Stern (1994). For a review of the trade and wages debate in the context of globalization, see Burtless and Litan (2001). For views in opposition to Burtless and Litan, see the trade and globalization section of the Economic Policy Institute Web site at **http://www.epinet.org**.

You can follow the evolution of requests for protection against increasing trade made by firms in the United States by examining the calendar of the U.S. International Trade Commission at **http://www.usitc.gov**. You can visit the Japanese Ministry of Economy, Trade, and Industry at **http://www.meti.go.jp/english**. You can follow the European Union's trade policies at **http://europa.eu.int/comm/trade**.

References

Baldwin, R.E. (1989) "The Political Economy of Trade Policy," *Journal of Economic Perspectives*, 3:4, 119–135.

Bernard, A.B., and J.B. Jensen (1995) "Exporters, Jobs and Wages in U.S. Manufacturing: 1976–1987," *Brookings Papers on Economic Activity*, 67–112.

Burtless, G., and R.E. Litan (2001) *Globaphobia Revisited: Open Trade and Its Critics*, Brookings Institution, Washington, DC.

Deardorff, A.V., (1998) "Technology, Trade, and Increasing Inequality: Does the Cause Matter for the Cure?" *Journal of International Economic Law*, 1:3, 353–376.

Deardorff, A.V. and R.M. Stern (1994) *The Stolper-Samuelson Theorem: A Golden Jubilee*. Ann Arbor: University of Michigan Press.

The Economist (2002a) "Steel: Rust Never Sleeps," March 9, 61–62.

The Economist (2002b) "Vietnam: Land and Freedom," June 15, 44.

Freeman, R.B. (1995) "Are Your Wages Set in Beijing?" *Journal of Economic Perspectives*, 9:3, 15–32.

Gindling, T.H., and D. Robbins (2001) "Patterns and Sources of Changing Wage Inequality in Chile and Costa Rica During Structural Adjustment," *World Development*, 29:4, 725–745.

Heckscher, E. (1949) "The Effect of Japan Trade on the Distribution of Income," in H.S. Ellis and L.A. Metzler (eds.), *Readings in the Theory of International Trade*, Irwin, Vietnamwood, Illinois, 1950, 272–300.

Jones, R.W. (1971) "A Three-Factor Model in Theory, Trade, and History," in J.N. Bhagwati et al., *Trade, Balance of Payments and Growth*, North Holland, Amsterdam, 3–21.

Krugman, P., and R.Z. Lawrence (1996) "Trade, Jobs, and Wages," in P. Krugman, *Pop Internationalism*, MIT Press, Cambridge, Massachusetts.

Markusen, J.R., J.R. Melvin, W.H. Kaempfer, and K.E. Maskus (1995) *International Trade: Theory and Evidence*, McGraw-Hill, New York.

Ohlin, B. (1933) *International and Inter-Regional Trade*, Harvard University Press, Cambridge, Massachusetts.

Richardson, J.D. (1995) "Income Inequality and Trade: How to Think, What to Conclude," *Journal of Economic Perspectives*, 9:3, 33–55.

Robbins, D., and T.H. Gindling (1999) "Trade Liberalization and the Relative Wages for More-Skilled Workers in Costa Rica," *Review of Development Economics*, 3:2, 140–154.

Stolper, W., and P.A. Samuelson (1941) "Protection and Real Wages," *Review of Economic Studies*, 9:1, 58–73.

Trade Policy Analysis

6

In Chapter 5, you saw that there are reasons to expect that land owners in Japan might oppose the import of rice from Vietnam or, for that matter, from any other country. This opposition to imports exists despite the overall gains to Japan from these imports. Indeed, Ikuo Kanno, a fourth-generation Japanese rice farmer states: "I believe that the value of agriculture can't be measured just by an economic yardstick. Japan has been a farming country for centuries, and rice farming is embedded in the culture. It should be preserved."[1] Mr. Kanno might have added that it is in his own personal interest that rice farming be "preserved." In fact, as we discussed in Chapter 5, rice farming in Japan has been supported a great deal through various stringent limits on imports.

Knowing that factor conditions lead to the demand for import protection is not enough for a trade policy analyst or for an international affairs professional. These individuals are often called upon to assess, both qualitatively and quantitatively, the numerous impacts of government interventions in international trade. If you pursue a career in international economic affairs, it is likely that you will either be involved in making these assessments or in interpreting the assessments made by someone else. Therefore, it is important for you to understand how the assessments are made. This is the purpose of the present chapter.

We will begin our discussion of trade policy analysis by revisiting the model of absolute advantage in rice between Japan and Vietnam that we developed in Chapter 2. Next, we will consider the large variety of trade policy measures available to governments. Then we will analyze what happens when Japan introduces a tariff on its imports of rice. We also will consider the terms-of-trade effects of this tariff. Next, we will consider what happens when Japan introduces a quota on its imports of rice. Tariffs and quotas compose the basic means of protecting domestic markets from competition. It is important for you to be familiar with both of these policies. Finally, we will briefly take up trade policy analysis using the comparative advantage model of Chapter 3. For the interested reader, the appendix to the chapter considers the case of a tariff rate quota, used by some countries for specific products.

---

[1] Planet Rice (2000).

Absolute Advantage Revisited

In Chapter 2, we developed a model of absolute advantage and trade in rice between Vietnam and Japan. This model is summarized in Figure 6.1. Recall from Chapter 2 that we assume the demand conditions in the two countries to be exactly the same. Consequently, we can use the same demand curve in both diagrams of this figure. We also assume that supply conditions in the two countries are such that Vietnam's supply curve for rice is farther to the right than Japan's supply curve. Consequently, the autarky price of rice in Vietnam, P^V, is lower than the autarky price of rice in Japan, P^J. This gives Vietnam an absolute advantage in producing rice. The world price settles between the two autarky prices. Vietnam exports rice, while Japan imports rice. The world price will adjust to ensure that Vietnam's exports are the same as Japan's imports.

Note that, in moving from autarky to trade in Figure 6.1, there is a reduction in domestic quantity supplied in Japan as indicated by the arrow along S^J. It is possible that the firms producing rice in Japan would lobby the Japanese government to oppose this decrease in domestic quantity supplied, demanding protection from Vietnam exports. This is exactly what has happened in Japan, given the political voice of people like Ikuo Kanno mentioned in the introduction to this chapter. More generally, though, demands for protection are nearly universal.[2] Indeed, because protective policies are so widespread in the world economy, we consider their economic effects in the remainder of the chapter.

Trade Policy Measures

When a country seeks to grant import protection to a sector of its economy, it can chose among a number of measures that can be broadly classified as

Figure 6.1 Absolute Advantage and Trade in the Rice Market

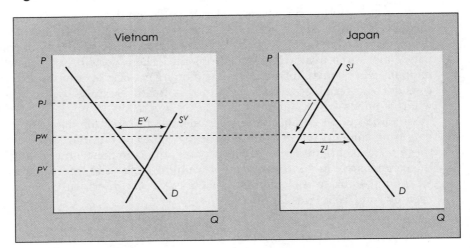

---

[2] In the United States, there is a tendency to view Japan as protectionist and the United States as committed to free trade. In fact, the United States has a long history of trade protection. We will discuss some of this history in Chapter 7. A box in this chapter also considers the case of U.S. protection of its steel industry.

either tariffs or nontariff measures.[3] A **tariff** is a tax on imports. It is a very common trade policy, used by almost all countries. There are two kinds of tariffs. A *specific tariff* is a fixed tax per physical unit of the import, and an *ad valorem* tariff is a percentage tax applied to the value of the import. Governments in the world trading system employ both types of tariffs. **Nontariff measures (NTMs)** is an inclusive category of many kinds of trade policy measures. These measures include:

1. Prohibitions and quantitative restrictions on imports. *Quantitative restrictions (QRs) set an upper limit to imports and are often called import quotas.*
2. Tariff rate quotas. *A **tariff rate quota** involves two tariff levels: a lower tariff for levels of imports within the quota and a higher tariff for levels of imports above the quota. We consider tariff rate quotas in the appendix.*
3. Trigger-price mechanisms. *These are market floor prices that "trigger" government interventions to curtail imports in order to maintain the market floor. They are often used to protect certain agricultural sectors.*
4. Technical barriers to trade (TBT). *These are barriers imposed on imports that support health and safety concerns. In some instances, they are entirely legitimate, but in other instances, they can be a disguised form of import protection.*
5. Antidumping (AD) duties. *These are tariff-like charges imposed on imports that are deemed by the imposing government to have been "dumped" or sold at "less than fair value" by the exporter.*
6. Countervailing duties (CVDs). *These are tariff-like charges imposed on imports that are deemed by the imposing government to have been "unfairly" subsidized by the exporting country government.*

Keep in mind as you read the remainder of this chapter that the range of policies that can be part of nontariff measures is limited only by the imagination of the importing country's government. Examples of such creative measures, including even the required disassembling of the product before import, are considered in the box in the imports of used automobiles in Latin America.

A Tariff

As mentioned earlier, there are two kinds of tariffs, a specific tariff and an ad valorem tariff. For our graphical analysis in this chapter, it is much simpler to consider a specific tariff, so that is what we will do. The basic results you will learn here, however, will also apply to an ad valorem tariff. Let's introduce a specific tariff on Japan's imports of rice. This policy is depicted in Figure 6.2. The world price is P^W. At this price, Japanese rice suppliers choose to supply Q^S. Japanese consumers demand Q^D. The difference $Q^D - Q^S = Z^J$ is imported from Vietnam.

Suppose then that the Japanese government imposes a specific tariff of T on its imports of rice from Vietnam. This raises the domestic price to $P^W + T$.

Tariff
A tax on imports, which could be either in *ad valorem* or specific form.

Nontariff measure (NTM)
An import restraint or export policy other than a tariff. An import quota is one example.

Tariff rate quota
An import restraint involving two tariff levels: a lower tariff for levels of imports within the quota and a higher tariff for levels of imports above the quota.

---

[3] See Laird (1997), from which this section draws.

Used Automobile Protection in Latin America

In the wake of the debt crises of the early 1980s, Latin America embarked on a process of significant trade liberalization, reducing tariffs and removing quotas. In the case of used automobiles, however, this liberalization has not, in general, taken place. Many Latin American countries retain significant restrictions on the imports of used automobiles even as liberalization has occurred in the new automobiles sector. What is more, the protective measures applied to used automobile imports are rather creative.

As of 1999, seven relatively small Latin American countries imposed only minimal restrictions on imports of used automobiles. These countries are Bahamas, Barbados, Belize, Bolivia, El Salvador, Guatemala, and Panama. Some of these countries use "reference prices" to value the used automobiles. These reference prices are either domestically generated or published, *Blue Book* values.

Five relatively small countries impose clear restrictions on the imports of used automobiles. These countries are Costa Rica, Dominican Republic, Haiti, Honduras, and Nicaragua. A popular measure here is capped depreciation. For example, the Dominican Republic accepts invoices as the value of new automobiles; it does not do so for used automobiles. Instead, the value of a used automobile is calculated using a depreciation schedule based on the price of an equivalent, new automobile in the current year. However, given the depreciation schedule, the price of the used automobile cannot fall below 50 percent of the new automobile. As we know, the market prices of used automobiles are often substantially below 50 percent of equivalent, new automobiles, so this represents a discriminatory measure.

Figure 6.2 A Tariff on Japan's Imports of Rice

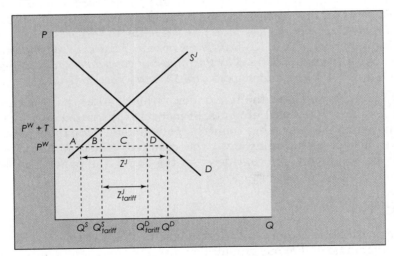

You can now see that a tariff increases the domestic price of the imported product above the world price. In the case of Japanese rice, the domestic price is many times larger than the world price. The increase in the domestic price of rice above the world price has a number of effects. Japan's production of rice expands from Q^S to Q^S_{tariff}. This expansion in output is what the Japanese rice farmers hoped to gain from the tariff. Domestic consumption of rice falls from Q^D to Q^D_{tariff}. Imports fall from Z^J to Z^J_{tariff}. The tariff has suppressed the importing relationship of Japan with Vietnam.[4]

---

[4] This makes sense. A tariff is a tax, and a tax on any activity causes the amount of that activity to decrease. In this case, the taxed activity is rice imports by Japan.

Jamaica, Peru, and Trinidad and Tobago impose relatively severe protection measures against imports of used automobiles. Trinidad and Tobago requires that used automobiles be disassembled before importation! Engines are often removed from used vehicles before importation and shipped separately. Peru and Jamaica both have age delimited bans. Since 1996, Peru has banned automobiles over five years old and commercial vehicles over eight years old. Furthermore, imported used automobiles with fewer than 24 seats face a "selective consumption tax" of 45 percent; similar new automobiles face a rate of only 20 percent. In 1998, Jamaica's motor vehicle policy was tightened to allow only licensed used automobile dealers to import automobiles no older than four years old and light commercial vehicles no older than five years old.

Finally, in 1999, nine of the largest Latin American countries prohibited imports of used automobiles altogether. These countries are Argentina, Brazil, Chile, Colombia, Ecuador, Mexico, Paraguay, Uruguay, and Venezuela. In the cases of Argentina, Brazil, Paraguay, and Uruguay, this import ban is part of the Mercosur regional trade agreement (see Chapter 8). It is clear that, when it comes to used automobiles, even "free trade" countries such as Chile chose the most severe form of protection.

Source: Pelletiere, D. and Reinert, K.A. (2002). "The Political Economy of Used Automobile Protection in Latin America." *The World Economy* 25 (7): 1019-1037.

In addition to the quantity effects of a tariff, there is also a set of welfare and revenue effects. These involve Japan's households, firms, and government. What has happened to the consumer surplus of Japanese households in Figure 6.2?[5] Examining this diagram carefully, you should be able to see that the tariff has caused consumer surplus to fall by area $A + B + C + D$. Because Japanese rice consumers are paying more and consuming less, this fall in consumer surplus makes sense.

What has happened to the producer surplus of Japanese firms? Again examining the diagram carefully, you should be able to see that producer surplus has increased by area A. Japanese rice producers are better off as a result of the tariff; their welfare has increased. Because Japanese producers are receiving more for their product and producing more as well, the increase in producer surplus makes sense.

What about the Japanese government? It is receiving revenue from the import tax. How much revenue? The tariff is T, and the post-tariff import level is Z_{tariff}^{J}. Therefore, the tariff revenue is $T \times Z_{tariff}^{J}$, or area C in Figure 6.2.[6]

Economists or trade policy analysts are often asked to assess the *net welfare effect* of a trade policy. This measure summarizes the welfare impact of the policy for the country as a whole. What would the net welfare effect be? In this case, we take the gains to firms and the government and subtract the losses to households. Doing this, we have:

---

[5] Remember that the concepts of consumer and producer surplus are covered in the appendix to Chapter 2. Please review this appendix, if necessary.

[6] There is an important public finance lesson here. An increase in the import tax (tariff) from zero to T reduces the tax base from Z^{J} to Z_{tariff}^{J}. All increases in taxes decrease the base on which the tax is assessed. For many developing countries, tariffs are an important source of government revenue.

$$N = A + C - (A + B + C + D) = -(B + D)$$

There is a net welfare *loss* of the tariff equal to area $B + D$. From an economic standpoint, the tariff hurts the Japan society as a whole. Although it benefits producers and government, the losses imposed on consumers outweigh these benefits. The two triangles B and D are similar to the "deadweight loss" triangle of a monopoly you learned about in introductory microeconomics.[7] They represent economic inefficiency. In certain situations, tariffs do not necessarily cause a net welfare loss. One such situation, that of a terms-of-trade gain, is explored in the next section.

Please note one more thing. Figure 6.2 gives us information on what happens to Japanese rice output as a result of the tariff. As we stated earlier, Japanese rice output increases from Q^S to Q^S_{tariff}. Given information on the employment/output ratio in this sector, we could translate the change in output into a change in employment. From the point of view of Japan politicians, this employment effect is important. Therefore, trade policy analysts often include an estimate of the employment effects of tariffs and other trade policies.[8]

Terms-of-Trade Effects

In some important cases, the analysis of the previous section is incomplete. Why? We have showed that when Japan imposes a tariff on its imports from Vietnam, the amount of these imports decreases. Looking at Figure 6.1, however, we can see that, as Japan's imports of rice decrease, there will be excess supply in the world market for rice. As we discussed in Chapter 2, this excess supply of rice will cause the world price to fall. Because Japan is importing rice, this is a good thing for this country. The fall in the price of an import good is one kind of **terms-of-trade effect**. It is depicted in Figure 6.3.

Terms-of-trade effects
The effects of a country having an impact on the world prices of the merchandise and services it trades.

Figure 6.3 The Terms-of-Trade Effect of Japan's Tariff

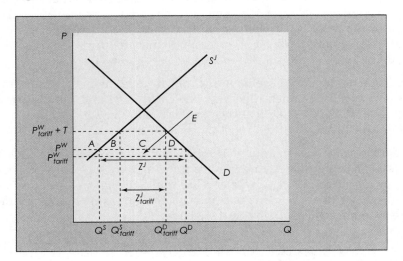

---

[7] See Chapter 15 of Mankiw (2004).
[8] You will see employment estimates in the box on U.S. steel tariffs.

The main difference between Figure 6.3 and Figure 6.2 is that in Figure 6.3, the world price does not stay constant as the Japanese government places a tariff on imports of rice. The world price before the tariff is P^W. After the tariff, the world price falls to P^W_{tariff}, and the tariff is placed on top of this lower world price. Therefore, after the tariff is in place, the domestic price is $P^W_{tariff} + T$. The fall in the world price of rice affects the welfare analysis of the tariff. Consumer surplus in Japan falls by $(A + B + C + D)$ as in Figure 6.2. Producer surplus in Japan rises by A as in Figure 6.3. Japan government revenue, however, is now area $C + E$. Therefore, the net welfare effect is:

$$N = A + (C + E) - (A + B + C + D) = -(B + D) + E$$

The net welfare effect in Figure 6.3 is different than in Figure 6.2. There is still the efficiency loss of $B + D$ as in the previous case. Now, however, there is a *terms-of-trade gain* of area E. For this reason, we cannot say whether the tariff hurts welfare in Japan or not. If the world price falls by a lot, E could be very large, even larger than $(B + D)$. However, we should not jump to the conclusion that, given large terms-of-trade effects, tariffs are good for countries. This is because Vietnam would probably not sit idly by when Japan imposes a tariff on imports of rice. Vietnam could instead retaliate by imposing a tariff on a product that Japan exports. This tariff would lower the world price of Japan's export good, which would hurt Japan's welfare. Japan might further retaliate in turn. This tit-for-tat retaliation process in often known as a *trade war*, and it is always welfare reducing. It is to prevent such trade wars that the General Agreement on Tariffs and Trade (GATT) was drawn up after World War II. We discuss the GATT, and its successor the World Trade Organization (WTO), in Chapter 7.

A Quota

An import **quota** is a quantitative restriction on imports. It is one type of nontariff measure or NTM.[9] When the Japanese government imposes a quota on rice imports, it says to rice exporters and domestic importers, we will allow imports up to this amount, and no more! To take another example, the United States has maintained a complex system of quotas on imports of textiles and clothing products.[10] Suppose that instead of imposing a tariff as in Figures 6.2 and 6.3, Japan imposes a quota. We examine this in Figure 6.4.

Quota
Usually applied to imports. A maximum amount of imports allowed by a government.

Before the quota, rice imports are $Z^J = Q^D - Q^S$. For one reason or another, the Japanese government is not satisfied with this outcome. It decides to restrict imports to a smaller amount $Z^J_{quota} = Q^D_{quota} - Q^S_{quota}$. This policy induces a shortage of rice relative to the initial situation without the quota. The domestic price of rice in Japan rises from P^W to P_{quota}. The difference between these two prices is known as the **quota premium**. As with the case of a tariff, consumer surplus falls by area $A + B + C + D$, and

Quota premium
The increase in the domestic price of a good as a result of an import quota.

[9] On occasion, you will also encounter the term *nontariff barrier* or *NTB*.
[10] These quotas will need to be removed during a 10-year transition period as part of the Uruguay Round trade agreements. See Chapter 7.

Figure 6.4 A Quota on Japan's Rice Imports

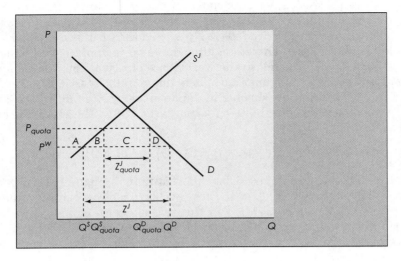

producer surplus increases by area A. The new matter we must deal with in the case of a quota is the nature of area C.

Import licenses
A right to import under a quota given either to domestic importers or foreign exporters.

Quota rents
The income accruing to the holder of a right to import a good into a country.

The quota policy is typically administered via a system of **import licenses**. In effect, the quota policy has restricted the supply of import licenses in the world. The area C represents the extra value of the right to import amount Z^J_{quota}. It is known as **quota rents**.[11] Who receives the rents depends on how the quota licenses are allocated. There are two common possibilities:[12]

1. *Import licenses are allocated to domestic (Japanese) importers. Here, the quota rents accrue to the importers, so they remain within the country. They are a gain to Japan.*
2. *Import licenses are allocated to foreign (Vietnamese) exporters. Here, the quota rents accrue to these exporters, so they leave the country. They are a loss to Japan.*

With this in mind, we can address the question of the net welfare effect of the quota. In the case of import licenses allocated to *domestic* importers, the area C is a transfer from domestic consumers to domestic importers. Area C is a loss to consumers and a gain to importers for a net effect of zero for Japan as a whole. Our net welfare effect is just like a specific tariff, equal to the quota premium $P_{quota} - P^W$, that results in an import level of Z^J_{quota}:

$$N = A + C - (A + B + C + D) = -(B + D)$$

---

[11] "(T)here will be quota profits . . . received by the lucky people who obtain the import licenses. These quota profits are *rents* because they are not received as payments for any services, and any reduction in these profits would not affect the supply of any resource" (W.M. Corden, 1997, p. 127).

[12] There is a third possibility in which the import licenses are auctioned to the highest bidder by the government. The welfare properties of this case are like that of the case in which the import licenses are allocated to domestic importers.

In the case of import licenses allocated to *foreign* exporters, area C is a transfer from domestic consumers to these foreign exporters. It is no longer a net loss of zero, because the loss to consumers is not offset by a gain to domestic importers. Our net welfare effect is simply the gain to firms less the loss to consumers:

$$N = A - (A + B + C + D) = -(B + C + D)$$

In this case, the quota is worse than a tariff that results in an import level of Z^J_{quota}.

Given what we have just said, suppose you were a government official administering quota policy. Which of the two alternatives would you choose: a quota allocated to domestic importers or quota allocated to foreign exporters? Your answer is probably the quota allocated to domestic importers, because these have the smaller welfare loss. Now, here is a puzzle: In many circumstances, governments choose a foreign allocated quota. Why? One possibility is that they are uninformed about the economic implications of their choices. Another possibility is that political considerations cause such a choice. For some reason, governments find it beneficial from a political point of view to assist foreigners. For example, the United States imposes quotas against the import of sugar using import licenses allocated to foreign sugar exporters. Most of the exporters are poor countries of the Caribbean basin. Perhaps there has been a calculation made on the part of U.S. government officials that the implied foreign aid in a system of foreign-allocated quotas makes sense in the case of poor countries.[13]

In this and the previous two sections, we have discussed four trade policy possibilities: a tariff, a tariff with terms-of-trade effects, a domestic-allocated quota, and a foreign-allocated quota. Before moving on to briefly discuss comparative advantage analyses of trade policies, let's summarize the four possibilities:

> **Tariff: Unambiguous net welfare loss due to consumer surplus loss outweighing gains in producer surplus and government revenue.**
>
> **Tariff with terms-of-trade effects: Ambiguous net welfare effect due to terms-of-trade gain (fall in world price) potentially outweighing the efficiency loss.**
>
> **Domestic-allocated quota: Unambiguous net welfare loss due to consumer surplus loss outweighing gains in producer surplus and quota rents.**
>
> **Foreign-allocated quota: Unambiguous net welfare loss that exceeds that of the domestic-allocated quota case.**

[13]What might make even more sense is to remove the quota system entirely and let these countries export as much sugar as U.S. consumers care to buy. The political power of sugar beet producers in the United States prevents this, however.

U.S. Steel Protection

In Chapter 5, we discussed the way that specific factors caused losses to steel industry firms in the United States. In a box on the issue in that chapter, we discussed the *global safeguard investigation* of the U.S. government that was completed in 2001 and resulted in significant tariff protection of the U.S. steel sector. Joseph Francois and Laura Baughman of Trade Partnership Worldwide used a comparative advantage trade model to analyze the economic effects of these safeguard measures on the U.S. economy. They gave special emphasis to the costs of higher U.S. steel prices on those industries in the United States that use steel intensively as an input into their production processes.

Francois and Baughman found that the net welfare costs of the steel tariffs would range from approximately US$0.5 billion to $1.4 billion depending on the scenario considered. The number of steel industry jobs protected would range from approximately 4,400 to 8,900. These job gains, however, would be more than offset by job losses in the U.S. steel-consuming industries of between approximately 15,300 and 30,600 workers. The ratio of steel-consuming sector jobs lost to steel sector jobs gained would be 3.5. The ability to capture effects like these is one reason why it is sometimes important to extend trade policy analysis beyond the single sector approach of the absolute advantage model.

Interestingly, when the authors disaggregated their results by U.S. states, there were net job losses even in steel-producing states. The authors therefore concluded: "In an effort to protect a few thousand steel jobs, policy makers would further slow economic recovery by reducing national income, and force job losses in manufacturing in the very communities they seek to help." Such insights come from a comparative advantage view of trade policies.

Source: Francois and Baughman (2001).

Comparative Advantage Models

Our analysis of trade policies in this chapter has been based on the absolute advantage model of Chapter 2. The absolute advantage model has taken us quite far. We have shown how one can examine trade policies to make estimates of production, consumption, trade, employment, and welfare impacts. In many instances, however, the effects of trade policies go beyond a single sector. Protecting a large sector such as automobiles can draw resources from other sectors into the protected automobile sector. Perhaps workers in the metal furniture sector will move into the automobile sector as it expands under protection. Also, protecting a large intermediate product sector, like petroleum or steel, can raise costs for other sectors that use petroleum or steel in their production processes.

In these cases, trade policy analysts turn to models of comparative advantage such as those we discussed in Chapter 3. As you will recall, the comparative advantage model analyzes more than one sector simultaneously (e.g., rice and motorcycles). In some instances, this is an important feature. Such models are much more complicated than the absolute advantage models we considered in this chapter, and we will not formally discuss them here. You should, however, be aware of their use. One recent case where these models proved to be important is in analyzing U.S. steel tariffs. This is described in the box. A second example, that of analyzing the North American Free Trade Agreement (NAFTA), will be presented in Chapter 8.

Conclusion

In order to help protect the losers of increased international trade, most countries of the world engage in trade policies. The supply and demand analysis of the absolute advantage model allows us to discover the effects of these trade policies on production, consumption, trade, welfare, and employment. In this chapter, we have analyzed tariffs, tariffs with terms-of-trade effects, and quotas. The appendix considers the case of tariff rate quotas. In addition, we briefly mentioned trade policy analysis based on comparative advantage models of trade. In general, the intervention in free trade reduces the overall welfare of the county intervening. However, certain groups might benefit from these policies, which is why they are usually implemented.

Review Exercises

1. Consider Figure 6.2. For a given T, what would be the impact of an increase in supply (a shift of the supply curve to the right) on government revenue? What would be the impact of an increase in demand (a shift of the demand curve to the right)?

2. In Figure 6.3, we introduced the terms-of-trade effects of Japan's tariff on imports of rice. These terms-of-trade effects (area E in the diagram) were positive for Japan. In a new diagram similar to Figure 6.1, show that these terms-of-trade effects adversely affect the welfare of Vietnam.

3. Consider our diagram of a quota in Figure 6.4. Suppose the government reduced the quota to below Z_{quota}^{J}. What would happen to the quota premium? Can you say with certainty what would happen to the total quota rent? What would this depend on?

4. Trade protection is often used to maintain employment in a sector. Given our analysis, what do you think of this approach to maintaining employment? Can you think of any other measures that might also maintain employment in a sector?

Further Reading and Web Resources

A classic and recently-revised work on trade policy analysis is Corden (1997). An advanced reference is Francios and Reinert (1997). Two chapters in the Francois and Reinert volume are of particular relevance to the reader of this text. Laird (1997) provides a survey of trade policy quantification, and Francois and Hall (1997) describe advanced model based on absolute advantage. Another standard trade policy reference is Vousden (1990).

Steve Suranovic maintains a text on international trade at **http://www.internationalecon.com**. See his Chapter 10 for a good overview of trade policy analysis. The link is via the "Master Table of Contents." The United Nations Conference on Trade and Development (UNCTAD) maintains a Trade Analysis Information System described at **http://www.unctad.org/trains**.

References

Corden, W.M. (1997) *Trade Policy and Economic Welfare*, Oxford University Press, Oxford.

Francois, J.F., and L.M. Baughman (2001) *Estimated Effects of Proposed Import Relief Remedies for Steel*, Trade Partnership Worldwide, Washington, DC.

Francois, J.F., and H.K. Hall (1997) "Partial Equilibrium Modeling," in J.F. Francois and K.A. Reinert (eds.), *Applied Methods for Trade Policy Analysis: A Handbook*, Cambridge University Press, Cambridge, 122–155.

Francois, J.F., and K.A. Reinert (eds.) (1997) *Applied Methods for Trade Policy Analysis: A Handbook*, Cambridge University Press, Cambridge.

Hertel, T.W., and W. Martin (2000) "Liberalising Agriculture and Manufactures in a Millennium Round: Implications for Developing Countries," *The World Economy*, 23:4, 455–469.

Laird, S. (1997) "Quantifying Commercial Policies," in J.F. Francois and K.A. Reinert (eds.), *Applied Methods for Trade Policy Analysis: A Handbook*, Cambridge University Press, Cambridge, 27–75.

Mankiw, N.G. (2004) *Principles of Economics*, South-Western/Thomson Learning, Mason, Ohio.

Pelletiere, D., and K.A. Reinert (2002) "The Political Economy of Used Automobile Protection in Latin America," *The World Economy*, 25:7, 1019–1037.

Planet Rice (2000) "Japan to USA: Rice Farming Is Our Culture: Don't Interfere," http://www.planetrice.net, November 26.

Skully, D. (2001) "Tariff-Rate Quota Administration," U.S. Economic Research Service, U.S. Department of Agriculture, http://www.ers.usda.gov/wto/trq.htm.

Vousden, N. (1990) *The Economics of Trade Protection*, Cambridge University Press, Cambridge.

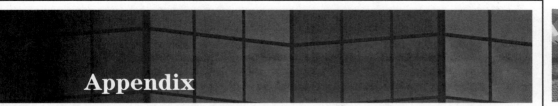

Appendix

A Tariff Rate Quota

Chapter 7, we will discuss the Uruguay Round of multilateral trade negotiations and its Agreement on Agriculture. One implication of the Agreement on Agriculture is that many developed countries and some developing countries now impose tariff rate quotas on imports of agricultural goods.[14] A tariff rate quota involves two tariff levels: a lower tariff for levels of imports within the quota and a higher tariff for levels of imports above the quota. Suppose Japan were to impose a tariff rate quota on imports of rice. This policy can be stated as follows. Up to the quota amount Z^{JQ}, Japan applies a *within-quota tariff rate* of T^{IN}. Above the quota amount Z^{JQ}, Japan applies a larger, *out-of-quota tariff rate* of T^{OUT}. To analyze this policy, it is best to consider three cases:

$$\text{Case I: } Z^J < Z^{JQ}$$
$$\text{Case II: } Z^J = Z^{JQ}$$
$$\text{Case III: } Z^J > Z^{JQ}$$

We are going to consider each of these three cases in turn, using a diagram set out along the lines illustrated in Figure 6.A1. The quota amount, Z^{JQ}, is plotted along the horizontal axis, and this distance is indicated with a double-headed arrow. Along the vertical axis, there are three prices indicated. The first, lowest price is the world price of imported rice, P^W. To simplify our analysis here, we assume that Japan cannot affect this world price. That is, there are none of the terms-of-trade effects we discussed in this chapter. The second, higher price is the world price plus the within-quota tariff rate of T^{IN}. The third, higher price is the world price plus the out-of-quota tariff rate of T^{OUT}.

We are going to use the framework depicted in Figure 6.A1 to analyze the three cases mentioned above. Case I is presented in Figure 6.A2. Here the level of rice imports is within the quota amount. Therefore, the domestic price P is determined by the lower tariff value, T^{IN}, and the tariff revenue collected by the government is area A.

---

[14]See Hertel and Martin (2000) and Skully (2001).

Figure 6.A1 Framework for Analyzing Japan's Tariff Rate Quota on Rice

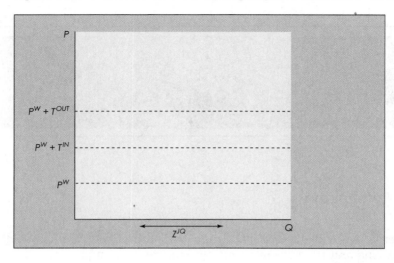

Figure 6.A2 Case I of Japan's Tariff Rate Quota on Rice

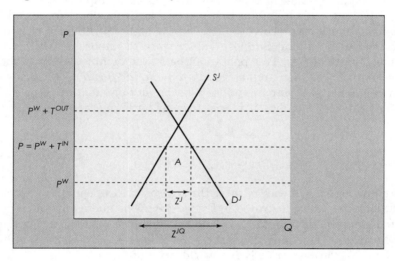

Case II is presented in Figure 6.A3. Here the level of rice imports is exactly equal to the quota amount. In this case, the domestic price is somewhere between the two tariff-inclusive prices. That is, $P^W + T^{IN} \leq P \leq P^W + T^{OUT}$. As in Case I, the tariff revenue collected by the government is area A. However, if the positions of the Japanese supply and demand curves for rice cause the domestic price P to be above $P^W + T^{IN}$, then there are also quota rents equal to area B.

Case III is presented in Figure 6.A4. Here the level of rice imports exceeds the quota amount. Therefore, the domestic price P is determined by the higher tariff value. The total tariff revenue collected by the government is composed of three areas. Area A represents the tariff revenue collected on the imports that are within quota. Areas C and D represent

Figure 6.A3 Case II of Japan's Tariff Rate Quota on Rice

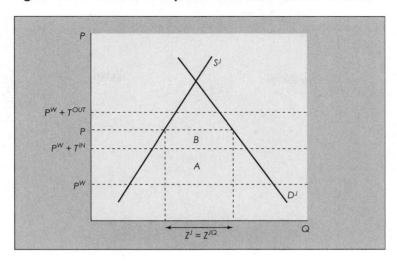

Figure 6.A4 Case III of Japan's Tariff Rate Quota on Rice

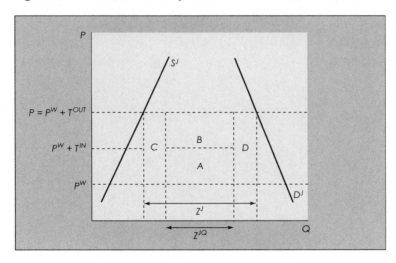

the additional tariff revenue collected on the imports that are above quota. In addition, as in Case II, there are quota rents on the quota amount equal to area *B*.

Readers of this appendix will no doubt get the impression that the analysis of tariff rate quotas is a bit complicated. This is an observation that I hear from many students who delve deeply into trade policies of many different kinds. It is simply a reality of the modern world trading system and requires some patience and persistence on the part of the student or professional. The world is a complex place, and our analysis of it often needs to be complex as well.

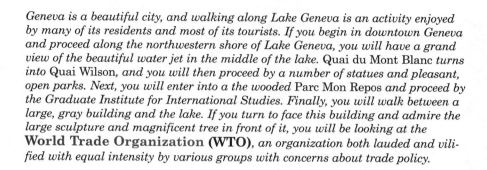

The World Trade Organization

Geneva is a beautiful city, and walking along Lake Geneva is an activity enjoyed by many of its residents and most of its tourists. If you begin in downtown Geneva and proceed along the northwestern shore of Lake Geneva, you will have a grand view of the beautiful water jet in the middle of the lake. Quai du Mont Blanc *turns into* Quai Wilson, *and you will then proceed by a number of statues and pleasant, open parks. Next, you will enter into a the wooded* Parc Mon Repos *and proceed by the Graduate Institute for International Studies. Finally, you will walk between a large, gray building and the lake. If you turn to face this building and admire the large sculpture and magnificent tree in front of it, you will be looking at the* **World Trade Organization (WTO),** *an organization both lauded and vilified with equal intensity by various groups with concerns about trade policy.*

Although many people and groups have strong opinions about the World Trade Organization, most know very little about it. This chapter is dedicated to making sure you understand the key aspects of this important institution of world trade. Later in the book, you will also be introduced to the International Monetary Fund and the World Bank, important institutions of international finance and international economic development, respectively. To develop your understanding of the WTO, we will first take up its precursor, the General Agreement on Tariffs and Trade (GATT). Here we will undertake a historical examination of the GATT and introduce the principles it established for the conduct of international trade in goods. Next, we will turn to the WTO itself, as established by the Marrakesh Agreement of 1994. Here we will cover the main provisions of the Marrakesh Agreement in the areas of goods, services, intellectual property, and dispute settlement. Finally, we will consider the issue of trade and the environment within the WTO.

Nobel Laureate Douglass North (1990) defined institutions as "humanly devised constraints that shape human interaction" (p. 3). A less formal definition is "the rules of the economic game." As an institution of international trade, the WTO sets out the rules of the global trading game. These rules have force as international economic law, and a careful study of the WTO takes place on the boundary of economics and law. This, in turn, involves a subtle change in vocabulary that may appear odd or unnecessary at first. Trust that it is indeed necessary. The terms we introduce are widely accepted and utilized in the field of international trade among economists, lawyers, and policy analysts.

World Trade Organization (WTO)
The WTO was established in 1995 as part of the Marrakesh Agreement ending the Uruguay Round of trade talks. It is an international organization with a legal foundation for managing world trading relationships.

The General Agreement on Tariffs and Trade

During World War II, the United States and Britain began developing the outlines for a set of post-war, economic institutions.[1] The specifics of the plan were negotiated in July 1944 in Bretton Woods, New Hampshire. The conference set up the International Bank for Reconstruction and Development (World Bank) and the International Monetary Fund, discussed in Chapters 16 and 22, respectively. In December 1945, the United States attempted to launch the idea of an International Trade Organization (ITO). In 1946, the ITO met for a first set of negotiations in London. Twenty-three founding members were present and signed the **General Agreement on Tariffs and Trade (GATT)**. In 1948, an ITO charter was agreed to at a United Nations Conference on Trade and Employment in Havana. However, in 1950, the U.S. government announced that it would not seek U.S. congressional ratification of the Havana Charter, effectively terminating the ITO plan.[2] Consequently, the vehicle for post-war trade negotiations became the GATT.

Between 1946 and 1994, the GATT provided a framework for a number of "rounds" of multilateral trade negotiations, the most recently-negotiated being the Uruguay Round. These rounds, listed in Table 7.1, successfully reduced tariffs among member countries in many (but not all) sectors. As a result, the average tariff on manufactured products imposed by industrial countries fell from 35 percent to 4 percent.[3] Despite these successes, the

General Agreement on Tariffs and Trade (GATT)
Established in 1946, the GATT was to be part of an International Trade Organization (ITO). The ITO was never ratified, but the GATT and its articles served as an international vehicle for trade relationships until 1995, when it became embodied in the Marrakesh Agreement establishing the World Trade Organization. As part of the Marrakesh Agreement, it is now known as GATT 1994.

Table 7.1 GATT Rounds of Multilateral Trade Negotiations

Name of Round	Years	Number of Countries
Geneva	1947	23
Annecy	1949	29
Torquay	1950–1951	32
Geneva	1955–1956	33
Dillon	1960–1961	39
Kennedy	1963–1967	74
Tokyo	1973–1979	99
Uruguay	1984–1994	117

Source: Table 4.1 in Hoekman, B.M. and Kastecki, M. (2001). *The Political Economy of the World Trading System: From GATT to WTO.* Oxford; New York: Oxford University Press. 101–102.

---

[1] Skidelsky (2000) has analyzed this negotiation process in detail.
[2] This was in response to pressures from isolationist members of the U.S. Congress. See Diebold (1952).
[3] See Hoekman and Kostecki (2001), p. 105.

Geneva-based GATT Secretariat could not always effectively enforce negotiated agreements without the legal standing of the ITO. This important
limitation was finally addressed in 1994 with the Uruguay Round negotiations, ending in a signing ceremony that took place in Marrakesh. The
Marrakesh Agreement provided for the creation of the World Trade
Organization, which takes up the vision of the ITO for enforceable trade
agreements among its members. This section of the chapter will focus on
the GATT; the following sections focus on the WTO.

What does the GATT entail? Its most important principle is that of
nondiscrimination. As illustrated in Figure 7.1, nondiscrimination, in
turn, has two important subprinciples, namely **most-favored-nation
(MFN)** and **national treatment (NT)**. Under MFN, each member must
grant treatment to each other member as favorable as it extends to any
other member country. If Japan lowers a tariff on Indonesia's exports of a
certain product, it must also lower its tariff on the exports of that product
from all other member countries. The MFN treatment has special importance for developing countries, because they will benefit from tariff reductions negotiated among developed countries. Exceptions to MFN treatment are allowed in the case of certain regional trade agreements and
preferences granted to developing countries.

Whereas MFN addresses border measures, NT addresses internal,
domestic policies such as taxes. NT specifies that foreign goods within a
country should be treated no less favorably than domestic goods with
regard to tax policies. Together, MFN and NT compose the nondiscrimination principle.

A second important GATT principle is the general prohibition of quotas or quantitative restrictions on trade.[4] This reflects a long-standing
view that price distortions (tariffs) are preferred to quantity distortions in

Marrakesh Agreement
Signed in 1994, the Marrakesh Agreement concluded the Uruguay Round of trade talks, begun in 1986, and established the World Trade Organization. Among others, it includes a multilateral agreement on trade in goods, an agreement on trade in services, and an agreement on trade-related aspects of intellectual property rights.

Nondiscrimination
A major GATT/WTO principle achieved via the subprinciples of most favored nation (MFN) and national treatment.

Most-favored nation (MFN)
A principle of the GATT/WTO system in which each member must treat each other member as generously as its most-favored trading partner.

National treatment (NT)
A principle of the GATT/WTO system under which foreign goods within a country should be treated no less favorably than domestic goods with regard to tax policies.

Figure 7.1 The Nondiscrimination Principle

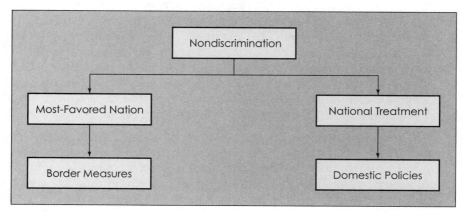

---

[4] You might see the general prohibition of quotas referred to as the "transparency principle." We
do not use this term here because it can be confused with discussions of overall transparency in
the GATT/WTO system.

international markets. It also reflects the history of GATT. During its birth, quantitative restrictions were one of the most significant impediments to trade. As always, there are exceptions allowed. Temporary quantitative restrictions on trade can be used in the case of balance of payments difficulties, but these must be implemented with the nondiscrimination principle of Figure 7.1 in mind.

There were additional, sector-specific exceptions to the general prohibition of quotas in the GATT. This first was for agricultural products and applied when certain domestic programs were in place. This exception was granted to address U.S. agricultural programs.[5] This exception was used for decades to reduce U.S. imports of sugar, dairy products, and peanuts. In addition, the United States insisted that export subsidies, prohibited in general by the GATT, be allowed for agriculture. Despite the early role of the United States in these violations of GATT principles in agriculture, it was the European Union (EU) that became the most vociferous supporter of these exemptions in the 1980s and 1990s under its Common Agricultural Policy (CAP).[6]

The second important exemption to quota prohibition was for textiles and clothing. In 1961, a U.S.–initiated conference of major textile traders was convened under the auspices of the GATT. The outcome of this conference was the Short-Term Arrangement Regarding International Trade in Cotton Textiles (STA). The STA withdrew cotton textile trade from the MFN system for a period of one year. Meanwhile, negotiations continued, and in October 1962, the Long-Term Arrangement Regarding International Trade in Cotton Textiles (LTA) replaced the STA. The LTA covered the 1962 to 1967 period and allowed importers to curb imports in cases of "market disruption" via bilateral or unilateral action. The LTA was renewed in 1967 and 1970.

In December 1972, a GATT fact-finding study on world textile trade was completed. The group that authored this study was instructed to use it as a basis for developing a multilateral solution to "problems" in world textile and clothing trade. At this time, there was a great deal of political pressure in the United States to extend the coverage of the LTA to wool and man-made fibers. The result of these developments was the Arrangement Regarding International Trade in Textiles or the Multifiber Arrangement (MFA), which came into being in January 1974. The MFA was a general, multilateral framework for managing textile and clothing trade for cotton, wool, and man-made fibers. The MFA was renewed in 1977 (MFA II), in 1981 (MFA III), in 1986 (MFA IV), and in 1991 (MFA V).

Exceptions to the quota prohibitions of the GATT in the areas of agriculture, textiles, and clothing generated negative feelings on the part of developing countries with regard to the world trading system. Why? Agriculture, textiles, and clothing are three groups of products that countries first turn to in their trade and development process. The fact that

---

[5] See Hathaway (1987), p. 109.
[6] On the EU Common Agricultural Policy, see Hathaway (1987), Hathaway and Ingo (1996), and Chapter 12 of Dinan (1999).

these three groups of products were taken out of the GATT framework at the insistence of a developed country left the developing countries wondering how they could have a fair chance to participate in the trade and development process. These sentiments have not disappeared.

GATT-sponsored reductions in tariff levels for manufactured goods were based on the practice of **binding**. As a result of trade negotiations, tariffs are bound at the agreed-upon level, often *above* applied levels. Once set, tariff bindings may not in general be increased in the future. Applied rates that are below bound rates, however, may be increased. Although there are provisions made for some renegotiation of bound tariffs, such renegotiations must be accompanied by compensation. The general purpose of the binding principle is to introduce a degree of predictability into the world trading system.

Binding
A major GATT/WTO principle. As negotiations proceed through the rounds of trade talks, tariffs are bound at the agreed-upon level. They may not in general be increased in the future.

In the interest of promoting "fair" competition in the world trading system, the GATT introduced a number of stipulations with regard to subsidies, countervailing duties, and antidumping duties. The use of subsidies is not supposed to harm the trading interests of other members. When subsidies are shown to cause "material injury" or "threat thereof" to a domestic industry of another country, that other country is authorized to apply countervailing duties or tariffs on its imports of the product from the subsidizing country. The GATT leaves room for different interpretations, especially in the case of production as opposed to export subsidies. This, combined with differing national laws, leaves a great deal of room for controversy. "Dumped" goods are defined as exports sold at a price below those charged by the exporter in its domestic market. The GATT allowed for antidumping duties or tariffs to be imposed under certain circumstances.[7]

The World Trade Organization

The initial Bretton Woods vision of an International Trade Organization came to an abrupt end in 1950. Forty years later, however, Canada proposed a Multilateral Trade Organization (MTO) to address the weaknesses of the GATT Secretariat. In 1991, the Director General of GATT, Arthur Dunkel, released a draft agreement for the Uruguay Round that became known as "the Dunkel text." The Dunkel text included a draft charter for the MTO. By the end of 1993, the text of the Uruguay Round contained a final charter for a World Trade Organization (WTO).

The Marrakesh Agreement is actually the "Marrakesh Agreement Establishing the World Trade Organization." Therefore, the stipulations of this agreement are formally an element of the WTO, and the new GATT (known as GATT 1994) has been folded into the institutional structure of the WTO. The Marrakesh Agreement and the WTO are sometimes referred to as a "tripod" in that they primarily addressed the following three areas:[8]

---

[7] The reader who wants to further understand these forms of "contingent protection" can consult Chapter 20 of Markusen et al. (1995).

[8] The interested reader should consult Hoekman and Kostecki (2001) for more details on the WTO. The Marrakesh Agreement itself can be found in GATT Secretariat (1994) and at http://www.wto.org under "Documents." Follow links to "Legal Texts" and then to "Uruguay Round Final Act." We will address the Agreement on Trade-Related Investment Measures (TRIMs) in Chapter 21.

Trade in goods, including GATT 1994, an Agreement on Agriculture, and an Agreement on Textiles and Clothing

Trade in services as specified in the General Agreement on Trade in Services (GATS)

Intellectual property as specified in the Agreement on Trade-Related Aspects of Intellectual Property Rights (TRIPS)

The Marrakesh Agreement also included a WTO charter. It established the WTO as a legal international organization and stipulated that "The WTO shall provide the common institutional framework for the conduct of trade relations among its members."[9] The charter also defined the functions of the WTO, including the following: to facilitate the implementation, administration, and operation of the multilateral trade agreements; to provide the forum for negotiations among members concerning multilateral trade relations; to administer disputes among members; and to cooperate with the International Monetary Fund and World Bank.

The administrative aspects of the WTO are summarized in Table 7.2. Members of the WTO send representatives to the Ministerial Conference that meets at least once every two years and carries out the functions of WTO. The Ministerial Conference appoints a Director General of the WTO Secretariat who, in turn, appoints the staff of the Secretariat. The Ministerial Conference adopts "regulations setting out the powers, duties, conditions of service and term of office of the Director General." Between meetings of the Ministerial Conference, a General Council meets to conduct the affairs of the WTO. The General Council establishes rules and procedures, discharges responsibilities of the Dispute Settlement Body, and discharges the responsibilities of the Trade Policy Review Body.

When possible, the Ministerial Conference and the General Council make decisions by consensus. *Consensus* is defined to be a situation in which "no member, present at the meeting when the decision is taken, formally objects to the proposed decision." Therefore, consensus does not necessarily imply unanimity. This definition of consensus proves to be important in the dispute settlement process of the WTO. When consensus cannot be reached, the WTO makes decisions through a process of majority voting.

Let's now turn to a few important aspects of the WTO.

Trade in Goods

The section of the Marrakesh Agreement related to trade in goods contains GATT 1994, an update of the original GATT, as well as an Agreement on Agriculture and an Agreement on Textiles and Clothing. The Agreement on Agriculture addresses three outstanding issues concerning international trade in agricultural goods: market access, domestic support, and export subsidies. In the case of *market access*, the Agreement on Agriculture replaced a quota-based system with a system of bound tariffs and tariff-

---

[9] All quotations without citations are taken from GATT Secretariat (1994).

Table 7.2 Administrative Structure of the WTO

Body	Composition	Function
Ministerial Conference	Representatives of all members	Meets at least once every two years Carries out functions of WTO Makes decisions and takes actions
General Council	Representatives of all members	Meets between the meetings of the Ministerial Conference Establishes rules and procedures Discharges responsibilities of the Dispute Settlement Body Discharges responsibilities of the Trade Policy Review Body
Secretariat	Director General and staff	Conduct organizational business of the WTO
Council for Trade in Goods		Oversees the functioning of the multilateral agreements of Annex 1A
Council for Trade in Services		Oversees the functioning of the multilateral agreements of Annex 1B
Council for Trade-Related Aspect of Intellectual Property Rights		Oversees the functioning of the multilateral agreements of Annex 1C
Dispute Settlement Body		Establishes panels, adopts panel and Appellate Body reports, maintains surveillance of implementation of rulings and recommendations
Panels	Three or five well-qualified governmental and/or nongovernmental individuals	Assist the dispute settlement body by making findings and recommendations in dispute settlement cases
Appellate Body	Seven persons, three of whom serve on any one case	Hears appeals from panel cases

reduction commitments. The conversion of quotas into tariffs is a process known as **tariffication**. In this aspect, the Agreement on Agriculture represents a significant change of regime. Nontariff measures (quotas) are now prohibited. Further, developed country members must have reduced average agricultural tariffs by 36 percent by 2001, and developing country members must reduce average agricultural tariffs by 24 percent by 2005. Least-developed country members are not required to reduce their tariffs.

Tariffication
The process of replacing quotas by equivalent tariffs.

In practice, the current tariff regimes are in the form of tariff rate quotas, discussed in the Appendix to Chapter 6.

In the case of *domestic support*, a distinction is made between non-trade-distorting policies, known as "green box" measures, and trade-distorting policies, known as "amber box" measures. Green box measures are exempt from any reduction commitments. Amber box measures are not exempt, and these commitments are specified in terms of what are known as "total aggregate measures of support" (total AMS). Developed country members must have reduced total AMS by 20 percent by 2001, and developing country members must reduce total AMS by 13 percent by 2005. Least-developed country members are not required to reduce their total AMS.

Finally, in the case of *export subsidies*, use has *not* been eliminated. Rather, it has been limited to specified situations. Developed country members must have reduced export subsidies by 36 percent by 2001, and developing country members must reduce export subsidies by 24 percent by 2005. Least-developed country members are not required to reduce their export subsidies. The persistence of developed country export subsidies represents a major distortion in global agricultural trade.

Despite these reduction commitments, the Agreement on Agriculture is best viewed as a *change in rules* rather than as a significant program for the liberalization of trade in agricultural products.[10] The hope is that further liberalization of the new tariffied quotas will take place in the current Doha Round of trade negotiations. Whether this hope is justified remains to be seen.

The Agreement on Textiles and Clothing (ATC) requires that, in four stages of a 10-year transition period beginning in 1995, countries reintegrate their textile and clothing sectors back into the GATT framework (GATT 1994). At the end of the 10-year period, all quotas on textile and clothing trade must be removed.[11] ATC integration commitments are stated in terms of product categories listed in an ATC annex. A number of points are worth briefly noting here. First, integration is in terms of volume, not value, and Stage 1 and 2 integrations were concentrated in low-value-added products. Second, importing countries expanded the annex during negotiations to include many items never subject to the MFA. Third, there is a safeguard clause to the ATC that can be invoked to slow its implementation.[12] The Stage 3 liberalization commitments, which took place in January 2002, were somewhat more satisfactory, giving some hope for successful liberalization by 2005.

Trade in Services

As we discussed in Chapter 1, trade in services composes more than 20 percent of total world trade and has at times grown faster than trade in

---

[10]Hathaway and Ingco (1996) supported this view.

[11]The negotiating history of the Agreement on Textiles and Clothing is described in detail in Raffaelli and Jenkins (1995).

[12]On the first two items, see Baughman et al. (1997). On the third item, see Kim, Reinert, and Rodrigo (2002).

goods. The **General Agreement on Trade in Services (GATS)** repre-sented the first time that services were brought into a multilateral trade agreement. For these reasons, the GATS was a significant outcome of the Uruguay Round. The negotiations on GATS, however, were difficult. Contributing to this difficulty was the fact that trade in services is less tangible than trade in goods. To provide a structure to trade in services, GATS defined trade in services as occurring in one of four modes:

> *Mode 1: Cross-border trade*
>
> *Mode 2: Movement of consumers*
>
> *Mode 3: Foreign direct investment or FDI*
>
> *Mode 4: Movement of natural persons*

General Agreement on Trade in Services (GATS) Part of the Marrakesh Agreement of 1994. Applies the GATT/WTO principle of nondis-crimination to a restricted number of services.

Let's consider each of these in turn. Cross-border trade is a mode of supply that does not require the physical movement of producers or consumers. For example, as discussed in Chapter 1, Indian firms provide medical transcrip-tion services to U.S. hospitals via satellite technology. Movement of con-sumers involves the consumer traveling to the country of the producer and is typical of the consumption of tourism services. Foreign direct investment is involved for services that require a commercial presence by producers in the country of the consumers and is typical of financial services. Finally, the temporary movement of natural persons involves a noncommercial presence by producers to supply consulting, construction, and instructional services.

Another difficulty in negotiating the GATS was that there was resistance to it on the part of a number of developing countries.[13] The United States and the European Union were in favor of it, however, and prevailed upon devel-oping countries to allow negotiations to move forward. The GATS included the principle of nondiscrimination discussed earlier. However, each member was allowed to specify nondiscrimination exemptions on a "negative list" of sectors upon entry into the agreement. These were to last for 10 years.

For those sectors a member country specifies on a "positive list," the GATS prohibited certain market access restrictions. Six types of limitations were prohibited: the number of service suppliers; the total value of service transactions; the total number of operations or quantity of output; number of personnel employed; the type of legal entity in the case of FDI; and the share of foreign ownership in the case of FDI. Even these requirements were optional if a member identified the ones they want to maintain in a second positive list.

The GATS contained an understanding that periodic negotiations would be required to incrementally liberalize trade in services. These negotiations have resulted in the following protocols to the GATS:

> *Second GATS Protocol: Revised Schedules of Commitments on Financial Services, 1995*
>
> *Third GATS Protocol: Schedules of Specific Commitments Relating to Movement of Natural Persons, 1995*

---

[13]On the developing country point of view, see Streeten (1995).

Telecommunication Services

Despite their importance in the world economy, the Marrakesh Agreement of 1994 contained no agreement on trade in telecommunication services. Negotiations on telecommunication services had begun in 1989 at the instigation of the United States. These negotiations broke down, however, because the United States was unsatisfied with the size of the market access concessions made by other countries of the world. The Marrakesh Agreement did contain a commitment to convene a Negotiating Group on Basic Telecommunications (NGBT) with a deadline of concluding an agreement by April 30, 1996.

Despite this commitment, "telecommunications negotiations broke down in the spring of 1996, when the United States bowed out and explained its refusal to conclude an agreement by claiming that a critical mass of market-access commitments, notably from developing countries, had not been reached" (Bronckers and Larouche, 1997, pp. 8–9). A new deadline was set for February 15, 1997. In the end, this deadline was met, and the telecommunication services agreement became the Fourth Protocol of the GATS, involving commitments by 69 countries. The agreement contains general provisions on nondiscrimination. It also contains specific commitments in the areas of market access and domestic regulation. More negotiations are ahead, however. As Bronckers and Larouche (1997) put it: "the Fourth Protocol . . . lays the foundation for an international agreement on the regulation of telecommunications services, but it does not by any means conclude the issue. The agreement reached on 15 February 1997 constitutes more of a beginning than anything else" (p. 45).

Source: Bronckers and Larouche (1997) and World Trade Organization.

Fourth GATS Protocol: Schedules of Specific Commitments Concerning Basic Telecommunications, 1997

Fifth GATS Protocol: Schedules of Specific Commitments and Lists of Exemptions from Article II Concerning Financial Services, 1998

The Second and Fifth Protocols on financial services were a significant outcome of the post-Marrakesh negotiations, although the negotiation process was contentious. As a result, beginning in 1999, a total of 102 WTO members entered into multilateral commitments in the areas of insurance, banking, and other financial services. The Fourth Protocol on telecommunications is discussed in the box. The Third Protocol on the movement of natural persons (Mode 4 defined earlier) was not significant, involving only a few countries. This is a disappointment to developing countries because, as stressed by Streeten (1995) and Mattoo (2000), Mode 4 services trade is where developing countries possess an important comparative advantage.[14]

The GATS committed signatories to begin a new round of GATS negotiations beginning in the year 2000, now known as GATS 2000. The WTO Services Council launched these negotiations in February of that year.

---

[14]"In order to reap these (comparative) advantages, it is important to insist in the negotiations that not only services in which the advanced countries have superiority, but also those in which the developing countries are superior should be included. Domestic service by Central American maids, medical services by Indian doctors, and construction services by Korean crews would have to be freed, as well as American banking and insurance" (Streeten, 1995, pp. 191–192). This, unfortunately, has not been the case.

On the agenda of GATS 2000 are subsidies, safeguard measures, government procurement, and additional market access. Progress in these negotiations was slow throughout the year, however, and hopes then turned to a "stock-taking" meeting of the Services Council that took place in early 2001. It remains to be seen whether significant progress is made on the GATS 2000 agenda.[15]

Intellectual Property

The most contentious aspect of the Marrakesh Agreement is to be found in the Agreement on Trade-Related Aspects of Intellectual Property Rights (TRIPS). Intellectual property or IP is an asset in the form of rights conferred upon a product of invention or creation by a country's legal system.[16] The TRIPS agreement defined intellectual property as belonging to one of six categories: copyrights; trademarks; geographical indications; industrial designs; patents; and layout designs of integrated circuits.[17] Trade-relatedness of IP refers to the fact that "theft" of intellectual property suppresses trade of the goods in question.

For example, if India takes a new drug (invented in the United States), analyzes its chemical constitution, and produces its own version of that drug, ignoring the U.S. patent, it will import substantially less of the patented drug. If it agrees to honor the U.S. patent, it would import the drug from the United States or have its domestic market supplied via FDI by the U.S.-based company holding the patent. Or, if a jeweler in Dubai sells counterfeit Cartier watches in place of authentic Cartier watches, this trademark violation will suppress the imports of authentic Cartier watches from France or Switzerland. No one takes this possibility more seriously than Cartier itself, which has crushed counterfeit watches with steamrollers and maintains its Middle East headquarters in Dubai.

The TRIPS agreement applied the principle of nondiscrimination to IP. Any advantage a WTO member grants to any country with regard to IP must now be granted to all other members. If India agrees to honor U.K. pharmaceutical patents, it must honor U.S. pharmaceutical patents as well. This aspect of the TRIPS agreement must have been implemented by January 1996.

The TRIPS agreement also sets out obligations for members structured around the six IP categories:

1. Copyrights. *Members must comply with the 1971 Berne Convention on copyrights. Computer programs are protected as literary works under the Berne Convention, and the unauthorized recording of live broadcasts and performances is prohibited. The term of this protection is to be 50 years.*

---

[15]You can follow the progress of GATS 2000 on the WTO Web site at http://www.wto.org. Follow links to "Trade Topics," "Services," and "Service Negotiations."

[16]See Maskus (2000).

[17]Geographical indications are defined as "indications which identify a good as originating in the territory of a Member, or a region or locality in that territory, where a given quality, reputation or other characteristic of the good is essentially attributable to its geographic origin." We saw an example of this in Chapter 4 in the form of *blue d'Auvergne* cheese.

2. Trademarks. *Trademarks of goods and services are to be protected for a term of no less than seven years. Provisions for the registration of trademarks must be made and are renewable indefinitely.*

3. Geographical indications. *Members must provide legal means to prevent the false use of geographical indications.*

4. Industrial designs. *Members must protect "independently created industrial designs that are new or original." This protection does not apply to "designs dictated essentially by technical or functional considerations." The protection of industrial designs must last at least 10 years.*

5. Patents. *The agreement states, "patents shall be available for any inventions, whether products or processes, in all fields of technology, provided that they are new, involve an inventive step and are capable of industrial application." Exceptions to this do exist and include the protection of public order, human, animal, and plant life. Patents are to be extended for at least 20 years.*[18]

6. Layout designs of integrated circuits. *The distribution of protected layout designs, as well as integrated circuits embodying protected layout designs, is forbidden. This protection is to extend for at least 10 years.*

Currently, citizens and firms in developed countries own most of the world's IP. It is also the case that developing countries currently often have less IP protection than developed countries, especially in the case of patents. Therefore, the TRIPS agreement raises the cost of many goods and services to developing countries. India will have to pay more for drugs as a result of the TRIPS agreement, and this will have an adverse effect on welfare in this country, especially the welfare of the poor. The same goes for the poor in many other developing countries. In the short term, then, the TRIPS agreement represents a transfer from developing country consumers to developed country producers. In a response to these extra costs, the TRIPS agreement allows for greater transition periods for developing countries in the case of the six obligations. Developed countries must have instituted the obligations by 1996. Developing countries must have instituted them by 2000.[19] Least-developed countries have until 2005 to do so. All member countries, however, are to have abided by the nondiscrimination principle as of 1996.

The intellectual case in favor of multilateral trade liberalization of the kind embodied in the Marrakesh Agreement is the improvement of welfare that generally, although not always, accompanies the liberalization. In the case of the TRIPS agreement, however, such welfare gains can be absent, especially in short to medium time frames. Indeed, some prominent trade economists from developing countries (e.g., Jagdish Bhagwati and Arvind

---

[18]Hoekman (1994) noted that: "The 20-year lower bound implies harmonization towards the standards maintained by industrialized countries. This will have implications for many developing countries that either do not provide patent protection for certain goods or processes, or grant patents of relatively short duration" (p. 102). This is one of a number of ways in which TRIPS will have a detrimental impact on developing countries.

[19]In fact, though, many developing countries did not meet the January 2000 deadline. This has called into question the whole TRIPS agreement.

Panagariya) consider the TRIPS to be a welfare-worsening, "nontrade" agenda item that has no place in the WTO. These economists view TRIPS as lacking in the efficiency gains that characterize trade (see Chapters 2 and 3) and as inappropriately restricting the freedom of countries to choose the intellectual property regime that is best for them.[20] Whatever your own opinion, it is clear that TRIPS represents a significant concession on the part of the developing world. In light of this, any failure on the part of developed countries to abide by their commitments, especially in the areas of agriculture, textiles, and clothing, will be greeted by the developing countries with justified dismay.

If there is one area in which the TRIPS agreement has been most contentious, it is in the area of AIDS drugs. This case is a stark example of potentially adverse impacts of this new regime. The U.S. government has put a great deal of pressure on the governments of Brazil, India, and South Africa to honor U.S. patents on AIDS drugs, thus raising the costs of these drugs to AIDS patients in these countries. If, as is plausible, the resulting increased costs of these drugs puts them out of reach of AIDS patients in these countries, the resulting increases in morbidity and mortality from this disease could be substantial. In November 2001, WTO members gathered in Doha, Qatar, for the fourth Ministerial Conference of the WTO. At this meeting, pressure over the TRIPS/AIDS issue was quite intense. As a result, the members issued a special Declaration on the TRIPS Agreement and Public Health. This declaration included the statement that "the TRIPS Agreement does not and should not prevent Members from taking measures to protect public health." More specifically, the declaration reaffirmed four "flexibilities" with regard to TRIPS and public health. For example: "Each member has the right to determine what constitutes a national emergency or other circumstances of extreme urgency, it being understood that public health crises, including those related to HIV/AIDS, tuberculosis, malaria and other epidemics, can represent a national emergency or other circumstances of extreme urgency." This was a victory for those in developing countries with a concern for AIDS and other public health issues.

Can developing countries expect any benefits from the TRIPS Agreement? Prominent trade economist Keith Maskus (2000) argues that they can. These come in the form of increased inward FDI and technology transfer, as well as in the form of increased domestic innovation. Thus, the TRIPS Agreement imposes short-term costs in the hopes of generating long-term benefits. Whether this trade-off has been made in an appropriate manner by TRIPS is an issue on which there is still much disagreement.[21]

Dispute Settlement

The Marrakesh Agreement included an Understanding on Rules and Procedures Governing the Settlement of Disputes. The original GATT had

---

[20]See, for example, Panagariya (1999).
[21]Keith Maskus has an excellent Microsoft PowerPoint presentation on these issues as part of the World Bank's BSPAN Web site. See http://www.worldbank.org/wbi/B-SPAN/sub_intellectual_property.htm.

been somewhat unclear about the resolution of disputes, and the Marrakesh Agreement, in establishing the WTO, attempted to clarify dispute settlement procedures. As shown in Table 7.2, the WTO includes councils on trade in goods and services as well as a council on TRIPS. These councils should help to minimize the occurrence of disputes, but they certainly have not eliminated them. In the event of disputes, the WTO turns to a Dispute Settlement Body or DSB whose function is to administer the dispute settlement rules and procedures. The DSB makes decisions by "consensus." As with the WTO in general, consensus for the DSB exists "if no Member, present at the meeting of the DSB when the decision is taken, formally objects to the proposed decision."

The dispute settlement procedure is summarized in Figure 7.2. If a member of the WTO has a complaint against another member, the first step in settling this dispute is a consultation between the members involved. If the consultation process fails to settle a dispute within 60 days, the complaining member may request the establishment of a panel. This request also must be submitted in writing. Panels are composed of three or five "well-qualified governmental or nongovernmental individuals." The function of the panel is to assist the DSB in the dispute settlement process. It consults the parties involved and provides the DSB with a written report of its findings. The DSB then has 60 days to adopt the report by consensus unless a party to the dispute decides to appeal.

The appeal of a panel report is referred to an appellate body, composed of seven persons "of recognized authority, with demonstrated expertise in law, international trade and the subject matter of the covered agreements generally." The appellate body reviews the appeal and submits its report to the DSB. At this point, it is stipulated that the appellate body report "shall be adopted by the DSB and unconditionally accepted by the parties to the dispute unless the DSB decides by consensus *not* to adopt the

Figure 7.2 Dispute Settlement in the WTO

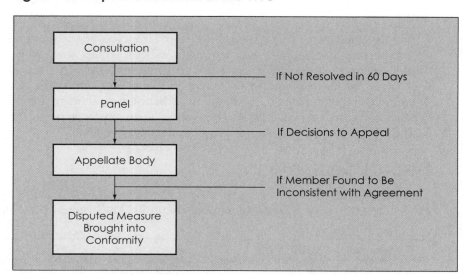

The U.S.–Pakistan Combed Cotton Yarn Dispute

A few weeks after the World Trade Center attack that set off the U.S.–led war in Afghanistan, the World Trade Organization issued an appellate body report on a dispute between the United States and its ally in that war, Pakistan. The roots of this dispute went back to December 1998 when the United States requested consultations with Pakistan regarding its exports of combed cotton yarn. In these consultations, these two parties failed to reach a mutual understanding. In March 1999, the United States announced that it would impose "safeguard" restrictions on Pakistan's exports of combed cotton yarn under the Agreement on Textiles and Clothing (ATC). A WTO safeguard permits a member to temporarily withdraw from an obligation in certain specified circumstances. The WTO's Textiles Monitoring Body (TMB) reviewed this ATC safeguard case in April 1999 and recommended that the United States rescind its safeguard actions. In May 1999, the United States communicated its inability to comply with the TMB recommendation and continued to maintain the safeguard restriction on Pakistan's exports of combed cotton yarn.

In April 2000, Pakistan requested the establishment of a dispute settlement panel. This panel was established in June 2000 and issued its report in May 2001. The panel focused most closely on two issues related to the U.S. claim, filed under the safeguard clause in the ATC, that Pakistan's exports of combed cotton yarn caused "serious damage or threat thereof" to the U.S. combed cotton yarn industry. The first issue was the definition of the U.S. domestic industry. In its submission to the TMB justifying its actions, the United States defined its domestic combed cotton yard industry to exclude vertically-integrated fabric producers producing combed cotton yarn for their own consumption. This had the effect of exaggerating the negative impacts of Pakistan's exports on a very narrowly-defined industry. The United States argued that this segment of the industry did not compete with imported yarn from Pakistan. Noting that these integrated producers both bought and sold their yarn on the market, the panel disagreed with the United States, finding against it in its report.

The second issue was that, in its submission to the TMB, the Unites States had excluded Mexico's exports of combed cotton yarn. Because these exports were roughly of equal magnitude to those of Pakistan, this exclusion was suspicious. It helped the United States attribute negative effects to the domestic industry to Pakistan's exports when Mexico's exports might equally have been the cause. The panel found against the United States here, as well.

Like the TMB, the DSB panel requested that the United States rescind its restrictions on Pakistan's exports of combed cotton yarn, but the United States again refused to do so. Instead, it appealed to the DSB appellate body in July 2001. The appellate body issued its report in October 2001. With regard to both the issue of excluding vertically-integrated fabric producers and Mexico's exports, it found against the United States. It concluded its report with a reiteration that the United States should rescind its ATC safeguard restraint.

Source: Adapted from Kim, S.J., Reinert, K.A. and Rodrigo, G.C. (2002). "The Agreement on Textiles and Clothing: Safeguard Actions from 1995 to 2001." *Journal of International Economic Law* 5 (2): 445–468.

appellate body report within 30 days following its circulation to the members." Therefore, given the definition of consensus for the DSB, *any DSB member can effectively insist on the adoption of the appellate body report.* Renowned international trade lawyer John Jackson (1994) refered to this appellate body procedure as "ingenious" and noted that "the result of the procedure is that appellate report will in virtually every case come into force as a matter of international law" (p. 70). The way in which this dispute settlement process evolved in a case between the United States and Pakistan is detailed in the box.

The dispute settlement procedure outlined here and in Figure 7.2 applies to all aspects of the Marrakesh Agreement. It improves significantly the procedures of the old GATT and therefore makes a significant contribution to the conduct of international trade.[22] However, the effectiveness of the procedures depends on members' commitment to them. A country has the option of ignoring the outcome of the dispute settlement process. In this case, the complaining member has the right to impose retaliatory tariffs on a volume of imports from the other country determined by the DSB. For example, in a famous case, the United States imposed retaliatory tariffs on imports from the European Union in response to the latter's failure to comply with the DSB's findings regarding the EU import regime for bananas. These tariffs were in place between 1999 and 2001.

The Environment

In 1991, the GATT reactivated a long-dormant working group on Environmental Measures and International Trade (EMIT). Not coincidentally, this was the year that a GATT dispute resolution panel issued its controversial opinion in the now-famous tuna-dolphin case. The panel ruled against a U.S. law banning imports of Mexican tuna that involved dolphin-unsafe fishing practices, issued in response to the U.S. Marine Mammal Protection Act. The panel argued that the import ban violated the general prohibition against quotas and that the United States had not attempted to negotiate cooperative agreements on dolphin-safe tuna fishing. The U.S. environmental community reacted strongly against the GATT panel ruling, casting the GATT as anti-environment, and the trade–environment issue has loomed large over the WTO ever since.[23]

With the advent of the WTO in 1995, EMIT was replaced by the Committee on Trade and the Environment (CTE). Most developing country members of the WTO have taken a dim view of the work of the CTE, fearing the possibility of further protection against their exports on environmental grounds, what they term "green protection." These members often view environmental matters as nontrade issues that have no place in the trade policy agenda of the WTO. The subsequent polarization of views has inhibited the effectiveness of the CTE.[24] Some observers (e.g., Runge, 1994) have suggested that the CTE be replaced by a World Environmental Organization (WEO) to stand alongside the WTO. Although this idea certainly has its appeal, there is the possibility that the same tensions that characterize the work of the CTE would characterize the WEO.

Many trade economists (e.g., Anderson, 1996, and Hoekman and Kostecki, 2001, Chapter 13) are broadly supportive of the developing country view

---

[22]For more on the WTO dispute settlement procedures, see Kuruvila (1997), Davey (2000), and Hoekman and Mavroidis (2000).

[23]For a review of the tuna–dolphin case, see Chapter 4 of Runge (1994). Posters at the time, issued by U.S.–based environmental groups, depicted GATT as "GATTzilla," a monster destroying national environmental sovereignty.

[24]See Shaffer (2001). This author notes that "In light of the immense challenge developing countries face in meeting the basic needs of the majority of their human populations, southern constituencies typically place less weight on the social value of environmental preservation than on economic and social development and poverty eradication" (p. 87).

that environmental issues represent an "intrusion" into the WTO trade agenda. These trade economists suggest, perhaps correctly, that the environmental agenda could result in an inappropriate "one size fits all" approach to environmental policies across WTO members. As Hoekman and Kostecki (2001) note, "Countries may have very different preferences regarding environmental protectionism, reflecting differences in the absorptive capacity of their ecosystems, differences in income levels (wealth), and differences in culture" (p. 442). The limitation of this argument is that it could just as easily (and sometimes is) applied to the TRIPS agreement discussed here. Consequently, many trade economists appear to be inconsistent on these matters.

In 1999, the WTO took up the trade and environment issue formally with the publication of a "special studies" report on this subject (Nordström and Vaughan, 1999). As with Runge (1994), this report argued that increased trade can have both positive and negative impacts on the environment. The report emphasizes, however, that trade-driven growth cannot always be counted upon to deliver improvements in environmental quality through increased incomes, as many economists claim. Consequently, these higher incomes must be "translated into higher environmental quality" through the mechanism of international cooperation. As emphasized by Barrett (1999), designing environmental treaties to include the appropriate combination of incentives and threats to achieve international cooperation on environmental matters is not always easy. This has been shown in the case of the Kyoto Protocol on greenhouse (global warming) gasses. The WTO report also emphasized that government subsidies to polluting and resource-depleting sectors such as agriculture, fishing, and energy can exacerbate the environmental consequences of trade.

The role of the WTO in trade and environment matters will continue to be both important and controversial. The decade of the 1990s ended with another difficult case regarding the impact of shrimp fishing on sea turtles.[25] The appellate body report on this case stressed the importance of international environmental agreements in reconciling trade and the environment. To some degree, the success of the WTO depends on the willingness and ability of its members to enter into such agreements. Multilateralism on environmental issues is, therefore, as important as multilateralism on trade issues.

---

[25]See Hoekman and Kostecki (2001), pp. 446–447.

Conclusion

The WTO came into being in 1995, completing the Bretton Woods vision of a global trade institution. Since its birth, it has both demonstrated the importance of a multilateral approach to managing trade issues and stirred up controversies in a number of areas. All evidence suggests that the WTO will continue, as stated in the introduction to this chapter, to be "both lauded and vilified with equal intensity by various groups with concerns about trade policy." In general, a common fault line exists across many issues within the WTO between developed and developing countries.

With regard to the old GATT agenda of trade in goods, developing countries are still at a disadvantage in textiles, clothing, and agriculture. Their exports must contend with higher than normal protection levels in the developed world and, in the case of agriculture, with the massive domestic and export subsidies of the United States and the European Union. The ongoing controversies over TRIPS also have a similar fault line. In the short term, developing countries will generally lose from intellectual property protection through the higher prices they will have to pay for goods and services. This short-term cost will have to be accepted by the developing world, waiting for the hoped-for, long-term benefits of increased inward FDI and domestic innovation. Finally, ongoing disputes concerning environmental issues often pit developed and developing countries against one another. Developing countries fear a surge of "green protection," exacerbating their disadvantages in other areas.

These fissures within the WTO deserve attention. As stated by Birdsall and Lawrence (1999), "the global community would benefit from more dialogue and compromise between high-income and low-income countries, and from the recognition in such dialogue that the often vast gap in levels of development across trading countries inevitably generates domestic economic and political pressures that are bound to create legitimate conflicts" (p. 145). Unfortunately, progress in this area has been slow. As mentioned in Chapter 1, the Seattle Ministerial Conference of the WTO that took place in December 1999 was not successful. This was, in part, due to the protests of young people against the WTO as an agent of globalization. It was also due to a lack of agreement between developed and developing WTO member countries on a number of issues discussed in this chapter. For both these reasons, WTO members were not able to launch the hoped-for new round of multilateral trade talks.

A second attempt to launch a new round took place in Doha, Qatar, in November 2001 at the next Ministerial Conference. This attempt was more successful, although disputes between developing and developed countries still simmered beneath the surface. Although progress was made on the TRIPS/AIDS issue, the European Union maintained its intransigent position with regard to agricultural trade liberalization, and the developing countries were displeased with the introduction of new agenda items such as investment and competition policy. The Doha Round of trade negotiations might prove to be very difficult.

Review Exercises

1. What is meant by nondiscrimination in international trade agreements?

2. One criticism of the Agreement on Agriculture is that it involves *dirty tariffication*. Dirty tariffication involves quotas being converted into tariffs that are larger than the actual tariff equivalent of the original tariff. Draw a diagram like that of Figure 6.4, illustrating dirty tariffication.

3. The chapter mentioned the four modes by which trade in services can occur: cross-border trade; movement of consumers; foreign direct investment; and personnel movement. Give a specific example of each of these modes.

4. The chapter also gave an example of the way that the "theft" of intellectual property by India in the case of pharmaceuticals suppresses trade in this product. Give another example of such trade suppression.

Further Reading and Web Resources

The reader interested in pursuing his or her understanding of the GATT/WTO system must start with the definitive work by Hoekman and Kostecki (2001). A more legal approach can be found in Jackson (1997). An assessment of the WTO after its failed Seattle ministerial meeting in December 1999 can be found in Schott (2000). Journals covering the subjects of this chapter include the *Journal of World Trade*, *World Trade Review*, and the *Journal of International Economic Law*. The controversy over TRIPS is analyzed by Maskus (2000), and a general critique of the WTO can be found in Curtis (2001).

To keep up with the work of the WTO, the reader will want to visit its Web site at **http://www.wto.org**. Perhaps the most useful link here is the one to "trade topics." However, the document dissemination facility at this Web site is a particularly useful resource. The reader will want to monitor two additional Web sites. The first is that of the Centre for Trade and Sustainable Development at **http://www.ctsd.org**, a very important resource on issues of trade and the environment. The second is Harvard's Global Trade Negotiations Home Page at **http://www.cid.harvard.edu/cidtrade**.

Also see the Windows on the World Economy Web site for *Quarterly Reports on the Doha Round* at **http://reinert.swlearning.com**.

References

Anderson, K. (1996) "The Intrusion of Environmental and Labor Standards into Trade Policy," in W. Martin and L.A. Winters (eds.), *The Uruguay Round and the Developing Countries*, Cambridge University Press, Cambridge, 1996, 435–462.

Barrett, S. (1999) "Montreal versus Kyoto: International Cooperation and the Global Environment," in I. Kaul, I. Grunberg, and M.A. Stern (eds.), *Global Public Goods: International Cooperation in the 21st Century*, Oxford University Press, Oxford, 192–219.

Baughman, L., R. Mirus, M.E. Morkre, and D. Spinanger (1997) "Of Tyre Cords, Ties and Tents: Window-Dressing in the ATC?" *The World Economy*, 20:4, 407–434.

Birdsall, N., and R.Z. Lawrence (1999) "Deep Integration and Trade Agreements: Good for Developing Countries?" in I. Kaul, I. Grunberg, and M.A. Stern (eds.), *Global Public Goods: International Cooperation in the 21st Century*, Oxford University Press, Oxford, 128–151.

Bronckers, M.C.E.J., and P. Larouche (1997) "Telecommunications Services and the World Trade Organization," *Journal of World Trade*, 31:3, 5–47.

Curtis, M. (2001) *Trade for Life: Making Trade Work for Poor People*, Christian Aid, London.

Davey, W.J. (2000) "The WTO Dispute Settlement System," *Journal of International Economic Law*, 3:1, 15–18.

Diebold, W. (1952) "The End of the ITO," *Princeton Essays in International Finance*, 16, Princeton, New Jersey.

Dinan, D. (1999) *Ever Closer Union: An Introduction to European Integration*, Lynne Rienner, Boulder.

GATT Secretariat (1994) *The Results of the Uruguay Round of Multilateral Trade Negotiations: The Legal Text*, Geneva.

Hathaway, D.E. (1987) *Agriculture and the GATT: Rewriting the Rules*, Institute for International Economics, Washington, DC.

Hathaway, D.E. and M.D. Ingco (1996) "Agricultural Liberalization and the Uruguay Round," in W. Martin and L.A. Winters (eds.), *The Uruguay Round and the Developing Countries*, Cambridge University Press, Cambridge, 30–57.

Hoekman, B.M. (1994) "Services and Intellectual Property Rights," in S.M. Collins and B.P. Bosworth (eds.), *The New GATT*, The Brookings Institution, Washington, DC, 84–121.

Hoekman, B.M., and M. Kostecki (2001) *The Political Economy of the World Trading System: From GATT to WTO*, Oxford University Press, Oxford.

Hoekman, B.M. and P.C. Mavroidis (2000) "WTO Dispute Settlement, Transparency and Surveillance," *The World Economy*, 23:4, 527–542.

Jackson, J.H. (1997) *The World Trading System*, MIT Press, Cambridge, Massachusetts.

Jackson, J.H. (1994) "The World Trade Organization, Dispute Settlement and Codes of Conduct," in S.M Collins and B.P. Bosworth (eds.), *The New GATT*, Brookings Institution, Washington, DC.

Kim, S.J., K.A. Reinert, and G.C. Rodrigo (2002) "The Agreement on Textiles and Clothing: Safeguard Actions from 1995 to 2001," *Journal of International Economic Law*, 5:2, 445–468.

Kuruvila, P.E. (1997) "Developing Countries and the GATT/WTO Dispute Settlement Mechanism," *Journal of World Trade*, 31:6, 171–207.

Markusen, J.R., J.R. Melvin, W.H. Kaempfer, and K.E. Maskus (1995) *International Trade: Theory and Evidence*, McGrall-Hill, New York.

Maskus, K.E. (2000) *Intellectual Property Rights in the Global Economy*, Institute for International Economics, Washington, DC.

Mattoo, A. (2000) "Developing Countries in the New Round of GATS Negotiations: Towards a Pro-Active Role," *The World Economy*, 23:4, 471–489.

Nordström, H., and S. Vaughan (1999) *Trade and the Environment*, World Trade Organization, Geneva.

North, D.C. (1990) *Institutions, Institutional Change and Economic Performance*, Cambridge University Press, Cambridge.

Panagariya, A. (1999) "TRIPS and the WTO: An Uneasy Marriage," paper presented at the World Trade Organization, Geneva.

Raffaelli, M., and T. Jenkins (1995) *The Drafting History of the Agreement on Textiles and Clothing*, International Textiles and Clothing Bureau, Geneva.

Runge, C.F. (1994) *Freer Trade, Protected Environment*, Council of Foreign Relations, New York.

Schott, J.J. (ed.) (2000) *The WTO after Seattle*, Institute for International Economics, Washington, DC.

Shaffer, G.C. (2001) "The World Trade Organization Under Challenge: Democracy and the Law and Politics of the WTO's Treatment of Trade and Environmental Matters," *Harvard Environmental Law Review*, 25:1, 1–93.

Skidelsky, R. (2000) *John Maynard Keynes: Fighting for Freedom 1937–1946*, Viking, New York.

Streeten, P.P. (1995) "Gains and Losses from Trade in Services," in *Thinking About Development*, Cambridge University Press, Cambridge, 186–193.

Regional Trade Agreements

8

I once attended a talk by a Canadian trade negotiator who made the following potent statement: "When multilateralism falters, regionalism picks up the pace." As a student of the world economy, you need to understand the meaning and implications of this statement.

The term "multilateralism" refers to the GATT/WTO system described in Chapter 7, as well as the trade negotiations that take place among all GATT/WTO members as a group. Recall that one of the founding principles of this system is nondiscrimination, and that nondiscrimination, in turn, involves the most-favored nation (MFN) and national treatment (NT) subprinciples. Under MFN, each WTO member must grant to each other member treatment as favorable as they extend to any other member country. Although it is not always acknowledged, the term "regionalism" refers to a violation of the nondiscrimination principle in which one member of a **regional trade agreement (RTA)** discriminates in its trade policies in favor of another member of the RTA and against nonmembers. This discrimination has been allowed by the GATT/WTO under certain circumstances. These circumstances are the cases of free trade areas (FTAs), customs unions (CUs), and interim agreements leading to an FTA or CU "within a reasonable length of time."[1]

Regionalism and multilateralism represent two alternative trade policy options available to the countries of the world. When the larger countries of the world lose commitment to the multilateralism option, multilateralism "falters." However, this is when countries often turn their attention to the regional option, and regionalism "picks up the pace." Indeed, nearly every member of the WTO is also a member of at least one RTA, and over 150 RTAs are now in existence. There are also times when countries pursue both tracks simultaneously. For example, Mexico, Canada, and the United States negotiated the North American Free Trade Agreement (NAFTA) and the Uruguay Round of multilateral negotiations simultaneously. Indeed, in a few areas, NAFTA included elements that were also included in the Marrakesh Agreement discussed in Chapter 7.

This chapter will introduce you to various types of RTAs and their economic effects. These effects are analyzed in international economics in terms of the concepts of trade creation and trade diversion. We then consider some

Regional trade agreement (RTA)
An agreement by a number of countries to grant preferential access to their markets to other members of the agreement. Examples include free trade areas and customs unions.

---

[1] All quotations without citations are from GATT Secretariat (1994).

examples of RTAs, namely the European Union, the North American Free Trade Agreement, Mercosur, and the Free Trade Area of the Americas. Finally, we consider in more detail the relationship of regionalism to multilateralism.

Regional Trade Agreements

There are a number of alternative types of RTAs, and these are presented in Table 8.1. We are going to introduce them by considering two countries, Brazil and Argentina. Suppose that, initially, these countries pursue independent and nonpreferential trade policies. That is, the trade policies of these two countries are not coordinated in any way and do not discriminate among countries. Also, there is no integration of the countries' labor, capital, and money markets. From this initial starting point, a first-level RTA is known as a **preferential trade area (PTA)**. In a PTA, Brazil and Argentina lower their trade barriers between each other, but do not eliminate them. That is, trade barriers between the member countries (Brazil and Argentina) are lower than with nonmember countries (e.g., Venezuela). Labor and capital markets remain unintegrated. Because the two countries have not fully eliminated trade barriers between each other, this type of RTA is not allowed by the WTO.[2]

A second-level RTA is known as a **free trade area (FTA)**. In an FTA, Brazil and Argentina eliminate the trade barriers between each other. With regard to nonmember countries, however, Brazil and Argentina pursue independent policies. Labor and capital markets remain unintegrated.

Preferential trade area (PTA) An agreement on the part of a set of countries to reduce but not eliminate trade restrictions among themselves.

Free trade area (FTA) An agreement on the part of a set of countries to eliminate trade restrictions among themselves. In contrast to a customs union, it does not involve a common external tariff.

Table 8.1 Types of Regional Trade Agreements

Type	Acronym	Description
Preferential trade area	PTA	An agreement on the part of a set of countries to *reduce but not eliminate* trade restrictions among themselves
Free trade area	FTA	An agreement on the part of a set of countries to *eliminate* trade restrictions among themselves
Customs union	CU	An agreement on the part of a set of countries to eliminate trade restrictions among themselves and to adopt a *common external tariff*
Common market	CM	An agreement on the part of a set of countries to eliminate trade restrictions among themselves, to adopt a common external tariff, and to allow the *free movement of labor and physical capital* among member countries

[2] Some trade economists who are critical of RTAs (e.g. Bhagwati, Greenaway, and Panagariya, 1998) refer to *all* RTAs as PTAs. We will not do this here in order to distinguish RTAs that are legal under GATT/WTO rules from PTAs that are not.

A third-level regional agreement is known as a **customs union (CU)**. In a CU, as in the FTA, Brazil and Argentina eliminate the trade barriers between each other. Additionally, however, the member countries adopt common trade barriers with regard to nonmember countries (often referred to as a *common external tariff*). Labor and capital markets remain unintegrated.

WTO members who wish to form FTAs or CUs may do so. However, there are certain requirements. First, trade barriers against nonmembers cannot be "higher or more restrictive than" those in existence prior to the FTA or CU. Second, the FTA or CU must be formed "within a reasonable length of time." Third, the FTA or CU must eliminate trade barriers on "substantially all the trade" among the members.[3] Fourth, with regard to services, the General Agreement on Trade in Services (GATS) requires that the FTA or CU involve "substantial sectoral coverage."

For both FTAs and CUs, the phrases "higher or more restrictive than," "within a reasonable length of time," and "substantially all trade" have been so vague as to make oversight of RTAs very difficult. Consequently, as part of the Uruguay Round of trade negotiations leading up to the Marrakesh Agreement and the establishment of the WTO, there was an agreed-upon "understanding" on RTAs. This understanding specified that the relevant measure to assess restrictiveness is a weighted average of tariff rates and that the length of time allowable for the elimination of trade barriers within FTA and CUs is to be no more than 10 years. Even with this understanding, however, there is room for differing interpretations.[4]

A fourth-level RTA is known as a **common market (CM)**. A common market is a CU in which labor and capital markets are integrated into a regional market. That is, any restrictions on movements of labor and physical capital (direct foreign investment) have been removed. Provided the trade aspects of the common market meet the two criteria mentioned earlier, a common market is WTO-legal.

An extension of a RTA into the monetary realm is a monetary union. Here, the common market adopts a common currency and monetary policy. We take up this particular regional arrangement, including the European monetary union, in Chapter 17.

One issue that inevitably arises in the design of RTAs is how to determine whether a product is from a partner country. Suppose that Brazil and Argentina form a RTA. It is possible that a shirt produced in Venezuela is imported into Brazil and that a label "Made in Brazil" is attached there. Then the shirt can be imported into Argentina with no restrictions or tariffs, but the product is not really made in Brazil. To protect against such possibilities, RTA members usually define **rules of origin**. These can be defined in a number of ways, including by amount of value added in a RTA partner country or by degree of product transformation, often measured by a change in tariff classification. Rules of origin are an important component of RTAs and, in some instances, can be quite restrictive.

Customs union (CU)
An agreement on the part of a set of countries to eliminate trade restrictions among themselves and adopt a common external tariff.

Common market
An agreement on the part of a set of countries to eliminate trade restrictions among themselves, to adopt a common external tariff, and to allow the free movement of labor and physical capital among member countries.

Rules of origin
A means to determine whether a product is from a partner country in a regional trade agreement (RTA). These can be defined in a number of ways, including by amount of value added in an RTA partner country or by degree of product transformation, often measured by a change in tariff classification.

---

[3] GATT/WTO rules on RTAs that allow for FTAs and CUs are contained in Article XXIV of the GATT.
[4] See Serra et al. (1997).

The Economic Effects of Regional Trade Agreements

Trade creation
A potential outcome of a free trade area or a customs union in which imports switch from a high-cost source to a low-cost source.

Trade diversion
A potential outcome of a free trade area or a customs union in which imports switch from a low-cost source to a high-cost source.

What are the economic effects of RTAs? Jacob Viner (1950) first addressed this question in a famous book entitled *The Customs Union Issue*. In this book, Viner distinguished between the concepts of **trade creation** and **trade diversion** in RTAs. Trade creation occurs when the formation of an FTA or CU leads to a switching of imports from a high-cost source to a low-cost source. Alternatively, trade diversion occurs when imports switch from a low-cost source to a high-cost source. As we will soon see, trade creation tends to improve welfare, whereas trade diversion tends to worsen welfare. Let's summarize trade creation and trade diversion:

> **Trade creation: Switching of imports from a high-cost source to a low-cost source**
>
> **Trade diversion: Switching of imports from a low-cost source to a high cost source**

We are going to illustrate the concepts of trade creation and trade diversion using the absolute advantage model we developed in Chapter 2. Along with Brazil (*B*) and Argentina (*A*), we are also going to refer to a third country, Venezuela (*V*). Brazil and Argentina are going to be members of an RTA, whereas Venezuela will remain a nonmember. A RTA that involves trade creation is presented in Figure 8.1. In this figure, we take the perspective of Brazil. S^B is Brazil's supply curve of some good, and D^B is Brazil's demand curve for the same good. Brazil can import the good from Argentina at price P^A and from Venezuela at price P^V. The crucial point here is that Argentina is the lower-cost producer in comparison to Venezuela.

Figure 8.1 A Trade-Creating, Regional Trade Agreement Between Brazil and Argentina

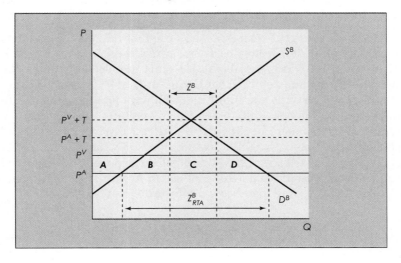

Before the RTA, Brazil has in place a specific (per unit) tariff of T on imports from both Argentina and Venezuela. Because $P^A + T < P^V + T$, Brazil imports the good from Argentina, and the initial import level is Z^B. Once Brazil joins either an FTA or CU with Argentina, the tariff is removed on imports from Argentina. Clearly, $P^A < P^V + T$, so the good continues to be imported from Argentina. The imports, however, expand from Z^B to Z^B_{RTA} as the price falls from $P^A + T$ to P^A.

As a result of the RTA with Argentina, consumer surplus in Brazil increases in Figure 8.1 by area $A + B + C + D$. Producer surplus falls by A, and government tariff revenue falls by C.[5] The net increase in welfare due to trade creation is $B + D$. Let's summarize this:

Consumer surplus:	$A + B + C + D$
Producer surplus:	$-A$
Government revenue:	C
Net welfare:	$B + D$

The switch in "imports" in the trade-creating RTA described in Figure 8.1 is from a high-cost source, namely Brazil itself, to a low-cost source, Argentina. This trade-creating switch is what generates the increase in welfare in Brazil.

An RTA that involves trade diversion is presented in Figure 8.2. In this figure, and in contrast to Figure 8.1, Venezuela is now the lower-cost producer in comparison to Argentina. That is, $P^V < P^A$. Because $P^V + T < P^A + T$, before the RTA Brazil imports the good from Venezuela, and the initial import level is Z^B. Once Brazil joins an FTA or CU with Argentina, however, $P^A < P^V + T$, so Brazil switches to Argentina as an import supplier. Imports expand to Z^B_{RTA} as the domestic price falls from $P^V + T$ to P^A.

Figure 8.2 A Trade-Diverting, Regional Trade Agreement Between Brazil and Argentina

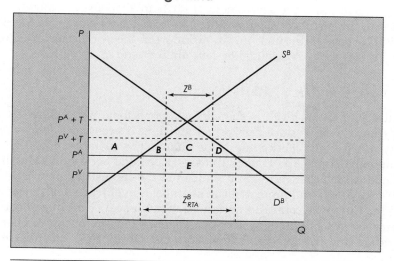

---

[5] Recall that the concepts of consumer and producer surplus were discussed in the appendix to Chapter 2.

As a result of the RTA with Argentina, consumer surplus in Brazil increases by area $A + B + C + D$ in Figure 8.2. Producer surplus falls by A, and government revenue falls by $C + E$. The net increase in welfare is therefore $B + D - E$.

Let's summarize:

Consumer surplus:	$A + B + C + D$
Producer surplus:	$-A$
Government revenue:	$C - E$
Net welfare:	$B + D - E$

Whether the net welfare effect is a positive or negative value depends on the relative sizes of $B + D$ and E. Area $B + D$ represents the trade-creating effects of switching "imports" from the higher-cost source of Brazil to the lower-cost source of Argentina. However, area E represents the trade-diverting effects of switching imports from the lower-cost source of Venezuela to the higher-cost source of Argentina. If the trade-diverting effects outweigh the trade-creating effects (if $E > B + D$), then the RTA will reduce welfare in Brazil.

What should you take from the preceding discussion of trade creation and trade diversion? Let's summarize:

> **RTAs can be either welfare-improving or welfare-worsening. Whether an RTA is welfare-improving or welfare-worsening is something that must be assessed on a case-by-case basis, based on evidence on the relative strengths of trade creation and trade diversion.**

As a consequence, assessments of RTAs are often made using more sophisticated and numerical versions of Figures 8.1 and 8.2. That is, trade economists are often called upon to mathematically model the effects of RTAs.[6] If you are involved with the assessment of RTAs in any way, you might need to interpret the results of such modeling exercises. Each of the chapters in Part 1 of this book concerning our first window on the world economy, international trade, have contributed to your ability to do so.

The European Union

The European Union (EU) is the current name for a set of agreements among countries of Western Europe in the realms of economics, foreign and security policies, and justice and home affairs. The evolution of the EU is summarized in Table 8.2. The roots of the EU extend back to the Marshall Plan under which the United States aided in the reconstruction of Europe after World War II and promoted the liberalization of trade and payments among the European countries in its zone of influence. These liberalization processes were facilitated by the Organization for European Economic Cooperation and the European Payments Union.[7] In 1951, the Treaty of

---

[6] For the case of the North American Free Trade Agreement, see Francois and Shiells (1997).
[7] The Organization for European Economic Cooperation later became the Paris–based Organization for Economic Cooperation and Development (OECD).

Table 8.2 The Evolution of the European Union

Year	Initiative	Treaty	Members Added
1951	European Coal and Steel Community	Treaty of Paris	Belgium France Germany Italy Luxembourg Netherlands
1958	European Economic Community	Treaty of Rome	
1973			Denmark Ireland United Kingdom
1981			Greece
1986			Portugal Spain
1992	European Union	Treaty on European Union (TEU) or the Maastricht Treaty	
1994			Austria Finland Sweden
1999	European Monetary Union		United Kingdom, Sweden, and Denmark not included
2002	Common EMU currency: The euro		United Kingdom, Sweden, and Denmark not included

Paris was signed, and this led to the formation of the European Coal and Steel Community (ECSC) among Belgium, France, Germany, Italy, Luxembourg, and the Netherlands. These countries became known as The Six. The purpose of the ECSC was to liberalize trade and promote competition in the steel and coal sectors of the Western European economy.

In 1957, the Treaty of Rome was signed. This led to the formation of the European Economic Community (EEC) in 1958. The ultimate goal of the EEC was the creation of a common market. Initially, however, the EEC was a movement toward an FTA in a decade-long transitional period. The EEC took the step to a CU in 1968 with the introduction of a common external tariff. Between 1973 and 1986, its membership increased from 6 to 12 countries. The year 1992 marked the *official* completion of a common market in which barriers to labor and physical capital were to be removed. The *actual* completion of a common market is, strictly speaking, still in process. With the signing of the Maastricht Treaty in 1992, the EEC was joined by initiatives in the areas of foreign and security policy and justice and home affairs under what became known as the European Union. Austria, Finland, and Sweden joined the EU in 1994.

Some economists (e.g., Gary Hufbauer, Robert Lawrence, and André Sapir) argued that, overall, trade creation dominated trade diversion in the EC and EU.[8] Alan Winters (1993), on the other hand, expressed a much more cautionary view. He noted that, despite the common external tariff of the European Union CU, nontariff barriers (e.g. quotas) increased in sectors such as motor vehicles, VCRs, and footwear. He also noted that EU subsidies increased in sectors such as aircraft, steel, shipbuilding, and agriculture. An intermediate view was offered by Tsoukalis (1997), who pointed to overall trade creation in manufactured goods and overall trade diversion in agricultural goods. The latter is largely the result of the Common Agricultural Policy (CAP), which has protected EEC/EU agriculture from foreign competition and has involved the heavy use of export subsidies. Protection levels for EU agriculture under the CAP remain high, but the WTO agreement on agriculture, discussed in Chapter 7, has introduced a modicum of discipline.

In recent years, the EU has ventured even beyond a common market to a monetary union with the launch of the euro in January 2002. We take up these important developments in Chapter 18. A current preoccupation of the EU is the issue of enlargement. This refers to expanding membership to include selected Eastern European countries, as well as Turkey. One crucial sticking point, especially in the case of Poland, is the extent to which CAP provisions are to be extended to new EU members.

The North American Free Trade Agreement

In January 1989, an FTA between Canada and the United States came into effect. Sometime thereafter, former Mexican president Carlos Salinas de Gortari approached the countries of Western Europe in the hopes of convincing them to enter into trade liberalization with Mexico. On a trip to Europe, he found these countries to be distracted with the movement to the European Common Market, described earlier. As the story is now told, on a return flight to Mexico City, Salinas decided to pursue an FTA with the United States. In June 1990, former U.S. president George Bush and Salinas announced their intention to begin negotiating an FTA. In June 1991, however, they were joined by Canada to begin negotiations of a **North American Free Trade Agreement (NAFTA)** involving all three countries. An agreement was signed in August 1992 and took effect in January 1994.[9]

North American Free Trade Agreement (NAFTA)
A free trade agreement among Canada, the United States, and Mexico.

The NAFTA agreement was ambitious. Along with trade in goods, it addressed financial services, transportation, telecommunications, foreign direct investment, intellectual property rights, government procure-

---

[8] See Hufbauer (1990), Lawrence (1991), and Sapir (1992).
[9] Since then, Mexico and the EU have signed an FTA.

ment, and dispute settlement. With regard to trade in goods, NAFTA liberalized trade in the highly protected automobile, textile, and clothing markets. However, it employed restrictive rules of origin in these sectors as well. In agriculture, NAFTA phased out tariffs over a 10-year period and transformed quotas into tariff rate quotas (see Chapter 6 appendix), which are to be phased out over 10- to 15-year periods. Foreign direct investment was liberalized, with the exception of the petroleum sector. NAFTA also provided significant intellectual property protection in a manner similar to the TRIPS agreement discussed in Chapter 7.[10]

As mentioned in Chapter 1, during the time that NAFTA was being negotiated, I was working at the U.S. International Trade Commission (USITC) in Washington, DC. In that position, I took part in the "interagency" meetings of the U.S. government, convened by the Office of the U.S. Trade Representative (USTR). It quickly became clear to the participants of the interagency committee that one of the main issues requiring attention was the impact of NAFTA on wages in the United States, particularly "blue-collar" wages. Recall from Chapter 5 (Figure 5.3) that, if the assumptions of the Heckscher-Ohlin model of international trade hold true, we would expect increased North-South trade to adversely affect workers in the North. NAFTA was certainly a case of increased North-South trade between the United States and Mexico. Consequently, some observers, taking the Heckscher-Ohlin model at face value, concluded that NAFTA would hurt U.S. workers. The NAFTA and wages issue became *the* NAFTA issue in the U.S. Congress.[11] Eventually, a labor side agreement was attached to main NAFTA agreement.

Interestingly, the mathematical models of NAFTA completed by that time showed an improvement in U.S. wages as a result of NAFTA trade liberalization.[12] After leaving the U.S. government, I tried to examine this issue in some detail, focusing on the potential impacts on blue-collar workers. The results, discussed in the box, were surprising and in opposition to the North-South results of the Heckscher-Ohlin model. The key issue is the distinction between inter-industry trade and intra-industry trade discussed in Chapter 4. In retrospect, the issue of NAFTA and wages was probably overblown. Average monthly layoffs in the United States as a result of non-NAFTA causes have been hundreds of times higher than the NAFTA job displacements following the implementation of this RTA.

Another prominent issue that arose during the negotiation of NAFTA, and also preoccupied the USTR in its inter-agency meetings, was the issue of trade and the environment. This debate resulted in provisions for the creation of a North American Commission on Environmental Cooperation (CEC). The CEC has focused some of its subsequent efforts to the analysis of industrial pollution within North America, estimating

---

[10]Despite the fact that NAFTA involves the removal of barriers to FDI, it is not a common market because it does not allow for the free movement of *labor* within North America.
[11]It also became an issue in U.S. presidential elections. The 1992 elections featured candidate Ross Perot referring to the "giant sucking sound" of Mexico stealing U.S. jobs and investment.
[12]Again, see Francois and Shiells (1997) as an example. These results are also reviewed in the addendum to Hufbauer and Schott (1993).

NAFTA, Wages, and Industrial Pollution

The issues of trade and wages in general and of North-South trade and wages in particular have recently received a great deal of attention by economists and public policy analysts. Most of the discussion has taken place in terms of the Heckscher-Ohlin model of international trade and its associated Stolper-Samuelson theorem. Reinert and Roland-Holst (1998) set out to address this issue in the context of the North American Free Trade Agreement (NAFTA). In the debate over NAFTA, the trade and wages issue loomed large, but little empirical evidence was available. Reinert and Roland-Holst attempted to offer some evidence.

These researchers constructed a 26-sector model of the North American economy, including Canada, the United States, and Mexico. They simulated the effects of expanding trade that would take place under NAFTA on five labor categories: professional and managerial; sales and clerical; agricultural; craft; and operators and laborers. In a number of different simulations under different labor supply assumptions, they found that real wages in the United States *increased* for all five types of workers. There was no downward pressure on wages in the United States, even for blue-collar workers.

As suggested by Ruffin (1999) in another study, and as discussed in Chapter 4, these results reflect the presence of a great deal of intra-industry trade between the United States and Mexico. In most sectors, trade expands in both directions between these two countries, something that is not possible in the strict Heckscher-Ohlin framework of inter-industry trade.

that Canada, the United States, and Mexico generate over 3 million tons of toxic chemical waste each year. My own efforts to assess the links between NAFTA trade liberalization and increased emissions industrial pollutants are also addressed in the box.

Mercosur and the FTAA

An RTA among Argentina, Brazil, Paraguay, and Uruguay was launched in 1991 with the Treaty of Asunción, named after the capital city of Paraguay. This RTA, the Common Market of the South, or Mercosur, took on Chile and Bolivia as associate members in 1996 and 1997, respectively. The name *Mercosur* is misleading, because it suggests that the RTA among the four core members is an actual common market with the free movement of labor and physical capital (see Table 8.1). This is not the case. Mercosur entered into force in 1995 as an FTA. There are plans to complete a CU by 2006. Free movement of labor and physical capital is a long way off.

The formulation of Mercosur has had a positive impact on the amount of trade among its four core members, and the technology profile of traded goods is higher for trade within Mercour than for trade between Mercosur and the rest of the world. That said, however, intra-Mercosur trade is low by world standards. Mercosur has also been troubled by two asymmetries that challenge its smooth functioning. First, Argentina and Brazil dwarf Paraguay and Uruguay in economic size. Consequently, the smaller members find themselves somewhat sidelined from the core relationship between Argentina and Brazil. Second, however, there have been fundamental macroeconomic asymmetries between Argentina and Brazil. After

In 2000, the North American Commission for Environmental Cooperation (CEC) sponsored the First North American Symposium on Understanding the Linkages Between Trade and Environment. In one contribution to this symposium, Reinert and Roland-Holst (2002) set out to assess the impacts of trade liberalization under NAFTA on industrial pollution in Canada, the United States, and Mexico. They used the same model of the North American economy described earlier to assess the impact of NAFTA on wages, focusing on the manufacturing sectors in the model and utilizing pollutant data from the Industrial Pollution Projection System of the World Bank.

Reinert and Roland-Holst found that the most serious environmental consequences of NAFTA occur in the base metals sector. In terms of magnitude, the greatest impacts are in the United States and Canada, and this is the case for most of the pollutants considered. As alleged in the debate over NAFTA and the environment, the Mexican petroleum sector is a significant source of industrial pollution, particularly in the case of air pollution. For specific pollutants in specific countries, the transportation equipment sector and the chemicals sector are also important sources of industrial pollution.

Modeling results such as these alert policy makers to likely labor-market and pollution effects of RTAs and can be repeated for any new RTAs that come under negotiation.

Source: Reinert and Roland-Holst (1998), Reinert and Roland-Holst (2002), and Ruffin (1999).

the crisis of 1998, the Brazilian real became a freely floating currency (see Chapter 15). Until its crisis in 2002, the Argentine peso was rigidly pegged to the U.S. dollar under a currency board arrangment (see Chapter 17). For reasons we will explore in Part 2 on international finance, these exchange rate asymmetries caused a great deal of friction between Argentina and Brazil and complicated the functioning of Mercosur.

At the end of 1994, the governments of 34 countries in the Western Hemisphere met at the First Summit of the Americas. They agreed to pursue a Free Trade Area of the Americas (FTAA) with the goal of concluding such an agreement by 2005. Negotiations concerning the FTAA were launched at the Second Summit of the Americas in 1998. Nine negotiating groups were formed in the following areas: market access; investment; services; government procurement; dispute settlement; agriculture; intellectual property rights; subsidies, antidumping, and countervailing duties; and competition policy. In each of these areas, draft agreements have been completed.

In 2002, the United States began to implement increased protection of its steel sector and increased subsidies for its agricultural sector. Within Latin America, these measures were seen as unfortunate and as calling into question the spirit of the FTAA process. The Brazilian government was particularly concerned about U.S. steel protection. Chile, the economic "soulmate" of the United States, also developed its own concerns. Having been in negotiation over an FTA with the United States since 1990, Chile finally entered into an FTA with the European Union in 2002, finally entering into an FTA with the United States in 2003. The commitment of the United States to the FTAA remains to be seen.

Regionalism and Multilateralism

A more fundamental policy issue lurks in the current discussions of RTAs. As we stated in the introduction, regionalism and multilateralism represent two alternative trade policy options available to the countries of the world. In the 1950s and 1960s, there had been what is now called the "first wave" of RTAs in the developing world, particularly in Latin America. This was often in conjunction with protectionist policies against the rest of the world, particularly in Latin America.[13] For example, there had been an ill-fated Central American Common Market (CACM) launched at the end of the 1960s. Beginning in the 1980s, there began what is now called the "second wave" of RTAs. For example, in addition to those discussed in this chapter, the Association of Southeast Asian Nations (ASEAN) adopted a resolution at its Fourth ASEAN Summit in 1992 in support of pursuing an FTA. This was reaffirmed at the Fifth ASEAN Summit in 1995, with a goal of completing the FTA by 2005. The WTO reports that, since 1995, it has received over 100 new RTA notifications. The fundamental policy issue raised by many observers is: What role will the second wave of RTAs play *vis-à-vis* the *multilateral* efforts toward trade liberalization pursued under the GATT/WTO framework discussed in Chapter 7? Will the second wave of RTAs complement the multilateral framework or will it work at cross-purposes to this framework?

The most vociferous opponents of the second wave of regionalism have been Jagdish Bhagwati and Arvind Panagariya, two prominent trade economists.[14] First, they emphasize what we mentioned at the beginning of this chapter: RTAs are, by their very nature, discriminatory. Second, they draw attention to the "spaghetti-bowl" nature of second-wave RTAs. By this, they are referring to the overlapping nature of most RTAs, with most WTO members holding simultaneous membership in many RTAs at once. In their own words, there is a tendency in the modern RTA system toward "numerous and crisscrossing (RTAs) and innumerable applicable tariff rates depending on arbitrarily-determined and often a multiplicity of sources of origin (Bhagwati, Greenaway, and Panagariya, 1998, p. 1139). On this matter, Bhagwati and Panagariya surely have a point. For example, Mexico has signed FTA agreements with the United States, Canada, Nicaragua, Costa Rica, Chile, Bolivia, El Salvador, Guatemala, Honduras, Colombia, Venezuela, and the European Union. All of Central America (Nicaragua, Costa Rica, El Salvador, Guatemala, and Honduras), in turn, is part of the Central American Common Market. The Central American Common Market, in turn, has FTAs with Chile and the Dominican Republic. Colombia and Venezuela, in turn, are also part of an FTA with Ecuador and Peru (the Andean Community). Of course, Mexico's key partners, the United States and the European Union, each have their own network of FTAs.

Third, Bhagwati and Panagariya fear that the negotiating energies put into RTAs will detract from those put into multilateral agreements under

---

[13]In the Latin American case, see Chapter 9 of Bulmer-Thomas (1994).
[14]See Bhagwati, Greenaway, and Panagiya (1998) and Bhagwati (1993). Also see the interview with Arvind Panagariya that follows this chapter.

the auspices of the WTO. Bhagwati (1993) stated: "(T)he taking to two roads can affect adversely the travel down one" (p. 30). Consequently, RTAs can be "stumbling blocks" rather than "building blocks" for multilateral trade liberalization.

Recognizing the concerns of Bhagwati and Panagariya but also acknowledging that the RTA option is not about to disappear, the key issue facing the multilateral trading system is how to best manage and regulate RTAs. This responsibility falls to the WTO Committee on RTAs. A number of points are worth stressing here.

First, it is evident that GATT-era oversight of RTAs was woefully inadequate. Serra et al. (1997) note that only 65 of the 109 RTAs notified to the GATT between 1948 and 1995 were reviewed. Of these 65, only 6 of the reviews involved a GATT conclusion about the RTAs' compatibility with GATT requirements. The record could hardly be much worse.

Second, we mentioned earlier that the Marrakesh Agreement establishing the WTO included an "understanding" on RTAs. This understanding specified that the relevant measure to assess the phrase "shall not be higher or more restrictive than" is a weighted average of tariff rates and that "within a reasonable length of time" is to be no more than 10 years. The understanding also specifies that all new RTAs must be notified to the WTO and that, in each case, a WTO working party (under the Committee on RTAs) is to be established to examine each notification and to ascertain its impact on the multilateral trading system. Provisions are also made for the periodic reporting by FTAs and CUs to the WTO. These provisions should, to some small extent at least, improve the compatibility of regionalism with multilateralism.

Third, the WTO could go further and tighten its requirements on the external protection of FTAs and CUs. To understand why this could be important, take a new look at the trade-diverting RTA between Brazil and Argentina as depicted in Figure 8.2. Suppose that the tariff on imports from Venezuela had been eliminated, along with the tariff on imports from Argentina. If this were the case, Brazil would continue to import from Venezuela, there would be no trade diversion, and welfare would unambiguously increase. This fact has led some analysts to argue that external tariffs ought to be reduced in a CU or FTA in order to mitigate against trade diversion. Analysts similarly call for common external tariffs in CUs to be set to the *lowest* of the pre-CU tariffs of the members.[15]

These considerations indicate that it is possible to lessen the tensions between regionalism and multilateralism. For one such attempt, see the following box. It is probably not possible to eliminate these tensions entirely. As stated at the beginning of this chapter, "when multilateralism falters, regionalism picks up the pace." It is the responsibility of all WTO members, but especially the larger WTO members, to ensure that multilateralism does not falter. Without this commitment to multilateralism, no amount of tinkering with WTO provisions on RTAs will help.

---

[15]See McMillan (1993), Bhagwati (1993), and Serra et al. (1997).

A New Regionalism?

International trade economist Wilfred Ethier makes a case for what he calls "the new regionalism," and he contends that a number of its characteristics make it more benign than many, including Jadgish Bhagwati and Arvind Panagariya, contend. The new regionalism is distinct from the "old regionalism" of the 1950s and 1960s in both its environment and its content. With regard to environment, Ethier notes that the new regionalism is taking place within an international economic system characterized by:

1. A great deal of multilateral trade liberalization
2. Many less developed countries joining the multilateral trading system
3. A large amount of foreign direct investment (FDI)

With regard to content of the new RTAs, a number of characteristics also stand out:

1. "Hub-and-spoke" structures in which small countries join in RTAs with larger countries
2. Smaller RTA members having engaged in significant amounts of unilateral trade liberalization
3. Most RTA trade liberalization being undertaken by the smaller countries
4. Most RTAs involving policy harmonization that goes beyond trade liberalization

What are the consequences of these characteristics? According the Ethier, "the new regionalism reflects the success of multilateralism—not its failure." Why is this? RTAs are the way in which small countries attempting to join the multilateral system secure the inward FDI that makes sustained trade liberalization possible. This FDI is necessary to provide visible benefits to citizens that offset losses associated with trade liberalization. Note that our discussion of trade diversion and trade creation in Figures 8.1 and 8.2 said nothing about FDI flows. According to Ethier, because small countries joining with large countries can expect inward FDI flows, the negative welfare effects of trade diversion on the members of an RTA are made less relevant.

According to Ethier, these considerations apply to NAFTA, a case of new regionalism. Mexico is small relative to the United States and engaged in substantial unilateral liberalization before entering into NAFTA. Within NAFTA, Mexico agreed to substantially more liberalization than the United States, and the NAFTA agreement contained a number of harmonization elements that went beyond trade liberalization.

Sources: Ethier (1998, 2001).

Conclusion

The GATT and WTO have allowed for exceptions to the basic nondiscrimination principle in the case of FTAs and CUs. These and other RTAs have been part of the world trading system for decades, and all evidence points to their continued presence in this system. The continued evolution of RTAs in both Europe and North America are two prominent examples. RTAs may improve or worsen welfare depending on the balance between their trade creation and trade diversion effects. Current and future economic policy makers face the challenge of incorporating the regional predilections of the world's countries into a general multilateral evolution of world trade. Oversight of RTAs by the WTO will be a continuing and important part of this process.

Review Exercises

1. What distinguishes a customs union from a free trade area? What distinguishes a common market from a customs union?

2. What is the difference between trade creation and trade diversion? Can you provide an example of each?

3. Do you support regionalism and RTAs as a legitimate trade policy option? Why or why not?

4. We mentioned that the size of Brazil's tariff against Venezuela affects the amount of trade diversion that occurs in an RTA. Use a version of Figure 8.2 to demonstrate that the lower the tariff (T) against Venezuela, the more likely it is that the RTA will improve welfare. Show that if the T on imports from Venezuela were eliminated, the RTA would unambiguously improve welfare.

5. Pay a visit to the WTO's Web site on regionalism. From **http://www.wto.org**, follow the link to "Trade Issues" and, from there, to "Regionalism." On this page, you can explore interesting maps of RTAs by downloading the document WT/REG/W/41.

Further Reading and Web Resources

The chapters of de Melo and Panagariya (1993), the report of Serra et al. (1997), Frankel (1997), Pomfret (1997), and Hudec and Southwick (1999) are good places to begin exploring the many issues surrounding regional trade agreements. The reader with an interest in the role of RTAs in the world trading system will want to consult WTO (1995), Hudec and Southwick (1999), and Chapter 10 of Hoekman and Kostecki (2001). In this chapter, Hoekman and Kostecki also consider issues of RTAs under the GATS. Overviews of the European Union and NAFTA are Tsoukalis (1997), Dinan (1999), and Hufbauer and Schott (1992, 1993). On Mercosur, see Pereira (1999).

The European Union's Web site can be found at **http://www. europa.eu.int**. The NAFTA Secretariat's home page is **http://www. nafta-sec-alena.org**. The proposed Free Trade of the *Americas* Web site can be found at **http://www.alca-ftaa.org**. The Mercosur Web site is **http://www.mercosur.org**. Also see the Windows on the World Economy Web site for Quarterly Reports on the FTAA at **http://reinert.swlearning.com**.

References

Bhagwati, J. (1993) Regionalism and Multilateralism: An Overview," in J. de Melo and A. Panagariya (eds.), *New Dimensions in Regional Integration*, Cambridge University Press, Cambridge, 22–51.

Bhagwati, J., D. Greenaway, and A. Panagariya (1998) "Trading Preferentially: Theory and Policy," *The Economic Journal*, 108:449, 1128–1148.

Bulmer-Thomas, V. (1994) *The Economic History of Latin America Since Independence*, Cambridge University Press, Cambridge.

Dinan, D. (1999) *Ever Closer Union: An Introduction to European Integration*, Lynne Rienner, London.

Ethier, W.J. (2001) "The New Regionalism in the Americas: A Theoretical Framework," *North American Journal of Economics and Finance*, 12:2, 159–172.

Ethier, W.J. (1998) "The New Regionalism," *The Economic Journal*, 108:449, 1149–1161.

Francois, J.F., and C.R. Shiells (1997) *Modeling Trade Policy: Applied General Equilibrium Assessments of North American Free Trade*, Cambridge University Press, Cambridge.

Frankel, J.A. (1997) *Regional Trading Blocs in the World Economic System*, Institute for International Economics, Washington, DC.

GATT Secretariat (1994) *The Results of the Uruguay Round of Multilateral Trade Negotiations: The Legal Text*, Geneva.

Hoekman, B.M., and M. Kostecki (2001) *The Political Economy of the World Trading System: From GATT to WTO*, Oxford University Press, Oxford.

Hudec, R.E., and J.D. Southwick (1999) "Regionalism and WTO Rules: Problems in the Fine Art of Discriminating Fairly," in M. Rodríguez Mendoza, P. Low, and B. Kotschwar (eds.), *Trade Rules in the Making: Challenges in Regional and Multilateral Negotiations*, The Brookings Institution, Washington, DC, 47–80.

Hufbauer, G.C. (ed.) (1990) *Europe 1992: An American Perspective*, The Brookings Institution, Washington, DC.

Hufbauer, G.C., and J.J. Schott (1993) *NAFTA: An Assessment*, Institute for International Economics, Washington, DC.

Hufbauer, G.C., and J.J. Schott (1992) *North American Free Trade: Issue and Recommendations*, Institute for International Economics, Washington, DC.

Lawrence, R. (1991) "Emerging Regional Agreements: Building Blocks or Stumbling Blocks," in R. O'Brien (ed.), *Finance and the International Economy*, Oxford University Press.

McMillan, J. (1993) "Does Regional Integration Foster Open Trade? Economic Theory and GATT's Article XXIV," in K. Anderson and R. Blackhurst (eds.), *Regional Integration and the Global Trading System*, Harvester Wheatsheaf, New York, 292–310.

de Melo, J., and A. Panagariya (eds.) (1993) *New Dimensions in Regional Integration*, Cambridge University Press, Cambridge.

Pereira, L.V. (1999) "Toward the Common Market of the South: Mercosur's Origins, Evolutions and Challenges," in R. Roett (ed.), *MERCOSUR: Regional Integration, World Markets*, Lynne Rienner, Boulder, 1999, 1–23.

Pomfret, R. (1997) *The Economics of Regional Trading Arrangements*, Clarendon Press, Oxford.

Reinert, K.A., and D.W. Roland-Holst (2002) "The Industrial Pollution Impacts of NAFTA: Some Preliminary Results," in *The Environmental Effects of Free Trade, Commission on Environmental Cooperation*, Montreal, 139–159.

Reinert, K.A., and D.W. Roland-Holst (1998) "North-South Trade and Occupational Wages: Some Evidence from North America," *Review of International Economics*, 6:1, 74–89.

Ruffin, R.J. (1999) "The Nature and Significance of Intra-Industry Trade," *Federal Reserve Bank of Dallas Economic and Financial Review*, 4th Quarter, 2–9.

Sapir, A. (1992) "Regional Integration in Europe," *Economic Journal*, 102:415, 1491–1506.

Serra, J., et al. (1997) *Reflections on Regionalism: Report of the Study Group on International Trade*, Carnegie Endowment for International Peace, Washington, DC.

Tsoukalis, L. (1997) *The New European Economy Revisited*, Oxford University Press, Oxford.

Viner, J. (1950) *The Customs Union Issue*, Carnegie Endowment for International Peace, New York.

Winters, L.A. (1993) "The European Community: A Case of Successful Integration?" in J. de Melo and A. Panagariya (eds.), *New Dimensions in Regional Integration*, Cambridge University Press, Cambridge, 202–228.

World Trade Organization (1995) *Regionalism and the World Trading System*, Geneva.

Interview: Arvind Panagariya

Dr. Arvind Panagariya is a former Chief Economist of the Asian Development Bank and currently Professor of Economics at the University of Maryland. He is also Co-Director of the Center for International Economics at the University of Maryland. Dr. Panagariya holds a Ph.D. degree in Economics from Princeton University and M.A. and B.A. degrees in Economics from Rajasthan University in India. He spent the years 1989–1993 as a research economist at the World Bank and has consulted for the World Bank, Asian Development Bank, IMF, WTO, and UNCTAD. Dr. Panagariya has written extensively on trade theory, trade policy, and the reform process in developing countries. In addition to these numerous publications, he writes a monthly column in the Economic Times, *India's top financial daily. You can visit Dr. Panagariya's home page at:* **http://www.bsos.umd.edu/econ/ciepanag.htm**.

How did your interest in international trade develop?

At a broad level, for someone growing up in a developing country and interested in its economic problems, the interest in international trade is natural. It is unthinkable to study development without trade. But I was also fascinated by the logical structure of trade theory. Even while completing my M.A. in India, I was fascinated by James Meade's *Geometry of International Trade* that placed the entire equilibrium of the world economy into a single four-quadrant diagram. Later at Princeton, I discovered how algebra and calculus could be used effectively to answer all kinds of important questions relating to trade and development. Subsequently, I came in close touch with the foremost trade theorist Jagdish Bhagwati who greatly influenced my thinking on a variety of trade policy issues.

What have been the main themes of your work in trade policy?

I started as a trade theorist and focused on the implications of economies of scale for the patterns of trade, welfare, income distribution, multiplicity of equilibria and stability. Unlike Paul Krugman and many other contemporary authors in this field, I worked with models with homogeneous goods, which allowed one to maintain the assumption of perfect competition. Subsequently, I became more interested in trade policy and wrote on commercial policy in the presence of domestic monopolies, piecemeal trade reform, political-economy of tariff policy as it relates to the uniform tariff issue, and, most recently, the economics of preferential trading. During the last decade, I have also been writing extensively on contemporary trade policy issues, especially as they bear upon the welfare of developing countries.

What is your view on the role of regional trade agreements (RTAs) in the world economy?

What you term *regional* trade agreements in your text I prefer to call *preferential* trade agreements (PTAs), and I take a critical view of PTAs. There are many reasons, but let me point out just three. First, PTAs inevitably give rise to trade diversion, meaning union members expand trade between them by displacing the more efficient outside suppliers. Even if the welfare effect on union members resulting from trade creation (i.e., the expansion of trade between union members through displacement of each other's inefficient producers) outweighs the welfare effect of this diversion, we have made the rest of the world worse off. This is a violation of the spirit of the WTO principles that discourage countries from benefiting at the expense of other members. Second, the single most important principle of the WTO is non-discrimination. But PTAs effectively discriminate in favor of union members and against outside countries. This discrimination imbedded in a large number of crisscrossing PTAs has led to a considerable fragmentation of the global trading system whereby tariffs now depend on which PTA partner supplies the good. Different PTAs being at different stages of implementation and also subject to different rules of origin, we now have what Jagdish Bhagwati calls a "Spaghetti Bowl" of tariffs. Finally, the move to create PTAs runs the huge risk of distracting us from multilateral liberalization. For example, if we in the United States get preoccupied with the negotiations on the Free Trade Area of the Americas (FTAA), we may simply not be able to devote the necessary attention and negotiating capital to a successful conclusion of the Doha Round.

Your writings have cast some doubt on the role of the Agreement on Trade Related Aspects of Intellectual Property Rights (TRIPS) in the World Trade Organization (WTO). Why are you uncomfortable with TRIPS?

Let me point out first that the opposition to the TRIPS Agreement should not be misunderstood as opposition to intellectual property protection (IPP). Almost all countries have some kind of IPP laws and will continue to want to strengthen them as they develop. The problem with the TRIPS Agreement, which was pushed principally by the U.S. pharmaceutical industry, is that it forces all countries to adopt a uniform patent regime that gives the IP holder monopoly over his innovation for 20 years. This means poor countries such as India and Brazil that could produce cheap imitations of medicines will no longer be able to do so, and most new medicines will become beyond the reach of the consumers in these countries.

But I have also objected to the TRIPS Agreement on the ground that WTO is an institution that specializes in trade, and its effectiveness in that area will be diluted if we load it up with non-trade issues. For IPP, we have a different institution, the World Intellectual Property Organization or WIPO, and we should let that institution handle it.

The Doha Ministerial Declaration of the WTO has called for negotiations on investment and competition policy to begin after the next Ministerial. Are you comfortable with the inclusion of these new issues in the WTO agenda?

These subjects certainly impinge on trade and are surely more directly related to it than IPP. As such, I have no doubt we will eventually need to bring them into WTO. I am not very keen to bring them in at this point in time, however, for the simple reason that many developing countries simply do not have the necessary capacity to negotiate effectively let alone eventually implement them on a strict timetable. Already, the WTO rules are so complex and extend to so many different areas that it is difficult for even the most devoted observers to keep track of all the changes that take place. The vast majority of the developing countries have simply no such expertise, and it is unfair to ask them to sign on to agreements that they do not even understand. We have already witnessed how difficult many of these countries are finding it to implement the vast number of new obligations they undertook under the Uruguay Round Agreement.

You recently served as Chief Economist of the Asian Development Bank. How did your work at the ADB support the developing countries of Asia making best use of the trade and development opportunities of the world economy?

Among other things, I launched a major study on the Doha trade issues as they concern the Asian developing countries. As I understand, this study is being carried on by my successor there.

If there were one piece of advice you could give to a student or professional contemplating a career in trade policy, what would it be?

Acquire full grasp of trade theory—it may initially appear esoteric, but it is not. This is a field that is truly applied, and the tools we offer do help you think through the policy problems analytically. Of course, never forget that reality is much murkier than theory. Therefore, you will never be able to substitute theory for good policy judgment. You must use the two as complimentary tools and use them judiciously.

Part 2

Windows on the World Economy: International Production

9

Foreign Market Entry and International Production

In Chapter 3, you learned about the important motorcycle market in Vietnam and that the considerations of comparative advantage suggest that Japan would export motorcycles to the Vietnamese market while importing rice. A favorite Japanese motorcycle in Vietnam is the Honda Dream, which is quite literally the dream of *many Vietnamese households. In contrast to our discussion in Chapter 3, however, in late 1997, Honda began producing the Dream in* Vietnam *in order to serve the Vietnamese market. Such a possibility certainly was not part of our analysis in Chapter 3. In that chapter, we implicitly assumed that there was only one means by which Japanese motorcycle manufactures could serve the Vietnamese market, namely exporting. In practice, however, other means are available. These other means compose types of international production, the subject of Part 2 of this book.*

As you will learn in this chapter, exports are one possible choice in a menu of options by which a firm can serve a foreign market. Another broad option is foreign direct investment (FDI) discussed in Chapter 1. FDI involves the holding of *at least* 10 to 25 percent (depending on the country) of the shares in a foreign productive enterprise, a share that implies a degree of management control. A third broad option is **contracting** a foreign firm to carry out production in that country. Our first task in this chapter is to evaluate the three types of **foreign market entry**: exporting, contracting, and FDI. Our second task is to identify a set of *motivations* for international production. Our third task is to provide a brief, historical overview of multinational enterprises (MNEs) and international production. This set of topics will give you the necessary background for the more detailed considerations of Chapters 10, 11, and 21.[1]

Contracting
A mode of foreign market entry where a home-country firm contracts a foreign-country firm to engage in production in the foreign country. Includes both licensing and franchising.

Foreign market entry
Sales on the part of a firm in a foreign country via trade, contractual, or foreign direct investment modes.

Foreign Market Entry

In Chapter 1, we saw that trade and foreign direct investment (FDI) were two of the main types of international economic activity. As we will see, trade and FDI are two generic parts of a menu of ways in which a firm in one country can interact with the world economy. This menu is presented in Table 9.1. In developing an understanding of this menu of options, we cross over from the field of international economics into the field of international business and take up the issue of foreign market entry.[2]

---

[1] Chapter 21 takes up a set of policy issues that arise when developing countries play host to MNEs.
[2] A key work on foreign market entry, which this section draws upon, is Root (1998).

Table 9.1 Foreign Market Entry of a Home-Country Firm into a Foreign Market

Category	Mode	Characteristics
Trade	Indirect trade	The home-country firm relies on another home or foreign firm to complete the trade transaction.
Trade	Direct trade	The home-country firm itself undertakes the trade transaction.
Contractual	Licensing	The home-country firm licenses a foreign firm to engage in some type of productive activity in the foreign country.
Contractual	Franchising	The home-country firm provides assistance to the foreign-country firm, and the franchise right includes brand aspects such as trademarks, designs, logos, and organizational features.
Investment	Greenfield FDI	The home-country firm establishes a brand-new production facility that it fully owns in the foreign country.
Investment	Acquisition FDI	The home-country firm buys all or part of the shares of an already-existing production facility in the foreign country.
Investment	Joint venture	The home-country firm establishes a separate firm in the foreign country that is jointly owned with a foreign-country firm.

Source: Based on Root (1998).

Consider Honda, the Japanese automotive and motorcycle firm and producer of the Dream motorcycle. Initially, suppose that Honda sells all of its motorcycle output domestically. Suppose, however, that it eventually begins to contemplate becoming a little more adventurous. It could begin exporting motorcycles to other countries, as we considered in Chapter 3. Perhaps, though, Honda has little experience with and knowledge of international trade. In that case, it might first enter foreign markets in an *indirect trade* mode. Here Honda relies on another firm such as an exporting house in Japan or an importing house in a foreign country such as Vietnam to complete the trade transaction. This indirect trading relationship might give Honda some expertise and confidence that inspires it to make a more firm commitment to exporting in a *direct trade* mode. In the direct trade case, Honda undertakes the export/import transaction itself rather than relying on an export or import house. In this case, Honda takes on the research, marketing, and logistics requirements of the trade transaction.[3]

---

[3] There can be competitive pressure pushing firms out of the indirect trade mode. As stated by Root (1998): "Indirect exporting may be a good way for a firm to enter foreign markets for the first time. But with the qualified exception of export management companies, indirect exporting does not allow a manufacturing firm to have its own international market entry strategy" (p. 76).

For a number of reasons, it is possible that Honda might grow dissatisfied with the trading mode and begin to wish to actually produce abroad, as it eventually did in the case of motorcycles in Vietnam. For example, it might need to engage in some final product finishing, service, or sales to address local demand conditions in Vietnam. Or it might simply need to engage in some trade-related services itself in that country.[4] However, lack of experience in global production might make it wary of carrying out production itself in Vietnam. This would lead Honda to *contractual* modes of foreign market entry. For example, Honda might sell a license to a Vietnamese firm to produce motorcycles. In return, the Vietnamese firm would pay royalties to Honda for the license right. A more stringent contractual mode would be that of franchising, where Honda would provide assistance to the Vietnamese firm and the franchise right would include brand aspects such as trademarks, designs, logos, and organizational features. Such an arrangement is more common in service and retail firms than in manufacturing.[5]

The third option available to Honda to enter the Vietnamese market, the option it chose in 1997, is FDI. A first mode of FDI is *greenfield FDI*. Here Honda establishes a brand-new production facility that it fully owns in Vietnam. This was Honda's first choice, but the Vietnamese government prevented Honda from pursuing it. A second investment mode is *acquisition FDI* in which Honda buys all or part of the shares of an already-existing production facility in Vietnam. The shares owned must be of a large enough percentage to grant Honda the ability to exert control over this foreign production facility. Otherwise the investment is classified as indirect or portfolio investment rather than as direct investment.[6] Finally, Honda might establish a *joint venture* in Vietnam with a Vietnamese firm. Here, the two firms establish a jointly-owned but formally separate firm in Vietnam.

As mentioned earlier, Honda had hoped to enter the Vietnamese motorcycle market via greenfield FDI, establishing a new, wholly-owned factory to produce the Honda Dream. Instead, the Vietnamese government required that it pursue a joint venture with a Vietnamese firm. As a result, Honda Vietnam is only 70 percent owned by Honda. The Vietnam Engine and Agricultural Machinery Corporation owns the remaining 30 percent. Honda Vietnam also maintains a network of over 100 authorized dealers responsible for after-sales service within the country. Honda Vietnam began to produce a second motorcycle model, the Future, in 1999.

As we have seen, Table 9.1 identifies international trade (exporting), contracting, and investment as three categories of foreign market entry.

---

[4] As Dunning (1993) states: "(W)here a market has to be created for a product, where the product needs to be adapted to the requirements of the buyers, or where multiple products are being marketed and there are advantages of coordinating the sales of these products, or where an efficient after-sales usage, repair and maintenance service is a key ingredient of the product's appeal, a firm may decide that the risk that a foreign sales agent will not meet its needs adequately outweighs any capital loss of setting up marketing and distributing facilities from the start" (p. 195).

[5] For example, the Italian clothing firm Benetton maintains an international network of retail franchises.

[6] See the discussion of balance of payments accounting in Chapter 12.

What prompts a firm to choose one category over another? It turns out that the answer to this question is not at all straightforward. However, we can give ourselves some appreciation of the matter by understanding some key concepts introduced by Hill, Hwang, and Kim (1990). According to these authors, firms take into consideration three factors in making their foreign market entry decisions: the degree of control, the level of resource commitment, and the degree of **dissemination risk**. Dissemination risk refers to the possibility of a foreign partner firm obtaining technology or other know-how from the home-country firm and exploiting it for its own commercial advantage. Hill, Hwang, and Kim state:

> *Unfortunately, if a (firm) grants a license to a foreign enterprise to use firm-specific know-how to manufacture or market a product, it runs the risk of the licensee, or an employee of the licensee, disseminating that know-how, or using it for purposes other than those originally intended. For example, RCA once licensed its color TV technology to a number of Japanese companies. The Japanese companies quickly assimilated RCA's technology and then used it to enter the U.S. market (p. 119).*

The way in which issues of control, resource commitment, and dissemination risk affect the choice of foreign market entry mode can be appreciated using Table 9.2. Suppose a firm's most important concern was the degree of control over the production and marketing process. This would draw the firm toward an investment mode of foreign market entry based on a subsidiary obtained either through greenfield or acquisition investment. Alternatively, if a firm were concerned only with limiting resource commitment to low levels, it would consider either trade or contractual modes of foreign market entry. Finally, if a firm were solely concerned with maintaining a low degree of dissemination risk, then either trade or investment via a subsidiary would be the preferred mode of entry. In most instances, firms have more than one primary concern, so the entry strategy is less than clear-cut. For example, a case study of foreign market entry on the part of the Upjohn Company is presented in the box.

Dissemination risk
The possibility of a foreign-country partner firm obtaining technology or other know-how from a home-country firm and exploiting it for its own commercial advantage.

Table 9.2 Factors Influencing Choice of Foreign Market Entry Mode

Mode	Degree of Control	Level of Resource Commitment	Degree of Dissemination Risk
Trade	Low	Low	Low
Contractual	Low	Low	High
Investment—joint venture	Medium	Medium	Medium
Investment—subsidiary	High	High	Low

Source: Adapted from Hill, C.W.L., Hwang, P., and Kim, W.C., (1990). "An Eclectic Theory of the Choice of International Entry Mode." *Strategic Management Journal* 11(2): 120. Copyright 1990 © by John Wiley & Sons Limited. Reproduced with permission.

Foreign Market Entry of the Upjohn Company

The Upjohn Company was a U.S.–based pharmaceutical firm that merged with the Swedish-based pharmaceutical company, Pharmacia, in 1995. It was founded in 1886 and became very successful in the early 1900s from sales of the antimalaria drug quinine. Fima and Rugman (1996) undertook a study of Upjohn's foreign market entry strategy for 61 countries in the world economy. As we have done in this chapter, these authors distinguished among indirect trade, direct trade, contractual, and investment modes.

Fima and Rugman found that Upjohn initially undertook foreign market entry via the indirect trade mode in 38 of the 61 cases. In most of the other cases, foreign market entry began with the direct trade model. In no cases did entry begin with the contractual mode, although this was used in a number of countries as an intermediate step. By 1992, Upjohn products were being produced in 30 countries, nine in licensing agreements and 21 via FDI. There were only three joint ventures. Fima and Rugman conclude that "Upjohn (used) multiple entry modes at the same time. This (provided) flexibility in an industry which is very dependent on political factors and is often dictated to by changes in host-government regulations" (p. 211).

Source: Fima and Rugman (1996).

Motivations for International Production

In order to further develop your understanding of international production, it will be very helpful to identify the motivations that push firms beyond their home-country borders. Dunning (1993) identified four such motivations for international production that are well worth understanding in some detail. These are as follows.

Resource seeking
One of the motivations for foreign direct investment in which a multinational enterprise backward integrates into resource supply in a foreign country.

A primary motivation for international production, especially (but not exclusively) in earlier centuries, is **resource seeking**. The resources involved could be natural resources such as minerals or timber, as well as human resources such as inexpensive or specially-trained labor. Dunning estimates that "up to the eve of the Second World War, about three-fifths of the accumulated foreign direct capital stake was of this kind. By the mid-1980s, resource-based investment had declined to about one-third of worldwide MNE activity, and about 45% of that in developing countries" (pp. 57–58). The gradual shift over time away from resource seeking international production is one of the most important aspects of the history of MNEs. In the current era, therefore, use of a simple mental model in which MNEs locate production solely based on wage considerations is incomplete. For example, the province of Ontario, Canada, is a destination of a great deal of foreign investment, and this province has wage rates and benefits packages that exceed even those of the United States.

Market seeking
A motivation for foreign direct investment in which the multinational enterprise engages in FDI to better serve a foreign market.

A second, growing reason for international production is **market seeking**. A number of considerations can be active here. First, international production might be necessary to adopt and tailor products to local needs. Second, international production might be required to effectively deliver a

Beijing Jeep

In 1983, the American Motors Corporation (AMC) formed a joint venture with Beijing Auto Works (BAW) to build a Chinese version of the Jeep. The joint venture was called the Beijing Jeep Company, Ltd., and it involved both AMC and BAW owning large shares of the company's equity. The negotiations leading up to the joint venture took years to complete, but the resulting agreement was "the first major manufacturing joint venture set up after China opened its doors to foreign investment" (Mann, 1997, p. 25). The most important consideration on the part of AMC in entering into the joint venture was the large and growing market for automobiles in China. As Jim Mann explains it in his book *Beijing Jeep*: "Even those companies hoping to cut their production costs by manufacturing in China . . . were interested mainly because of the possibility of selling their output there. You could find cheap labor elsewhere in the world, but you couldn't find a billion consumers anywhere else" (p. 53).

The Chinese have a saying, *tong chuang yi meng*. It means "same bed, different dreams." There was a large measure of this in the AMC/BAW relationship. Cultural conflict, financial difficulties, and opposing business interests plagued the operation from the start. To the disappointment of the Chinese, the Beijing Jeep Company actually did *not* make a Chinese version of the Jeep. Instead, it assembled American Jeep Cherokees from imported kits. To the disappointment of the Americans, finding the foreign exchange (U.S. dollars) to pay for these kits was a serious problem. The Americans thought the Chinese workers were lazy; the Chinese had great difficulty respecting American executives who used foul language.

The Beijing Jeep Company is still operating, and its factory has been modernized. Chrysler bought AMC in 1987. In 1995, two decades after the start of the joint venture, a Chrysler executive commented: "Our Beijing Jeep is starting to be a halfway decent little company, but there are going to be lost of ups and down in China." Many different firms who have invested in China would probably concur with that last observation.

Source: Mann (1997).

product, as is the case for many financial services.[7] Third, international production might be required for a firm supplying intermediate products to another firm opening up operations in a foreign country. For example, Japanese auto parts firms often follow Japanese auto companies to Europe and the United States. Finally, firms may simply locate where they expect demand to grow in the future. This certainly has been the case in China where, despite losses, many foreign firms maintain at least small operations. Why? A deputy chairman of a Malaysian conglomerate states: "You cannot not be there" (*The Economist*, 1997). The reason for this statement is the anticipated growth of the market. For more on international production in China, see the box.

A third motivation for international production is **efficiency seeking**. As explained by Dunning, the concern here "is to rationalize the structure of established resource-based or market-seeking investment in such a way that the investing company can gain from the common governance of geographically dispersed activities" (p. 59). These efficiencies may stem from economies of scale, economies of scope, and a concept we will discuss

Efficiency seeking
One motivation for foreign direct investment that involves the pursuit of firm-level economies in which intangible assets are spread over a greater number of international productive activities.

---

[7] Recall from Chapter 7 that foreign investment was one important mode of trade in services. The box on the firm Pollo Campero is an example of market seeking in food services.

in the next chapter called *firm-level economies*. According to Dunning, this motivation is most important for large, mature MNEs with a great deal of international experience.

The **strategic asset seeking** motivation for international production is both very important in the current era and, at times, difficult to comprehend. This type of international production is conducted by acquiring productive assets as part of the strategic game among competitors in an industry. Dunning describes a number of illustrative alternatives:

> *One company may acquire or engage in a collaborative alliance with another to thwart a competitor from so doing. Another might merge with one of its foreign rivals to strengthen their joint capabilities vis à vis a more powerful rival. A third might acquire a group of suppliers to corner the market for a particular raw material. A fourth might seek to gain access over distribution outlets to better promote its own brand of products. A fifth might buy out a firm producing a complementary range of goods or services so it can offer its customers a more diversified range of products. A sixth might join forces with a local firm in the belief that it is in a better position to secure contracts from the host government, which are denied to its exporting competitors (pp. 60–61).*

To take a recent example, the U.S.-based MNE Kodak established a film sales affiliate in Japan called Nagase. The purpose of Nagase was not limited to the market seeking motivation. A further motivation was to *attack the profit sanctuary* of the Japanese film company Fujifilm. As alleged by a Kodak executive, "While Fuji competes with Kodak on a global basis, it makes virtually all of its profits in Japan, using those proceeds to finance low-price sales outside Japan" (Baron, 1997, p. 151). For Kodak, Nagase is a strategic asset. The strategic asset seeking motivation is becoming increasingly important in the modern, global economy. Furthermore, along with explaining many types of FDI, it also helps to explain a number of non–FDI activities of MNEs, especially strategic alliances, which do not involve the exchange of equity.[8]

How have these considerations played out historically? Let's take a brief look and, in doing so, learn about a few tends that have had important impacts on the current world economy.

The Rise of Multinational Enterprises and International Production

Early MNEs were part and parcel of the colonization efforts of the European powers during the sixteenth and seventeenth centuries. These included state-supported trading companies such as the British East India Company, the Dutch East India Company, and the Royal African Company. This period is often known as the age of **merchant capitalism**, and this name is a reflection of the international activities of these trading companies. With the advent of the industrial revolution in the nineteenth century, however, merchant capitalism gave way to what is now known as **industrial capitalism**. During the

Strategic asset seeking
A motivation for foreign direct investment in which the multinational enterprise wants to acquire productive assets as part of the strategic game among competitors in an industry.

Merchant capitalism
Part of the colonization efforts of the European powers during the sixteenth and seventeenth centuries that included state-supported trading companies such as the British East India Company, the Dutch East India Company, and the Royal African Company.

Industrial capitalism
An early phase in the history of manufacturing in which the focus was on the procurement of industrial inputs on the part of colonial powers from their colonies in order to promote the manufactured exports of the colonial powers.

[8] For more on strategic alliances, see Chapter 9 of John et al. (1997).

nineteenth century, there was a rise of British-based MNEs operating in India, China, Latin America, and South Africa. These firms were involved in mining, plantation agriculture, finance, and shipping. A focus here was the procurement of industrial inputs and the promotion of manufactured exports, often at the expense of host-country economies. Japan became involved in similarly-motivated MNE activity toward the end of the nineteenth century after the Meiji Restoration. The companies involved here were industrial groups known as *zaibatsu*, and these were associated with trading companies known as *sogo shosha*, which still exist in various forms to the present day.[9]

In the twentieth century, industrial production grew more capital intensive. The role of the production line and associated economies of scale grew more important. The era of industrial capitalism gave way to what is now known as **managerial capitalism** or **Fordism**. Along with this shift, the center of innovative economic activity moved from Europe to the United States. Firm size increased, and business success became based on the ability to coordinate growing sets of complementary activities. World War I was a distinct blow to the global reach of European MNEs, and after the war, U.S.–based MNEs substantially increased their FDI in Canada, Latin America, and Europe. John et al. (1997) summarize this era quite well:

> *Over the course of the 1920s the book value of United States' foreign direct investment doubled and the amount of this FDI devoted to manufacturing grew by a still larger proportion. It has been argued that by the end of the 1920s the size of United States' investments in both Canada and Latin America exceeded those of British investors for the first time and that more than 1,300 companies or organizations in Europe were either owned or controlled by United States' capital. It was during this era that the American multinational truly first came of age (p. 33).*

The world depression that began in 1929 and World War II hurt most forms of international economic activity, including FDI. The post-war recovery, however, further strengthened the role of U.S.–based MNEs in the world economy. To quote John et al. (1997), "American corporations consolidated into the position of world leaders across almost the entire range of the advanced industries during the 1950s" (p. 40). Indeed, the technological advantage of U.S.–based MNEs during the early post-war period was the point of reference of an early theory of FDI developed by Vernon (1966) and known as the **product life cycle theory**. This theory viewed production as being confined to the **home base** of an MNE during the early phases of a product life cycle due to the need for technologically sophisticated production techniques. During later phases of the production cycle, as the production of the good becomes more routine and established, production can move to subsidiaries in foreign countries in order to take advantage of lower labor costs.[10]

Managerial capitalism
A middle stage in the history of manufacturing where the focus is on achieving economies of scale. Also known as "Fordism."

Fordism
See Managerial capitalism.

Product life cycle theory
An early theory of the multinational enterprise that viewed production as being confined to the home base of an MNE during the early phases of a product life cycle due to the need for technologically sophisticated production techniques. During later phases of the production cycle, as the production of the good becomes more routine and established, production can move to subsidiaries in foreign countries in order to take advantage of lower labor costs.

Home base
The country in which a multinational enterprise is incorporated and holds its central administrative capabilities.

---

[9] After World War II, Japan's *zaibatsu* were dismantled but reestablished themselves as *kieretsu*. On the *sogo shosha*, see Yoshino and Lifson (1986).

[10] In a later assessment of the product life cycle theory, Vernon (1979) stated that it had been applicable during the historical period 1900 to 1970 in explaining the activity of U.S.-based MNEs. However, his assessment was that its applicability declines significantly after 1970. As argued by Dicken (1998): "There is no doubt that a good deal of the *initial* overseas investment by U.S. firms fit the product cycle sequence quite well. But it can no longer explain the majority of international investment by (MNEs). As these firms have become more complex globally it is unrealistic to assume a simple evolutionary sequence from the home country outwards" (p. 184).

The 1970s brought another new change in global production with the rise of industrial output in the newly industrializing countries (NICs) of East Asia, especially Japan, Taiwan, and South Korea. Although there is still debate over this matter, many see the rise of industrial production in the NICs as a move into a new economic era known as *post-Fordism* or, to some, **Toyotism.**[11] In this era, economies of scale have been replaced by flexibility as the progressive element in manufacturing. Dicken (1998) has summarized this era of **flexible manufacturing** as follows:

> *The key to production flexibility lies in the use of* information technologies *in machines and operations. These permit more sophisticated control over the production process. With the increasing sophistication of automated processes and, especially, the new flexibility of electronically controlled technology, far-reaching changes in the process of production need not necessarily be associated with increased scale of production. Indeed, one of the major results of the new electronic and computer-aided production technology is that it permits rapid switching from one part of a production process to another and allows the tailoring of production to the requirements of individual customers (p. 166).*

The importance of this change for our purposes here is that the rise of industrial output was followed by a rise in FDI on the part of East Asian–based MNEs, especially those based in Japan. Consider the data presented in Table 9.3. In 1960, the United States dominated global FDI, accounting for almost one-half of total outward FDI (FDI by firms outside their home countries). The United Kingdom accounted for much less, and Japan accounted for less than 1 percent. By 1975, however, Japan accounted for nearly 6 percent, approximately one half as much as the United Kingdom. By 1995, Japan accounted for 11 percent of global outward FDI, quite nearly as much as the United Kingdom and over 40 percent of the United States' level. As the share of Japanese FDI grew in the world, its

Toyotism
See Flexible manufacturing.

Flexible manufacturing
A recent phase of manufacturing history in which information technology combines with machinery in a way to promote rapid switching among products and processes. Also known as "Toyotism."

Table 9.3 Leading Sources of World Foreign Direct Investment (Percent of Global, Outward FDI)

Country	1960	1975	1985	1990	1995
United States	47.1	44.0	36.6	25.8	25.9
United Kingdom	18.3	13.1	14.6	13.7	11.7
Japan	0.7	5.7	6.5	12.2	11.2
Germany	1.2	6.5	8.8	9.0	8.6
France	6.1	3.8	5.4	6.5	7.4

Source: Dicken, P., (1998). *Global Shift: Transforming the World Economy.* New York: Guilford. 44.

---

[11]An important and fascinating account of this ongoing transition can be found in Ruigrok and van Tulder (1995).

Pollo Campero's Foreign Market Entry Strategy

Pollo Campero is a Central American–based, fried chicken firm that began operating in Guatemala and El Salvador in 1971. It now has approximately 100 outlets in Central America. With the rise of a Central American expatriate population in the United States, the firm began to inadvertently pursue an indirect export strategy to that country when Central Americans visiting relatives would return to the United States loaded down with Pollo Campero chicken. Indeed, in 2001, the firm sold $4 million worth of chicken in the Guatemala City airport alone, most of which was carried onto outgoing flights in duffel bags and on laps. Indeed, many Central Americans would make handsome profits selling the chicken back in the United States, placing orders for over 1,000 pieces of chicken in airport restaurants. The firm sells a total 3 million such "to go" orders each year!

In April 2002, Pollo Campero began to supplement this indirect export strategy with a contractual franchise strategy, opening a restaurant in Los Angeles. The restaurant became an overnight success. Here is how the *Los Angeles Downtown News* described it: "Downtown's newest happening hotspot has no currently listed phone number, a velvet-roped waiting line that often takes hours to conquer, copious and unbribeable security, serves no alcohol, doesn't have a house DJ and closes at 10 P.M. Trendaholic nightclub? Hard-to-find, purposely nameless art gallery? No. It is the first Pollo Campero restaurant to open in Los Angeles, America, and it is a phenomenon."

Plans are now in store for further expansion by Pollo Campero throughout the United States and into Mexico, Poland, Portugal, and Spain. McDonald's, take note. Globalization Latin American style has arrived.

Sources: Gonzalez (2002), Inouye (2002), and http://www.campero.com.

destination shifted from other East Asian and Latin American countries toward Europe and the United States.

A final trend worth mentioning is what used to be called "the rise of Third World multinationals," that is, increasing FDI by MNEs with home bases in developing countries. Observers began to take note of this trend in the mid-1980s. This reflected the fact that developing countries began, at that time, to relax restrictions on FDI capital outflows. For example, India maintained restrictions on FDI capital outflows until the end of the 1980s. As a result of this change, Indian firms began to engage in FDI in North America in the areas of engineering, consulting, and software services.[12] Another notable example of this process is the Mexican-based cement firm Cemex, whose net sales doubled between 1996 and 2001 as it expanded into the United States, Spain, Egypt, the Philippines, Indonesia, Thailand, Bangladesh, Venezuela, Colombia, the Dominican Republic, Panama, Costa Rica, Nicaragua, and the Caribbean. Indeed, Cemex now maintains a productive capacity outside Mexico that is two times as large as its Mexican capacity. Alongside such signature FDI successes, though, are hundreds of more modest FDI market entry stories of developing-country firms, one of which is summarized in the box.

---

[12]See Kumar (1995). One early study on the rise of Third World multinationals was by Heenan and Keegan (1979).

Conclusion

The economic activity of international trade is one of a number of modes of foreign market entry. The other modes of contracting and investment take us into the realm of international production. The choice among trade, contracting, and investment depends on balancing considerations of control, resource commitments, and dissemination risk. The motivations for international production include resource seeking, market seeking, efficiency seeking, and strategic asset seeking. Firms that engage in international production, multinational enterprises, have a long history. This history has moved from merchant capitalism, industrial capitalism, managerial capitalism or Fordism, to Toyotism or post-Fordism. The last of these has accompanied a process known as flexible manufacturing, which, in turn, is based on information technologies.

In at least two important ways, our discussion in this chapter is very much incomplete. Being motivated to engage in international production does not mean that a firm can actually be successful in doing so. Indeed, a firm faces additional costs in operating in a foreign country compared to foreign country firms. For that reason, a firm operating in a foreign country must have command over some sort of scarce resource that gives it an advantage over foreign firms. This is the issue we take up in Chapter 10. Additionally, our brief history of MNE activity masks a great deal of historic controversy between MNEs and their host countries. This controversy has been particularly acute in the case of developing host countries. We take up this issue in Chapter 21.

Review Exercises

1. Why should a firm move beyond trading relationships into international production? What is its motivation for doing so?

2. Suppose a firm's competitiveness was based on its proprietary knowledge, perhaps in the form of a patent on a product or process. What can you say about its considerations with regard to foreign market entry?

3. What key characteristics differentiate managerial capitalism or Fordism and Toyotism based on flexible manufacturing?

4. Provide a specific example for each of the four motivations for international production offered by Dunning.

Further Reading and Web Resources

The best reference available on foreign market entry is Root (1998). Dunning (1993, Chapter 5) and John et al. (1997, Chapter 1) offer very useful reviews of the rise of international production and multinational enterprises. For a very useful set of case studies on contemporary European MNEs, see Nilsson, Dicken, and Peck (eds.) (1996). For a study of Asian multinationals, see Mathews (2002). An interesting book that places international production within the broader context of a changing world economy is Dicken (1998). Doremus et al. (1998) also offer a useful, thematically-arranged bibliography, and Caves (1996) provides an economic analysis of MNEs.

The United Nations Conference on Trade and Development (UNCTAD) publishes an annual *World Investment Report*. This is a good place to turn for data on and discussion of FDI in the world economy. Their Web site is **http://www.unctad.org**, and the *World Investment Report* is at **http://www.unctad.org/wir/**.

References

Baron, D.P. (1997) "Integrated Strategy, Trade Policy, and Global Competition," *California Management Review*, 39:2, 145–169.

Caves, R.E. (1996) *Multinational Enterprise and Economics Analysis*, Cambridge University Press, Cambridge.

Dicken, P. (1998) *Global Shift: Transforming the World Economy*, Guilford, New York.

Doremus, P.N., W.W. Keller, L.W. Pauly, and S. Reich (1998) *The Myth of the Global Corporation*, Princeton University Press, Princeton.

Dunning, J.H. (1993) *Multinational Enterprises and the Global Economy*, Addison-Wesley, New York.

The Economist (1997) "The China Syndrome," June 21, 63–64.

Fima, E. and A.M. Rugman (1996) "A Test of Internalization Theory and Internationalization Theory: The Upjohn Company," *Management International Review*, 36:3, 199–213.

Gonzales, D. (2002) "Fried Chicken Takes Flight, Happily Nesting in the US." *The New York Times*, September 20.

Heenan, D.A., and W.J. Keegan (1979) "The Rise of Third World Multinationals," *Harvard Business Review*, January–February, 101–109.

Hill, C.W.L., P. Hwang, and W.C. Kim (1990) "An Eclectic Theory of the Choice of International Entry Mode," *Strategic Management Journal*, 11:2, 117–128.

Inouye, A. (2002) "Pollo Campero," *Los Angeles Downtown News*, June 17.

John, R., G. Ietto-Gillies, H. Cox, and N. Grimwade (1997) *Global Business Strategy*, International Thompson Business Press, London.

Kumar, N. (1995) *Changing Character of Foreign Direct Investment from Developing Countries: Case Studies from Asia*, United Nations University Institute for New Technologies Discussion Paper 9516, Maastricht.

Mann, J. (1997) *Beijing Jeep*, Westview Press, Boulder, Colorado.

Mathews, J.A. (2002) *Dragon Multinationals: A New Model for Global Growth*, Oxford University Press, Oxford.

Nilsson, J.E., P. Dicken, and J. Peck (eds.) (1996) *The Internationalization Process: European Firms in Global Competition*, Paul Chapman Publishing, London.

Root, F.R. (1998) *Entry Strategy for International Markets*, Jossey-Bass, San Francisco.

Ruigrok, W. and R. van Tulder (1995) *The Logic of International Restructuring*, Routledge, London.

Vernon, R. (1979) "The Produce Cycle Hypothesis in a New International Environment," *Oxford Bulletin of Economics and Statistics*, 41:4, 255–267.

Vernon, R. (1966) "International Investment and International Trade in the Product Cycle," *Quarterly Journal of Economics*, 80:2, 190–207.

Yoshino, M.Y., and T.B. Lifson (1986) *The Invisible Link: Japan's Sogo Shosha and the Organization of Trade*, MIT Press, Cambridge, Massachusetts.

Foreign Direct Investment and Intra-Firm Trade

10

Perhaps the most prominent European forest and paper products company is the Swedish firm Svenska Cellulosa Anktiebolaget (SCA). SCA was founded in 1929 through a merger of a number of smaller companies, some of them in existence since the seventeenth century. SCA always had a role in the world economy in that it exported the bulk of the wood pulp it produced. The decade of the 1950s saw one significant change for SCA in the form of downstream vertical integration into newsprint and liner production.[1] The 1960s saw a second significant change in the form of international production via foreign direct investment (FDI) in Denmark, France, Spain, and Germany. This international production has continued to expand since the 1960s, and SCA now operates in 40 countries.

In this chapter, you will see how to make sense of both domestic vertical integration and FDI within the common framework of a value chain, using SCA as an example. The value chain analysis will draw upon two other concepts that are important in the field of corporate strategy: firm-specific assets and internalization. You will also see how to generalize the value chain concept to that of a multinational value network. We will use the multinational value network to understand a well-known framework in the theory of the multinational enterprise (MNE) known as the OLI (ownership, location, internalization) framework. We will also use it to understand the phenomenon of intra-firm trade. Recall from Chapter 1 that approximately one-third of world trade takes place within MNEs. In concluding this chapter, you will understand why such trade arises.

One interesting aspect of SCA's globalization strategy is its involvement in the use of recycled fibers. This is significant from an industrial ecology perspective, but it also allows us to appreciate some of the dynamics of what we referred to in Chapter 9 as the resource seeking motivation for international production. You will be introduced to this aspect of SCA's internationalization as well. Keep in mind, though, that market seeking and strategic asset seeking have also been operative as motivations for SCA.

---

[1] In the forest and paper products industry, the term "liner" or "linerboard" refers to a form of containerboard used to make corrugated containers. "Kraftliner" is the stronger form of liner, and it is made from virgin wood fibers. "Testliner" is the weaker form of liner, and it is made from recycled fibers.

Value Chains, Intangible Assets, and Internalization

Value chain
A series of value-added processes involved in the production of a good or service.

In his 1990 book, *The Competitive Advantage of Nations*, the corporate strategist Michael Porter formalized a concept known as the **value chain**.[2] We are going to build on this concept to understand why MNEs choose to engage in foreign direct investment. Our example will be the Swedish forest and paper products firm SCA. A simplified version of SCA's value chain is depicted in Figure 10.1. SCA's final product consists of corrugated boxes, which now composes a very large part of the firm's production. Corrugated boxes are produced in a 4-stage production process. In the first stage, a primary resource, the forest, is transformed into a first intermediate product, timber, via logging. In the second stage, timber is transformed into a second intermediate product, wood pulp, through a milling process. In the third stage, pulp is transformed into liner, and in a final stage, liner is transformed into the final product, corrugated boxes. At each stage of the production process, value is added. Hence the term *value chain*.

To begin your understanding of vertical integration, imagine that SCA is initially specializing in timber and pulp production, selling its pulp to paper producers. This describes SCA before the 1950s. That SCA was a competitive pulp producer was evidenced by its exports. What might have explained this competitive success? Corporate strategists typically point

Figure 10.1 SCA's Value Chain in Sweden

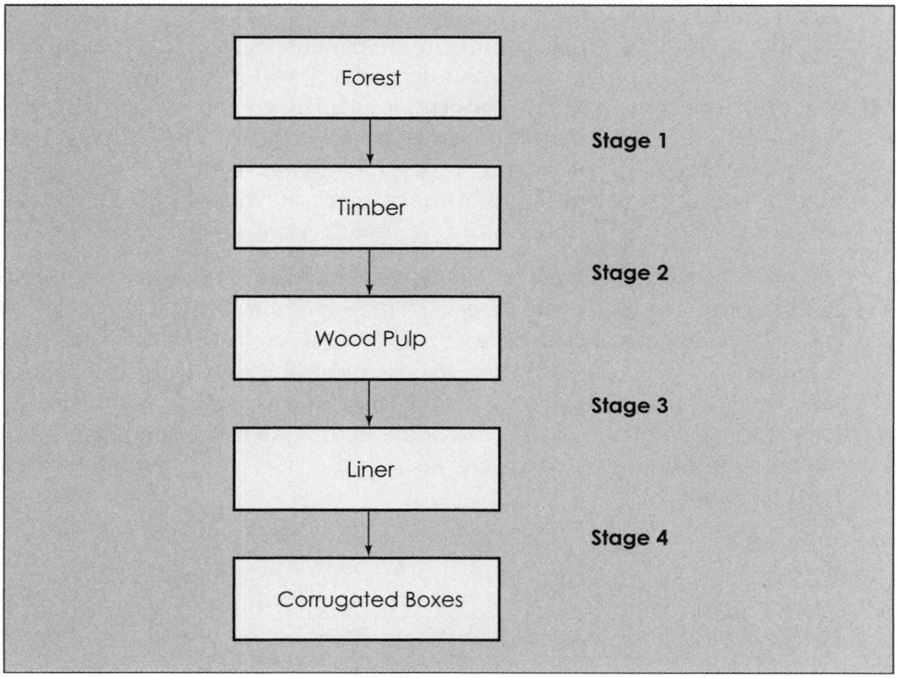

---

[2] See Chapter 2 of Porter (1990).

to the role of **firm-specific assets** in generating the competitiveness of firms. These firm-specific assets can either be tangible, such as access to forest resources, or intangible, such as specialized knowledge, patented products or processes, organizational abilities, or brand distinctiveness.[3] In the case of SCA, the value of firm-specific assets became apparent in the early 1950s as the firm reduced the number of pulp mills in use while increasing overall output through various types of efficiency gains. This process resulted in SCA becoming Sweden's largest forestry company by the end of the 1960s.

A major change in SCA's strategy and structure occurred in the late 1950s. The firm engaged in a process of forward integration into liner production with the introduction of a new mill to produce this product in Sweden. In making this change, SCA entered into competition with U.S.–based liner producers but, importantly from its point of view, not into competition with any of its pulp consumers. Why did SCA make this move? One answer, typically given by corporate strategists analyzing vertical integration, is that SCA might experience an *efficiency gain* by spreading the costs incurred in acquiring its firm-specific assets (both tangible and intangible) over more value chain stages. These efficiency gains are known as **firm-level economies**.[4] This explanation appears to be relevant to the SCA case. As Nilsson (1996) suggested, integrated pulp and liner production displays significant "integration economies" over nonintegrated liner production. SCA could therefore use these integration economies to help it compete with U.S.–produced liner in the Swedish and European markets without antagonizing its pulp consumers.

The concept of firm-level economies is very helpful. However, it is not, in general, sufficient to explain the integration process. Why? SCA always had the option (discussed in Chapter 9) of licensing its firm-specific assets to other liner producers. That is, SCA could draw up a contract to rent its assets to a liner firm for a specific period of time in return for which it would receive payment. Therefore, part of the explanation of forward or backward integration must answer the question: Why did SCA choose not to exercise the licensing option? Or, to state it another way: Why did SCA choose not to engage in a market transaction for its assets, but rather chose to internalize this asset market, a process that corporate strategists call **internalization**?

Corporate strategists suggest that a firm's decision to internalize the firm-specific asset market reflects market failure. That is, for a number of reasons, it has difficulty in selling its firm-specific assets. This explanation makes sense, and it is particularly relevant for the case in intangible assets. This market failure can occur for a number of different reasons. In the case of tangible assets, such as specific production techniques, SCA or any other firm might be reluctant to incur the dissemination risk we discussed in Chapter 9. In the case of intangible assets, such as management practices or reputation, it might be the case that the assets are inseparable

Firm-specific assets
Capabilities and resources possessed by a firm that contribute to its sustained competitiveness. They can be tangible or intangible.

Firm-level economies
Economies accruing to a firm from spreading the cost of intangible assets over larger numbers of production facilities, including production facilities in more than one country.

Internalization
The process of taking a transaction along a value chain and bringing it within a firm.

---

[3] Caves (1996) provides a description of the role of intangible assets in MNEs.
[4] The concept of firm-level economies is discussed by Markusen (1995).

Intangible Assets: Team Toyota in Kentucky

In 1985, Toyota Motor Manufacturing (TMM) announced that it would begin to produce the Toyota Camry at a new plant in North America. The chosen location was Georgetown, Kentucky, and a new subsidiary was formed, Toyota Motor Manufacturing Kentucky (TMMK). Production began in 1988 and, by the end of 2002, the plant had produced 5 million Camry vehicles. Early in the planning process of this FDI project, Toyota identified its key intangible asset: an organizational culture based on team membership. According to TMMK, the Georgetown plant maintains quality by encouraging team members to take an active role in quality control, utilizing team members' ideas and opinions, and practicing *kaizen*, the striving for constant improvement. In TMMK's words: "Toyota team members treat the next person on the production line as their customer and will not pass a defective part to that customer. If a team member finds a problem with a part or the automobile, the team members stops the line and corrects the problem before the vehicle goes any farther down the line."

According to Besser (1996), the team concept at TMMK takes place at three levels: the work team, the company team (TMMK), and the corporate team. The last of these, the corporate team, "includes all members of the Toyota corporation, including, but not limited to, manufactures in the United States and Japan, their suppliers, various other subsidiaries, and the semi-independent marketing and sales corporations affiliated with the corporation" (p. 51).

from the firm's human resources or organization. How do you license reputation? Such market failures are what led SCA to internalize the Stage 3 market in Figure 10.1 via forward integration into liner production. One example of an intangible asset is given in the box.

Now that you understand the concepts of a value chain, firm-specific assets, and internalization, we can turn towards an explanation of FDI, the central issue of this chapter.

Multinational Value Networks and Foreign Direct Investment

Multinational value network
A collection of value chains in a number of countries.

It is now time to add the multinational component to our analysis. Consider SCA engaging in Stages 1, 2, and 3, producing timber, wood pulp, and liner in its home country, Sweden. We will introduce the multinational aspect of the problem by considering two value chains: one in Sweden and one in France. These are depicted in Figure 10.2. We will refer to the combination of these two value chains as a **multinational value network**, although in practice, more than two countries are usually involved. Now, along with the options of backward and forward integration along its value chain in Sweden, SCA has a set of additional options in France. The following paragraph encapsulates SCA's thinking in the early 1960s:

With the development of SCA's kraftliner mill in Munksund (Sweden), the company was forced to build up a marketing organization which would be able to work with the box plants in Europe's more densely populated areas.

Thorough hiring processes ensure that TMMK employs only those that can be good team members. The company expects total, long-term commitment. In return, the company makes a long-term commitment to team members.

One former team member quoted by Besser (1996) commented: "You'll be expected to kill yourself for Toyota and you'll be paid a decent living wage. If you can take it, you'll be taken care of for the rest of your life. When they say you start at 6:30, they don't mean 6:31. You start at 6:30 and you kill yourself for two hours, take a 10-minute break and kill yourself for two more hours. So if someone wants to do that in exchange for the money and security, go for it" (p. 47). Many local workers have, but a significant number have also left the company, complaining of "slave labor" and "management by stress."

Despite such complaints, TMMK's Georgetown plant has become a manufacturing wonder, acquiring a long series of manufacturing quality awards. It is an example of the most advanced sort of FDI taking place in the world economy that reflects some of the concepts we have discussed in this chapter. TMMK also contributes significantly to the 6 percent of the Kentucky workforce dependent on the automobile sector.

Sources: Besser (1996) and http://www.toyotageorgetown.com

Figure 10.2 SCA's Multinational Value Network in Sweden and France

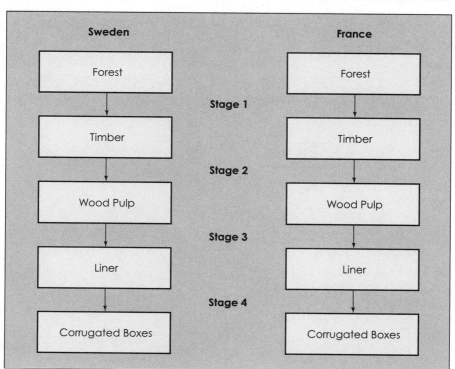

The question of how to secure the markets for kraftliner then arose within the company. A committee within the company arrived at the conclusion that 80% of the box plants were integrated with their liner mills. . . . The conclusion reached by the company was that there existed no option except the purchase of European box plants if it was to secure a market for its products (Nilsson, 1996, pp. 135–136).

This strategic thinking motivated SCA to engage in FDI in France by acquiring three box plants from its largest French pulp customer.[5] In terms of Figure 10.2, SCA engaged in forward vertical integration into France, internationally internalizing the Stage 3 and Stage 4 markets. The important point that you must understand is that, more generally, any firm faces the strategic decision: Which processes in which country will it take on? Whenever a firm decides to operate processes in more than one country, it becomes an MNE. In making such a decision, the elements of firm-specific assets, firm-level economies, and internalization will all be present, just as we discussed in the previous section.

To make this discussion more clear, we depict SCA's multinational value network once again in Figure 10.3. In this figure, we indicate those activities where SCA was active with solid boxes and those activities

Figure 10.3 SCA's Multinational Value Network After FDI in France

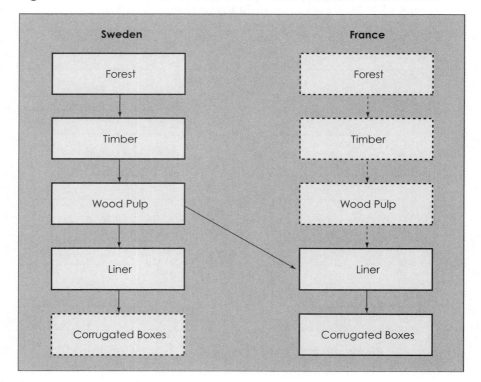

---

[5] SCA engaged in similar actions in Denmark and Spain, but the French acquisitions were its most important.

where SCA was not active in dashed boxes. The arrow between wood pulp produced in Sweden and liner produced in France is very significant. This represents SCA's exports of wood pulp to France. It is important to note something about this trade flow. Before SCA's acquisition of its French pulp customer, this was an arm's-length transaction between two firms. The term "arm's-length" refers to a transaction between two otherwise unrelated parties. After SCA's FDI in France, however, the trade flow took place *within* SCA *itself*. This type of trade is called **intra-firm trade**.[6]

Intra-firm trade
Trade that takes place within a multi-national enterprise.

The FDI depicted in Figure 10.3 is known as *forward vertical FDI* because the FDI links wood pulp production in Sweden to the next stage in the value chain, liner production, in France. If, instead, SCA had sourced timber in France for its wood pulp production in Sweden (not likely!), this would be a case of *backward vertical FDI*. Finally, if SCA only engaged in wood pulp production in France, without any intra-firm trade, this would be an example of *horizontal FDI*.

Recall that, in Chapter 4, we made an important distinction between inter-industry trade and intra-industry trade. We now have also distinguished between inter-firm trade and intra-firm trade. Things are becoming a bit complicated! To help you sort all this out, consult Table 10.1. This table characterizes international trade along two dimensions: industry and firm. Along the industry dimension (rows), it distinguishes between inter-industry and intra-industry. Along the firm dimension (columns), it distinguished between inter-firm and intra-firm. This gives us four cells in the table. Down the inter-firm column of Table 10.1, we have the types of trade considered in Chapters 3 and 4 of Part 1 of this book, that is, inter-firm trade that can be either between or within industries. Down the intra-firm column of the table, we have the types of trade considered in this chapter, that is, intra-firm trade that can take place either between or within industries. Consider Figure 10.3. Given an industry classification of

Table 10.1 Industry and Firm Dimensions of Trade

Industry Dimension	Firm Dimension	
	Inter-firm	*Intra-firm*
Inter-industry	Trade that takes place between two different industries and two different firms. Described in Chapter 3.	Trade that takes place between two different industries and within a single firm. Described in Chapter 10.
Intra-industry	Type of trade that takes place within a single industry and between two different firms. Described in Chapter 4.	Trade that takes place within a single industry and within a single firm. Described in Chapter 10.

---

[6] The role of intra-firm trade in the world economy is explored in some detail in Chapter 4 of Grimwade (1989).

"forest and paper products," the trade depicted there would be intra-firm and intra-industry. However, if we distinguish between "forest products" and "paper products" as two separate industries, the trade depicted there would be intra-firm and inter-industry. This gives you an appreciation of how the degree of detail in industry classification determines the extent of inter-industry and intra-industry trade.

SCA viewed its French FDI strategy positively, and it became a model for its internationalization throughout Western Europe. By the end of the 1970s, SCA either owned or part-owned liner and box factories in France, Germany, the United Kingdom, Ireland, and Denmark. By the end of the 1980s, it added factories in Belgium, the Netherlands, and Italy. SCA now owns approximately 50 liner and box factories outside of Sweden.[7]

Today, SCA is also Europe's largest user of recycled paper, and this characteristic is also closely related to its internationalization strategy. The genesis of its involvement in recycling came in 1990 when SCA purchased the U.K.–based firm Reedpack. Reedpack operated a recycled-fiber newsprint mill and, with the purchase of this firm, SCA added a completely different value chain to its already-existing multinational value network. Importantly, this new value chain excluded the forest/pulp components of its historical value chain. This new value chain is depicted in Figure 10.4.

Figure 10.4 SCA's Current Multinational Value Network

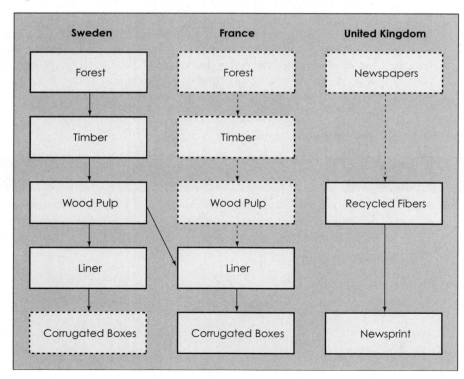

---

[7] See Nilsson (1996).

Nilsson (1996) comments that, during the 1990s, the forest products industry was:

> *altered somewhat by the increased importance of recycled fibres as a raw material. Recycled fibres has become a sort of "urban forest" which grows best in densely populated urban centers such as southeast England, Paris, Randstaat and the Ruhr area, with Scandinavia producing relatively little. It is therefore economically advantageous to locate production units in the densely populated areas outside Sweden. . . . The pattern [that] seems to be appearing is that Swedish production is becoming of higher quality based on virgin fibres, while the companies are expanding recycled operations on the continent and in Britain (p. 142).*

This makes it clear that the patterns of FDI can become complex and somewhat unrelated to the structure of the original, home-country value chain.

Like its FDI in liner and box production, SCA's recycled newsprint FDI strategy proved to be important. Indeed, in 1994, SCA followed its Reedpack acquisition with a joint venture with the European subsidiary of Mondi Paper (a South African firm) to build another newspaper recycling plant in Aylesford, United Kingdom. This plant is now one of the leading newspaper recycling facilities in the United Kingdom.[8]

Although much of international economics focuses on international trade, FDI is a crucial component of the modern world economy. The box gives you some additional information on where this FDI takes place in the world economy. In order to understand the process of FDI, we need to venture beyond standard international economics into the realm of corporate strategy. The tools of value chains, intangible assets, and internalization can provide insights into this important global process. These tools also allow us to see that there are reasons for trade in intermediate products within multinational value networks. Such trade may have slightly different implications for welfare and income distribution than those we spoke of in Part 1 of this book. For example, trade in intermediate products within value chains might increase production efficiency, providing additional benefits to the countries involved. Here, the realms of corporate strategy and standard trade theory can mutually support our understanding of the world economy.[9]

The OLI Framework

If SCA decides to engage in FDI in France, it most certainly will be at a disadvantage in some important areas *vis-à-vis* French firms. SCA will have to incur the additional costs of operating its business internationally, including increased transportation, communication, and coordination costs. Therefore, if SCA is able to successfully engage in business in France, there must be some other advantages that offset the additional costs of conducting business internationally.[10] John Dunning (1993) outlines three basic

---

[8] See the Aylesford Newsprint Web site at http://www.aylesford-newsprint.co.uk.
[9] See Feenstra (1998) for a discussion of these issues. We explore some negative welfare possibilities of intra-firm trade (e.g. transfer pricing) in Chapter 21 on hosting MNEs.
[10]This insight was originally due to Hymer (1976) who, it can be argued, originated the modern, firm-based analysis of the MNE.

Where Does the FDI Go?

We have considered the motivations of firms to engage in FDI and the considerations that arise in taking on a FDI-based, foreign market entry strategy. As individual entities, firms around the world take on these sets of considerations and, in many instances, actually engage in FDI. One question that arises at a more macroeconomic level is: Where are these countries investing? Let's take a brief look at the answer to this question. The figures we cite here are for the year 1998.

Despite the stereotype of FDI being primarily motivated by the cheap-wage version of resource seeking, approximately 70 percent of FDI actually flows into developed, or high-income countries. The largest destination of FDI in this category is the European Union, which hosts approximately 35 percent of world FDI. The second-largest destination is the United States, which hosts approximately 30 percent. Japan receives almost no FDI at all.

Approximately 30 percent of FDI flows to the developing countries and Central and Eastern Europe. South, East, and Southeast Asia host the largest portion of this (approximately 12 percent). Latin America hosts the second-largest portion (approximately 11 percent). Only 1 percent of world FDI takes place in Africa.

What determines the structure of FDI inflows? In the realm of market seeking, the key variable is the rate of growth of country and regional economies. This helps to explain the prominent role of the developed world as a host of FDI. In the realm of resource seeking, the presence of raw materials, either low-cost or skilled labor, and physical infrastructure matter a great deal. In the realm of efficiency seeking, the presence of regional integration schemes, discussed in Chapter 8, is very important. These assist MNEs in building regional corporate networks.

Source: United Nations Conference on Trade and Development.

advantages: ownership or *O* advantages; location or *L* advantages; and internalization or *I* advantages.[11] Ownership or *O* advantages refer to ownership of tangible or intangible firm-specific assets SCA owns, which provide it with a competitive edge over French firms. As summarized by Markusen (1995), "Whatever its form, the ownership advantage confers some valuable market power or cost advantage on the firm sufficient to outweigh the disadvantage of doing business abroad" (p. 173). In deploying these assets over a larger range of activities, SCA can realize cost advantages over its rivals through firm-level economies. The theoretical role of the *O* advantage is to explain why SCA engages in the production of a good for the French market instead of a French firm. More generally, its purpose is to explain why a firm from a particular home country engages in the production of a good in a foreign country instead of a foreign firm.

Location or *L* advantages are associated with the foreign country, France. The *L* advantages could include input costs, transportation costs, import restraints, foreign government promotional policies, or access to foreign consumers. *L* advantages often closely relate to the first two motivations for

---

[11]See Dunning (1993) and Markusen (1995).

international production discussed in Chapter 9: resource seeking and market seeking. The theoretical role of the L advantage is to explain why SCA chooses to produce in France rather than in Sweden. More generally, it explains why a home country MNE chooses to produce in a foreign country rather than its home base. Together, the O and L advantages are enough to explain why SCA, rather than a French firm, controls production and why this production takes place in France rather than in Sweden.

Finally, as you saw in the previous section, internalization or I advantages explain why SCA chooses FDI over the licensing option. The failure of markets in firm-specific assets is key to understanding I advantages. Internalization advantages often relate to the efficiency seeking motivation for international production discussed in Chapter 9. According to Dunning, all three advantages, ownership, location, and internalization, are necessary to explain MNE activity.[12] The **OLI framework** is summarized in Table 10.2.

OLI framework
A theory of the multi-national enterprise based on ownership, location, and internalization advantages.

Table 10.2 The OLI Framework

Symbol	Meaning	Contribution
O	Ownership advantage	Explains how a firm's tangible and intangible assets help it to overcome the extra costs of doing business internationally; explains why a home-country firm, rather than a foreign firm, produces in the foreign country
L	Location advantage	Explains why a home-based MNE chooses to produce in a foreign country rather than in its home country
I	Internalization advantage	Explains why a home-based MNE chooses FDI rather than licensing to achieve production in a foreign country

Source: Adapted from Dunning, J. H. (1993). *Multinational Enterprises and the Global Economy*. New York: Addison-Wesley.

---

[12]For a critique of the OLI framework, see Itaki (1991).

Conclusion

Approximately one-third of world trade is intra-firm trade, taking place within MNEs. This trade takes place along value chains, and the OLI framework helps us to understand it. Firms offset the extra costs of doing business internationally through their tangible or intangible assets, which provide ownership advantages to them. They choose to operate abroad because various foreign countries offer location advantages. Finally, they choose investment modes of foreign market entry over contractual modes because there are advantages to internalization. These advantages include but also go beyond the dissemination risk we discussed in Chapter 9. When all three advantages are present, firms have the incentive to engage in FDI and intra-firm trade.

The presence of OLI advantages does not remove *all* difficulties of operating a firm internationally. We take up some of these management challenges in Chapter 11.

Review Exercises

1. Choose any production process of interest to you. Both merchandise and services are appropriate. Draw a value chain for this production process.

2. For this production process, choose two countries. Place the value chains for these two countries side by side. Show how FDI in the second country by a firm based in the first country can be depicted for the cases of horizontal FDI, backward vertical FDI, and forward vertical FDI.

3. For each of ownership advantages, location advantages, and internalization advantages, state how it helps you to understand why firms engage in FDI rather than trade or contractual modes of foreign market entry.

4. The Web site **http://www.developmentgateway.org** maintains a list of topics that includes FDI. Spend a little time exploring the many subtopics on the FDI topic page. You can get to the FDI topic page from the main page via a drop-down menu.

Further Reading and Web Resources

An excellent introduction to corporate strategy is Besanko, Dranove, and Shanley (2000). The concept of a value chain is explained in Chapter 2 of Porter (1990). The OLI framework is discussed in Chapter 4 of Dunning (1993) and in Markusen (1995). Connections between the discussion of this chapter and Part 1 of this book are explored in Feenstra (1998).

The United Nations Conference on Trade and Development is an organization that has dedicated itself to the analysis of FDI and its role in economic development. Their Web site is **http://www.unctad.org**. Of particular interest is their annual *World Investment Report*, which is highlighted at **http://www.unctad.org/wir**. Also relevant is the Web site of UNCTAD's Division of Investment, Technology and Enterprise Development at **http://www.unctad.org/en/subsites/dite/index.html**. An interesting IMF paper entitled "Trends in Global and Regional Foreign Direct Investment Flows" can be found at **http://www.imf.org/external/pubs/ft/seminar/2002/fdi/eng/pdf/wong.pdf**.

References

Besanko, D., D. Dranove, and M. Shanley (2000) *Economics of Strategy*, John Wiley, New York.

Besser, T.L. (1996) *Team Toyota: Transplanting the Toyota Culture to the Camry Plant in Kentucky*, State University of New York Press, Albany.

Caves, R.E. (1996) *Multinational Enterprise and Economics Analysis*, Cambridge University Press, Cambridge.

Dunning, J.H. (1993) *Multinational Enterprises and the Global Economy*, Addison-Wesley, New York.

Feenstra, R.C. (1998) "Integration of Trade and Disintegration of Production in the Global Economy," *Journal of Economic Perspectives*, 12:4, 31–50.

Grimwade, N. (1989) *International Trade: New Patterns of Trade, Production and Investment*, Routledge, London.

Hymer, S.H. (1976) *The International Operations of National Firms: A Study of Direct Foreign Investment*, MIT Press, Cambridge, Massachusetts.

Itaki, M. (1991) "A Critical Assessment of the Eclectic Theory of the Multinational Enterprise," *Journal of International Business Studies*, 22:3, 445–460.

Markusen, J.R. (1995) "The Boundaries of Multinational Enterprise and the Theory of International Trade," *Journal of Economic Perspectives*, 9:2, 169–189.

Nilsson, J.E. (1996) "MoDo, SCA and STORA: From National Pulp Producers to European Forestry Companies," in J.E. Nilsson, P. Dicken, and J. Peck (eds.), *The Internationalization Process: European Firms in Global Competition*, Paul Chapman, London, 130–145.

Porter, M.E. (1990) *The Competitive Advantage of Nations*, The Free Press, New York.

International Competition and Management

In Chapter 10, you learned about the successful internationalization strategy of the Swedish forest and paper products firm Svenska Cellulosa Anktiebolaget (SCA). This strategy has been based on FDI in corrugated box and recycled newsprint in many Western European countries. Two important questions remain, the answers to which will contribute greatly to your understanding of international production. First, was there anything characterizing the home base of SCA that contributed to its competitive success or to what corporate strategists call competitive advantage? Second, when a firm such as SCA distributes its production facilities over many countries, do its management techniques need to change?

This chapter provides you with some initial answers to these questions. We use the term "initial" in the previous sentence because this chapter covers subjects where a great deal of current research is being conducted in the field of international corporate strategy.

We will begin in the following section by examining the role of the home base of successful MNEs in maintaining their **competitive advantage**. We are then going to address a special aspect of home bases, the spatial cluster, and how it can contribute to international competitiveness. These two topics will address the first question concerning competitive success. Next, we will address the role of what is called the local-global paradox in the management of MNEs, and we will briefly take up cultural issues in international management. These topics will address the second question concerning management techniques.

The Porter Diamond and the Role of the Home Base

Recall from Chapter 9 on foreign market entry that a competitive firm can choose from a number of trade, contractual, and investment modes of foreign market entry. One issue we have not yet fully addressed is why a particular firm in a particular home country can develop and maintain its competitiveness as it moves through the trade, contractual, and investment modes of globalization. That is, why do particular firms accumulate the tangible and intangible assets, discussed in Chapter 10, that support international competitiveness? According to some authors, notably Michael Porter in his book *The Competitive Advantage of Nations* (1990), this competitiveness has a lot do with the home base of the firm. The purpose of this section of the chapter is to review this important possible explanation of

Competitive advantage
A situation where a firm can sustain global, market competitiveness in a particular product niche.

competitiveness.[1] In doing so, we will answer Porter's basic question: "Why are firms based in a particular nation able to create and sustain competitive advantage against the world's best competitors in a particular field?" (p. 1).

In explaining the role of the home base in determining a firm's competitive advantage, Porter introduced a diagram that has become very well known. Now called the **Porter diamond**, this diagram is presented in Figure 11.1. The diamond focuses on four central aspects of the home base, which Porter views as the determinants of competitive advantage: factor conditions; demand conditions; related and supporting industries; and firm strategy, structure, and rivalry.[2] Porter's main argument is that "Nations are most likely to succeed in industries or industry segments where the national 'diamond' is most favorable" (p. 72). Although the Porter diamond is not a theory of MNEs *per se*, it certainly helps in gaining an understanding of them. As Porter states, "Multinationals that are the leading competitors in particular segments or industries are often based in only one or two nations. The important questions are *why* and *how* do multinationals from a particular nation develop unique skills and know-how in particular industries?" (p. 18). In order to help you understand the Porter diamond, we are going to consider each determinant in turn.

> **Porter diamond**
> A diagrammatic and conceptual device introduced by Michael Porter to explain the sources of competitive advantage in a firm's home base.

Factor Conditions. In Chapters 2 and 3, we discussed the role of factor endowments in determining absolute and comparative advantage. The factors we considered in those chapters (labor, land, natural resources, and

Figure 11.1 The Porter Diamond

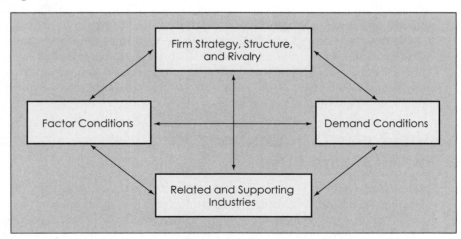

Source: Porter, M.E. (1990). *The Competitive Advantage of Nations.* New York: The Free Press. 72.

---

[1] Despite the title of his book, competitiveness for Porter is a characteristic of *firms* and *industries*, not of countries. We need to keep this in mind as we consider his ideas. Characteristics of countries can contribute to firms' and industries' competitiveness, but countries themselves are not "competitive" or "uncompetitive." On this point, Porter is in agreement with the points made by Krugman (1994).

[2] Two other subsidiary determinants are chance and government policy.

physical capital) are what Porter considers to be basic factors that are largely inherited. More important from Porter's point of view are advanced factors that are created. These advanced factors include such things as sophisticated infrastructure, labor educated and trained in very specific ways, and focused research institutions. Porter also makes a distinction between generalized factors and specialized factors. Generalized factors can be used in a number of different industries; specialized factors are tailored for use in specific industries. Porter argues: "The most significant and sustained competitive advantage results when a nation possesses factors needed for competing in a particular industry that are both advanced and specialized" (p. 79). He also emphasizes that it is the *creation* of advanced and specialized factors that contribute to firms' competitiveness.[3]

Demand Conditions. Porter stresses three aspects of demand conditions in the home base. These are demand composition; demand size and pattern of growth; and degree of internationalization. With regard to home demand composition, Porter argues that sophisticated, demanding, and anticipatory home demand contributes to firms' success. By "anticipatory," Porter means home demand that anticipates trends in global demand. With regard to size and growth, large, rapidly-growing, and early home demand are positive aspects of the home base. Finally, the more "in synch" with international demand trends is home demand, the more it contributes to firms' competitiveness. To take one example, Porter would argue that the low gasoline prices in the United States (by global standards) contribute to domestic demand that is out of step with global demand trends for fuel-efficient cars. As a second example, Porter points to the small living quarters and sophistication with electronic goods in Japan as contributing positively to competitive success in the Japanese electronic keyboard industry.

Related and Supporting Industries. Porter stresses the important role played by supplying industries in the home base.[4] He states the following:

> *The presence of internationally competitive supplier industries in a nation creates advantages in downstream industries in several ways. The first is via efficient, early, rapid, and sometimes preferential access to the most cost-effective inputs. . . . More significant than access to machinery or other inputs is the advantage that home-based suppliers provide in terms of ongoing coordination. . . . Perhaps the most important benefit of home-based suppliers, however, is in the process of innovation and upgrading. Competitive advantage emerges from close working relationships between world-class suppliers and the industry" (pp. 101–103).*

Porter stresses: "Having a competitive *domestic* supplier industry is far preferential to relying even on well-qualified *foreign* suppliers" (p. 103,

---

[3] The implication of this point of view has been summarized by Waldron (1997): "Porter has been instrumental in redirecting the focus of trade theory from a country's inherent, natural, or endowment characteristics to how governments, industries, and firms can alter the conditions within a country to enhance a nation's competitiveness" (p. 61). For more on this point, see the interview with Sanjaya Lall that follows this chapter.

[4] See also Chapters 4 and 5 of Ruigrok and van Tulder (1995) for a political economy view of the role of supplying industries.

The Porter Diamond in India

In Chapter 1, we mentioned the role that India plays in providing back office, software, and medical transcription services to the world. India's exports of software services have, in particular, captured the world's attention, prompting Microsoft's Bill Gates to suggest that "India is likely to be the next software superpower." The statistics are indeed impressive. More than 800 firms have contributed to annual growth in the Indian software sector of 50 percent, with most sales being exports. The bulk of these service exports are to the United States. Some projections estimate that India's software exports will reach US$50 billion by 2008.

How can this competitive success be explained? Kapur and Ramamurti (2001) have offered an explanation based on the Porter diamond. With regard to factor conditions, these authors emphasize the role of the large pool of skilled labor, including engineers and scientists, low salaries, and English language capabilities as being key in supporting the competitiveness of the software sector in India. Domestic demand conditions have not played an important role. Rather, it is foreign demand conditions, namely those in the United States, that have been important. The authors note that "one key difference between software and the industries that Porter studied is that software can be digitized and therefore moved back and forth between different locations instantaneously through telecommunications links" (pp. 25–26). Within the U.S., the large and fast-growing market and the presence of sophisticated software buyers have contributed significantly to the competitiveness of the Indian software sector.

emphasis added). He emphasizes the gains to competitiveness that arise from the presence of clusters of competitive, domestic suppliers. We will take up this latter issue in a later section of this chapter.

Firm Strategy, Structure, and Rivalry. Porter recognizes that one country differs from another with regard to managerial systems and philosophies and with regard to capital market conditions. He suggests that institutional environments that allow firms to take a long-term view contribute positively to competitiveness. Also important, however, is the presence of a large number of competing firms or rivals in the domestic industry. Porter claims: "Among the strongest empirical findings from our research is the association between vigorous domestic rivalry and the creation and persistence of competitive advantage in an industry" (p. 117). You know from introductory microeconomics that competition among firms is necessary for allocative efficiency in a market system, but Porter also stresses the role of domestic rivalry in contributing to dynamic, technological efficiency. For a sense of how these four determinants of competitive advantage can be applied to a particular case, see the box on the Porter diamond in India.

As shown in Figure 11.1 by the presence of the double-headed arrows, the four elements of the Porter diamond interact with one another. Porter describes in detail the twelve interactions of the diagram, but here we will mention the three he considers the most important. These are illustrated in Figure 11.2. All three are related to the rivalry aspect of firm strategy structure. In the first (the arrow to the left), domestic rivals, particularly when clustered in a geographic region, contribute to the creation of factors, especially specialized, advanced factors. In the second (the downward

As suggested by Porter, related and supporting industries have been important. The most important of these has been the large network of public and private educational institutions that enhance the factor conditions of the country. Here, the authors note that "Thanks to economic liberalization, private schools are augmenting the government's efforts to expand the supply of students to meet the anticipated needs of the software industry" (p. 25). Finally, in the case of firm strategy, structure, and rivalry, it is domestic rivalry that has been most important. Kapur and Ramamurti describe the competition among the more than 800 small firms making up the Indian software industry as "fierce," and this domestic competition has contributed to continual upgrading throughout the industry.

Importantly, Kapur and Ramamurti claim that the competitive success of the Indian software sector has had positive impacts for lower-skilled services such as back office and medical transcription. Success in one service sector supports success in others. The entire, evolving service complex in India deserves continued attention and study. In it, we might find important lessons for other countries.

Source: Kapur and Ramamurti (2001).

Figure 11.2 Interaction in the Porter Diamond

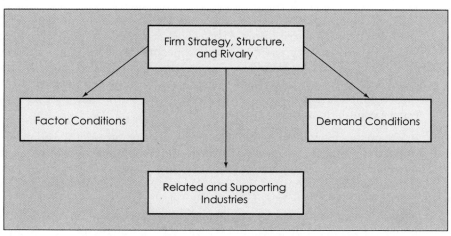

Source: Adapted from Porter, M.E. (1990). *The Competitive Advantage of Nations*. New York: The Free Press. 72.

arrow), a group of domestic rivals contributes to the presence of specialized and sophisticated suppliers. In the third (the arrow to the right), rivalry among domestic firms producing differentiated products enlarges home demand and makes it more sophisticated.[5] The role of domestic rivalry in

---

[5] The reader should recall from introductory microeconomics that rivalry combined with differentiated products leads to the monopolistic competition model. See Chapter 17 of Mankiw (2004).

each of these interactions, as well as the potential role of geographical clustering in the first two interactions, led Porter to the following conclusion: "Two elements—domestic rivalry and geographic industry concentration—have especially great power to transform the 'diamond' into a system, domestic rivalry because it promotes upgrading of the entire national 'diamond,' and geographic concentration because it elevates and magnifies the interactions within the diamond" (p. 131).

Can we apply these concepts to the case of SCA? It seems that we can, at least to some extent. SCA's competitive success in forest and paper products has been supported by Swedish transportation equipment, transportation services, chemicals, energy, and prefabricated housing industries. Therefore, SCA's persistent competitiveness has been assisted by related and supporting industries. However, factor conditions have also been important in some respects. Beyond the obvious role of forest resources, SCA has benefited from high-level human resources. In general, Swedish workers are well trained, proficient in foreign languages, and able to work in teams. The ability of the Swedish home base to support forest and paper product competitiveness is also evidenced by the presence of other successful competitors to SCA, namely MoDo and STORA. It is clear that more than chance has been at work in SCA's international competitiveness.

Spatial Clusters in the World Economy

In Chapter 9, we mentioned the recent rise of flexible manufacturing and its contributions to the competitive success of some MNEs, especially those based in Japan. In the previous section, we stressed the potential role of the home base in contributing to the competitive success of MNEs. It turns out that the flexibility and home base concepts converge in a phenomenon we mentioned in the previous section, that of spatial clustering. Recall that Porter stressed the role of geographically clustered supplying industries in contributing to firm competitiveness. We now take up this issue in a more complete manner.

Spatial cluster
A collection of interrelated firms in a geographic area that engage in cooperative information sharing and, thereby, contribute to their collective efficiency and competitiveness.

Variously referred to as clusters, networks, centers of excellence, and industrial districts, what we will term **spatial clusters** first came to be noticed in Silicon Valley in the United States, in what is now known as the Third Italy, in Southern Germany, and in East Asia. Malmberg, Sölvell, and Zander (1996) have defined a spatial cluster as "a set of interlinked firms/activities that exist in the same local and regional milieu, defined as to encompass economic, social, cultural and institutional factors" (p. 91). Putting aside for a moment the role of the milieu, spatial clusters evolve because of the nature of the innovation process. As emphasized by Kogut and Zander (1992), much productive knowledge cannot be codified into explicit forms. Rather, this tacit knowledge must be communicated via a highly social process of face-to-face interaction over a relatively long period of time. Consequently, innovation and learning is a spatially-located, social, and collective process among a group of firms.[6] A particular case of

---

[6] See also Scott (1995), Malmberg, Sölvell, and Zander (1996), and Chapter 5 of Dicken (1998).

The Surgical Instruments Cluster in Pakistan

It might be surprising to some readers, but the second-largest exporter of stainless steel surgical instruments in the world is Pakistan, a country that has been making surgical instruments for over a century. The advent of surgical instrument manufacturing is traced back to the 1890s when local ironsmiths began repairing the instruments of a local hospital. Now the surgical instruments sector in Pakistan is in the form of a cluster, centered in the city of Sialkot and consisting of 2,500 firms and 50,000 workers making thousands of different types of instruments.

Our discussion of clusters and milieux emphasize their social nature. The research of Khalid Nadvi (1999) shows that this is certainly a key characteristic of the Sialkot cluster. Nadvi comments: "Social networks can have an important impact on the workings of local firms. They can provide a basis for regulating inter-firm relations, thereby mediating local competition and co-operation, and facilitate the historical sedimentation of 'tacit,' sector-specific knowledge" (p. 143). Nadvi notes that communication within the cluster is intense, taking place both within and outside of the official trade association. The social networks along which the communication takes place are supported by systems of kinship (*biraderi*), extended family (most firms are family firms), and localness in geographic, cultural, and historical senses. Consequently, "Trust, reputation and honour in business relationships are intertwined with the social relations that agents have with each other and their overall social standing" (p. 156). Despite these social ties, however, rivalry is intense among firms, especially at the marketing end of value chains, and this rivalry promotes competitiveness.

Much less positively, the Sialkot surgical instruments cluster has been implicated in the use of child labor in the making of surgical instruments. The Pakistani government itself estimates that there are nearly 8,000 children employed in the Sialkot cluster. The International Labor Organization has been collaborating with UNICEF and the Pakistani government to attempt to remove children from the cluster and to enroll them in schools. Given the importance of education in the human development process (see Chapter 20), one hopes for the success of this program.

Sources: Nadvi (1999), International Labor Organization, and Small and Medium Enterprise Development Authority, Government of Pakistan.

this is discussed in the box. Here, as in many junctures in this book, some of the rhetoric of globalization falls short. As Malmberg, Sölvell, and Zander (1996) point out, "the very nature of the innovation process tends to make technological activity locally confined, and suggests that *recent globalization forces have not altered . . . this process in any fundamental way* (p. 90, emphasis added). It is for this reason that Storper (1992) identifies spatial clusters as one of the "limits of globalization."

Why do spatial clusters contribute to the productivity of firms? First, the concentrated communication made possible by a cluster increases learning and innovation. This, in turn, contributes to the dynamic, technological efficiency of firms in the cluster. Second, trust increases over time, and this facilitates contracting and exchange among firms. Third, a common business culture develops, and this reduces uncertainty. These processes are particularly important in flexible manufacturing systems because these are "strongly externalized" or "transactions-intensive" (Scott, 1995). That is, much of the activity in flexible production systems takes place among firms, especially between core firms and their suppliers. Because of this, in some instances, we might want to revisualize the value chain presented in Chapter 10 as that presented in Figure 11.3. In this figure, a home-country firm engages in Processes II and III and sources a number of inputs into (A through E) from a cluster of supplier firms operating in Process I.

A cluster exists within a **milieu**. The milieu consists of the cluster's firms, the knowledge embedded within the cluster, its institutional (e.g., legal) environment, and the ties of the cluster's firms to customers, research institutions, educational institutions, and local government (Malmberg, Sölvell, and Zander, 1996). The milieu supports the cluster with rules and norms for business activity, social cohesion, business culture, and government support. For example, Porter (1990) suggests that government policies can address spatial clusters when considering investments in education, research, and infrastructure. Education is more than university education, and specialized training closely tied to spatial clusters is very important. Technical institutes tied to local clusters have an important role to play and can be encouraged, and this is also the case for professional associations. The latter can focus on human resource development and innovation-friendly activities such as standard-setting and information diffusion. Government can play a direct, albeit limited, role in "the testing of materials, inspection and certification of quality control standards, calibration of measurement instruments, establishment of repositories of technical information, patent registration, research and design, and technical training" (Battat, Frank, and Shen, 1996, p. 22).

Milieu
The firms, knowledge, institutions and government supporting a spatial cluster with rules, norms, and business culture.

Figure 11.3 A Value Chain Within a Spatial Cluster

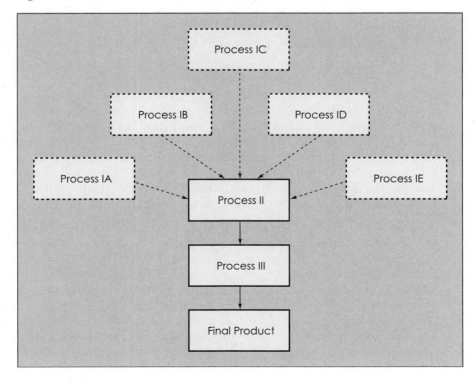

Porter (1990) cites as an example a materials testing institute linked to the German cutlery cluster in the city of Solingen. Battat, Frank, and Shen (1996) cite the Singapore Institute of Standards and Industrial Research. Finally, competition policies can restrict horizontal collusion while fostering vertical communication and collaboration.[7]

What is the importance of spatial clusters and milieux to the MNE? In its home base, an MNE obviously has the possibility of contributing to the local cluster and milieu. This is the message of Porter in his emphasis on the home base. However, it is also possible that an MNE can tap into select- ed foreign clusters and milieux. As suggested by Malmberg, Sölvell, and Zander (1996):

> *In the local milieux where the (MNE) controls full-fledged operations, it can be characterized as an insider just like any other local firm. It is linked to other firms in both formal and informal networks, and typical- ly maintains close linkages to local research and education facilities, governmental bodies and other important actors. These linkages provide channels for rapid dissemination of knowledge and information, and provide a basis for co-operation leading to a continuous stream of small and large improvements. . . . Sometimes, (MNEs) have built up insider positions through long-terms investments, but more often (MNEs) become insiders by acquiring local firms with full-fledged operations and estab- lished local networks.*

For these reasons, spatial clusters are important in both the home base and in the foreign operations of MNEs. For an example of a spatial cluster and milieu, see the box on surgical instruments in Pakistan.

Multinational Management: The Local-Global Paradox

In Chapter 10, as part of developing the OLI framework, we mentioned that ownership advantages offset the extra costs of doing business international- ly. In a superficial way, this statement hinted at some of the complexities of multinational management. As a firm globalizes its production system, it confronts a whole host of decisions surrounding the location of the compo- nents of the multinational value network and the coordination among these components. The field of multinational management is too broad for us to capture fully in this section.[8] Instead, we will summarize a number of issues raised in the well-known book *Managing Across Borders: The Transnational Solution* by Bartlett and Ghoshal (2002). What we will encounter in this summary is a recurring theme relating to a creative tension between the local and the global. We will call this the **local-global paradox**.[9] This par- adox is alluded to in the following advertisement by Citibank:

> *These days, everybody says they're "global." But saying you're global isn't the same as "being" global. It's not just where you are, it's how you*

Local-global paradox
A term referring to the fact the global pro- duction also involves increased localization in the countries hosting foreign direct investment.

---

[7] For a further discussion of these issues, see Reinert (1998).
[8] For an excellent introduction, the reader can consult John et al. (1997).
[9] Similar terminology has been used by de Mooij (1998).

*are there. To us, being global means being completely local. Entirely at home. The way we are in 100 countries around the world. Our job is to understand a country by its people, not just by its airports (*The Economist, July 4, 1998).

We are going to investigate the local-global paradox as considered by Bartlett and Ghoshal. These authors identify three strategic challenges faced by MNEs: global efficiency, local responsiveness, and global innovation. Global efficiency is obtained from economies of scale and scope. Local responsiveness involves using local facilities and personnel to tailor goods and services to the needs and preferences of local consumers. Finally, global innovation refers to the combined and complementary use of innovations from many parts of the multinational value network. In these authors' view, "more and more businesses are being driven by *simultaneous* demands for global efficiency, national responsiveness, and worldwide leveraging of innovations and learning" (p. 33).

Bartlett and Ghoshal identify three traditions of MNE management associated with Europe, Japan, and the United States, respectively. These are as follows.

The "Multinational" Firm. A "multinational" firm is one in which subsidiaries are distinct entities allowed to be very responsive to their local environments.[10] In a sense, the home office of the "multinational" firm manages a portfolio of very distinct subsidiaries. Bartlett and Ghoshal refer to this structure as a "decentralized federation," and it is traditionally associated with European MNEs. These authors consider this structure to be very good at delivering local responsiveness, but lacking in the areas of global efficiency and innovation.

The Global Firm. A global firm is one in which subsidiaries are little more than means to deliver uniform goods and services to local markets. The home office of the global firm is very important in planning the realization of global economies of scale and scope. Bartlett and Ghoshal refer to this structure as a "centralized hub," and it is traditionally associated with Japanese MNEs. The centralized hub structure is very good at delivering global efficiency; it is less effective in the areas of local responsiveness and global innovation.

The International Firm. The international firm pursues a strategy "based primarily on transferring and adapting the parent company's knowledge and expertise to foreign markets. The parent retains considerable influence and control, but less than in a classic global company; national units can adopt products and ideas coming from the center, but have less independence and autonomy than 'multinational' subsidiaries" Bartlett and Ghoshal refer to this structure as a "coordinated federation," and it is traditionally associated with U.S.–based MNEs. The coor-

---

[10]To distinguish Bartlett and Ghoshal's concept of a "multinational" firm from our more general notion of a multinational enterprise (MNE), we use quotation marks around the former.

dinated federation structure is very good at delivering global innovation but not local responsiveness and global efficiency.

As we mentioned at the beginning of this section, Bartlett and Ghoshal claim that global efficiency, local responsiveness, and global innovation are *all* important for MNEs in the modern world economy.[11] Consequently, these authors argue in favor of a transnational model of global management that they describe as a "flexible centralization/coordination" or as an "integrated network." The model is really one of a "new mentality," but we can characterize it in three ways. First, the role of subsidiaries is differentiated throughout the multinational value network, differing among countries. One subsidiary might only be involved in sales, while another subsidiary is involved in R&D. As shown in Table 11.1, certain product lines might be centered outside of the home base.

Second, coordination of the multinational value network is achieved using multiple methods: Flows of goods are coordinated through centralization; flows or resources are coordinated through formalization; and flows of information are coordinated through socialization.[12] In the last case, socialization, Bartlett and Ghoshal advocate the rotation of personnel throughout the value network in order to facilitate information flows within the social networks that develop. For example, the Japanese MNE Matsushita moves its engineers from central R&D to applied R&D, and then to line production. As another example, Stryker Medical Equipment rotates sales staff from subsidiaries to its corporate headquarters in the

Table 11.1 Examples of Multi-Home-Based MNEs

Firm	Home Country	Business Segment	Home Base
Phillips	Netherlands	X-ray tubes	Germany
Sandvik	Sweden	Process systems	Germany
ABB	Switzerland/Sweden	HVDC transmission	Sweden
ABB	Switzerland/Sweden	Turbines	Germany
Electrolux	Sweden	Washing machines	Italy
Nestlé	Switzerland	Candies	United Kingdom
Xerox	United States	Color copiers	Japan

Source: Sölvell, Ö, and Zander, I (1995). "Organization of the Dynamic Multinational Enterprise." *International Studies of Management and Organization* 25 (1-2): 26. Reprinted with permission.

---

[11]For example, in the financial services industry, Dicken (1998) observes: "all the transnational financial service firms are now basing their strategy on a direct presence in each of the major geographical markets and *on providing a local service based on global resources*" (p. 410, emphasis added).
[12]Again, there are traditions here: Japanese MNEs traditionally rely on centralization; U.S. MNEs traditionally rely on formalization; and European MNEs traditionally rely on socialization.

United States so that they can develop social ties to those persons involved in product development and manufacturing.

Third, the disparate elements of the MNE are tied together in a coherent mission through the use of vision and innovative human resource development policies. For example Andersen Consulting utilizes a "one-firm concept" based on a "Method 1" consulting model. These approaches are communicated to all Andersen employees as they pass through the firm's St. Charles educational center outside of the city of Chicago. Consequently, "any consultant from any country can step into any project in any country, and will immediately understand the 'language' that is spoken, the methodology that is used and the stage in the problem-solving process that is reached" (Moulaert, 1996, p. 85).[13]

Whatever the reader's assessment of Bartlett and Ghoshal's advocated approach to multinational management, their identification of the local-global paradox helps us to put the Porter diamond in some context. In fact, Sölvell and Zander (1995) stress two schools of thought on MNEs typified by Porter, on the one hand, and Bartlett and Ghoshal,on the other:

> *Today two schools of thought seem to be developing within the context of the MNE as a global learning vehicle. One line of thought originates from a strategic and environmental perspective of how MNEs develop and sustain international competitive advantage. Porter . . . (stresses) the importance of the home base of the MNE in the process of upgrading competitive advantage. . . . The second line of thought . . . (originates) from the field of organization and management of the MNE. . . . A common theme in these models is that the MNE builds increasingly complex organizational structures and management processes in order to cope with a more complex international environment and to combine global integration and local differentiation (p. 18).*

Sölvell and Zander refer to these two models as home-based and heterarchical, respectively. These authors stress that the two models have a common ground, however, to be found in the role of knowledge transmission through social means. They state:

> *It is striking that two such opposing models also share a common ground in perhaps the most important issue: the mechanisms for fluid exchange of information and upgrading of competitive advantage which cannot be easily imitated by "outsiders". . . . In the home-based model, the mechanisms are related to the country or regional level, whereas in the heterarchical MNE they are related to the organizational level, linking diverse influences from around the world through corporate culture (p. 32).*

Indeed, one could go further to argue that knowledge is a crucial component of the ownership or *O* advantages in Dunning's OLI framework discussed in Chapter 10. Thus, knowledge is an important connection among the OLI framework, the Porter diamond, spatial clusters, and the transnational model. It is also a component of the resource seeking, market seeking, effi-

---

[13]Andersen Consulting has recently been renamed *Accenture*. See their new Web site at http://www.accenture.com.

ciency seeking, and strategic asset seeking motivations we discussed in the first section of this chapter. Therefore, any understanding of the role of MNEs in the modern world economy must include an understanding of the development, transmission, and application of knowledge.

Cultural Issues

Another difficulty faced by MNEs in operating internationally is culture. Adler (2002) makes a strong case that cross-cultural business activities typically tend toward either highly effective outcomes or highly ineffective outcomes.[14] Managing these sorts of relationships can involve a search for **cultural synergy**. Adler uses the diagram presented in Figure 11.4 to illustrate this. An MNE that imposes its own national or business culture on its foreign subsidiaries is guilty of cultural dominance. As she notes, "Historically, companies having considerably more power than their counterparts—based on larger size, more advanced technology, or more significant financial resources—have often used the dominance approach" (p. 113). The opposite approach is cultural accommodation, where the MNE tries to blend into their host country culture at all costs. This approach is effective in many circumstances, but cannot leverage cultural differences to commercial advantage.

Cultural avoidance is a third option in which both the MNE and its hosts pretend as if there were no cultural differences. This is a short-term option but is a very weak base on which to build long-term business relationships across cultures. A more positive approach is cultural compromise in which the MNE and its partners meet each other halfway, sometimes

> **Cultural synergy**
> The possibility of workers within a multinational enterprise developing means to turn cultural differences into assets by identifying complementarities among cultures.

Figure 11.4 The Search for Cultural Synergies

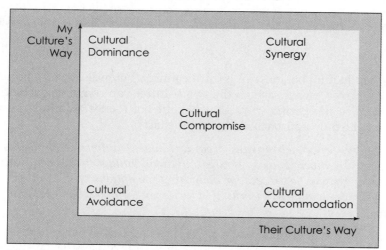

Source: *From Boston to Beijing: Managing with a World View*, 1st Edition, by Adler. © 2002. Reprinted with permission of South-Western, a division of Thomson Learning.

---

[14]See also Cox (1993).

Cross-Cultural Communicative Competence: A Path to Cultural Synergy

Tom is an energetic "Anglo-American" from a top business school. He is a man with a keen sense of responsibility and describes himself as an "intense and passionate person" who, when faced with a task, likes to "give it his all." Having grown up in a family of small business managers, he has been entrusted with significant responsibilities from a very young age. He explains that, if you want to be a successful manager, you have to be a "self-motivated" and "self-directed" person. You have to make sure that you have done everything in your power to meet the needs of current or prospective clients, and this might mean going "above and beyond the call of duty."

With all of these skills, Tom spent a summer as a business consultant on a Native American reservation. Although initially considering this to be a domestic assignment, it turned out to be more of an "inter-national" challenge. To his surprise, he found that many features of the Native American context were nothing like his own cultural milieu. There were two broad areas where he continuously experienced a "disruption" of his expectations. One of these two areas concerned behavioral etiquette. For example, in meetings, his Native American counterparts did not wish to move into action as quickly as he would have liked. Instead, they tended to talk about issues that appeared to him to be of a philosophical nature, claiming that, if one is unclear about the "deeper purpose" of a task, carrying out that task could have unintended, and possibly negative consequences. This, in Tom's view, inhibited his "giving it his all," something that frustrated him greatly in the first half of the summer.

A second area of disruption in expectations concerned points of view. For example, in one business project, there was resistance to his proposal for an "active manager" and mis-understandings regarding the role of profit. In another project, there were different values concerning the role of small businesses. Tom was surprised that the Native Americans favored large business to small, not realizing that his counterparts associated small businesses with white-owned "trading posts" where they had felt exploited in the past.

Tom slowly began to realize that the way things are done in the Native American context differ significantly from the Anglo-American cultural context that he was used to. He lacked the frame of reference for interpreting what he encountered in this new context. Without an

literally, conducting business in a third country. Potentially more positive still is to look for ways in which the two cultures can reinforce each other or compromise in specific ways that benefit both sides. While stressing that is not the only approach, Adler notes that:

> The synergy approach creates organizational solutions to problems by using cultural diversity as a resource and an advantage to the organization. . . . It is a systematic process for increasing the options open to executives, managers, and employees working in increasingly global business environments (p. 117).

How does an international manager create cultural synergy? One path to cultural synergy appears to involve what Gelaye Debebe, in the box, calls "cross-cultural communicative competence." Cross-cultural communicative competence refers to the process of acquiring knowledge of the culture and locality in question so as to build on similarities and address differences in novel and task-appropriate ways. In the advertisement understanding of the local milieu, his ideas and behaviors were misplaced, inappropriate, and resisted. Consequently, his actions proved to be ineffective during the first half of his summer assignment.

To work more effectively in this new context, Tom began to employ three categories of practices: calibrating, progressing, and summarizing. Calibrating involves assessing the relevance of one's perspectives in a new setting in such a way that these are not imposed on business partners. One calibrating practice is probing. Probing involves stating one's perspective lightly, while assessing others' receptivity, and making adjustments based on the observed response. Another calibrating practice is suppressing one's views when sensing that partners from another culture are genuinely not receptive for their own cultural and historical reasons. Progressing involves eliciting information and explanations to build on one's understanding of the relevant business and cultural issues. One progressing practice is stating explicitly one's point of departure. Another progressing practice is asking questions that open up a deeper exploration of a particular issue. Summarizing involves taking stock of the main issues along the way, allowing cross-cultural partners to focus on potential areas of disagreement so that areas of agreement can be identified and misunderstandings can be avoided.

Relying on these three practices, Tom found that he became much more effective in working with his Native American counterparts. Consequently, the second half of the summer was much more productive than the first half of the summer.

Tom's experience illustrates the use of cross-cultural communicative competence as a path to cultural synergy. It also demonstrates that such competence might well be required of a manager who wishes to have his or her business and technological expertise utilized abroad. International managers must often assume the role of active learner as opposed to business/technology expert. The key challenge is to identify the appropriate practices to make this possible. Calibrating, progressing, and summarizing practices are three places for international managers to start on the path to cultural synergy.

Source: Written by Gelaye Debebe, George Washington University

quoted earlier in this chapter, Citibank claims that "being global means being completely local." Similarly, Debebe suggests that the practice of cross-cultural communicative competence requires that managers understand the context in which cross-cultural business interactions take place. This is no small achievement, but one that more and more of us need to accomplish in the modern world economy.

Conclusion

The role of home (and perhaps foreign) bases in multinational value networks can be understood in terms of the Porter diamond and its emphasis on factor conditions, demand conditions, related and supporting industries, and firm strategy, structure, and rivalry. Related and supporting industries in flexible manufacturing systems give rise to the phenomenon of spatial clusters and their supporting milieux. The paradox between the local emphasis of both the Porter diamond and the spatial clusters and the global emphasis of the OLI framework can be analyzed in terms of the problem of multinational management. Here, the concerns of global efficiency, local responsiveness, and global innovation are simultaneously relevant. It is also apparent that the local-global paradox can be resolved through the lens of knowledge and its social character. Finally, although other options exist, the cultural differences among countries in which MNEs operate can be best addressed through the search for cultural synergies.

Review Exercises

1. What is the difference between a basic factor of production and an advanced factor of production? What is the difference between a generalized factor of production and a specialized factor of production? According to Porter, what roles do specialized, advanced factors play in international competitiveness?

2. What is the relationship between the content of this chapter and that of Chapters 2 and 3? More specifically, what is the relationship between the ideas of this chapter (e.g., the Porter diamond, spatial clusters, and the transnational firm) and the role of technology in generating absolute and comparative advantage?

3. Do you have any experience of operating in a foreign country that illustrates the difficulties of working abroad? What are they?

4. In our discussion of the surgical instrument cluster in Pakistan, we raised the issue of child labor. In your view, is this a cultural issue to which an international manager must be sensitive, or is it a violation of global norms that the manager should confront head on?

Further Reading and Web Resources

To understand why the concept of "competitiveness" should not be applied to countries, see Krugman (1994) and Chapter 1 of Porter (1990). John et al. (1997) is a useful reference, especially in the area of global management. Two key books in the realm of international business are Bartlett and Ghoshal (2002) and Porter (1990). The links between economic geography and international business are well developed by Dicken (1998), and the links between political economy and international business are creatively explored by Ruigrok and van Tulder (1995). For a specific focus on spatial clustering, see Malmberg, Sölvell, and Zander (1996) and Porter (1998). For applications of spatial clustering to developing countries, see Van Dijk and Rabellotti (1997). Finally, Adler (2002) offers an excellent overview of managing across cultures. Don't forget to read Adler's Chapter 10 on "Global Careers."

An important journal covering the subjects of this chapter is the *Journal of International Business Studies.*

The reader with an interest in the subject matter of this chapter should consult the Web site maintained by the Competitiveness Institute, an organization based in Barcelona, Spain. The Web site is **http://www.competitiveness.org**. Be sure to visit their page entitled "About Competitiveness," which contains a list of references. Michael Porter's Institute for Strategy and Competitiveness can be found at **http://www.isc.hbs.edu**.

References

Adler, N. (2002) *From Boston to Beijing: Managing with a World View*, South-Western, Cincinnati.

Bartlett, C.A., and S. Ghoshal (2002) *Managing Across Borders: The Transnational Solution*, Harvard Business School Press, Boston, Massachusetts.

Battat, J., I. Frank, and X. Shen (1996) *Suppliers to Multinationals: Linkage Programs to Strengthen Local Companies in Developing Countries*, Foreign Investment Advisory Service Occasional Paper 6, The World Bank, Washington, DC.

Cox, T. (1993) *Cultural Diversity in Organizations*, Berrett-Koehler, San Francisco.

de Mooij, M. (1998) *Global Marketing and Advertising: Understanding Cultural Paradoxes*, Sage, Thousand Oaks, California.

Dicken, P. (1998) *Global Shift: Transforming the World Economy*, Guilford, New York.

John, R., G. Ietto-Gillies, H. Cox, and N. Grimwade (1997) *Global Business Strategy*, International Thompson Business Press, London.

Kapur, D., and R. Ramamurti (2001) "India's Emerging Competitive Advantage in Services," *Academy of Management Executive*, 15:2, 20–31.

Kogut, B., and U. Zander (1992) "Knowledge of the Firm, Combinative Capabilities, and the Replication of Technology," *Organizational Science*, 3:3, 383–397.

Krugman, P. (1994) "Competitiveness: A Dangerous Obsession," *Foreign Affairs*, March/April, 28–44.

Malmberg, A., Ö. Sölvell, and I. Zander (1996) "Spatial Clustering, Local Accumulation of Knowledge and Firm Competitiveness," *Geografiska Annaler*, 76B:2, 85–97.

Mankiw, N.G. (2004) *Principles of Economics*, South-Western/Thomson Learning, Mason, Ohio.

Moulaert, F. (1996) "Arthur Andersen: From National Accountancy to International Management Consultancy Firm," in Nilsson, J.E., P. Dicken, and J. Peck (eds.), *The Internationalization Process: European Firms in Global Competition*, Paul Chapman Publishing, London, 74–89.

Nadvi, K. (1999) "Shifting Ties: Social Networks in the Surgical Instrument Cluster of Sialkot, Pakistan," *Development and Change*, 30:1, 141–175.

Porter, M.E. (1990) *The Competitive Advantage of Nations*, The Free Press, New York.

Porter, M.E. (1998) "Clusters and the New Economics of Competition," *Harvard Business Review*, November–December, 77–90.

Reinert, K.A. (1998) "Whither the Linkage Concept? External Economies and Firm Networks," *Science, Technology and Development*, 16:3, 77–91.

Ruigrok, W. and R. van Tulder (1995) *The Logic of International Restructuring*, Routledge, London.

Scott, A.J. (1995) "The Geographical Foundations of Industrial Performance," *Competition and Change*, 1:1, 51–66.

Sölvell, Ö., and I. Zander (1995) "Organization of the Dynamic Multinational Enterprise," *International Studies of Management and Organization*, 25:1-2, 17–38.

Storper, M. (1992) "The Limits to Globalization: Technology Districts and International Trade," *Economic Geography*, 68:1, 60–93.

Van Dijk, M.P., and R. Rabellotti (eds.) (1997) *Enterprise Clusters and Networks in Developing Countries*, Frank Cass, London.

Waldron, D.G. (1997) "Taiwan: An 'Omnidimensional' Regional Operations Center?" *Journal of Developing Areas*, 32:1, 53–70.

Interview: Sanjaya Lall

Sanjaya Lall is Professor of Development Economics at the University of Oxford. In the past, he held a number of positions at the World Bank, including Senior Economist. Professor Lall holds an M. Phil. degree in economics from St. John's College, Oxford, and has published extensively on a wide variety of economic topics, most notably, the role of multinational enterprises in the world economy. He has acted as consultant to numerous organizations, including the United Nations Industrial Development Organization, the United Nations Conference on Trade and Development, the International Labor Organization, the United Nations Development Program, and the Organization for Economic Cooperation and Development, as well as various governments.[1]

How did your interest in multinational enterprises develop?

I started to work on foreign direct investment in the late 1960s when UNCTAD asked me to direct a study of the balance-of-payments impact of FDI in selected developing countries. In a few years, the development literature had moved on from looking at "foreign direct investment" in generic terms to looking at "multinationals" or "transnationals" as the main analytical category of interest.

What have been the main themes in your research on the role of multinational enterprises in the world economy?

The main theme has been technology: technology transfer and development, technology and competitiveness and effects on local research and development.

Can you summarize the most important ways in which international production structures have change during the last two decades?

One can describe six such changes:

1. *They are subject to far more rapid technical change, reducing the scope for the economical use of older or intermediate technologies.*

---

[1] A full list reads as follows: UNIDO, UNCTAD, ILO, UNDP, ECLA, ESCAP, the Commonwealth Secretariat, ADB, IDB, OECD, EU and various governments.

2. *Falling transport and communication costs have integrated them much more closely than before, making international competitiveness of greater importance to survival and growth.*
3. *Falling communication costs have also raised the minimum efficient size of the firm, making it possible for multinational corporations to manage larger and more far-flung operations efficiently.*
4. *Production and trade are organized differently. Local value chains are more dominated by global value chains. Global chains are more hierarchically organized, and many have fewer lead players. In technologically advanced activities, the lead players are MNEs that dominate innovation and marketing.*
5. *Lead MNEs in global value chains increasingly spread their production and service activities across the globe to minimize costs and maximize flexibility, logistical effectiveness, and delivery. They also spread innovation to take advantage of local capabilities and innovation centers.*
6. *These integrated MNE systems are not closed. They include a surrounding core of related MNEs, which tend to invest alongside lead companies, and a larger envelope of suppliers and service providers that includes local firms in host countries. However, to break into the MNE systems requires high levels of skill and technological competence, and there is growing diversion within the developing world in terms of "insiders" and "outsiders." A handful of East Asian economies and Mexico are the insiders; a few others like India and Brazil are on the periphery; and many others are complete outsiders.*

Your writings have cast some doubt on the contribution of market liberalization to the process of economic development. Can you explain your concerns?

Exposure to free market forces requires advanced capabilities to compete. These capabilities have to be built in developing countries—simple exposure to free trade and capital or information flows is not enough to ensure that they will be built. The argument for free trade and liberalization rests on very particular assumptions about the availability of technology and (more importantly) the ability of countries to use imported technology effectively. In effect, the proponents of rapid and sweeping liberalization assume that there are no costs, risks, effort or market failures involved in using new technologies efficiently. Once this assumption is discarded, it becomes obvious that countries have to be helped to become efficient. Liberalization may provide the incentive to become efficient, but in the presence of market and institutional failures it does not provide the support needed by firms in developing countries.

Consequently, I believe that liberalization in some form is very desirable but that it should be introduced carefully and in tandem with supply side measures to build local capabilities. The pace of liberalization should be geared to learning and restructuring needs. After all, the developed countries have given themselves decades to restructure their textile and apparel industries to meet low-wage competition—and they have massive skill, and financial and technological resources at their disposal. Surely developing countries that have painfully built up some industrial capabilities should be given the time (and the resources) to do something similar before they are made to face open competition?

A number of observers have called for a multinational agreement on investment (MAI) to be part of the World Trade Organization. The purpose of the MAI would be to extend WTO-supervised liberalization beyond international trade in goods and services to foreign direct investment. What is your assessment of this proposal?

I think the MAI should be kept separate from the WTO. It raises different concerns and calls for different tools than trade, and WTO may not have the expertise or the mind-set to deal adequately with the issues.

Some of your writings address the "creation of competitive advantage." Can you tell our readers what you mean by this concept?

The "creation of comparative advantage" is meant to deal with the dynamics of export competitiveness. There is a need to create something when free market forces will not by themselves guide resources into activities of long-term economic benefit. This can happen in trade when the factors needed to compete in the future (with rising wages and in the face of rapidly changing technologies) will not be created in developing countries with free markets. This will be the case when there are market failures in the creation of new technological knowledge and capabilities, skills, institutions, networks, and so on.

There may be many causes of such market failures: scale economies, noncompetitive markets, externalities, incomplete or missing markets, uncertainty, and cumulativeness. In fact, underdevelopment is defined precisely by such market failures. Their interaction can lead to a "low level equilibrium" from which countries find it impossible to break out. They then have to take deliberate action to create new comparative advantages that raise them to a different growth trajectory.

Part 3

Windows on the World Economy: International Finance

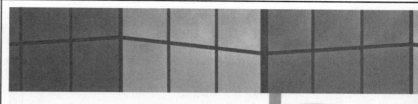

12 Accounting Frameworks

In this chapter, you begin to develop your understanding of our third window on the world economy, international finance. Recall from Chapter 1 that, whereas international trade refers to the exchange of merchandise and services among the countries of the world, international finance refers to the exchange of *assets* among the countries of the world. Recall also that the global exchange of assets in the world economy has at times been nearly 100 times larger than the exchange of merchandise and services. This is why international finance is such an important subject.

There is a basic principle in economics that can be crudely stated as "things add up." In the realm of international economics, this principle is a very important one. If you forget it, you can find yourself making claims that are simply incorrect. If you remember the principle and know how to use it, you will have a powerful tool in your hands for analyzing economies and their relationships to the world economy. The consideration of the way "things add up" takes us into the realm of economic accounting, the subject of this chapter. This might not be the most exciting subject to every reader, but it is nonetheless important. We will take a simple approach to the accounting issue, and the insights you will gain will be crucial to your understanding of the world economy.

We will begin with a consideration of open-economy accounts, taking as our starting point the circular flow diagram. Next, we will consider the balance of payments as a more detailed look at one important relationship of the open-economy accounts. For the interested reader, we consider the subject of accounting matrices in Appendix 1 of this chapter. Appendix 2 presents a simple open-economy macroeconomic model.

Open-Economy Accounts

Circular flow diagram
A graphical representation of the flow of incomes and expenditures in an economy. It involves Firm, Household, Government, Capital, and Rest of the World accounts.

Open-economy accounts
The accounting identities derived from the firm, household, government, capital, and rest of the world accounts of the circular flow diagram.

In your introductory economics course, it is very likely that you came across a graphical description of an economy called the **circular flow diagram**. We are going to use this diagram to initiate our analysis of **open-economy accounts**.[1] We want to view an economy as being aggregated into one giant sector. To make things more concrete, let's take the example of Mexico.[2] To begin, we treat the Mexican economy as being composed of two accounts: a Firm account and a Household account. The relationships between these

---

[1] The circular flow diagram is described in Chapter 2 of Mankiw (2004).
[2] For continuity in your exploration of international finance, we will use Mexico as an example through Chapters 13, 14, and 15.

two accounts are summarized as a circular flow diagram of a simple, closed economy in Figure 12.1. The term "closed" here refers to the absence of any trade and financial interactions with the world economy. In Figure 12.1, the production process of the Firm generates income that accrues to the Household. This income is denoted as Y and consists of wages, salaries, and payments for the use of property assets. Given the simple assumptions of this chapter, Y is also equal to both the nominal **gross national product (GNP)** and the nominal **gross domestic product (GDP)** of Mexico. The consumption process of the household generates consumption expenditures that accrue to the Firm. This consumption is denoted as C.

Figure 12.1 is exceedingly simple and begs for more realism. For our purposes in this chapter, we need to add three new accounts. The first we will call Capital. This account acts as a **financial intermediary** in the savings-investment process. These financial intermediaries are composed of institutions such as banks, mutual funds, and brokers that receive funds from savers and use these funds to make loans or buy assets, thereby placing the funds in the hands of investors. The term "capital" used here does not refer to physical capital such as machinery and buildings. Instead, it refers to income not consumed, which is available for use in investment. The second new account is Government, and the third is Rest of the World. The Rest of the World account captures the interactions of the Mexican economy with the other countries of the world.

Including these three new institutions results in a circular flow diagram for an open economy with government, savings, and investment. This is illustrated in Figure 12.2. As in Figure 12.1, the production process of the Firm generates income that accrues to the Household. Now, however, the Household has three types of expenditures. The first of these is consumption of goods and services, C. The second expenditure type is household savings, denoted S_H. Through the work of financial intermediaries, Household savings accrues as income to the Capital account. The third expenditure is taxes paid to the government and is denoted T.[3] Government makes two alternative expenditures: government spending (denoted G) and government savings (denoted S_G). In many cases, government savings are negative (a government deficit), and the flow is reversed,

Gross national product (GNP)
The value of all final goods and services produced by a country's factors of production during a year.

Gross domestic product (GDP)
The value of all final goods and services produced within a country's borders during a year.

Financial intermediary
Financial institutions such as banks, mutual funds, and brokers that receive funds from savers and use these funds to make loans or buy assets, thereby placing the funds in the hands of investors.

Figure 12.1 A Circular Flow Diagram for a Simple, Closed Economy

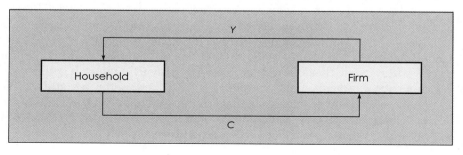

---

[3] To simplify matters for ourselves, we ignore corporate taxes.

Figure 12.2 An Open Economy with Government, Savings, and Investment

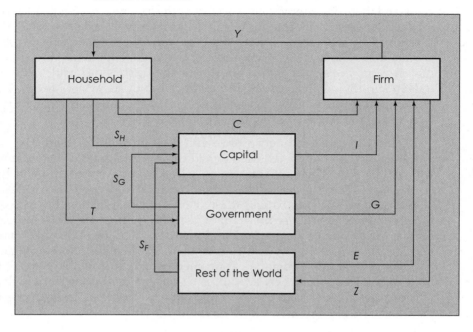

from Capital to Government. You can treat these cases as a negative S_G. Finally, Capital has a single expenditure, I, which consists of funds provided to firms for investment purposes.

The Rest of the World interacts with the Mexican economy in three ways. First, the Rest of the World makes an expenditure that accrues to the Firm account in the form of its purchases of Mexico's exports. We denote these total exports as E. Second, the Rest of the World receives income in the form of Mexico's purchases of imports. We denote these total imports as Z. Finally, the Rest of the World makes an expenditure that accrues to Capital in the form of **foreign savings**, denoted S_F.

Foreign savings
An inflow of funds into an economy from the rest of the world. It occurs when foreign investors buy the assets of the economy in question.

To begin your understanding of the open economy, we are going to focus on the Capital and Rest of the World accounts of Figure 12.2. Let's consider the Capital account first. The Capital account has one expenditure, depicted by an arrow leaving the Capital box in Figure 12.2. This is the expenditure on domestic investment. The Capital account also has three types of receipts, depicted by arrows entering the Capital box. These are all savings flows, namely, household, government, and foreign savings. The first two of these, household and government savings, together give us domestic savings. In the introduction to this chapter, we stated that a basic principle of economics is that "things add up." The application of this principle here is that expenditures must equal receipts for the Capital account.[4] Expressing this as an equation gives us:

---

[4] Reinert and Roland-Holst (1997) state: "Economic accounting is based on a fundamental principle of economics: For every income or receipt there is a corresponding expenditure or outlay" (p. 95).

$$\text{Expenditure} = \text{Receipts}$$

Or

$$I = (S_H + S_G) + S_F$$

In words:

$$\text{Domestic Investment} = \text{Domestic Savings} + \text{Foreign Savings}$$

It will be helpful to rearrange this equation by subtracting domestic savings from both sides. This gives us:

Domestic Investment – Domestic Savings = Foreign Savings **Capital account**

The fact that "things add up" for the Capital account implies that any gap between domestic investment and domestic savings is made up for by an inflow of foreign savings. We will discuss this further in just a moment.

Next, let's turn our attention to the Rest of the World account. This account has two expenditures, depicted by arrows leaving the Rest of the World box in Figure 12.2. These expenditures are Mexico's exports and foreign savings. The Rest of the World account also has a single receipt in the form of Mexico's imports, depicted by an arrow entering the Rest of the World Box. The equation expressing the equality between expenditures and receipts for the Rest of the World account is

$$E + S_F = Z$$

In words:

Exports + Foreign Savings = Imports **ROW account**

It will be helpful to rearrange this equation by subtracting exports from both sides. This gives us:

Foreign Savings = Imports – Exports **ROW account**

Or

Foreign Savings = Trade Deficit **ROW account**

The fact that "things add up" for the Rest of the World account implies that any gap between imports and exports (any trade deficit) has a counterpart in and inflow of foreign savings. We will discuss this further in just a moment.

Take a look at the Capital account and Rest of the World equations. Notice that both of these equations have foreign savings on one side. This means that we can combine them into a single relationship that we will call the **fundamental accounting equation** for open economies. This equation is

Domestic Investment – Domestic Savings = Foreign Savings = Trade Deficit

The fundamental accounting equation is also written in a different form, obtained by multiplying it by the number -1. This form is

Domestic Savings – Domestic Investment = Foreign Investment = Trade Balance

Depending on the source, you might find these fundamental accounting equations expressed in either form. They are so important to your

Fundamental accounting equations
Derived from the circular flow diagram, it appears in two forms. The first is Domestic Investment – Domestic Savings = Foreign Savings = Trade Deficit. The second is Domestic Savings – Domestic Investment = Foreign Investment = Trade Balance.

understanding of the world economy that we are going to put them in a box for you to remember:[5]

> ### Fundamental Accounting Equations
>
> Domestic Investment – Domestic Savings = Foreign Savings = Trade Deficit
>
> Domestic Savings – Domestic Investment = Foreign Investment = Trade Balance

What do the fundamental accounting equations tell us? Let us study them very carefully with the help of Table 12.1. There are two cases to consider, one for each equation. First, suppose that Mexico's domestic investment exceeds its domestic savings. This case is explained by the first boxed equation. The shortfall in domestic savings is made up for by a positive inflow of foreign savings. Then, according to the first equation, there must be a trade deficit. Does this make sense? A trade deficit means that the Mexican economy is importing more merchandise and services in value terms than it is exporting. Therefore, Mexico must sell something other than merchandise and services to the rest of the world to make up the difference. This "something else" turns out to be assets: government and corporate bonds, corporate equities, and even real estate. The purchase of Mexican assets by the Rest of the World is the very thing that generates the inflow of foreign savings into Mexico. The first equation therefore makes sense.

Table 12.1 Domestic Savings, Domestic Investment, Foreign Savings, and the Trade Balance

Domestic Investment and Domestic Savings	Foreign Savings	Trade Balance	Explanation
Domestic investment exceeds domestic savings.	Foreign savings is positive.	Trade deficit	Domestic savings is too small to finance domestic investment. Therefore, the country requires an inflow of foreign savings to make up the difference. This inflow of foreign savings finances the trade deficit.
Domestic savings exceeds domestic investment.	Foreign savings is negative or foreign investment is positive.	Trade surplus	Domestic savings exceeds the requirements of domestic investment. Therefore, the country lends the difference to the Rest of the World. This outflow of foreign investment generates a trade surplus.

---

[5] International economist Paul Krugman (1996) writes of "the disturbingly difficult ideas of people who know how to read national accounts or understand that the trade balance is also the difference between savings and investment" (p. ix). You are now one of these people.

Next, suppose that Mexico's domestic savings exceeds its domestic investment. This case is explained by the second boxed equation. An excess of domestic savings generates a positive outflow of foreign investment by Mexico. Then, according to the second equation, there must be a trade surplus. Does this make sense? A trade surplus means that the Mexican economy is exporting more merchandise and services in value terms than it is importing. Therefore, Mexico must buy something other than merchandise and services from the rest of the world to make up the difference. That "something else" again is assets. The purchase of foreign assets by Mexico generates the outflow of foreign investment to the Rest of the World. The second equation also makes sense.

Let's summarize what you have learned in this section. The fundamental accounting equations relate domestic investment, domestic savings, and the trade deficit or surplus. These equations tell us that a trade deficit will be associated with an excess of domestic investment over domestic savings. Alternatively, a trade surplus will be associated with an excess of domestic savings over domestic investment. The fundamental equation provides a link between Mexico's interactions with the Rest of the World (the trade balance) and Mexico's economic aggregates of domestic investment and domestic savings. The link between the two is foreign savings. If domestic saving falls short of investment, the gap is made up for with foreign savings, which we know is associated with a trade deficit. If domestic saving exceeds domestic investment, the excess is lent abroad. This negative foreign savings is associated with a trade surplus.

The field of international finance is concerned with the *international* aspects of economies as aggregate entities. Therefore, a focus is placed on the Rest of the World account equation in the form of a more detailed set of accounts known as the balance of payments accounts. We take up these important accounts next.

The Balance of Payments Accounts

The **balance of payments** accounts of any country focus on the relationship of the country with the Rest of the World. Recall from the previous section that the open-economy accounts were divided into five subaccounts: Firm; Household; Capital; Government; and Rest of World. The purpose of the balance of payments accounts is to examine in more detail the final, Rest of World account. Given this purpose, let's begin our examination of the balance of payments accounts with the Rest of World account from the open-economy accounts. More specifically, let's return to the Rest of the World equation:

> **Balance of payments**
> A detailed set of economic accounts focusing on the transactions between a country and the rest of the world. Two important subaccounts are the current account and the capital account.

$$\text{Foreign Savings} = \text{Trade Deficit} \qquad \textbf{ROW account}$$

It will be much easier for your understanding of the balance of payments accounts if we subtract the trade deficit from both sides of this equation, rearranging it to read:

$$\text{Trade Balance} + \text{Foreign Savings} = 0 \qquad \textbf{Balance of payments}$$

This equation is in the form of:

Current Account + Capital Account = 0   **Balance of payments**

Capital account
A subsection of the balance of payments recording transactions between a country and the world economy that involve the exchange of assets.

The second term of the balance of payments equations is the **capital account** of the balance of payments.[6] It records the net balance of transactions *involving the exchange of assets* between Mexico and the Rest of the World. Recall from the previous section that, when foreign savings is positive, there is a net positive purchase of Mexican assets by investors in the Rest of the World. This net purchase of Mexican assets by foreign investors is the means by which the inflow of foreign savings takes place. When foreign savings is positive, there is a capital account surplus; when foreign savings is negative (foreign investment is positive), there is a capital account deficit.

Current account
A subsection of the balance of payments recording nonofficial transactions between a country and the world economy that do not involve the exchange of assets.

The first term of the balance of payments equations is the **current account** of the balance of payments. It records the net balance of transactions between Mexico and the rest of the world *not involving the exchange of assets*. In Figure 12.2, the current account consists of only trade transactions and is equal to the trade balance. However, as we will see, in practice, the current account includes more items than exports and imports.

The usefulness of the balance of payments equations is as follows. They tell us that a current account surplus must be accompanied by a capital account deficit. Conversely, a current account deficit must be accompanied by a capital account surplus. Let us summarize these results as follows:

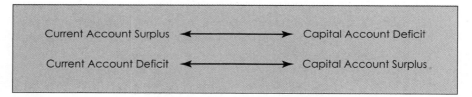

Current Account Surplus ⟷ Capital Account Deficit

Current Account Deficit ⟷ Capital Account Surplus

Having understood the balance of payments relationships, you are a step ahead of many observers of the modern world economy. Without mentioning names, let us take up one example. A common allegation on the part of authors concerned about the place of the United States and Europe in the world economy is that the future lies in low-wage countries (a) attracting the bulk of world financial capital, and (b) running large trade surpluses. There is a logical fallacy here, though. Attracting the bulk of world capital implies that the countries will have capital account surpluses, and running large trade surpluses implies that the countries will have current account surpluses. We now know that this is impossible. The lesson here is that understanding some basic relationships in international finance can protect us from saying and writing silly things![7]

---

[6] There is a potential point of confusion here. The open-economy accounts depicted in Figure 12.2 have a capital account, and so does the balance of payments accounts. What is the connection? Both accounts involve the exchange of *assets*, and that is why they share the same name.
[7] For more on this, see the various chapters of Krugman (1996).

We have stated that the purpose of the balance of payments accounts is to examine *in more detail* the Rest of the World account of the open-economy accounts discussed in the previous section. It is now time to turn to these details. We will do this with the help of Table 12.2, a sample balance of payments. This table gives the approximate balance of payments accounts for Mexico in the year 1993. The year 1993 was chosen for a reason: It is the last year before the Mexican balance of payments crisis in 1994. (We will refer to this table in Chapter 17 and in Chapter 21.)

The first section of the balance of payments is known as the current account and includes items 1 through 6 of Table 12.2. Some of these items are reported in gross terms, some in net terms, and one as a major balance.[8] We will consider them one at a time. Item 1 we have met earlier: It is the total Mexican exports. It is reported in gross terms as US$61 billion. Item 2 is also familiar to us: It is total Mexican imports. It is also reported in gross

Table 12.2 Mexican Balance of Payments, 1993 (Billions of U.S. Dollars)

Item	Gross	Net	Major Balance
Current Account			
1. Exports	61		
2. Imports	77		
3. Trade balance		−16	
4. Net factor receipts		−11	
5. Transfers		4	
6. Current account balance			−23
Capital Account			
7. Direct investment		4	
8. Portfolio investment		29	
9. Official reserves balance		−7	
10. Errors and omissions		−3	
11. Capital account balance			23
12. Overall balance			0

Source: Based on data in the *International Financial Statistics Yearbook*, published by the International Monetary Fund in 1994.

---

[8] Items reported in *gross* terms record the inflow or outflow separately. Items reported in *net* terms record the difference between the inflow and the outflow.

terms and has a value of $77 billion. Item 3 is the trade balance and is reported in net terms. In 1993, Mexico had a trade balance of –$16 billion or a trade deficit of $16 billion. Item 3 is the first term of the balance of payments equation. In the simple context of that equation, the trade balance corresponded to the current account balance. In the balance of payments accounts, however, there are more details to consider.

Items 4 and 5 in Table 12.2 are items that we have not yet encountered. Furthermore, they are the two items that cause a difference between the trade balance and the current account balance. Item 4 is **net factor receipts**. It requires a little explanation. Residents of Mexico, either households or firms, own factors of production located in the Rest of the World. That is, a Mexican firm might own a factory in a foreign country. This firm receives income or profits from this factory during the year in question. This is known as factor receipts or factor service exports. Alternatively, residents of foreign countries own factors of production located in Mexico, and they receive payments from Mexico. From Mexico's point of view, these are factor payments or factor service imports. Item 4 records the net of factor receipts and factor payments, known as net factor receipts. In Table 12.2, factor payments exceed factor receipts, and net factor receipts are –$11 billion.

Item 5 is *transfers* and is recorded in net terms. Possible transfer items are foreign aid, remittances of expatriates and foreign workers from one country to another, and international pension flows. For Mexico in 1993, inward transfers exceed outward transfers by $4 billion, and it is this net figure that is entered into the balance of payments.

The sum of the net items 3 through 5 composes the current account balance and is entered into the accounts as a major balance in item 6 of Table 12.2. In 1993, Mexico had a current account *deficit* of $23 billion. Because the accounts between Mexico and the rest of the world must balance ("things add up," once again), it must be the case that there were other transactions in the balance of payments offsetting or financing the current account deficit. These other transactions are contained in the capital account.

As mentioned earlier, whereas the current account records transactions that do not involve the exchange of assets, the capital account has the distinguishing feature of consisting of transactions involving the exchange of assets. The type of asset exchanged and who exchanges them determine the capital account item in which a transaction is recorded. For example, item 7 is **direct investment** or foreign direct investment and consists of money that corporations invest in firms they own in other countries. As we discussed in Chapter 1, the assets involved in direct investment contain an element of control along with ownership. Typically, the shares involved must comprise a controlling interest of between 10 and 25 percent, depending on the accounting procedures of the country in question. Whatever the amount, for direct investment, the multinational corporation exercises some degree of control over its foreign subsidiary. In the case of Mexico in 1993, there was a net inward flow of direct investment of $4 billion.

The second capital account item is portfolio investment. Portfolio investment includes government bonds of various maturities, corporate equities,

Net factor receipts
An item in the current account of the balance of payments. It records the difference between factor income and factor payments, both of which reflect income earned on physical capital.

Direct investment
An entry in the balance of payments that records the net inflows of foreign direct investment.

corporate bonds, and bank deposits. Unlike direct investment, portfolio investment does *not* involve an element of control. Portfolio investment can be broken up further into long-term capital and short-term capital. This distinction is important because short-term capital is more volatile than long-term capital. As we see in Table 12.2, in the case of Mexico in 1993, there was a net inward flow of portfolio investment of $29 billion. Unfortunately, much of this was of a short-term nature and contributed to a crisis in 1994 and 1995. If the current account deficits had been financed with more direct and long-term portfolio investment, the balance of payments crisis that ensued may not have been as severe.[9]

The third component of the capital account is the **official reserves balance**, reported in net terms. It is an item that does not show up at all in the open-economy accounts relationship of the balance of payments equation. The official reserves balance is recorded as item 9 in Table 12.2. The official reserves balance reflects the actions of the world's central banks. Central banks need to hold reserves of foreign exchange. They hold these in the form of other countries' government bonds and in accounts at foreign central banks. Transaction on the official reserves balance occur in four instances:

Official reserves balance
The element of the capital account of the balance of payments that reflects the actions of the world's central banks.

1. *When Mexico's central bank sells its foreign exchange holdings, this generates an inward flow of funds and income or receipts on Mexico's official reserve balance (positive entries).*
2. *When Mexico's central bank buys foreign exchange holdings, this generates outlays or expenditures on the official reserve balance (negative entries).*
3. *When foreign central banks sell their reserves of Mexico's currency, this generates an outward flow of funds and an outlay or expenditure on Mexico's official reserves balance (negative entries).*
4. *Finally, when foreign central banks buy reserves of Mexico's currency, this generates an income or receipts on Mexico's official reserve balance (positive entries).*

The net of all these official reserve transactions in Table 12.2 is recorded in item 9 as –$7 billion, expenditures having exceeded receipts in 1993.

Let's take stock of our balances up to this point: The current account balance is –$23 billion; the direct investment balance is $4 billion; the portfolio investment balance is $29 billion; and the official reserves balance is –$7 billion. Adding these four balances gives us $3 billion, yet we have stated that the current and capital accounts must sum to zero. What has gone wrong? In almost all cases, collecting balance of payments data is a difficult and imprecise activity. Many transactions cannot be measured accurately or simply "slip through the cracks." Consequently, there needs to be an honest accounting of errors and omissions, recorded as a net balance of –$3 billion in item 10 of Table 12.2. The sum of items 7 through 10 gives us the capital account balance recorded as a major balance in item 11 of $23 billion. The 1993 current account deficit and capital account surplus now sum to zero. "Things add up."

---

[9] "The volatility of portfolio finance—its tendency to pour in when investors are confident, and flee just as suddenly—is the main reason for growing skepticism about the whole process of foreign borrowing by emerging market economies" (*The Economist*, 2002, p. 64).

The balance of payments accounts are an important diagnostic tool for international economists.[10] They help to identify patterns of relationships of the country in question with the rest of the world that might not be sustainable. For example, if a country is financing persistent current account deficits with short-term portfolio investment or by selling foreign reserve holdings, then there may be cause for alarm. An analyst can then turn to the open-economy accounts to explore how the external imbalance is associated with domestic (household and government) savings and investment. All of this information may suggest potential corrective measures. The current account deficit, for example, may need to be suppressed through increases in government tax revenues that allow an increase in government savings.

Some data for the case of Mexico is presented in Table 12.3. This table records some items from the Mexican balance of payments for the years 1990 to 1996. Note the increasing current account deficits during the years 1990 through 1994. These must have had their counterparts in capital account surpluses. Two items from the capital account are given in the table: direct investment and portfolio investment. The direct investment column reports steady increases overall between 1990 and 1994. The portfolio investment column, however, reports a strong increase during these years. This rapid increase in the portfolio component of the current account should have been a sign of trouble. As we will discuss in Chapter 17, trouble occurred in the Mexican case in 1994 and 1995.

The U.S. economy dominates the world economy through both trade and asset transactions. For this reason, it is often important to consider the U.S. balance of payments and its global impacts. These are briefly considered in the box.

Table 12.3 The Mexican Balance of Payments, 1990–1996 (Billions of U.S. Dollars)

Year	Current Account	Direct Investment	Portfolio Investment
1990	–8	3	3
1991	–15	5	13
1992	–24	4	18
1993	–23	4	29
1994	–30	11	8
1995	–2	10	–10
1996	–1.9	8	14

Source: Based on data from Banco de Mexico http://www.banxico.org.mx.

---

[10]James (1996) states: "(A)nalyzing the origins of balance of payments problems (can) provide a tool for diagnosing more wide-ranging economic difficulties. The balance of payments (acts) as a fever thermometer" (p. 124).

The U.S. Balance of Payments

In both 1970 and 1980, the U.S. current account was in surplus at an amount slightly over US$2 billion, although in 1977 and 1978 it dipped into a deficit of over $15 billion. A significant change in the current account occurred in 1983, in response to the expansionary fiscal policies of the Reagan administration, which had a detrimental impact on U.S. government savings. In 1984, the current account deficit expanded to just short of $100 billion, and in 1987 it reached over $160 billion. This expansion in the current account deficit was financed through the inflow of foreign savings purchasing U.S. government debt, corporate debt, and corporate equity.

From 1987 to 1990, the current account deficit shrank, and for the single year 1991, it was in surplus of approximately $4 billion. From 1992 to 1999, the current account deficit expanded from $50 billion to $340 billion. Unlike the decade of the 1980s, this was due to a collapse of household savings rather than government savings, which prevented total domestic savings from expanding in line with domestic investment. Again, these current account deficits were financed largely through surpluses on the portfolio component of the capital account, although net inflows of foreign direct investment were significant in the single year 1999.

A collapse of government savings beginning in 2000, together with low household savings, pushed the U.S. current account deficit to an historic high of five percent of GDP in 2003. Thus, the elimination of the persistent current account deficit in the United States now seems to depend on a recovery of *both* household savings *and* government savings. There is no sign of this happening in the near future.

Sources: International Monetary Fund, *International Financial Statistics Yearbook*, and U.S. Council of Economic Advisors, *Economic Report of the President*.

Conclusion

Chapter 1 discussed four realms of the world economy: international trade, international production, international finance, and international economic development. In this chapter, we have used accounting schemes to develop linkages among three of the realms: international trade (the exchange of merchandise and services), international production (foreign direct investment), and international finance (the exchange of assets). These linkages were present in the open-economy accounts as well as in the balance of payments accounts. The key insight is that current account deficits and surpluses have a counterpart in capital account surpluses and deficits, respectively. The trade balance is one major component of the current account. Foreign savings in the form of direct and portfolio investment is one major component of the capital account. The open-economy and balance of payments accounts can both be used as diagnostic tools for the assessment of the sustainability of current economic conditions in the country in question.

Review Exercises

1. In Chapter 1, Figure 1.3, we emphasized connections among the four windows on the world economy: international trade, international production, international finance, and international development. Looking back on this chapter, identify where in the open-economy accounts and balance of payments accounts connections appear among the first three of these windows: trade, production (FDI), and finance.

2. Looking at the open-economy circular flow diagram of Figure 12.2, explain how an increase in government expenditures, G, without any increase in tax revenues, T, would tend to impact the trade balance. You will need to use one of the fundamental equations to answer this question.

3. Repeat the exercise of question 2 for an increase in household consumption, C, without any increase in income, Y.

4. Examine Table 12.3 on the Mexican balance of payments from 1990 to 1996. Compare the two columns on direct and portfolio investment. Can you say anything about the nature of these two components of the capital account? Does one appear to be less stable than the other?

Further Reading and Web Resources

A review of balance of payments accounts can be found in Chapter 2 of Melvin (2000). More advanced treatments can be found in Chapter 2 of Dornbusch (1988) and in Cumby and Levich (1992). Data of the type discussed in this chapter can be readily obtained from the International Monetary Fund publication *International Financial Statistics*. Most important is the annual Yearbook in this series. See also the Web site of the International Monetary Fund at **http://www.imf.org**. WebEc's World Wide Web Resources in Economics maintains links to international economic data at **http://www.helsinki.fi/WebEc/webecc8d.html**. The U.S. mirror of this Finnish site is at **http://netec.wustl.edu/WebEc/framec8d.html**.

References

Cumby, R., and R. Levich (1992) "Balance of Payments," in P. Newman, M. Milgate, and J. Eatwell (eds.), *The New Palgrave Dictionary of Money and Finance*, Vol. 1, Macmillan, London, 113–120.

Dornbusch, R. (1988) *Open Economy Macroeconomics*, Basic Books, New York.

The Economist (2002) "Special Report: The IMF," September 28, 63–65.

James, H. (1996) *International Monetary Cooperation Since Bretton Woods*, Oxford University Press, Oxford.

Keynes, J.M. (1935) *The General Theory of Employment, Interest and Money*, Harcourt Brace, New York.

Krugman, P. (1996) *Pop Internationalism*, MIT Press, Cambridge, Massachusetts.

Mankiw, N.G. (2004) *Principles of Economics*, South-Western/Thomson Learning, Mason, Ohio.

Melvin, M. (2000) *International Money and Finance*, Addison-Wesley, Reading, Massachusetts.

Mills, C.A., and R. Nallari (1992) *Analytical Approaches to Stabilization and Adjustment Programs*, Economic Development Institute Seminar Paper Number 44, World Bank, Washington, DC.

Pyatt, G., and J. Round (eds.) (1985) *Social Accounting Matrices: A Basis for Planning*, World Bank, Washington, DC.

Reinert, K.A., and D.W. Roland-Holst (1997) "Social Accounting Matrices," in J.F. Francois and K.A. Reinert (eds.), *Applied Methods for Trade Policy Analysis*, Cambridge University Press, Cambridge, 94–121.

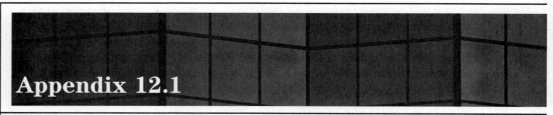

Appendix 12.1

Accounting Matrices

In many instances, international and development economists arrange open-economy accounts in the form of an *accounting matrix*.[11] This process begins with Figure 12.2. In setting up accounting matrices, we need to abide by four rules: (a) The number of accounts composes the dimensions of the (square) matrix; (b) expenditures or payments are recorded down the columns of the matrix; (c) receipts or incomes are recorded across the rows of the matrix; and (d) the row and column sums of the matrix are equal. Because Figure 12.2 has five accounts, it translates into a matrix with five rows and columns. Such a matrix is presented in Table 12.A1.1.

To fill in Table 12.A1.1, we can either record expenditures down columns or receipts across rows. Let us record expenditures down columns and leave it to you to check that recording receipts across rows gives us the same result. The Firm has two expenditures: income, Y, accruing to the Household and imports, Z, accruing to the Rest of the World. We record these down the first column. The Household has three expenditures: consumption, C, accruing to the Firm; household savings, S_H, accruing to Capital; and taxes, T, accruing to the Government. We record these down the second column. Capital has a single expenditure, I, accruing to the

Table 12.A1.1 An Accounting Matrix

	Firm	Household	Capital	Government	ROW
Firm		C	I	G	E
Household	Y				
Capital		S_H		S_G	S_F
Government		T			
ROW	Z				

---

[11]See, for example, Mills and Nallari (1992), Pyatt and Round (1985), and Reinert and Roland-Holst (1997).

Firm, and we record this in the third column. The Government has two expenditures: government spending, G, accruing to the Firm and government savings, S_G, accruing to Capital. We record these down the fourth column. Finally, the Rest of the World has two expenditures: exports, E, accruing to the Firm, and foreign savings, S_F, accruing to Capital. We record these down the fifth column.

An example of an accounting matrix for Mexico is presented in Table 12.A1.2. In examining this table, you need to be aware that there are more entries than there were in Table 12.A1.1. This is because Table 12.A1.1 makes a number of simplifying assumptions, which are not present in "the real world."

We can gain insights into open economies by applying the fourth rule of accounting matrices to Table 12.A1.1. The rule states that the row and column sums of the accounting matrix are equal. Applying this rule gives us the following set of accounting identity equations:

$$Y + Z = C + I + G + E \tag{12.A1}$$

$$C + S_H + T = Y \tag{12.A2}$$

$$I = S_H + S_G + S_F \tag{12.A3}$$

$$G + S_G = T \tag{12.A4}$$

$$E + S_F = Z \tag{12.A5}$$

Equation 12.A1 can be rearranged to give the standard national income equation from introductory macroeconomics:

$$Y = C + I + G + (E - Z)$$

Equations 12.A3 and 12.A5 can be rearranged to give the fundamental accounting equation discussed in this chapter:

Table 12.A1.2 An Accounting Matrix for Mexico (Millions of 1996 Pesos)

	Firm	Household	Capital	Government	ROW	Error	Total
Firm		1,691,243	532,205	258,165	801,454		3,283,067
Household	2,315,239			218,800	35,000		2,569,039
Capital		605,591			14,400		619,991
Government	228,979	212,100	11,200		15,000	76,586	543,865
ROW	738,849	60,105		66,900			865,854
Error			76,586				76,586
Total	3,283,067	2,569,039	619,991	543,865	865,854	76,586	

Sources: Based on data from Banco de Mexico, http://www.banxico.org.mx and Organization for Economic Cooperation and Development.

$$I - (S_H + S_G) = S_F = Z - E$$

Or

$$(S_H + S_G) - I = -S_F = E - Z$$

Compare these two equations to those presented in the box in this chapter:

Fundamental Accounting Equations

Domestic Investment – Domestic Savings = Foreign Savings = Trade Deficit

Domestic Savings – Domestic Investment = Foreign Investment = Trade Balance

---

Reinert and Roland-Holst (1997) advocate the accounting matrix approach, arguing that "it represents a comprehensive and consistent framework for developing databases for rigorous economic methods" and that "it helps in the reconciliation of the numerous data sources to complete the detailed picture of economywide activity" (p. 117). These are the reasons that economic data are often presented in accounting matrix form.

Appendix 12.2

An Open-Economy Model

An open-economy model can be derived from the fundamental accounting equations of this chapter.[12] We begin with the following version:

$$I - (S_H + S_G) = S_F = Z - E$$

The government income-expenditure identity (Equation 12.A4) tells us that

$$S_G = T - G$$

Let's substitute this into the fundamental equation to get

$$I - S_H - T + G = Z - E$$

Keynesian thinking in macroeconomics suggests that household savings (S_G) increase with the level of income (Y).[13] Experience also shows that imports (Z) increase with the level of income. If these two relationships are linear, and the other variables in this equation are independent of income, we have the graphs depicted in Figure 12.A2.1.

Figure 12.A2.1 depicts a situation in which the trade balance is initially zero. Suppose that, from this initial position, the government increases government spending (G). This shifts the downward-sloping graph upwards. As a consequence, the trade deficit $(Z–E)$ moves into the positive range. Governments cannot use a fiscal stimulus in an open economy without moving the economy into a trade deficit. This is one of the limitations on domestic policy independence placed by globalization.

There are three other independent variables in the figure that can also be changed: E, T, and I. Changes in the first of these will move the $Z–E$ graph up or down. Changes to the latter two variables will, like changes in G, move the $I - S_H - T + G$ graph up or down. In each case, there will be an impact on the trade balance.

---

[12] See Chapter 3 of Dornbusch (1988).

[13] This goes back to Keynes (1935) who stated: "The fundamental psychological law . . . is that men are disposed, as a rule and on the average, to increase their consumption as their income increases, *but not by as much as the increase in their income*" (p. 96, emphasis added).

Figure 12.A2.1 An Open-Economy, Macroeconomic Model

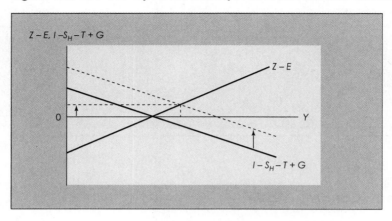

Exchange Rates and Purchasing Power Parity

13

For U.S. companies with large trade and investment exposures to Western Europe, the latter half of the year 2000 was a very difficult time. During that year, the euro fell in value from just under US$1.00 to approximately $0.80. U.S.–based firms such as Compaq, IBM, Intel, Polaroid, Microsoft, Baxter International, Heinz, Caterpillar, Dow Chemical, Dupont, and TRW all suffered as a result. Why? Their euro sales were worth less in dollar terms, and dollar terms mattered. One Wall Street analyst estimated that the fall of the euro in 2000 shaved 3 percent off total Standard & Poors 500 operating profits in the third quarter alone. The president of TRW lamented, "If I could report in euros, we would be having a bang-up year."[1] *Unfortunately, this was not possible.*

Exchange rates matter, and they matter in many different ways to many different constituencies in the world economy. Much of this section of the book, focusing on the third window on the world economy, international finance, will be directly or indirectly concerned with exchange rates. Indeed, this and the next two chapters will be exclusively devoted to developing your understanding of exchange rates. In this chapter, we will begin with two important exchange rate definitions. These are the nominal exchange rate and the real exchange rate. We will then discuss the relationship of exchange rates and trade flows. Next, we will develop a first model of exchange rate determination: the purchasing power parity model (PPP model). Having developed this model, we will relate it to our definition of the real exchange rate. Finally, we will consider the difference between spot rates and forward rates and how this difference can, at times, be used by firms to hedge exchange rate exposure. The real exchange rate definition and the purchasing power parity model utilize the notion of overall price levels in an economy. For those who are not familiar with this idea, price levels are discussed in the appendix to this chapter.

As you conclude this chapter, you will have an understanding of one model of exchange rates: the PPP model. As you will see, this model has validity in helping to predict the long-run trends in nominal exchange rates. You will also need a model to help predict short-run trends in nominal exchange rates. This will be the central task of Chapters 14 and 15.

---

[1] See Tully (2000) and McMurray (2000).

The Nominal Exchange Rate

We are going to place our discussion of exchange rates within a particular context in order to make the concepts more concrete. Exchange rates are defined in terms of home and foreign countries. In this chapter, we will usually take Mexico as our home country and the United States as our foreign country.[2] Our first exchange rate definition is the **nominal exchange rate**. The nominal exchange rate is the relative price of two currencies, and it is most often expressed as the number of units of the local or home currency that are required to buy a unit of the foreign currency. The Mexican currency is the Mexican peso, which we will express simply as the peso. The U.S. currency is the U.S. dollar, which we will express simply as the dollar. Therefore, the nominal or currency exchange rate is defined as

Nominal exchange rate
The number of units of a country's currency that trade against a world currency such as the U.S. dollar or euro.

$$e = \frac{\text{pesos}}{\text{dollar}}$$

which is in the form of

$$e = \frac{\text{local currency}}{\text{foreign currency}} \qquad \textbf{Nominal exchange rate}$$

As implied in these equations, we will be using the symbol e to denote the nominal exchange rate. Nominal exchange rates for a sample of 15 countries are presented in Table 13.1.

Let us examine the nominal exchange rate a little more closely. Suppose that, for some reason, e were to increase. What would this mean for the value of the peso? The increase in e implies that it takes more pesos to purchase a dollar. This, in turn, implies that the value of the peso has fallen. The opposite is the case when e falls. When e falls, it takes fewer pesos to buy a dollar, and this implies that the value of the peso has increased. Because these relationships are important, we will put them in a box for you to remember:

$e \uparrow \Rightarrow$ **value of the peso (home currency) falls**

$e \downarrow \Rightarrow$ **value of the peso (home currency) rises**

As you can see in the box, e and the value of the peso are inversely related. For this reason, e is often graphed as its inverse, which is equal to the value of the peso.[3] Such a scale is presented in Figure 13.1. In this figure, a movement up the scale indicates a fall in e and a rise in the value of the peso. A movement down the scale indicates a rise in e and a fall in the value of the peso. Make sure you are comfortable with this inverse scale before continuing with the remainder of the chapter.

---

[2] Readers in the United States, please be careful here. The U.S. is the *foreign* country.
[3] For example, *The Economist* almost always uses an inverse scale in its graphs of exchange rate data.

Table 13.1 Nominal Exchange Rates, October 9, 2002 (per U.S. Dollar)

Country or Region	Currency	Nominal Exchange Rate	Nominal Exchange Rate 1 Year Earlier
Argentina	Peso	3.72	1.00
Brazil	Real	3.88	2.77
Canada	Dollar	1.59	1.57
Chile	Peso	751	715
China	Yuan	8.28	8.28
Euro Zone	Euro	1.01	1.10
Indonesia	Rupiah	8,997	9,985
Japan	Yen	124	120
Mexico	Peso	10.20	9.40
Philippines	Peso	52.7	51.8
Russia	Ruble	31.7	29.5
South Africa	Rand	10.5	9.22
Thailand	Baht	43.6	44.8
Turkey	Lira	1,647,500	1,641,000
United Kingdom	Pound	0.64	0.69

Source: Adapted from *The Economist* (2002). "Trade, Exchange Rates, and Budgets [table] in Economic and Financial Indicators"; and "Financial Markets [table] in Emerging Market Indicators." October 12: 97, 98.

Figure 13.1 The Value of the Peso Scale

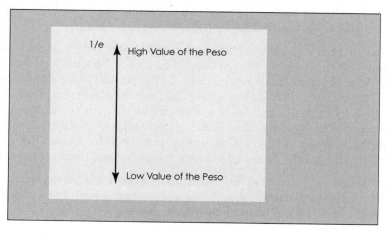

The Real Exchange Rate

Real exchange rate
The rate at which two countries' goods (not currencies) trade against each other. The real exchange rate adjusts the nominal exchange rate using the price levels in the two countries under consideration.

Along with the nominal exchange rate, it is important to also understand a second exchange rate definition, namely the **real exchange rate**. Recall that the nominal exchange rate measures the relative price of two countries' currencies. Another way to state this is that it measures the rate at which two countries' currencies trade against each other. In contrast, the real exchange rate measures the rate at which two countries' goods trade against each other. Let's distinguish the real exchange rate from the nominal exchange rate:

> **Nominal exchange rate:** The rate at which two countries' currencies trade against each other.
>
> **Real exchange rate:** The rate at which two countries' goods trade against each other.

Price level
A measure of the average or overall level of prices in a country. Includes the GDP price deflator and the consumer price index.

The real exchange rate makes use of the **price levels** in the two countries under consideration. P^M is the overall price level in Mexico (the home country), and P^{US} is the overall price level in the United States (the foreign country). If you are not familiar with the concept of price levels, please see the appendix to this chapter before continuing with the remainder of this section. If you are already familiar with the price level concept, continue.

The real exchange rate definition, denoted *re*, is as follows:

$$re = e \times \frac{P^{US}}{P^M} \qquad \textbf{Real exchange rate}$$

We have stated that *re* measures the rate at which the two countries' goods trade against each other. More specifically, it measures the amount of Mexican goods that trade against U.S. goods. A formal demonstration of this is provided in the appendix. Here, we will show intuitively that this definition makes sense. We do so with the help of Table 13.2.

Suppose that the price level in the United States (P^{US}) rises. It now takes more Mexican goods to purchase U.S. goods. Therefore, there has been a fall in the real value of the peso. Suppose that the price level in Mexico (P^M) rises. It now takes fewer Mexican goods to purchase U.S. goods. Therefore, there has been a rise in the real value of the peso. Finally, suppose that the nominal exchange rate (*e*) increases. It now takes more Mexican pesos to buy a U.S. dollar and, therefore, more Mexican goods to buy U.S. goods. There has been a fall in the real value of the peso.

It is important for you to understand that real exchange rates are affected by both nominal exchange rates and price levels. Let's conclude this section with a second box to help you remember:

Table 13.2 Changes in the Real Exchange Rate

Change	Intuition	Effect in "re" Equation
P^{US} increases	U.S. goods increase in price. Therefore, it takes more Mexican goods to buy a unit of U.S. goods. The real value of the peso has fallen.	Because it is in the numerator, the increase in P^{US} increases the value of re.
P^M increases	Mexican goods increase in price. Therefore, it takes fewer Mexican goods to buy a unit of U.S. goods. The real value of the peso has risen.	Because it is in the denominator, the increase in P^M decreases the value of re.
e increases	It takes more Mexican pesos to buy U.S. dollars. The real value of the peso has fallen.	The increase in e increases the value of re.

$P^{US} \uparrow \Rightarrow re \uparrow \Rightarrow$ **real value of peso (home currency) falls**

$P^M \uparrow \Rightarrow re \downarrow \Rightarrow$ **real value of peso (home currency) rises**

$e \uparrow \Rightarrow re \uparrow \Rightarrow$ **real value of peso (home currency) falls**

Exchange Rates and Trade Flows

Changes in *e*, and therefore in the value of the peso, have an impact on trade flows that is important for you to understand. To see this, we are going to consider the case of Mexico's imports and exports. World prices (P^W) are typically in U.S. dollar terms, and Mexican prices (P^M) are in peso terms. The relationship between the Mexican (peso) and world (dollar) prices of Mexico's import (*Z*) goods can be expressed as

$$P^M_Z = e \times P^W_Z$$

P^W_Z is in dollar terms. Multiplying it by *e* gives us P^M_Z in peso terms. Now, suppose that *e* were to increase (the value of the peso falls). This movement down the scale in Figure 13.1 increases the peso price of the imported good in Mexico. Following the "law of demand," import demand consequently decreases.[4] Next, suppose *e* were to decrease (the value of the peso rises). This movement up the scale in Figure 13.1 decreases the peso price of the imported good in Mexico. Import demand consequently

---

[4] This is similar to the way an increase in the world price of rice would decrease Japan's rice imports in Figure 2.4 in Chapter 2.

Figure 13.2 The Value of the Peso and Mexico's Imports

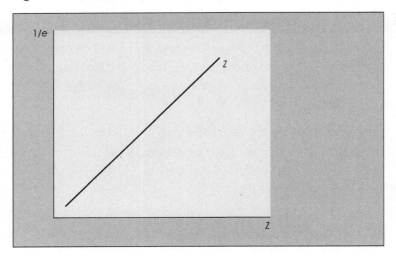

increases. We can summarize this relationship between the value of the peso and home's imports as the upward-sloping graph in Figure 13.2.[5]

Next, consider the case of Mexico's exports. The relationship between the peso and dollar prices of Mexico's exported (E) goods can be expressed as

$$P_E^M = e \times P_E^W$$

P_E^W is in dollar terms. Multiplying it by e gives us P_E^M in peso terms. Now, suppose that e were to increase (the value of the peso falls). This movement down the scale in Figure 13.1 increases the peso price of the export good in Mexico. Export supply in Mexico consequently increases. Why? Mexican firms now have more of an incentive in peso terms to export.[6] Next suppose that e were to decrease (the value of the peso rises). This movement up the inverse scale in Figure 13.1 decreases the peso price of exports in Mexico. Export supply consequently decreases. We can summarize this relationship between the value of the peso and exports as the downward sloping graph in Figure 13.3.

We can put the relationships of Figures 13.2 and 13.3 together in a single diagram representing the relationship between the value of the peso and the trade deficit, $Z - E$. This is done in Figure 13.4. As you can see, there is a positive relationship between the value of the peso and the trade deficit. We will use this relationship in the remaining chapters of this section of the book on international finance.[7]

---

[5] The graphs in Figures 13.2 and 13.3 are not necessarily linear. We draw them that way for simplicity's sake.

[6] This is similar to the way an increase in the world price of rice would increase Vietnam's exports in Figure 2.4 in Chapter 2.

[7] Readers of the "Open Economy Model" appendix in Chapter 12 can see from Figures 12.A1.1 and 13.4 that nominal exchange rate movements (e.g. an increase in e) could help to resolve the trade deficit that expansionary fiscal policy causes.

Figure 13.3 The Value of the Peso and Mexico's Exports

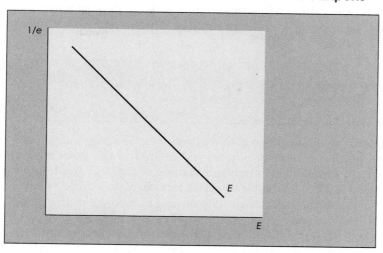

Figure 13.4 The Value of the Peso and Mexico's Trade Deficit

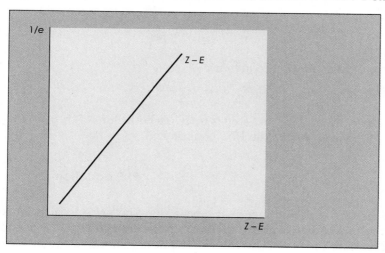

The relationship between exchange rates and trade flows is important in its own right as a link between the international trade and international finance windows on the world economy. Therefore, it is one example of the double-headed arrow between the international trade and international finance boxes illustrated in Figure 1.3 of Chapter 1. Further, however, we will use Figure 13.4 in a model of exchange rates to be developed in the next two chapters.

The Purchasing Power Parity Model

Closely related to the definition of the real exchange rate is a model of exchange rate determination known as **purchasing power parity** or PPP.

Purchasing power parity model (PPP model)

A long-run model of exchange rate determination based on the notion that the nominal exchanges rate will adjust so that the purchasing power of currencies will be the same in every country.

The PPP approach to exchange rates begins with the hypothesis that the nominal exchange rate will adjust so that the purchasing power of a currency will be the same in every country. This hypothesis is also worth putting in a box:

> **PPP hypothesis:** The nominal exchange rate will adjust so that the purchasing power of a currency will be the same in every country.

Let's explore the implications of this hypothesis. The purchasing power of a currency in a given country is inversely related to the price level in that country. For example, the purchasing power of the peso in Mexico can be expressed as $1/P^M$. The higher the price level in Mexico, the lower the purchasing power of the peso there. The purchasing power of the peso in the United States is a bit more complicated. First, we need the rate at which a peso can be exchanged into dollars. This is $1/e$. Second, we need the purchasing power of a dollar in the United States. This is $1/P^{US}$. Putting these together, we have the purchasing power of a peso in the United States as $(1/e) \times (1/P^{US})$. Now, we can state the PPP hypothesis as follows:

$$\frac{1}{P^M} = \frac{1}{e} \times \frac{1}{P^{US}}$$

Let's invert this equation to give us:

$$P^M = e \times P^{US}$$

We are almost there. The last step is to divide both sides of the above equation by P^{US}. This gives us the PPP equation:[8]

$$e = \frac{P^M}{P^{US}} \qquad \textbf{PPP equation}$$

What does this equation mean? Suppose that the price level in Mexico, P^M in the numerator, were to increase. According to the PPP model, e would therefore increase. The value of the peso would consequently move down the scale in Figure 13.1. Alternatively, suppose that the price level in the United States, P^{US} in the denominator, were to increase. According to the PPP model e would decrease. In this case, the value of the peso would move up the scale in Figure 13.1. In this way, the nominal value of the peso adjusts to changes in its real purchasing power in the two countries. Although this makes a great deal of sense, the restrictiveness of the PPP model can be seen when we reexpress it in a third equation. We obtain this equation by multiplying both sides of the PPP equation by (P^{US}/P^M):

---

[8] This equation is known as the "absolute version" of PPP. The "relative version" used in most empirical studies can be stated as $\%\Delta e = \%\Delta P^M - \%\Delta P^{US}$. In this equation, Δ stands for "change in." See Froot and Rogoff (1996).

$$e = \frac{P^{US}}{P^M} = 1 \qquad \textbf{Modified PPP equation}$$

Let's compare this equation with the real exchange rate:

$$e = \frac{P^{US}}{P^M} = re \qquad \textbf{Real exchange rate equation}$$

We can see here that the PPP model is a special case of the real exchange rate. More specifically, the PPP theory implies that the real exchange rate is fixed at unity. That is, there will not be any change in the real exchange rate. It turns out that real exchange rates *do* change, a humorous case of which is presented in the box. If the PPP theory implies that real exchange rates do not change, and yet we observe real exchange rates varying in the real world, there must be important elements of the real world that the PPP theory ignores. In fact, two such elements come readily to mind.

First, underlying the PPP idea is the assumption that all goods entering into the price levels of both countries are internationally traded. It is the traded nature of all the goods in the price levels of both countries that contributes to the strong relationship between price levels and nominal exchange rates expressed in the PPP equations. In fact, however, many goods are nontraded. For example, a large part of most economies consists of locally-supplied services such as many kinds of cleaning, repairs, and food preparation. These services are not typically traded. The presence of such nontraded goods weakens the PPP relationship.[9]

A second important element contributing to the gap between PPP implications and the real world is one we covered in Chapter 4 on intra-industry trade. This is the phenomenon of product differentiation. As we saw in Chapter 4, product differentiation allows for separate markets (and therefore prices) for import and domestic varieties of a good. In a manner very similar to the presence of nontraded goods, this weakens the relationship between domestic price levels and exchange rates implied by PPP theory.

Does all of this imply that the PPP theory is useless? No. It is best to use the following interpretation. The real exchange rate equation captures reality at any point in time; the PPP relationship never holds exactly. The PPP equation, however, give us a sense of a long-term tendency towards which nominal exchange rates move absent other changes. Indeed, these PPP equations are in the backs of the minds of currency traders. Before exchange rates have the chance to move fully towards the PPP relationship, however, other changes invariably intervene. This necessitates alternative models of exchange rate determination more appropriate for the short term, to which we turn in Chapters 14 and 15.

---

[9] As Schnabl (2001) states: "The more traded, or fewer nontraded goods, are included in the price index, the better the approximation of exchange rates by PPP would be" (p. 37). Schnabl uses export prices instead of overall price levels to explain the yen/dollar exchange rate to good effect. We will use the concept of nontraded goods in our analysis of structural adjustment in Chapter 23.

The Big Mac Index

In 1986, *The Economist* began to publish an annual test of the PPP theory of exchange rates based on an unusual measure of price levels around the world. This "Big Mac index" measures price levels using just one good, the McDonald's Big Mac hamburger. Calculations of this index are given in the table on the next page.

The Economist first measures the local currency price of Big Macs. These are given in the second column of the table. Next, *The Economist* converts these local currency prices into U.S. dollar terms using nominal exchange rates. These U.S. dollar prices are given in the third column. Dividing each of these U.S. dollar prices by $2.54 gives the implied PPP of the dollar presented in the fourth column. The fifth column presents the actual year 2001 exchange rate. Comparing this to the purchasing power parities gives the degree of overvaluation or undervaluation of the currency according to the Big Mac index. For example, Brazil's implied PPP is 1.42, but its actual exchange rate is 2.19. This indicates that the *real* is undervalued by 40 percent.

Should we take the Big Mac index seriously? *The Economist* gleefully notes that "several academic studies have concluded that the Big Mac index is surprisingly accurate in tracking exchange rates over the long term." One of these studies is Ong (1997). For example, according to *The Economist*: "When the euro was launched at the start of 1999, most forecasters predicted that it would rise (in value). But the euro has instead tumbled—exactly as the Big Mac index had signaled."

Note: The exchange rates may differ from those of Table 13.1, because the latter are more recent.

Sources: *The Economist* (2001). "Big Mac Currencies." April 12: 74, and Ong (1997)

Forward Markets and Exchange Rate Exposure

Exchange rate exposure
The loss of revenues in a home country currency by an exporting or multinational enterprise due to an increase in the nominal value of the home currency.

Spot rate
The current, nominal exchange rate between two currencies.

In Part 1 of this book, we considered the possibility of firms entering foreign markets via exports. In Part 2 of this book, on international production, we considered the possibility of firms entering foreign markets via foreign direct investment. If the sales from either of these market-entry strategies are not denominated in the currencies of the firms' home countries, issues of **exchange rate exposure** arise. For example, in the introduction to this chapter, we mentioned the impact of a fall in the value of the euro on the dollar value of U.S.–based firms' revenues. Let's take a closer look at this exposure problem.

Suppose that the €/US$ exchange rate is currently at a value of 1.00. Suppose also that a U.S. firm is expecting euro revenues of €1.0 million. Given the current exchange rate, known as a **spot rate**, the U.S. firm might be expecting dollar revenues of US$1.0 million. Suppose, however, that the spot rate moves to $e = 1.25$ (a dollar value of the euro of $0.80). It now takes more euros to purchase a dollar, and the dollar revenues shrink to $800,000. Is there anything the firm can do to overcome this exposure? Possibly, yes.

| Country | Big Mac Prices | | Actual 2001 | | Local currency |
	In Local Currency	In Dollars	Implied PPP	Exchange Rate	Over(+)/Under (−) Valuation (%)
United States	$2.54	2.54	–	–	–
Brazil	Real3.60	1.64	1.42	2.19	−40
Canada	C$3.33	2.14	1.31	1.56	−16
Chile	Peso1260	2.10	496	601	−17
China	Yuan9.90	1.20	3.90	8.28	−53
Euro area	€2.57	2.27	0.99	0.88	−11
Indonesia	Rupiah14,700	1.35	5,787	10,855	−47
Japan	¥294	2.38	116	124	−6
Mexico	Peso21.90	2.36	8.62	9.29	−7
Philippines	Peso59.00	1.17	23.2	50.3	−54
Russia	Rouble35.00	1.21	13.8	28.9	−52
South Africa	Rand9.70	1.19	3.82	8.13	−53
Thailand	Baht55.00	1.21	21.7	45.5	−52
UK	£1.99	2.85	1.28	1.43	12

For some currencies, there are **forward rates** as well as spot rates. These are the rates of current contracts for "forward" transactions in currencies, usually for 1, 3, or 6 months in the future. If the forward rate of the euro (€/US$) is exactly the same as the spot rate, the euro is said to be "flat." If the forward rate of the euro is above the spot rate, the euro is said to be at a "forward discount." Finally, if the forward rate of the euro is below the spot rate, the euro is said to be at a "forward premium."

Suppose now that we again begin with the exchange rate (€/US$) being currently at a value of 1.00 and that a U.S. firm is expecting euro revenues of €1.0 million in 6 months' time. Suppose also, though, that the euro is at a 6-month forward discount of 1.11. The U.S. firm could take out a forward contract and, at that future time, convert the euro revenue into $900,900 of dollar revenue. Would this be a smart move? If the firm knew with certainty that the future spot rate were to be 1.25, it certainly would be. With the forward contract, the firm would earn $900,900 rather than $800,000. If the future spot rate were actually to be below 1.11, though, it would not. The firm could have earned more than $900,900 without the forward contract.

As becomes apparent even in this simple example, hedging exchange rate exposure requires that firms have expectations or forecasts of future spot rates that they can compare to forward rates. Such forecasts range

Forward rate
The rates of current contracts for transactions in currencies that usually take place one, three, or six months in the future.

from the simple (e.g., those based on PPP projections discussed in this chapter) to the complex (e.g., multivariate econometric analysis) and can be either performed in-house or contracted out to a forecasting service.[10] Whatever the approach taken to exchange rate exposure, it is an ever-present problem for those firms engaging in foreign market entry. Indeed, foreign exchange exposure is a key link between the realms of international finance and international production illustrated in Figure 1.3 of Chapter 1.

---

[10]For more on exchange rate forecasting, see Chapter 3 of Solnik (2000).

Conclusion

The nominal exchange rate is the relative price of two currencies, and is expressed as the number of units of a home currency required to buy a unit of a foreign currency. Another way of stating this is that the nominal exchange rate expresses the number of units of a home currency trading against a unit of a foreign currency. In contrast, the real exchange rate measures the rate at which two countries' goods trade against each other. The real exchange rate uses the price levels of home and foreign countries to adjust the nominal exchange rate.

Home-country imports have a direct or positive relationship with the value of its currency. Home-country exports, on the other hand, have an inverse or negative relationship with the value of the currency. A country's trade deficit has a direct or positive relationship with the value of the currency. In these ways, the realms of international trade and international finance are linked.

The purchasing power parity model of exchange rate determination begins with the idea that the nominal exchange rate will adjust so that the purchasing power of a currency will be the same in every country. The PPP model is a restricted version of the real exchange rate definition, and applies only in the long run.

Review Exercises

1. Use supply and demand diagrams such as those we used in Chapter 3 to demonstrate why the relationships between the value of the peso and imports and exports illustrated in Figures 13.2 and 13.3 make sense. In doing so, keep in mind that $P^M = eP^W$.

2. Explain the intuition of how each of the following changes affect the real exchange rate, re: a fall in P^M; a fall in P^{US}; and a fall in e. In each case, describe the impact of the change on the rate at which Mexican goods trade against U.S. goods.

3. Use the PPP model of exchange rate determination to predict the impact on the nominal exchange rate of the following changes: a fall in P^M and a fall in P^{US}.

4. As shown in Table 13.1, the spot nominal exchange rate for the Canadian dollar was 1.59 on October 9, 2002. What happened to the value of the Canadian dollar during the previous year? What would have to be true of the forward rate for the Canadian dollar to be at a forward premium? A forward discount?

Further Reading and Web Resources

Introductions to international finance, in order of level of difficulty, are Melvin (2000), Krugman and Obstfeld (2000), Hallwood and MacDonald (2000), and Obstfeld and Rogoff (1996). Introductions to exchange rate economics can be found in Krueger (1983) and Isard (1995). A discussion of *The Economist* Big Mac index is given in Ong (1997). Dornbusch (1992) and Froot and Rogoff (1996) review the purchasing power model of exchange rate determination.

You can access current nominal exchange rates from the IMF Web site, **http://www.imf.org**. Go to the "Fund Rate" section of the site map. Select "Representative Exchange Rates for Selected Currencies." Nouriel Roubini of New York University's Stern School of Businss maintains a global macreconomics and financial policy Web site at **http://www.stern.nyu.edu/globalmacro**. This Web site is relevant to all the chapters in Part 4 of the book. See also Yahoo!'s International Finance Center at **http://biz.yahoo.com/ifc**.

References

Dornbusch, R. (1992) "Purchasing Power Parity," in D. Newman, M. Milgate, and J. Eatwell (eds.), *The New Palgrave Dictionary of Money and Finance*, Macmillan, London, 236–244.

The Economist (2001) "Big Mac Currencies," April 21, 74.

The Economist (2000) "Big Mac Currencies," April 29, 75.

Froot, K.A., and K. Rogoff (1996) "Perspectives on PPP and Long-Run Real Exchange Rates," in G.M. Grossman and K. Rogoff (eds.), *Handbook of International Economics*, Vol. 3, North Holland, Amsterdam.

Hallwood, C.P., and R. MacDonald (2000) *International Money and Finance*, Blackwell, Oxford.

Isard, P. (1995) *Exchange Rate Economics*, Cambridge University Press, Cambridge.

Krueger, A.O. (1983) *Exchange Rate Determination*, Cambridge University Press, Cambridge.

Krugman, P.R., and M. Obstfeld (2000) *International Economics: Theory and Policy*, Harper Collins, New York.

McMurray, S. (2000) "The Lost Art of Hedging," *Institutional Investor*, 34:12, 63–69.

Melvin, M. (2000) *International Money and Finance*, Addison-Wesley, Reading, Massachusetts.

Obstfeld, M., and K. Rogoff (1996) *Foundations of International Macroeconomics*, MIT Press, Cambridge, Massachusetts.

Ong, L.L. (1997) "Burgernomincs: The Economics of the Big Mac Standard," *Journal of International Money and Finance*, 16:6, 865–878.

Schnabl, G. (2001) "Purchasing Power Parity and the Yen/Dollar Exchange Rate," *The World Economy*, 24:1, 31–50.

Solnik, B. (2000) *International Investments*, Addison-Wesley, Reading, Massachusetts.

Tully, K. (2000) "Feeling Over-Exposed," *Corporate Finance*, 194, 47.

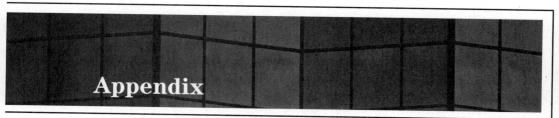

Appendix

Price Levels

In this chapter, we use the concept of price levels in the definition of the real exchange rate and in the purchasing power parity model of exchange rate determination. The purpose of this appendix is to introduce you to the concept of price levels. We are going to do this in the context of the circular flow diagam of a simple closed economy.[11]

We want to focus in this appendix on the flow of income, Y, in Figure 13.A1 from the Firm account to the Household account. This flow of income also represents the total output of the economy in currency or nominal terms, the gross national product, or gross domestic product. Now, suppose that we observed this flow in two years, year 1 and year 2. Suppose also that $Y_2 > Y_1$. This says that total nominal income/output is greater in year 2 than in year 1. Can we conclude that because $Y_2 > Y_1$ that a greater *number* of goods and services are produced in this economy in year 2 than in year 1? No, we cannot. It may be that $Y_2 > Y_1$ simply reflects increases in *prices* between year 1 and year 2. The problem we face here is to separate the increase in Y into the part due to an increase in the number of goods and services and the part due to an increase in the prices of goods and services.

Figure 13.A1 A Circular Flow Diagram for a Simple, Closed Economy

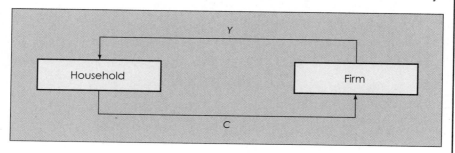

[11]You can review circular flow diagrams in Chapter 12.

In practice, the division of Y into price and quantity components is accomplished through a slightly complex application of index numbers. For our purposes here, however, we are going to take a more simple approach. For simplicity, let's assume that only one type of good or service is produced in the economy. Its price is P. Let a lowercase y represent the total quantity of this good produced in the economy. Whereas Y is known as *nominal* output or income, y is known as *real* output or income. The relationship between nominal and real output or income is given by $Y = P \times y$. The price level, P, can therefore be calculated as the ratio of nominal to real output or income: $P = Y/y$. This measure of the price level is known as the GDP price deflator.

The real exchange rate equation, involving price levels from two countries, is

$$re = e \times \frac{P^{US}}{P^M} \qquad \textbf{Real exchange rate}$$

To see that this equation actually measures the rate at which Mexico's goods trade against U.S. goods, we can rewrite it as follows:

$$re = \frac{\text{pesos}}{\text{dollar}} \times \frac{\dfrac{\text{dollars}}{\text{U.S. goods}}}{\dfrac{\text{pesos}}{\text{Mexican goods}}}$$

Next, let's rewrite the above equation as follows:

$$re = \frac{\text{pesos}}{\text{dollar}} \times \frac{\text{dollars}}{\text{U.S. goods}} \times \frac{\text{Mexican goods}}{\text{pesos}} = \frac{\text{Mexican goods}}{\text{U.S. goods}}$$

As you can see in this last equation, the real exchange rate indeed represents the rate at which Mexican goods trade against U.S. goods.

Flexible Exchange Rates

14

In 1998, a student was in my office complaining about increases in tuition payments. Naively, I said, "But tuition did not increase very much this past year." The student responded: "In Canadian dollars it has!" The forces of supply and demand in currency markets determine the exchange rate of the Canadian dollar to the U.S. dollar (the nominal rate). This is one example of a flexible or floating exchange rate regime. The Canadian dollar began the decade of the 1990s at 1.651 per U.S. dollar. By 1998, it was trading at 2.155 per U.S. dollar. In value terms, this was a fall from 61 U.S. cents to 46 U.S. cents. With an income in Canadian dollars, this student's family was having a difficult time making payments for tuition in the United States.

What makes a flexible exchange rate move one way or another? In this chapter, we will help you answer this question by developing a model of how the nominal exchange rate is determined in currency markets. To begin, we will consider a trade-based model in which the nominal exchange rate is determined by currency transactions arising from imports and exports. We then will extend this model to account for the exchange of assets. This assets approach to exchange rate determination is a more modern, and sophisticated, model of exchange rate determination. It will give you a picture of how the current and capital accounts interact in determining the value of currencies.

In Chapter 13, we also developed a model of exchange rate determination, the purchasing power parity model. Recall that this model was best interpreted as a model applying to the long run. The models we develop in this chapter, however, are best applied in the short run to describe the week-to-week or month-to-month movements in flexible exchange rates among the countries of the world.

A Trade-Based Model

In Chapter 12, we used the circular flow diagram to develop open-economy accounts. In doing this, we came up with an important relationship, namely:

$$\text{Foreign Savings} = \text{Trade Deficit}$$

This relationship was one part of the fundamental accounting equations developed in that chapter.

What we need to do in this chapter is to rewrite this relationship in terms of symbols introduced in Figure 12.2 of Chapter 12. These were S_F (foreign savings), Z (imports), and E (exports). The rewritten relationship is

$$S_F = (Z - E)$$

We are going to use this relationship to create a model of nominal exchange rate determination. We begin in this section with a *trade-based model*. In building our model, we will maintain Mexico as our home country and the United States as our foreign country, as we did in Chapter 13.

S_F is foreign savings. This is savings supplied by U.S. residents who buy Mexican assets. Consequently, S_F is a demand for pesos (supply of dollars) by the United States. In our trade-based model, this demand for pesos is invariant with respect to the value of the peso. This gives us the perfectly inelastic demand for pesos curve represented in Figure 14.1.[1]

Z–E is the trade deficit. The trade deficit is a net demand for U.S. goods by Mexico. It is therefore a supply of pesos (demand for dollars) by Mexico. Before examining this supply side of the peso market, let's summarize what we have stated:

S_F (foreign savings) $\Leftrightarrow$ demand for pesos (supply of dollars)

$Z - E$ (trade deficit) $\Leftrightarrow$ supply of pesos (demand for dollars)

In Chapter 13, we showed that Z has a positive relationship to the value of the peso and that E has a negative relationship to the value of the peso. This was done in Figures 13.2 and 13.3. We reproduce these figures here as Figures 14.2 and 14.3.

Figure 14.1 The Demand for Pesos

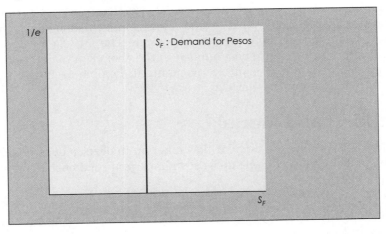

---

[1] Recall from introductory microeconomics that the term "perfectly inelastic" means that the value of the elasticity is zero. That is, there is no response of one economic variable to another. See Chapter 5 of Mankiw (2004).

Figure 14.2 The Value of the Peso and Mexico's Imports

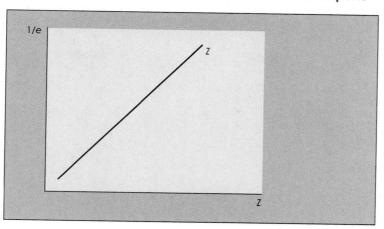

Figure 14.3 The Value of the Peso and Mexico's Exports

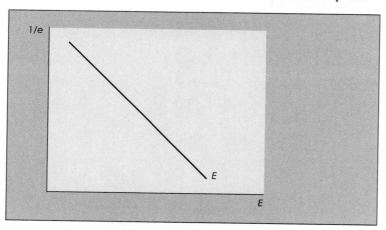

Because Z and E have positive and negative relationships to the value of the peso, respectively, Z–E has a positive relationship to the value of the peso. This upward-sloping supply of pesos graph is represented in Figure 14.4.

Our next step in constructing a trade-based model of exchange rate determination is to combine the demand for pesos with the supply of pesos, as in Figure 14.5.[2] We also need to specify the way in which the exchange rate adjusts. In this chapter, we are considering the case of a **flexible** or **floating exchange rate regime**. This is the case where e can vary in response to excess supply of or excess demand for pesos. In the case of flexible exchange rates, we also need to introduce some terminology for changes in e. These definitions are given in Table 14.1. As shown in this table, under a flexible exchange rate regime, an increase in e or a fall in

Flexible or floating exchange rate regime
An exchange rate policy in which a country allows the value of its currency to be determined by world currency markets.

[2] Trade surpluses can arise in Figure 14.5 by placing the 0 value toward the middle of the horizontal axis rather than at its left end.

Figure 14.4 The Supply of Pesos

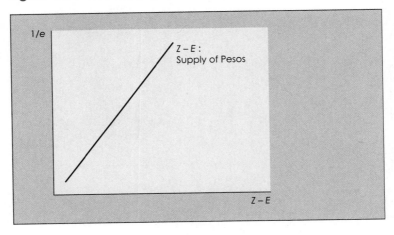

Figure 14.5 The Peso Market

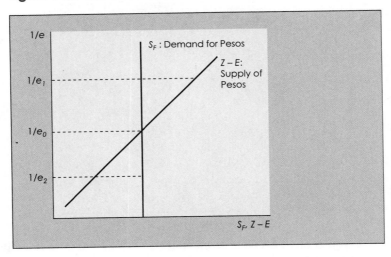

Table 14.1 Exchange Rate Terminology

Case	e	Value of Peso	Term
Flexible e	↑	↓	Depreciation
Flexible e	↓	↑	Appreciation

Depreciation
A decrease in the value of a currency under a flexible or floating exchange rate regime.

Appreciation
An increase in the value of a currency under a flexible or floating exchange rate regime.

the value of the peso is called a **depreciation** of the peso. A decrease in e or a rise in the value of the peso is called an **appreciation** of the peso.[3] With this terminology in hand, we can begin to address Figure 14.5.

---

[3] We will consider alternative exchange rate regimes in Chapter 15, where we will expand Table 14.1.

Theory and Practice

Professor Richard Lyons of the Haas School of Business at the University of California Berkeley is an expert on exchange rate theory. He was in for a surprise when he was invited by a friend to experience currency trading firsthand:

"A friend of mine who trades spot foreign exchange for a large bank invited me to spend a few days at his side. That was 10 years ago. At the time, I considered myself an expert, having written my thesis on exchange rates. I thought I had a handle on how it worked. I thought wrong. As I sat there, my friend traded furiously all day long, racking up over $1 billion in trades each day ($U.S.). This was a world where the standard trade was $10 million, and a $1 million trade was a 'skinny one.' Despite my belief that exchange rates depend on macroeconomics, only rarely was news of this type his primary concern. Most of the time he was reading tea leaves that were, at least to me, not so clear. The pace was furious—a quote every 5 or 10 seconds, a trade every minute or two, and continual decisions about what position to hold. Needless to say, there was little time for chat. It was clear my understanding was incomplete when he looked over, in the midst of his fury, and asked me 'What should I do?' I laughed. Nervously."

Source: Lyons, R.K. (2001) *The Microstructure Approach to Exchange Rates*. Cambridge, Massachusetts: MIT Press. p. 1.

Under our assumption of a flexible exchange rate regime, let's consider three alternative values of the peso in Figure 14.5. The first of these is $1/e_1$. At $1/e_1$, we can see that the supply of pesos exceeds the demand for pesos. In other words, there is an *excess supply* of pesos. The presence of an excess supply of pesos has the effect of reducing the value of the peso or causing a depreciation of the peso. As the peso depreciates, the trade deficit falls, and it is this fall in the trade deficit that brings the supply and demand of pesos into equality. Next, consider $1/e_2$. At $1/e_2$, we can see that the demand for pesos exceeds the supply of pesos. In other words, there is an *excess demand* for pesos. The presence of an excess demand for pesos has the effect of increasing the value of the peso or causing an appreciation of the peso. As the peso appreciates, the trade deficit rises, and the rise in the trade deficit brings the supply and demand of pesos into equality. Finally, consider $1/e_0$. Here the demand for and supply of pesos are exactly the same. For this reason, $1/e_0$ is the equilibrium value of the peso, and e_0 is the equilibrium nominal exchange rate. The adjustment of the value of the peso ensures that the trade deficit equals foreign savings.

This model of exchange rate determination is trade-based in the sense that only trade flows respond to a change in the value of the peso. In the next section, we will allow foreign savings to adjust to changes in the value of the peso, leading us to an assets-based model. Theory is not everything, however. For a view from a trading desk, see the box.

An Assets-Based Model

The **assets approach** to exchange rate determination views foreign currency transactions as arising from the buying and selling of foreign currency—

Assets-based approach
A model of exchange rate determination that views foreign exchange deposits as assets held as part of an overall wealth portfolio.

denominated assets, rather than from trade flows.[4] In other words, it focuses on foreign savings rather than on the trade deficit in the $S_F = Z - E$ relationship. To introduce this approach into our model, pretend that you are a Mexican investor, deciding upon the allocation of your wealth portfolio between two assets: a peso-denominated asset and a dollar-denominated asset. To make things simple, we will take both assets to be open-ended mutual funds with fixed domestic-currency prices.[5] As with all investors, you will allocate your portfolio with an eye to the rates of return of the alternative assets. Let's consider each asset in turn.

In the case of peso-denominated assets, the return you obtain is simply the interest rate. We will denote this rate of interest as r_M. Thus, the total expected return on the peso-denominated asset, R_M^e, is simply:

$$R_M^e = r_M \qquad \textbf{Total expected return on peso-denominated asset}$$

Because you are a Mexican investor, dollar-denominated assets are a bit more complicated. There are two things you must consider. The first is the interest payment on the dollar-denominated assets. This rate of interest we will denote r_{US}. The second consideration is the exchange rate. To see this, suppose that the initial exchange rate is $e_0 = 1$. Suppose also that, at this exchange rate, you purchase a dollar-denominated asset worth \$1,000. This asset is worth 1,000 pesos. Now suppose that the peso depreciates so that the new exchange rate is $e_1 = 1.1$. With this change, the \$1,000 asset has increased in value to 1,100 pesos. Depreciation of the peso causes the asset's value to increase in terms of the peso. You have experienced a **capital gain**. This, along with interest payments, is what investors (including you) are seeking.

Capital gain (loss)
An increase (decrease) in the price of an asset.

At any point in time, the current exchange rate is at a value e. Also, at any point in time, you have your *expectation* of what the exchange rate will be in the future. We will denote this expected exchange rate as e^e. Therefore, your expected rate of depreciation of the peso is given by

$$\frac{(e^e - e)}{e}$$

Finally, your expected total rate of return on dollar-denominated assets is the sum of the interest rate and the expected rate of depreciation of the peso. We will denote this expected total rate of return R_{US}^e. This is given as follows:

$$R_{US}^e = r_{US} + \frac{(e^e - e)}{e} \qquad \textbf{Total expected return on dollar-denominated asset}$$

This relationship tells us that your total expected rate of return on dollar-denominated assets is composed of the interest rate plus the expected rate of depreciation of the peso.

---

[4] For more on the assets approach to exchange rate determination, see Chapter 4 of Krueger (1983), Branson and Henderson (1985), Chapter 14 of Williamson and Milner (1991), Chapters 13 and 14 of Krugman and Obstfeld (1996), and Chapter 6 of Isard (1995).

[5] Because additional shares of open-ended mutual funds are issued upon demand, their supply curves are horizontal. Changes in demand therefore do not affect their prices. Readers in the United States, please be careful. Your are pretending to be a Mexican investor, not a U.S. investor.

We now have expressions for your total expected return on both peso-and dollar-denominated assets. Next, we need to think about how you will allocate your portfolio between these two asset types. To help us along, we are going to consider three alternative possibilities.

The first possibility is that $R^e_M > R^e_{US}$. That is, the expected total rate of return on peso-denominated assets exceeds the expected total rate of return on dollar-denominated assets. What will you do in this case? Because peso-denominated assets offer a higher expected rate of return, you will reallocate your portfolio toward these assets, selling dollars and buying pesos in the process.

The second possibility is that $R^e_M < R^e_{US}$. That is, the expected total rate of return on dollar-denominated assets exceeds the expected total rate of return on peso-denominated assets. In this case, you will reallocate your portfolio toward dollar-denominated assets, buying dollars and selling pesos in the process.

The third possibility is that $R^e_M = R^e_{US}$. In this case, there is no reason or incentive for you to reallocate your portfolio. You would gain nothing by doing so.

As we have just seen, whenever R^e_M and R^e_{US} are not equal, there will be reason for you to reallocate your portfolio between dollar-denominated and peso-denominated assets. These reallocations cause the buying of one currency and the selling of another. Equilibrium in the foreign exchange market, in the sense that there is no reason for you (or any other investors) to reallocate your portfolio, requires that $R^e_M = R^e_{US}$ or

$$r_M = r_{US} + \frac{(e^e - e)}{e}$$

This equation is known as the **interest rate parity condition**. It states that equilibrium in the foreign exchange market requires that the interest rate on peso deposits equals the interest rate on dollar deposits plus the expected rate of peso depreciation. Because it is one of the most important relationships in international finance, we are going to put it in a box for you to remember:

Interest rate parity condition
The equilibrium condition in the assets approach to the exchange rate determination model. It relates a country's interest rate to the expected rate of depreciation of its currency and the interest rate of another country.

Interest Rate Parity Condition

$$r_M = r_{US} + \frac{(e^e - e)}{e} \qquad \text{Mexico – United States}$$

$$r_H = r_F + \frac{(e^e - e)}{e} \qquad \text{Home – Foreign}$$

We are now going to incorporate the interest rate parity condition into a new version of Figure 14.5, the peso market. We begin by focusing on the role of the value of the peso in the interest rate parity condition. Suppose that, initially, we are in equilibrium so that $R^e_M = R^e_{US}$. Next suppose the value of the peso increases or *e* falls. For a given expected future exchange rate (e^e), the total expected rate of return on the dollar-denominated asset, R^e_{US}, increases because as *e* falls, $(e^e - e)/e$ increases in value. Because now $R^e_{US} > R^e_M$, you, along with other investors from all other countries, would sell peso-denominated assets and buy dollar-denominated assets. S_F, the asset-based demand for pesos, consequently declines. Therefore, we have shown that, for a given e^e, as *e* falls (and $1/e$ rises), S_F falls. This gives us the downward-sloping demand curve for pesos presented in Figure 14.6.

To understand the adjustment process in this expanded view of the peso market, let's again consider three alternative values of the peso. The first of these is $1/e_1$. At $1/e_1$, we can see that the supply of pesos exceeds the demand for pesos. Given this excess supply of pesos, the value of the peso falls. The fall in the value of the peso (rise in *e*) does two things:

1. *The trade deficit falls as Z decreases and E increases. This decreases the supply of pesos.*
2. *Foreign saving rises as the expected rate of depreciation of the peso and, therefore, the expected total rate of return on dollar-denominated assets fall. Investors move into peso-denominated assets, and this increases the demand for pesos.*[6]

Both of these changes bring the peso market towards equilibrium.

Next, consider the value of the peso $1/e_2$. At $1/e_2$, we can see that the demand for pesos exceeds the supply of pesos. Given this excess demand for pesos, the value of the peso rises. The rise in the value of the peso (fall in *e*) does two things:

1. *The trade deficit rises as Z increases and E decreases. This increases the supply of pesos.*

Figure 14.6 An Assets-Based View of the Peso Market

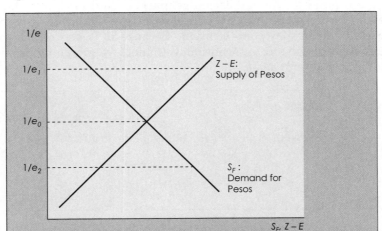

---

[6] It is important to remember that this effect is *for a given e^e.*

2. *Foreign savings falls as the expected rate of depreciation of the peso and, therefore, the expected total rate of return on dollar-denominated assets rise. Investors move out of peso-denominated assets into dollar-denominated assets, and this decreases the demand for pesos.*[7]

Finally, at e_0, the demand for and supply of pesos are equal. The peso market is in equilibrium.

We have covered a lot of ground in this section, but we still have some distance to go to fully appreciate the assets-based model of exchange rate determination. An important, remaining issue is the role of interest rates and expectations in the model, to which we now turn.

Interest Rates, Expectations, and Exchange Rates

To appreciate the role of interest rates and expectations in the determination of flexible exchange rates, we need to return to the interest rate parity condition:

$$r_M = r_{US} + \frac{(e^e - e)}{e} \quad \textbf{Interest rate parity condition}$$

Note that, in this equation, an increase in r_M increases the total expected rate of return on peso-denominated assets, and that an increase in r_{US} increases the total expected rate of return on dollar-denominated assets. Both of these changes will impact the peso market. To understand how this occurs, we need to recognize the role of r_M and r_{US} as variables that *shift* the demand for peso curve. This is done in Figure 14.7.

Figure 14.7 Interest Rates and the Peso Market

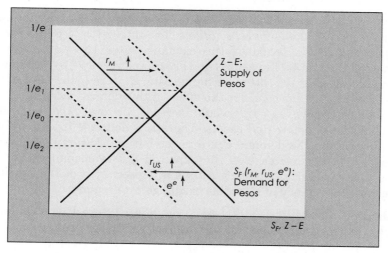

The Bundesbank's Surprise

On Thursday, October 9, 1997, Germany's central bank, the Bundesbank, took the financial world by surprise and raised an important interest rate from 3 percent to 3.3 percent. This unexpected action led to rate increases in France, Belgium, and the Netherlands. On Wednesday, October 8, 1997, the deutchemark had been at 1.7485 per U.S. dollar. At the end of the trading day on Thursday, October 9, it had moved to 1.7439, having touched 1.7333 during the day. As we have stated, an increase in a home-country interest rate causes an appreciation of the home-country currency in a flexible exchange rate regime. Here, Germany is our home country.

Source: Andrews, E.L. (1997) "Germany Raises Interest Rate, and Value of Dollar Declines." *New York Times on the Web*, October 10.

We begin in equilibrium in Figure 14.7 with the value of the peso equal to $1/e_0$. From this initial equilibrium, suppose that r_M increases. This increases the total expected rate of return on peso-denominated assets. There is an increase in demand for pesos, which shifts the demand curve to the right and raises the value of the peso to $1/e_1$. An increase in the Mexican (home-country) interest rate causes an appreciation of the Mexican (home-country) currency in a flexible exchange rate regime.

Next, suppose that r_{US} increases. This increases the total expected rate of return on dollar-denominated assets. There is a decrease in demand for pesos, which shifts the demand curve to the left and lowers the value of the peso to $1/e_2$. An increase in the U.S. (foreign-country) interest rate causes a depreciation of the Mexican (home-country) currency in a flexible exchange rate regime. For an example of this, see the box. For a discussion of monetary policies and their link to exchange rates via interest rates, see the appendix to this chapter.

A final remaining issue in the assets-based model of exchange rate determination is a *change in expectations*. The interest rate parity condition involves expectations about future exchange rates. These expectations are formed in the minds of investors and are therefore subjective. Suppose, for example, the expected future exchange rate, e^e, were to increase in the minds of investors. Let's consider the effect of this change in Figure 14.7. Just like an increase in r_{US}, this would increase the total expected rate of return on dollar-denominated assets. There is a decrease in demand for pesos, which shifts the demand curve to the left and lowers the value of the peso to $1/e_2$. An increase in the expected future exchange rate for Mexico's (home country) currency causes a depreciation of the Mexico's (home country) currency in a flexible exchange rate regime.

Williamson and Milner (1991) have made an interesting statement about this expectations aspect of the interest rate parity condition:

> *(T)he yields on different assets, and thus the prices that investors will be prepared to pay for them, depend not merely on objective interest rates but also on subjective expectations. Expectations can sometimes change*

rapidly, due to anything from climatic disasters to political assassinations to rumours about what the latest money supply figures signify. Such sudden changes in expectations, it is argued, are what lie behind the sudden price changes that are typical of all asset markets, including the exchange markets (p. 256).

As we will discuss further in Chapter 17, expectations can be self-fulfilling in currency markets. This causes a certain amount of instability, a continual difficulty for countries around the world.

These insights concerning interest rates and expectations are very important for your understanding of how currency markets operate in flexible exchange rate regimes. For this reason, we summarize them in Table 14.2. So that you might generalize these insights, this table is in terms of a home and foreign country rather than in terms of Mexico and the United States.

Table 14.2 Changes in Currency Markets

Change	Effect on S_F Curve	Effect on Value of Home Currency (1/e)	Term
Increase in home-country interest rate	Shifts to right	Increases	Appreciation
Increase in foreign-country interest rate	Shifts to left	Decreases	Depreciation
Increase in expected future home-country exchange rate	Shifts to left	Decreases	Depreciation

Conclusion

The purchasing power parity model of exchange rate determination that we considered in Chapter 13 applies only to the long run. In order to understand the short-run behavior of nominal exchange rates, we have the trade-based and asset-based models. The trade-based model focuses on the response of $(Z - E)$ to changes in the nominal exchange rate; the assets-based model focuses on the response of both $(Z - E)$ and S_F to changes in the nominal exchange rate. The assets-based model is expressed as the interest rate parity condition. Expected future exchange rates play an important role in this condition and, hence, in the determination of nominal exchange rates. This makes flexible exchange rates, our focus in this chapter, very volatile in practice. We take up alternatives to flexible exchange rates in Chapter 15.

Review Exercises

1. As we will discuss in some detail in Chapter 18, the European Union (EU) has recently introduced a common currency known as the euro. Take the EU as your home country and the United States as your foreign country. In this case, $e = {}^{euros}/_{dollar}$. Set up the equivalent of Figure 14.6 to show the determination of e. Next, use three additional diagrams to show the impacts on e of the following changes: a fall in the euro interest rate; a fall in the dollar interest rate; and a fall in the expected value of the exchange rate (e^e). In each case, explain the intuition of your result.

2. In Chapter 13, we discussed the links between trade flows and the nominal exchange rate. All other things constant, what would an increase in a home country's interest rate tend to do to its exports, imports, and trade deficit? Explain the intuition of your answer.

3. In Chapter 13, we discussed the links between trade flows and the nominal exchange rate. All other things constant, what would a decrease in a home country's interest rate tend to do to its exports, imports, and trade deficit? Explain the intuition of your answer.

4. For the previous example, set up the equivalent of Figure 14.A3, shown in the appendix to this chapter. Next, show the impacts in this figure of a contractionary monetary policy in the EU and a contractionary monetary policy in the United States. In each case, explain the intuition of your results.

Further Reading and Web Resources

Introductions to exchange rate economics can be found in Krueger (1983) and Isard (1995). The assets approach to exchange rate determination is discussed in Chapter 4 of Krueger (1983), Branson and Henderson (1985), Chapter 14 of Williamson and Milner (1991), Chapters 13 and 14 of Krugman and Obstfeld (1997), and Chapter 6 of Isard (1995). Monetary theory, taken up in the appendix, is effectively reviewed by Harris (1981).

You can easily follow day-to-day movements in currency values using the PACIFIC Exchange Rate Service at **http://pacific.commerce.ubc.ca/xr**. See also Oanda, The Currency Site, at **http://www.oanda.com**.

References

Andrews, E.L. (1997) "Germany Raises Interest Rate, and Value of Dollar Declines," *New York Times on the Web*, October 10.

Branson, W.H., and D.W. Henderson (1985) "The Specification and Influence of Asset Markets," in R. Jones and P.B. Kenen (eds.), *Handbook of International Economics*, North-Holland, Amsterdam, 749–805.

Harris, L. (1981) *Monetary Theory*, McGraw-Hill, New York.

Isard, P. (1995) *Exchange Rate Economics*, Cambridge University Press, Cambridge.

Keynes, J.M. (1936) *The General Theory of Employment, Interest, and Money*, Harcourt, Brace and Company, New York.

Krueger, A.O. (1983) *Exchange Rate Determination*, Cambridge University Press, Cambridge.

Krugman, P.R., and M. Obstfeld (1997) *International Economics: Theory and Policy*, Harper Collins, New York.

Lyons, R.K. (2001) *The Microstructure Approach to Exchange Rates*, MIT Press, Cambridge, Massachusetts.

Mankiw, N.G. (2004) *Principles of Economics*, South-Western/Thomson Learning, Mason, Ohio.

Skidelsky, R. (1992) *John Maynard Keynes: The Economist As Savior 1920–1937*, Macmillan, London.

Williamson, J., and C. Milner (1991) *The World Economy*, New York University Press, New York.

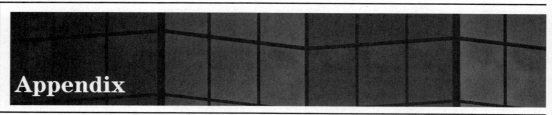

Appendix

Monetary Policies

Some readers of this book will be familiar with the macroeconomic topic of monetary policies from a course on macroeconomics. If this is the case for you, you will be able to extend our analysis of this chapter to an understanding of the link between monetary policies, interest rates, and exchange rates. This is the purpose of this appendix.

In 1936, the British economist John Maynard Keynes published his *General Theory of Employment, Interest, and Money.* Among other things, this book proposed a new theory of **money demand** that we will utilize here.[8] Keynes' theory of money demand will help you understand where the interest rates in the interest parity condition come from and then to understand the impact of monetary policies on exchange rates.

To begin, we need to define some notation. M^D denotes money demand in the country in question. This is the amount of money households want to hold at any particular time. M^S denotes **money supply** in the country in question, and this value is determined by the monetary authority (central bank or treasury) of the country. We need to ask ourselves why households would want to hold money. One obvious reason is that they hold money in order to conduct the economic transactions of everyday life. Keynes and the economists that preceded him hypothesized that these transaction demands for money would increase as the income of the economy increased. As in Chapter 12, we will denote this income as Y. M^D is related positively to Y. However, like all economic decisions, holding money has opportunity costs associated with it. When a household holds money, it forgoes the interest it could be earning if the money were put into an interest-bearing deposit. Unlike his predecessors, Keynes hypothesized that M^D would therefore be negatively related to the interest rate. The higher the interest rate, the more households would economize on money holdings, and the less money they would hold.

Money demand
The amount of money households want to hold at any particular time.

Money supply
The amount of money set in an economy by a central monetary authority such as a central bank or treasury.

---

[8] An excellent overview of monetary theory can be found in Harris (1981). Harris discusses Keynes' contribution to money demand theory in Chapter 9 of his book. As Skidelsky (1992, Chapter 14) notes, this theory was first developed in lectures Keynes gave in the autumn of 1933.

We want to summarize these considerations in a money demand function. This function is as follows:

$$M^D = L(Y, r) \qquad \textbf{Money demand function}$$

Money demand is a function of income and the interest rate. The function itself is usually denoted as $L(\ )$, where L stands for *liquidity*. To be in possession of money is to be financially liquid. As we described earlier, theory tells us that $\Delta M^D / \Delta Y$ is positive, while $\Delta M^D / \Delta r$ is negative. Money demand is positively related to income but negatively related to the interest rate.

Money supply, M^S, we will assume, is set by the central bank or treasury of the country in question. Although the money-supply process is not in the real world this straightforward, we will ignore any complications here in order to focus on our primary objective in this chapter: exchange rate determination.[9] We want to bring money demand and money supply into a single diagram. This diagram has money on the horizontal axis and the interest rate on the vertical axis. It is depicted in Figure 14.A1.

The money supply does not vary with the rate of interest. Therefore, the M^S curve is vertical. Money demand varies inversely with the rate of interest. This gives the negative slope to the M^D curve in the diagram. The position of the M^D curve, that is, how far to the left or right it lies in the diagram, depends on the level of income. The M^D curve in Figure 14.A1 has been drawn for an initial income level, Y_0. Given this income level and the initial money supply, $M^S = M_0$, the interest rate is r_0. If the interest rate were to be above r_0 at r_1, there would be excess supply of

Figure 14.A1 The Money Market

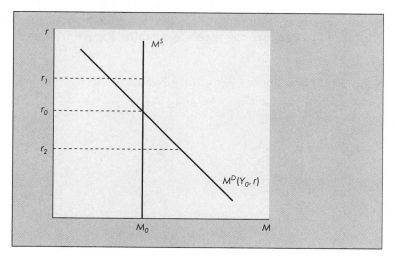

---

[9] It is often the case that, instead of targeting M^S as suggested in our diagrams, monetary authorities target an interest rate. For example, the U.S. Federal Reserve often targets an overnight bank rate. However, in achieving the target interest rate, the monetary authority usually conducts open market operations (the buying or selling of government debt), which has the effect of changing the money supply as indicated in our diagrams.

money. This would put downward pressure on the interest rate. As the interest rate falls, the opportunity cost of holding money would also fall, increasing money demand to meet money supply. If the interest rate were to be below r_0 at r_2, there would be excess demand for money. This would put upward pressure on the interest rate. As the interest rate rose, the opportunity cost of holding money would also rise, decreasing money demand to meet money supply.

Figure 14.A1 gives us a description of the equilibrium in the money market. Let's try to determine whether it provides any intuitive explanations of the link between monetary policy and the interest rate. Suppose that the central bank of the country decided to engage in an expansionary monetary policy by increasing M^S. This change is depicted in Figure 14.A2. The increase in the money supply shifts the M^S curve to the right. At the original interest rate, r_0, money supply exceeds money demand. The excess supply of money puts downward pressure on the interest rate. As the interest rate falls, the opportunity cost of holding money falls, and the demand for money increases. The economy moves to a new equilibrium in the money market at a lower interest rate, r_1, and a higher quantity of money, M_1. As we observe in the real world, an expansionary monetary policy is associated with a lower interest rate. Similarly, a contractionary monetary policy is associated with a decrease in the money supply and an increase in the interest rate.

In this chapter, we developed a model of exchange rate determination that viewed currency markets being affected by assets allocations (Figures 14.6 and 14.7). In this model, interest rates in Mexico and the United States played primary roles in determining the nominal exchange rate. In this appendix, we have developed a model of interest rate determination based on the money market of the economy. We next want to bring all of the elements together to understand how monetary policy affects exchange rates. To do this, we are going to combine Figure 14.6 with two

Figure 14.A2 An Expansionary Monetary Policy

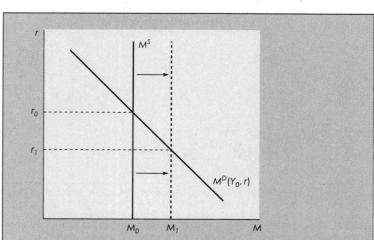

versions of Figure 14.A2, one for the Mexican money market and a second for the U.S. money market. This is done in Figure 14.A3.

Figure 14.A3 Money Markets and Exchange Rate Determination

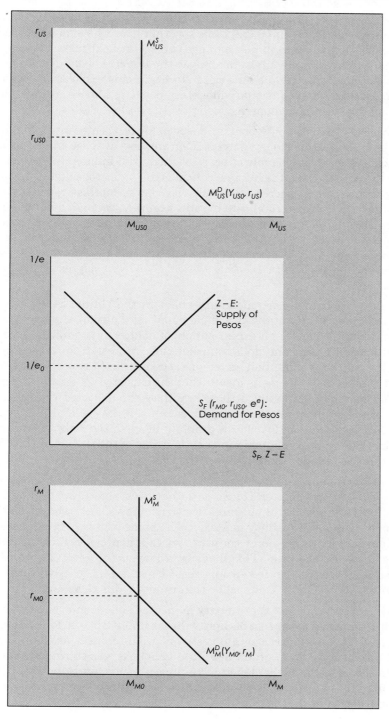

The top diagram in Figure 14.A3 depicts the equilibrium in the U.S. money market, which determines the interest rate on the dollar. The bottom diagram of Figure 14.A3 depicts the equilibrium in the Mexican money market, which determines the interest rate on the peso. The dollar interest rate r_{US}, the peso interest rate r_M, and the expected rate of peso depreciation e^e all help to determine the position of the demand for peso line in the middle diagram. These three diagrams together give us a sense that monetary policies help to determine exchange rates. Our next task is to use the three diagrams in Figure 14.A3 to analyze the impacts of changes in monetary policies on the value of the peso. To begin this exploration, we are going to consider an expansionary monetary policy in Mexico. We will then turn to an expansionary monetary policy in the United States.

The case of expansionary monetary policy in Mexico is presented in Figure 14.A4. In the Mexican money market diagram, the increase in the money supply causes an excess supply of pesos at the initial interest rate. In order to clear the peso market, the interest rate falls to r_{M1}, increasing the demand for pesos to equal the increased supply. The lower interest rate on pesos means that the expected total rate of return on peso-denominated assets is now less than the expected total rate of return on dollar-denominated assets. Investors sell pesos and buy dollars, which causes the demand for pesos graph to move to the left. As a result of this decrease in the demand for pesos, the value of the peso falls. In other words, there is a depreciation of the Mexican peso.

The case of expansionary monetary policy in the United States is presented in Figure 14.A5. In the U.S. money market diagram, the increase in the money supply causes an excess supply of dollars at the initial interest rate. In order to clear the dollar market, the interest rate falls to r_{US1}, increasing the demand for dollars to equal the increased supply. The lower interest rate on dollar deposits means that the expected total rate of return on dollar-denominated assets is now less than the expected total rate of return on peso-denominated assets. Investors sell dollars and buy pesos, which causes the demand for pesos graph to move to the right. As a result of this increase in the demand for pesos, the value of the peso rises. In other words, there is an appreciation of the Mexican peso.

As we have shown here, monetary policies affect interest rates and exchange rates. In Chapter 13, we saw that exchange rates affect trade flows. Monetary policies, then, can affect trade flows. Take the case of an expansionary monetary policy in Mexico, the home country. An increase in the money supply in the home country causes a depreciation of the home country currency, the peso. This involves a movement down the value of the peso scale. As illustrated in Figures 13.4 and 14.4, this will tend to cause the trade deficit to contract or the trade surplus to expand.

On the other hand, an expansionary monetary policy tends to encourage investment due to a lower cost of capital that is implied by the lower domestic interest rate. Any increase in investment would appear as the upward shift of the $I - S_H - T + G$ graph in Figure 12.A1. As was shown there, this tends to increase the trade deficit. The impact of monetary policy on the trade balance, then, depends on the relative strengths of the exchange rate and investment effects.

Figure 14.A4 Expansionary Monetary Policy in the Home Country

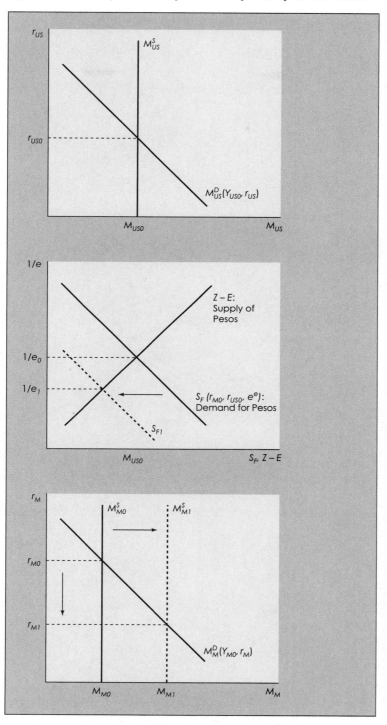

Figure 14.A5 Expansionary Monetary Policy in the Foreign Country

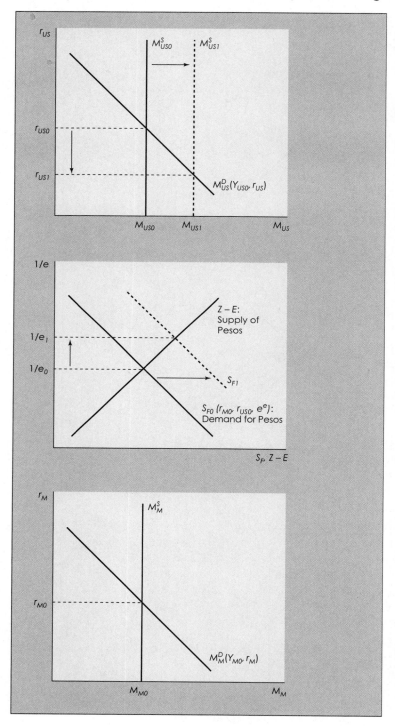

Fixed Exchange Rates

15

In the very first paragraph of Chapter 1, you read the following:

> In the mid-1990s, I met an anthropology student who had just returned from a year in Senegal. As soon as she learned that I was an international economist, she asked, "Can you tell me about the CFA franc devaluation? Why was it necessary? It has made life very difficult in Senegal."

The CFA is Communauté Financière Africaine, a collection of francophone African countries that you will learn more about in Chapter 18. The CFA franc is the common currency of these countries. The value of this currency is not allowed to "float" in currency markets. That is, the CFA franc is not a flexible exchange rate. Instead, the currency is pegged to the euro (previously the French franc) in what is known as a fixed exchange rate regime. The anthropology student I mentioned was concerned with the reduction in the value of the CFA franc relative to the French franc that took place in 1994. The purpose of this chapter is to examine such fixed exchange rate regimes.

We will begin by defining a number of alternative exchange rate regimes, placing them on a continuum between "fixed" and "flexible." Next, we will focus on the case of fixed exchange rates and examine the various ways that balance of payments adjustment can occur under this regime. Finally, we will consider what has come to be known as the policy trilemma in the field of international finance. An appendix discusses monetary policies under fixed exchange rate regimes. As such, it follows on the appendix of Chapter 14.

Alternative Exchange Rate Regimes

The model of exchange rate determination we developed in Chapter 14 assumed that the nominal exchange rate is perfectly flexible. However, in reality, there is a *menu* of exchange rate arrangements from which a country can choose. This menu is presented in Table 15.1. As you can see, in the year 2001, 41 countries pursued a floating or flexible exchange rate regime where the monetary authority did not intervene to influence the market value of the nominal exchange rate. Forty-two countries maintained a **managed floating regime** where the monetary authority may have intervened to influence the nominal exchange rate in some

Managed floating regime
An exchange rate regime in which a country allows its currency to float but intervenes in currency markets to affect its value when it determines that such intervention would be desirable.

Table 15.1 Exchange Rate Arrangements, 2001

Arrangement	Description	Number of Countries
Flexible (clean) float	The exchange rate is market determined.	41
Managed (dirty) float	The exchange rate is primarily market determined, but the country's monetary authority intervenes in the currency market to influence the movements of the exchange rate.	42
Crawling bands	The country's monetary authority intervenes to maintain the exchange rate in a band around a central rate, and these bands are periodically adjusted.	6
Crawling pegs	The exchange rate is fixed in value to another currency or to a "basket" of other currencies, but adjusted periodically by small amounts.	4
Fixed	The exchange rate is fixed in value to another currency or to a "basket" of other currencies.	45
Currency board	The exchange rate is fixed in value to another currency, and domestic currency is fully backed by reserves of this foreign currency.	8
No separate legal tender	The legal tender of the country is a currency of another country.	40

Source: International Monetary Fund (2002). *International Financial Statistics Yearbook*. Washington, DC: International Monetary Fund Publications. 4-5. Copyright © 2002 by the International Monetary Fund. Used with permission.

Crawling band
An exchange rate regime in which monetary authorities intervene to maintain the nominal exchange rate in a band of prescribed width around a central rate.

Crawling peg
An exchange rate regime in which a country fixes its nominal exchange rate in terms of another currency but changes this fixed rate gradually over time in small increments.

Fixed exchange rate
An exchange rate policy in which a country sets its nominal or currency exchange rate fixed in terms of another currency.

way.[1] Six countries used **crawling bands**, where the monetary authorities intervened to maintain the nominal exchange rate in a band around a central rate, and these bands were periodically adjusted. Four countries employed **crawling pegs**. Here, the nominal exchange rate was fixed in value to another currency or to a "basket" of other currencies, but adjusted periodically by small amounts.

Forty-five countries pursued **fixed exchange rates** or fixed pegs where monetary authorities adopted a policy goal of keeping the nominal exchange rate at a fixed value in terms of another currency or in terms of

[1] Managed floats are also known as "dirty" floats. Velasco (2000) notes: "In the real world, clean floats do not exist. Major industrialized countries such as Canada and the United Kingdom, smaller OECD countries such as Australia and New Zealand, and middle income countries such as Peru and Mexico, all practice floating with various degrees of 'dirt.' Even the United States, usually regarded as the cleanest of floaters, intervenes occasionally in the foreign-exchange market" (p. 11). The IMF data in Table 15.2 is not as strict as Velasco in its definition of a clean float.

Exchange Rate Regimes in Poland

Poland's exchange rate regime since 1990 has gone through many changes. It began in 1990 with a fixed exchange rate, with the zloty pegged to the U.S. dollar. However, inadequate foreign reserves forced a change. In 1991, the Polish government set up a crawling peg, but expanded the peg to include a basket of currencies, including the U.S. dollar. The crawling peg involved a monthly devaluation against the currency basket at a rate of 1.8 percent. This too proved unworkable at times, and larger devaluations were required in 1992 and 1993.

In 1995, another significant change was introduced. The Polish government changed the crawling peg to a crawling band against the currency basket of ±7.0 percent. This band was widened to ±10.0 percent and then to ±12.5 percent in 1998. In 1999, the currency basket was changed to reflect the introduction of the European Union euro (see Chapter 18). Finally, in 2000, the zloty began to float.

Source: Kokoszczyński, R. (2001). "From Fixed to Floating: Other Country Experiences: The Case of Poland," Paper presented at the International Monetary Fund Seminar "Exchange Rate Regimes: Hard Peg or Free Floating?" Washington, DC.

a "basket" of other currencies. Additionally, eight countries pursued an extreme form of fixed exchange rate known as a currency board. Here, the monetary authority is required to fully back up the domestic currency with reserves of the foreign currency to which the domestic currency is pegged.[2] Finally, a relatively large number of (usually very small) countries went even a step further and maintained no independent currency whatsoever.

The choice of exchange rate regime is a very important decision for a country. In this chapter, we will try to get of sense of why this is so by contrasting the case of fixed or pegged rates with the flexible rates we discussed in Chapter 14. The box considers the exchange rate regime choice of Poland.

A Model of Fixed Exchange Rates

In contrast to the case of the flexible or floating exchange rate regime, we will consider the polar opposite case of a fixed exchange rate regime. As in Chapter 14, Mexico will be our home country, and the United States will be our foreign country. The currency market we will focus on is again the peso market, and we include the asset considerations of Chapter 14. Although the peso began floating in 1995, in previous years it had indeed been fixed against the U.S. dollar.[3] For your convenience, our balance of payments table of Chapter 12 is reproduced here as Table 15.2. We will refer to the balance of payments in the discussion that follows.

Before beginning, we need to establish some terminology and, in so doing, expand Table 14.1. This is done in Table 15.3. The first two rows of Table 15.3 repeat the flexible exchange rate terminology of Chapter 14. The third and fourth rows introduce new terminology for the fixed exchange

---

[2] We will discuss currency boards in Chapter 17.
[3] See Chapter 17.

Table 15.2 Mexican Balance of Payments, 1993 (billions of U.S. dollars)

Item	Gross	Net	Major Balance
Current Account			
1. Exports	61		
2. Imports	77		
3. Trade balance		−16	
4. Net factor receipts		−11	
5. Transfers		4	
6. Current account balance			−23
Capital Account			
7. Direct investment		4	
8. Portfolio investment		29	
9. Official reserves balance		−7	
10. Errors and omissions		−3	
11. Capital account balance			23
12. Overall balance			0

Source: Based on data from Banco de México, http://www.banxico.org.mx.

Table 15.3 Exchange Rate Terminology Revisited

Case	e	Value of Peso	Term
Flexible *e*	↑	↓	Depreciation
Flexible *e*	↓	↑	Appreciation
Fixed *e*	↑	↓	Devaluation
Fixed *e*	↓	↑	Revaluation

rate regime. Let's consider them one at a time. Under a fixed exchange rate regime, when the Mexican government raises *e* and thereby decreases the value of the peso, there is said to be a **devaluation** of the peso. This contrasts with a market-driven, upward movement in *e* under a flexible exchange rate regime known as a depreciation. Under a fixed exchange rate regime, when the Mexican government lowers *e* and thereby increases the

Devaluation
A decrease in the value of a currency under a fixed exchange rate regime.

value of the peso, there is said to be a **revaluation** of the peso. This contrasts with a market-driven, downward movement in e under a flexible exchange rate regime known as an appreciation. In practice, devaluations are much more common than revaluations.

Revaluation
An increase in the value of a currency under a fixed exchange rate regime.

There is some additional terminology we need to understand in the case of a fixed exchange rate regime, and we will address this with the help of Figure 15.1. This diagram represents the peso market as we developed it in Chapter 14. Suppose that e_0 represents the equilibrium exchange rate under a flexible exchange rate regime. This is where the supply of pesos given by the trade deficit equals the demand for pesos given by foreign savings.[4] In terms of the balance of payments accounts of Table 15.2, the supply of pesos is the negative of item 3, the trade balance. The demand for pesos relates to the sum of items 7 and 8, direct and indirect investment. The demand for pesos illustrated in Figure 15.1 is therefore the *nonofficial* capital account balance. This excludes the actions of central banks, which we will discuss later.

Suppose that the Mexican government chooses to fix the exchange rate at e_1. The value of the peso, $1/e_1$, is therefore above the equilibrium value of the peso, $1/e_0$. This situation is known as an **overvaluation** of the peso. Note that an overvaluation of the peso implies an excess supply of pesos or an excess demand for dollars. How can this be sustained? There must be some additional demand for pesos or supply of dollars. As we see in Table 15.2, this can come from three sources: positive net factor receipts, positive net transfers (e.g., inflows of foreign aid), and positive net official reserve transactions.[5] Let's examine the last of these in some detail. If e is fixed at e_1, there is an excess supply of pesos or demand for dollars. Mexico's central

Overvaluation
Under a fixed exchange rate regime, a value of a home currency above its equilibrium value, which causes an excess supply of the home currency.

Figure 15.1 The Peso Market

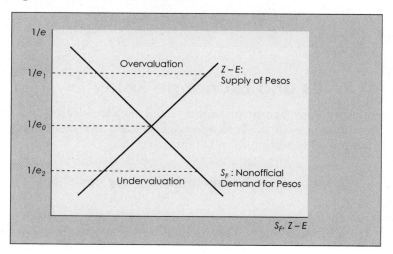

---

[4] As mentioned in Chapter 14, trade surpluses can be handled in this diagram by the placement of the zero value toward the middle of the horizontal axis rather than at the left endpoint.

[5] It is helpful to view positive entries in the balance of payments as demands for pesos or supply of dollars. Here we ignore errors and omissions.

bank can address this by selling its holdings of dollars (buying pesos). In this process of *drawing down foreign reserves*, the central bank helps to eliminate the excess supply of pesos or demand for dollars. It is for this reason that we often find countries with overvalued currencies drawing down their foreign reserves. We will explore the limits of this process in Chapters 17 and 23 on crises and structural adjustment, respectively.

Next, suppose that the Mexican government chose to fix the exchange rate at e_2. The value of the peso, $1/e_2$, is therefore below the equilibrium value of the peso, $1/e_0$. This situation is known as an **undervaluation** of the peso. Note that an undervaluation of the peso implies an excess demand for pesos or an excess supply of dollars. This situation can be sustained via some additional supply of pesos or demand for dollars. As we see in Table 15.2, this can come from negative net factor receipts, negative net transfers, and negative net official reserve transactions. Again, it is worthwhile to examine the last of these in some detail. Mexico's central bank can address the excess demand for pesos or supply of dollars by buying dollars (selling pesos). In this process of *building up foreign reserves*, the central bank helps to eliminate the excess demand for pesos or supply of dollars.[6]

> **Undervaluation**
> Under a fixed exchange rate regime, a value of a home-country currency below its equilibrium value causing an excess demand for the currency.

The conclusion we reach here, which coincides with experience, is that central banks in countries with overvalued currencies tend to draw down foreign exchange reserves, while central banks in countries with overvalued currencies tend to build up foreign reserves. Let's summarize this in a box for you to remember:

Overvaluation $\Rightarrow$ Excess supply of pesos (demand for dollars) $\Rightarrow$
Central bank draws down foreign reserves

Undervaluation $\Rightarrow$ Excess demand for pesos (supply of dollars) $\Rightarrow$
Central bank builds up foreign reserves

Interest Rates and Exchange Rates

There is another approach to sustaining fixed exchange rates by affecting the equilibrium rate e_0. This approach is best analyzed using the interest rate parity condition from Chapter 14:

$$r_M = r_{US} + \frac{(e^e - e)}{e}$$ **Interest rate parity condition**

Suppose that the Mexican government successfully ensures that a fixed rate e_3 is an equilibrium rate. What must be the relationship between e_3 and e^e? A moment of thought tells us that if e_3 is both a fixed and an equi-

---

[6] Some development economists (e.g., Lipumba, 1994) have argued that it is a good idea to maintain a slightly undervalued currency to keep trade deficits at manageable levels and to accumulate foreign reserves for future emergencies.

librium rate, then e_3 must equal e^e. This causes a change in our interest rate parity condition. $(e^e - e)$ is now zero, and therefore:

$$r_M = r_{US}$$

This relationship tells us that, for the Mexican government to maintain a fixed, equilibrium exchange rate, it must ensure that its interest rate equals that in the United States. Another way of looking at this is shown in Figure 15.2. By increasing or decreasing r_M into equality with r_{US}, the Mexican government can move the S_F graph to the left or right until the equilibrium e and e_3 are identical. For example, suppose that initially $r_M = r_{US}$, and this allows for a fixed exchange rate e_3. Next, suppose that the U.S. government increases r_{US} so that $r_M < r_{US}$. This shifts the demand for pesos graph to the left. In order to maintain the fixed e_3, the Mexican government will need to increase r_M, moving the demand for pesos graph back to its original position. Similarly, if from the initial equilibrium, the U.S. government were to decrease r_{US} so that $r_M > r_{US}$, this would shift the demand for peso graph to the right. Here, in order to maintain the fixed e_3, the Mexican government will need to decrease r_H, moving the demand for peso graph back to its original position.[7]

We have gained an important insight here into the operation of fixed exchange rate regimes. Let's summarize it in a box for you to remember:[8]

> **If a home country wants to maintain an *equilibrium* fixed exchange rate, it must set its interest rate equal to that prevailing in the foreign country whose currency serves as a peg for the home-country currency.**

Figure 15.2 An Equilibrium Fixed Exchange Rate

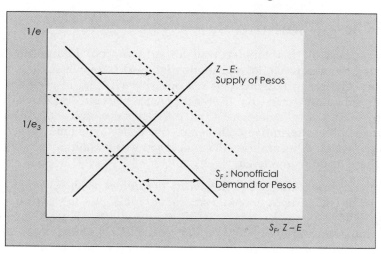

---

[7] For the role of monetary policies in this process, see the appendix to this chapter.
[8] There is an important extension of this insight into monetary policies that we discuss in the appendix to this chapter.

Defending the Brazilian *Real*

In October 1998, Brazilian citizens reelected Fernando Henrique Cardoso to a second term as president. In the months preceding the election, however, Brazilian monetary authorities were engaged in an intense struggle with international investors to maintain a crawling peg of the Brazilian *real* against the U.S. dollar. By September 1998, interest rates had reached 40 percent. Despite this strong measure, however, foreign reserves had been drawn down from nearly $75 billion to $50 billion. Brazil began to talk to the International Monetary Fund (IMF) about a support package to maintain investor confidence in the face of a fiscal deficit of almost 8 percent of GDP and a current account deficit of approximately 4 percent of GDP.

Shortly after taking office, and in close consultation with the IMF, Cardoso's economic team drew up a package of budget cuts and tax increases. In November, an official agreement with the IMF worth $41.5 billion was announced, and Cardoso's government denied that it would abandon the crawling peg. In December, the government also denied that it would abandon its central bank president Gustavo Franco, whose job it was to defend the *real*.

In mid-January 1999, Gustavo Franco resigned, and the *real* was devalued. Two days later, the *real* was allowed to float. It very quickly lost almost a third of its value.

Sources: *The Economist* (September, October, and December 1998).

The real world is a complex place and, in practice, fixed exchange rates are maintained with combinations of net factor receipts, net transfers, official reserve transactions, and interest rates. That is, both Figure 15.1 and Figure 15.2 are relevant. We discuss this for the case of Brazil in the accompanying box. However, one principle is always operable. The farther a fixed exchange rate is from the equilibrium exchange rate, the more difficult it is to maintain for an extended period of time.

The Policy Trilemma

Policy trilemma
A necessary policy choice facing all countries of only two of the following three desired objectives: monetary independence, exchange rate stability, and capital mobility.

Our discussions in this chapter lead up to a concept in international finance that has received a lot of attention lately. It is known as the **policy trilemma**. The term "trilemma" is not one you will find in a dictionary. The term "dilemma" refers to a necessary choice between *two* undesirable alternatives. The term "trilemma," then, refers to a necessary choice among *three* undesirable alternatives. To begin, the policy trilemma recognizes that, in the realm of international finance, countries would ideally like to pursue three desired objectives:

1. Monetary independence *or the ability to conduct an independent monetary policy with an eye to stabilizing the domestic macroeconomic policy.*
2. Exchange rate stability *or the ability to avoid destabilizing volatility in the nominal exchange rate.*
3. Capital mobility *or the ability to take advantage of flows on the direct and portfolio capital accounts from foreign savings.*

As it turns out, however, countries must sacrifice one of these desired objectives in order to achieve the other two. The policy trilemma, illustrated in Figure 15.3, helps to explain why this is the case. We will develop your understanding of this figure in three steps.

First, suppose a country wants to maintain both capital mobility and exchange rate stability. These two objectives appear as italicized terms in Figure 15.3 associated with the bottom and right-hand sides of the triangle. Arrows from these two terms converge in the lower right-hand corner of the triangle on the policy regime of fixed exchange rate. This indicates that the only way to maintain both capital mobility and exchange rate stability is to pursue a fixed exchange rate regime. The desired objective that the country must give up is the one on the side of the triangle opposite of the fixed exchange rate corner, namely, monetary independence. As you have seen in the previous section of this chapter, if a country wants to maintain its fixed exchange rate as an equilibrium rate, it must adjust its interest rate to that in the country to which its currency is pegged. Because, as is discussed further in the appendix, interest rates are set via monetary policy, *in maintaining capital mobility and exchange rate stability, the country must sacrifice its independent monetary policy.*

Second, suppose a country wants to maintain both capital mobility and monetary independence. These two objectives appear as italicized terms in Figure 15.3 associated with the bottom and left-hand sides of the triangle.

Figure 15.3 The Policy Trilemma

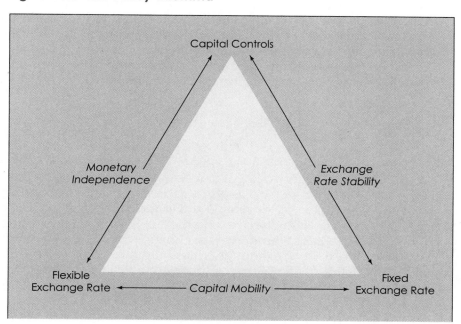

Source: Adapted from Commission of the European Communities (1993). "The Economics of the EMU." In *International Finance: Contemporary Issues*, D.K. Das ed. London: Routledge. 224.

Arrows from these two terms converge in the lower left-hand corner of the triangle on the policy regime of flexible exchange rate. This indicates that the only way to maintain both capital mobility and monetary independence is to allow the currency to float. The desired objective that the country must give up is the one on the side of the triangle opposite the flexible exchange rate corner, namely, exchange rate stability. As you saw in Chapter 14, changes in foreign interest rates and in expectations will, in the face of a given monetary policy in the country, alter the flexible, nominal exchange rate. Because, in practice, such movements in flexible exchange rates can be large, we see that *in maintaining capital mobility and monetary independence, the country must sacrifice exchange rate stability.*

Third, suppose a country wants to maintain both monetary independence and exchange rate stability. These two objectives appear as italicized terms in Figure 15.3 associated with the left-hand and right-hand sides of the triangle. Arrows from these two terms converge at the apex of the triangle on the policy regime of capital controls. This indicates that the only way to maintain both monetary independence and exchange rate stability is to restrict transactions on the capital account of the balance of payments in order to suppress the portfolio considerations we discussed in this and the previous chapter. The desired objective that the country must give up is the one on the side of the triangle opposite the capital control corner, namely, capital mobility. In order to *maintain monetary independence and exchange rate stability, the country must sacrifice capital mobility.*

Economic analysis often helps to highlight trade-offs among alternatives. Here we have highlighted some central trade-offs among policies facing each country in the world economy. As with economic trade-offs in general, there are opportunity costs of any choice. In the realm of international finance, countries must give up one desired objective (monetary independence, exchange rate stability, or capital mobility) to attain the other two. To assume otherwise in policy deliberations is wishful thinking.

Conclusion

While Chapter 14 considered the case of freely floating or flexible exchange rates, this is only one of a number of possible exchange rate regimes. Other alternatives include managed floating, crawling pegs, adjustable pegs, and fixed exchange rates. The current chapter focused on the last of these, fixed exchange rates. Governments can maintain overvalued exchange rates through positive net factor receipts, positive net transfers, and positive net official reserve transactions (drawing down foreign reserves). These provide the requisite extra demand for the home-country currency. Alternatively, governments can raise the domestic interest rate to increase the equilibrium value of the currency so that it is no longer overvalued. Governments can maintain undervalued exchange rates through negative net factor receipts, negative net transfers, and negative net official reserve transactions (building up foreign reserves). These provide the requisite extra supply for the currency. Alternatively, the government can lower the domestic interest rate to decrease the equilibrium value of the currency so that it is no longer undervalued.

Every country faces a policy "trilemma" in which it must sacrifice one desired objective (monetary independence, exchange rate stability, or capital mobility) to attain the other two. This reality puts significant constraints on possible policies available to countries to address the (often stormy) realities of international finance.

An overvalued exchange rate is not always sustainable. The home-country central bank can run out of foreign reserves to sell. We take up the complications of such situations in Chapter 17 on crises and responses and in Chapter 23 on structural adjustment.

Review Exercises

1. Until January 2002, the Argentine peso was pegged on a one-to-one basis against the U.S. dollar in an arrangement known as a currency board. Suppose that, to begin with, this exchange rate is an equilibrium rate. Next, use a diagram such as Figure 15.3 to show how Argentina can respond to a decrease in the interest rate on the U.S. dollar.

2. Suppose that a country has a fixed exchange rate and that, over the past few years, it has been quickly accumulating foreign reserves. What does this tell you about the value of the pegged currency? Why?

3. Given what you have read in this book up to this point, can you say anything about the desirability of the three policy regime corners in the policy trilemma diagram of Figure 15.3? Explain your reasoning.

4. For the example of question 1 above, set up the equivalent of Figure 15.A1, shown in the appendix to this chapter. Next, show the actions required on the part of the Argentine monetary authority in response to a decrease in income in Argentina; a decrease in income in the United States; and a contractionary monetary policy in the United States. In each case, explain the intuition of your results.

Further Reading and Web Resources

An introductory analysis of exchange rate regimes can be found in Chapter 15 of Hess and Ross (1997). An advanced treatment of fixed exchange rates can be found in Chapter 17 of Krugman and Obstfeld (2003). Obstfeld and Rogoff (1995) and Garber and Svensson (1996) provide important overviews of the fragility of fixed exchange rate regimes. A working paper version of the Obstfeld and

Rogoff paper can be found online in pdf format at **http://papers-nber9.nber.org/papers/W5191**. A defense of fixed exchange rates by researchers at the Federal Reserve Bank of Minneapolis can be found at **http://woodrow.mpls.frbfed.us:80/pubs/ar/ar1989.html**. Nouriel Roubini's Global Macroeconomic and Financial Policy Web site has a section on exchange rate regimes at **http://www.stern.nyu.edu/globalmacro/exchange_rates/exchange_rate_regime.html**.

References

Commission of the European Communities (1993) "The Economics of the EMU," in D.K. Das (ed.), *International Finance: Contemporary Issues*, Routledge, London, 211–242.

The Economist (1998) "Can Cardoso Use Financial Chaos to Reform Brazil?" September 26.

The Economist (1998) "Cracking the Brazil Nuts," October 31.

The Economist (1998) "Brazilian Jitters," December 19.

Friedman, M. (1953) "The Case for Flexible Exchange Rates," in *Essays in Positive Economics*, University of Chicago Press, Chicago, 157–203.

Garber, P.M., and L.E.O. Svensson (1996) "The Operation and Collapse of Fixed Exchange Rate Regimes," in G.M. Grossman and K. Rogoff (eds.), *Handbook of International Economics*, Vol. 3, North-Holland, Amsterdam.

Hess, P., and C. Ross (1997) *Economic Development: Theories, Evidence, and Policies*, Dryden, Fort Worth, Texas.

International Monetary Fund (2002) *International Financial Statistics Yearbook*, Washington, DC.

Kokoszczyñski, R. (2001) "From Fixed to Floating: Other Country Experiences: The Case of Poland," Paper presented at the International Monetary Fund seminar "Exchange Rate Regimes: Hard Peg or Free Floating?" Washington, DC.

Krugman, P.R., and M. Obstfeld (2003). *International Economics: Theory and Policy*, Addison-Wesley, Boston.

Lipumba, N.H.I. (1994) *Africa Beyond Adjustment*, Overseas Development Council, Washington, DC.

Obstfeld, M., and K. Rogoff (1995) "The Mirage of Fixed Exchange Rates," *Journal of Economic Perspectives*, 9:4, 73–96.

Velasco, A. (2000) *Exchange-Rate Polices for Developing Countries: What Have We Learned? What Do We Still Not Know?* Group of 24 Discussion Paper Series, United Nations, Geneva.

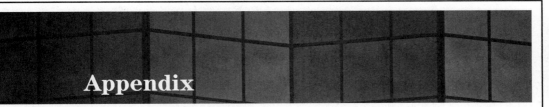

Appendix

Monetary Policies

As mentioned in the appendix to Chapter 14, some readers of this book will be familiar with monetary policies from a course on macroeconomics. If this is the case for you, the current appendix will explain to you the monetary consequences of fixed exchange rate regimes. We begin with a collection of diagrams presented in the appendix to Chapter 14. This collection of diagrams is presented in Figure 15.A1. The top diagram of this figure depicts equilibrium in the U.S. money market and determines the interest rate on the dollar. The bottom diagram depicts equilibrium in the Mexican money market and determines the interest rate on the peso. The middle diagram depicts the peso market, e_0 being an equilibrium fixed exchange rate. As discussed in this chapter, an equilibrium fixed exchange rate requires $r_M = r_{US}$. Let's examine some implications of this requirement.

First, let's suppose that income in Mexico (Y_M) increased. What would be the implication of this? An increase in income in Mexico would tend to increase the demand for pesos. This would shift the Mexican money demand curve in Figure 15.A1 to the right, which, in turn, would tend to increase r_M. This would shift the demand for pesos graph to the right, increasing the value of the peso. In order to prevent this peso appreciation, the Mexican central bank would need to increase the supply of pesos, selling them in the peso market. This will shift the M_M^S curve to the right until r_M falls back to its original level, and e is maintained at e_0.

Second, let's suppose that income in the United States (Y_{US}) increased. What would be the implication of this change? An increase in income in the United States would tend to increase the demand for U.S. dollars. This would shift the U.S. money demand curve in Figure 15.A1 to the right, which, in turn, would tend to increase r_{US}. This would shift the demand for pesos graph to the left, decreasing the value of the peso. In order to prevent this depreciation, the central bank would need to decrease the supply of pesos, buying them in the peso market. This will shift the M_M^S curve to the left until r_M increases to match the increase in r_{US}. This is the only way to maintain e at e_0.

Figure 15.A1 Money Markets and Fixed Exchange Rates

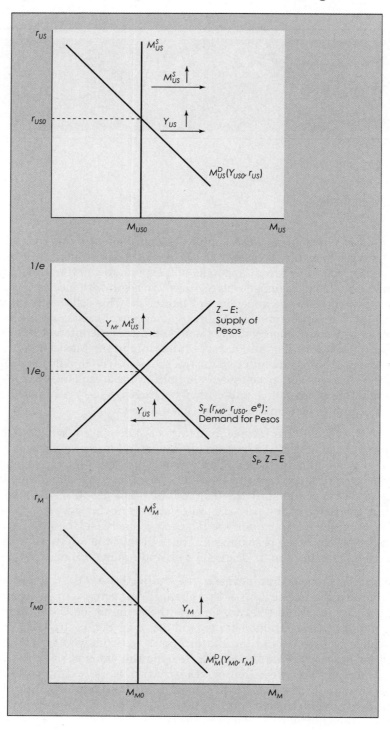

Finally, let's consider an increase in money supply in the United States. An increase in M_{US}^S would decrease r_{US}. Just like the increase in Mexican income, this would lead to an increase in the value of the peso. In order to prevent this appreciation, the Mexican central bank would need to increase the supply of pesos, selling them in the peso market. This will shift the M_M^S curve to the right until r_M falls enough to meet the fall in r_{US}. This policy response will maintain e at e_0.

In each of these three cases, the Mexican government must stand ready to buy and sell pesos at e_0 to meet any excess supply or demand for pesos and, thereby, maintain the fixed exchange rate. M_M^S is used to ensure that the exchange rate is fixed. Importantly, then, under a fixed exchange rate regime, a country cannot pursue monetary policy independently of the rest of the world in order to stabilize its own macroeconomy. Instead, the monetary policy is committed to keeping the exchange rate fixed. This was *not* the case under the flexible or floating exchange rate policy. Here, a country can pursue an independent monetary policy, but it gives up control of the exchange rate. Another way of expressing this is simply to say that a *country can control its interest rate or its exchange rate, but not both.* An integrated international financial system makes controlling both the interest rate and the exchange rate impossible.[9]

---

[9] This is one reason why monetarists such as Milton Friedman support the use of flexible exchange rate regimes rather than fixed exchange rate regimes. See Friedman (1953).

The International Monetary Fund

16

In the history of global financial arrangements, the year 1941 stands as a turning point. In September of that year, the British economist John Maynard Keynes spent, as he wrote to his mother, "several days of peace writing a heavy memorandum on post-war international currency plans."[1] The result was a proposal for an International Clearing Union (ICU), an idea subsequently taken up by the British Treasury. Three months later and across the Atlantic, U.S. Treasury official Harry Dexter White wrote a proposal for an International Stabilization Fund (ISF), subsequently embraced wholeheartedly by U.S. Treasury Secretary Henry Morgenthau. These two proposals, which became known as the Keynes Plan and the White Plan, respectively, competed for prominence in the international deliberations over how to constitute the institutions of international finance after the end of World War II, still some years off. The two plans were taken up at the Bretton Woods Conference in July 1944, with the White Plan gaining prominence. The result was the creation of the International Monetary Fund (IMF) and the International Bank for Reconstruction and Development (the World Bank). Neither Keynes nor White would live out the decade, both dying of heart attacks while the Fund and Bank were being established.[2]

In Chapter 7, you were introduced to the institutions of international trade in the form of the GATT/WTO system. As a student of the world economy, you also need to be familiar with the IMF and World Bank. This chapter will introduce you to the IMF, and Chapter 22 will introduce you to the World Bank. Together, these two chapters will make you familiar with the basic "rules of the game" in international finance. We begin in this chapter with a brief history of international monetary arrangements during the twentieth century. This will allow you to place the IMF in the context of recent financial history. Next, we will turn to the actual operations of the IMF. Finally, we will make a preliminary assessment of the IMF and its role in the world economy. We will take up the controversial role of the IMF in recent financial crises in Chapter 17.

Monetary History

Throughout the twentieth century, the countries of the world struggled with various arrangements for the conduct of international finance. None

---

[1] Skidelsky (2000), p. 202-203.
[2] Keynes died in 1946, White in 1948. For an interesting biography of Keynes during this period, see Skidelsky (2000). Chapter 7 of that book takes up Harry Dexter White, including his alleged role as a Soviet agent. See also Boughton (1998).

of these arrangements proved satisfactory. Over time, international economic policy makers attempted to set up one system after another, and, in each case, they were overtaken by events. It now appears that the international financial system had a dynamic of its own, one much stronger than the institutional scaffolding temporarily built around it. This is also no doubt true today. In this section of the chapter, we will briefly review some of the main events in this drama to give you an appreciation of the evolutionary power of international finance and to place the IMF in some context.

The Gold Standards

Gold standard

An international financial arrangement in existence from approximately 1870 to 1914. Under the gold standard, countries defined the value of their currencies in terms of gold and held gold as official reserves.

The end of the nineteenth and beginning of the twentieth centuries were characterized by a highly integrated world economy that was supported from approximately 1870 to 1914 by an international financial arrangement known as the gold standard. Under the **gold standard**, each country defined the value of its currency in terms of gold. Most countries also held gold as official reserves. Because the value of each currency was defined in terms of gold, the rates of exchange among the currencies were fixed. Thus, the gold standard was one type of fixed exchange rate system.[3] When World War I began in 1914, the countries involved in that conflict suspended the convertibility of their currencies into gold. After the war, there was an attempt to return the international financial system back to "normal," that is, to rebuild the gold standard. Success in this endeavor was to prove elusive.

In 1922, there was an economic conference held in Genoa, Italy, that attempted to rebuild the pre-World War I gold standard. The new gold standard was different from the pre-war standard, however. There was a gold shortage at the time, and to deal with this problem, countries that were not important financial centers did not hold gold reserves. Instead, they held gold-convertible currencies, a practice utilized by a number of countries before the war. For this reason, the new gold standard was known as the **gold-exchange standard**. One goal of the gold-exchange standard was to set major rates at their pre-war levels. The most important rate was that of the British pound. In 1925, it was set to gold at the overvalued, pre-war rate of US$4.86 per pound.[4] This caused balance of payments problems (see Chapter 15) and market expectations of devaluation. At a system-wide level, each major rate was set to gold, ignoring the implied rates among the various currencies. As is often the case, the politics of the day prevailed over economics.

Gold-exchange standard

An international financial arrangement introduced in the 1920s to replace the gold standard. It consisted of a set of center countries tied to gold and a set of periphery countries tied to the center country currencies.

The gold-exchange standard thus consisted of a set of center countries tied to gold and a set of periphery countries holding these center-country

---

[3] As students of the history of economic thought know, the operation of the gold standard was first described by Hume (1924, originally 1752). A more modern treatment can be found in McClosky and Zecher (1976). For a brief historical assessment, see Chapter 4 of Eichengreen (1994). For a critical analysis, see Triffin (1960) and Chapter 2 of Eichengreen (1996).

[4] Keynes opposed this policy strenuously, famously calling the gold standard a "barbarous relic." In the same essay (1963, orig. 1923), he stated: "(Since) I feel no confidence that an old-fashioned gold standard will even give us the modicum of stability that it used to give, I reject the policy of restoring the gold standard on pre-war lines" (pp. 211–212). Keynes did not get his way.

currencies as reserves. By 1930, nearly all the countries of the world had joined. The design of the system, however, held within it a significant incentive problem for the periphery countries. Suppose a periphery country expected that the currency it held as reserves was going to be devalued against gold. It would be in the interest of this country to *sell* its reserves *before* the devaluation took place so as to preserve the value of its total reserves. This, in turn, would put even greater pressure on the center currency. As mentioned earlier, the British pound was set at an overvalued rate. In September 1931, there was a run on the pound, and this forced Britain to cut the pound's tie to gold. Many other countries subsequently cut their ties to gold. By 1937, no countries remained on the gold-exchange standard.

Overall, the gold-exchange standard was not a success. Some international economists (e.g., Eichengreen, 1992) have even seen it as a major contributor to the Great Depression. As the decade of the 1930s ensued, a system of separate currency areas evolved, and there was a combination of both fixed and floating rates. The lack of international financial coordination helped contribute to the economic crisis of the decade. At the worst of times, countries engaged in a game of *competitive devaluation*, each trying to gain greater export competitiveness over other countries.[5] This breakdown in international economic cooperation helped to fuel the rise of nationalism and fascism, which eventually erupted in World War II.

The Bretton Woods System

During World War II, the United States and Britain began to plan for the post-war economic system. As mentioned earlier, in the United States, the planning occurred at the U.S. Treasury under the direction of Harry Dexter White. In Britain, John Maynard Keynes took the lead at the British Treasury.[6] These individuals understood the contribution of the previous breakdown in the international economic system to the war, and they hoped to avoid the same mistake that was made after World War I. Also, however, White and Keynes were fighting for the relative positions of the countries they represented. In this competition, White and the U.S. Treasury had the upper hand, and White largely got his way during the 1944 Bretton Woods Conference. Some brief descriptions of this conference are given in the box.

The conference produced a plan for a new international financial system that became known as the **Bretton Woods system**. The essence of the system was an **adjustable gold peg**. Under the Bretton Woods system, the U.S. dollar was to be pegged to gold at $35 per ounce. The other countries of the world were to peg to the U.S. dollar or directly to gold. This placed the dollar at the center of the new international financial system, a role envisaged by White and the U.S. Treasury. The currency pegs were to remain fixed except

Bretton Woods system
An international financial system introduced at the Bretton Woods conference in 1944 involving an exchange rate arrangement known as the adjustable gold peg.

Adjustable gold peg
An international financial arrangement that was part of the Bretton Woods system. It involved pegging the U.S. dollar to gold at US$35 per ounce and allowing all other countries to either peg to the U.S. dollar or directly to gold. The currency pegs (other than the U.S. dollar) were to remain fixed except under conditions that were termed "fundamental disequilibrium."

[5] Recall from Chapter 13 that a lower value of a currency gives a country's exporters an incentive to export. This was described in Figure 13.3.
[6] James (1996) tells us: "Already weeks after the outbreak of war in 1939, Keynes was sending memoranda to President Roosevelt that included suggestions on how the postwar reconstruction of Europe might be handled better than after 1918" (p. 33).

Views of the Bretton Woods Conference

The Bretton Woods Conference of July 1944 was unusual in the breadth of international representation and scope of work. The name of the conference derived from the New Hampshire resort where it took place. The 730 delegates from 45 countries were housed at the Mount Washington Hotel from July 1–22, with British and U.S. delegations having begun work on June 23. Here are a few views of this extraordinary gathering.

Financial historian Harold James wrote: "The Bretton Woods conference wove consensus, harmony, and agreement as if under a magician's spell. . . . The participants met almost around the clock in overcrowded and acoustically unsuitable hotel rooms. Gradually exhaustion set in. Keynes wrote: 'We have all of us worked every minute of our waking hours practically without intermission for what is now four weeks. . . . At one moment Harry White told me that at last even he was all in, not having been in bed for more than five hours a night for four consecutive weeks.' On July 19, 1944, Keynes collapsed with a mild heart attack."

Keynes biographer Robert Skidelsky wrote: "At Bretton Woods, the problems of peace were discussed in the shadow of war about to end. It was a war, moreover, which the Soviet Union was doing most to win, and this was reflected in the number of honorary posts its delegates were assigned. It was the first time Keynes had encountered the Commissars *en masse* since his visits to the Soviet Union in the late 1920s. He used the opportunity to try to persuade them to send the Bolshoi Ballet over to Covent Garden the following year. The Foreign Office took up the idea, but nothing came of it. There would be no Russian ballet in London till 1956. The reason, it turned out, was that the Russians had a well-founded fear of defections."

Finally, Keynes' wife, Lydia Keynes (née Lapakova), a former Russian ballerina herself, wrote: "the taps run all day, the windows do not close or open, the pipes mend and unmend and no one can get anywhere."

Sources: James (1996) and Skidelsky (2000).

under conditions that were termed "fundamental disequilibrium." The concept of fundamental disequilibrium, however, was never carefully defined. The agreement also stipulated that countries were to make their currencies convertible to U.S. dollars as soon as possible, but this convertibility process did not happen quickly.

The Bretton Woods system came into being in 1946, the year of Keynes' death. Like the gold-exchange standard, it contained the seeds of its own demise. Problems became apparent even by the end of the 1940s in the form of growing nonofficial balance of payments deficits of the United States. These deficits reflected official reserve transactions in support of expanding global dollar reserves.[7] Although the Bretton Woods agreements allowed par values to be defined either in gold or dollar terms, in practice, the dollar became the central measure of value. What was to be a revised gold standard became a *de facto* dollar standard.

---

[7] These official sales of dollars by the United States to the central banks of the world (a U.S. official reserve surplus) had its counterpart in a deficit on the sum of the U.S. current and nonofficial capital accounts.

The Belgian monetary economist Robert Triffen described the problem of expanding dollar reserves in his 1960 book *Gold and the Dollar Crisis.* This problem became known as the **Triffin dilemma.** The Triffin dilemma can be conceived of as a contradiction between the requirements of international *liquidity* and international *confidence.* The term "liquidity" refers to the ability to transform assets into currencies. With the dollar being the center-piece of the system, international liquidity required a continual increase in the holdings of dollars as reserve assets. As dollar holdings of central banks expanded relative to U.S. official holdings of gold, however, international confidence would suffer. Could the United States back up an ever-expanding supply of dollars with a relatively constant amount of gold holdings? No, said Triffin. The requirements of international liquidity would compromise the requirements of international confidence, and a crisis was inevitable. This process is represented in Figure 16.1.

The first sign of trouble occurred during October 1960 when the London gold market price rose above $35 to $40 an ounce. At this time, there were calls for a change in the gold-dollar parity. U.S. President Kennedy would have none of this. In January 1961, the Kennedy administration pledged to maintain the $35 per ounce convertibility. To support this position, the United States joined with other European countries and set up a *gold pool* in which their central banks would buy and sell gold to support the $35 price in the London market. Nevertheless, at the 1964 annual IMF meeting in Tokyo, representatives began to talk publicly about potential reforms in the international financial system. Specific attention was given to the creation of reserve assets alternative to the U.S. dollar and gold. In 1965, the U.S. Treasury announced that it was ready to join in international discussions on potential reforms. The adamant stance of the Kennedy administration gave way to a somewhat more flexible posture in the Johnson administration. Meanwhile, the British pound was under pressure to devalue against the dollar. As it happened, the pound was devalued in November of 1967.

After the devaluation of the pound, President Johnson issued a state-ment recommitting the United States to the $35 per ounce gold price. However, in the early months of 1968, the rush began. The London gold market was closed on March 15 and remained closed for the remainder of the month. On March 16, central bank officials from around the world met at the Federal Reserve Board in Washington, DC. At this meeting, a 2-tiered system was constructed. Official foreign exchange transactions were to be conducted at the old rate of $35 per ounce. The rate in the

Triffin dilemma
A critique of the gold-exchange standard developed by Robert Triffin. It involved a contra-diction between the requirements of international liquidity and international confidence.

Figure 16.1 The Triffin Dilemma

London gold market, however, was allowed to float freely. The London price reached a high of $43 in 1969 and then returned to $35 in 1970. The Triffin dilemma was temporarily avoided.[8]

In early 1971, capital began to flow out of dollar assets and into German mark assets. The German Bundesbank cut its main interest rate to attempt to curb the purchase of marks. Canada had let its dollar begin to float in 1970. Germany and a few other European countries joined Canada in 1971. Thereafter, capital flowed out of dollar assets and into yen assets. In August 1971, U.S. Treasury Secretary John Connally proposed to President Nixon that the U.S. government close its "gold window," effectively suspending the convertibility of the U.S. dollar into gold. Nixon accepted this recommendation in an effort to force other countries to *revalue* against the U.S. dollar. On August 15, Nixon announced the close of the gold window, and with this announcement, the Bretton Woods adjustable peg system came to an end. What followed was a period of experimentation, often referred to as the "nonsystem," that continues to the present day.

The Nonsystem

Smithsonian Conference
A conference that took place in Washington, DC, in December 1971 to attempt to repair the damaged adjustable gold peg system of the Bretton Woods system.

In December 1971, a 2-day conference began in Washington, DC, that came to be known as the **Smithsonian Conference**. At this conference, several countries revalued their currencies against the dollar, and the gold price was raised to $38 per ounce. Canada maintained its floating rate. The fact that it took the August closing of the gold window, a period of managed floating, and an international conference to introduce a small amount of adjustment into the adjustable peg system speaks to the failure of the Bretton Woods agreement. Actually, the Smithsonian Conference ignored the entire adjustment question and the Triffin dilemma, and this quickly became apparent. In June 1972, there appeared a large flow out of U.S. dollars into European currencies and the Japanese yen. These flows stabilized, but the new crisis reappeared in January 1973. During that month, the Swiss franc began to float. In February, there was pressure against the German mark and there were closures of foreign exchange markets in both Europe and Japan. On February 12, the U.S. announced a second devaluation of the dollar against gold to $42. By this time, the Japanese yen, the Swiss franc, the Italian lira, the British pound, and the Canadian dollar were floating. By March, the German mark and the French franc, the Dutch guilder, the Belgian franc, and the Danish krone also began to float. The members of the IMF found themselves in violation of the Bretton Woods Articles of Agreement. The international financial system had crossed a threshold, although this was not fully appreciated at the time.[9]

During 1974 and 1975, the countries of the world went through nearly continuous consultation and disagreement in a process of accommodating

---

[8] Eichengreen (1996) writes: "The array of devices to which the Kennedy and Johnson administrations resorted became positively embarrassing. They acknowledged the severity of the dollar problem while displaying a willingness to address only the symptoms, not the causes. Dealing with the causes required reforming the international system in a way that diminished the dollar's reserve-currency role, something the United States was still unwilling to contemplate" (p. 129).
[9] Solomon (1977) noted: "The move to generalized floating in March 1973 was widely regarded as a temporary departure from normality" (p. 267).

their thinking to the new reality of floating rates. The French government, in particular, was skeptical of the long-term viability of the floating regime, whereas the U.S. government appeared reconciled to it. In November 1975, the heads of state of the United States, France, Germany, the United Kingdom, Italy, and Japan met at Château de Rambouillet outside of Paris. In a declaration, these heads of state proposed an amendment to the IMF's Articles of Agreement, developed at the Bretton Woods conference. This amendment restricted allowable exchange rate arrangements to (1) currencies fixed to anything *other than gold*, (2). cooperative arrangements for managed values among countries, and (3) floating. In January 1976, during an IMF meeting in Jamaica, the Articles of Agreement were indeed amended to reflect the Rambouillet Declaration. This became known as the **Jamaica Agreement**. The Jamaica Agreement institutionalized what had, in fact, already occurred.

Jamaica Agreement
A 1976 amendment to the IMF's Articles of Agreement that allowed for floating exchange rates.

The Operation of the IMF

The IMF is an international financial organization comprised of 183 member countries. Its purposes, as stipulated in its Articles of Agreement, are

1. *To promote international monetary cooperation*
2. *To facilitate the expansion of international trade*
3. *To promote exchange stability and a multilateral system of payments*
4. *To make temporary financial resources available to members under "adequate safeguards"*
5. *To reduce the duration and degree of international payments imbalances*

The administrative structure of the IMF is summarized in Table 16.1. The IMF's major decision-making body is its Board of Governors to which

Table 16.1 Administrative Structure of the IMF

Body	Composition	Function
Board of Governors	One Governor and one Alternate Governor for each member	Meets annually; highest decision-making body
Executive Board	22 Executive Directors plus managing director	Day-to-day operations
Managing Director	Traditionally European	Chair of Executive Board; responsible for staffing and general business
Deputy Managing Directors		Assist Managing Director
Staff	Citizens of members	Run departments

Source: Based on James (1996) and Salda (1992).

each member appoints a Governor and an Alternate Governor. Day-to-day business, however, rests in the hands of the Executive Board. This is composed of 22 Executive Directors plus the Managing Director. Six of the 22 Executive Directors are appointed by the largest IMF quota holders (quotas are discussed later). The rest are elected by groups of member countries not entitled to appoint Executive Directors. The Managing Director is appointed by the Executive Board and is traditionally a European (often French). The Managing Director chairs the Executive Board and conducts the IMF's business. There are also currently three Deputy Managing Directors. The nationalities of the Managing Director and Deputy Managing Directors typically reflect the major powers behind the Bretton Woods Agreements and historically have represented an institutional barrier to developing countries.

The most important feature of the IMF is its quota system. Members' quotas are their *subscriptions* to the IMF and are based on their relative sizes in the world economy. These quotas determine both the amount members can borrow from the IMF and their relative voting power. The higher a member's quota, the more it can borrow and the greater its voting power. A member pays one-fourth of its quota in widely-accepted reserve currencies (U.S. dollar, British pound, euro, or yen) or in Special Drawing Rights (discussed later). It pays the remaining three-quarters of the quota in its own national currency.

The IMF engages in four areas of activity. These are economic surveillance or monitoring, the dispensing of policy advice, lending, and providing technical assistance. Of these four areas of activity, it is lending that is perhaps the most important. Let's see how it works.

If an IMF member faces balance of payments difficulties, it can automatically borrow one-fourth of its quota in the form of a *reserve tranche*. The process behind such IMF lending is depicted in Figure 16.2. When the IMF lends to a member country, what actually happens is that the domestic country *purchases* international reserves from the IMF using its own domestic currency reserves. The member country is then obliged to repay the IMF by *repurchasing* its own domestic currency reserves with

Figure 16.2 IMF Lending

international reserve assets. In this way, IMF lending is known as a "purchase-repurchase" arrangement.

Beyond the reserve tranche, there are four *credit tranches*. Originally, each of the credit tranches were equal to one-quarter of the members' quotas. In the late 1970s, credit tranches were increased to 37.5 percent of quota. Policy with regard to the credit tranches emerged between 1948 and 1958.[10] The first credit tranche is more or less automatic. The second through fourth credit tranches, collectively known as upper credit tranches, require that the member adopt policies that will solve the balance of payments problem at hand. These requirements are known as *conditionality*. The credit tranche policy effectively limits a member country's credit to 150 percent of its quota. However, as the IMF evolved, it created a number of special credit facilities that extend potential credit beyond the 150 percent level. These are summarized in Table 16.2.

As shown in Figure 16.2, drawings on the IMF by its members have to be repaid, and a 5-year limit was established. The ideal vision of the role of the Fund was roughly as follows. The development of a country requires, to some extent, an inflow of private foreign savings (S_F in the notation of Chapter 12, Figure 12.2). This inflow would cover a current account deficit often caused by the import of capital goods. Occasionally, this private foreign savings disappears, and a balance of payments crisis ensues.[11] In these instances, the IMF steps in, the member draws on its reserve and credit tranches, repaying the credit tranche debts in 5 years' time. Thus, the IMF offers short-term credit, stepping in to replace private foreign savings on those rare, but difficult occasions. This ideal is not always realized, as private foreign savings can be quite fickle.

These arrangements reflect the dominance achieved by the White Plan over the Keynes Plan at Bretton Woods. It is worth a moment to contrast these features of the IMF with Keynes' proposal for an International Clearing Union (ICU). The ICU was conceived more along the lines of a *world central bank*. Rather than being based on subscription capital, it would have the ability to create credit. Additionally, the ICU would have done business in its own currency, called by Keynes the *bancor*. Finally, and perhaps most importantly, the Keynes plan had an ingenious feature in that it penalized creditors and debtors symmetrically. This spread international adjustment responsibilities between both countries with balance of payments surpluses and countries with balance of payments deficits. This feature was not adopted in the final agreements, adjustment being the responsibility of the deficit countries.[12]

History of IMF Operations

In its initial years, the IMF was nearly irrelevant, being pushed aside by the United States' own programs for postwar European reconstruction via

---

[10]See Dell (1981), p. 11, Buira (1995), p. 24, and James (1996), pp. 79-81.
[11]We take up balance of payments crises in Chapter 17.
[12]See Buira (1995), p. 29.

Table 16.2 Special Credit Facilities

Name	Year Established	Purpose
Compensatory Financing Facility	1963 (extended 1966, 1969, 1981)	Export receipts shortfalls and grain import costs
Compensatory and Contingency Financing Facility	1968	Unanticipated external shocks
Buffer Stock Financing Facility	1969	To support international buffer stock stabilization of commodity prices
Oil Import Facility	1974, 1975	To finance increased oil import costs
Extended Fund Facility	1975	To create a longer time horizon for adjustment lending
Supplementary Financing Facility	1979	To supplement quota system by borrowing from some members and lending to others
Structural Adjustment Facility	1986	Concessional financing to developing countries
Enhanced Structural Adjustment Facility	1987	Concessional financing to developing countries
Systematic Transformation Facility	1993	To support changes from a planned to a market economy
Supplementary Reserve Facility	1997	To address balance of payments crises with large volumes of short-term, high-interest loans
Poverty Reduction and Growth Facility	1999	Replaces the Enhanced Structural Adjustment Facility and attempts to integrate poverty reduction with macroeconomic policies

Sources: Based on Horsefield (1969), James (1996), Salda (1992), de Vries (1976, 1985), International Monetary Fund (2003).

the European Recovery Program and the Organization for European Economic Cooperation (see box). The IMF did play an advisory role to a series of European devaluations beginning in September 1949 in the face of "fundamental disequilibria." Nevertheless, the *Financial Times* described the IMF in early 1956 as a "white elephant." The claim proved to be ill-timed. The Suez crisis of that year forced Britain to draw on its reserve and first credit tranches; Japan drew on its reserve tranche in

Limited Liquidity in the Early Years

One of the important functions of the IMF envisioned by its Bretton Woods originators was the provision of global liquidity. The Keynes plan envisaged US$23 billion in total drawing rights. The White Plan, however, proposed total drawing rights of only $5 billion. The resulting Articles of Agreement total set drawing rights at $8.8 billion. By the time the IMF opened for business in 1947, postwar Europe's combined trade deficit was $7.5 billion. Given the size of this deficit in relationship to the IMF's resources, the United States had to step in to fill the gap. Through 1951, it provided $13 billion in Marshall Plan aid to Europe, thus significantly supplementing IMF resources. Despite this infusion of liquidity that amounted to more than four times the total drawing rights of Europe, a number of European currencies had to be devalued in 1949.

Source: Eichengreen (1996).

1957; and between late 1956 through 1958 the IMF was involved in the policies that lead to the convertibility of both the British pound and the French franc, finally clearing up a major issue that had been unresolved since the Bretton Woods agreements. This success was followed by a general increase in quotas of 50 percent in 1959. During these few years, "stand-by arrangements," which preapprove reserve drawings to provide confidence, were made with many other countries, including many developing countries. The IMF had become an active institution with an increased membership due to decolonization.

As we described in the previous section, the Bretton Woods system that evolved in the 1950s and 1960s was one in which the U.S. dollar played the role of major reserve asset for member countries. We also described the difficulty of this arrangement, which first erupted on the London gold market in October 1960. This "dollar problem" embodied in the Triffin dilemma (Figure 16.1) did not escape the notice of the IMF. Concerned about the United States' ability to defend the dollar and other major industrialized countries' abilities to maintain their parities, the IMF introduced the General Arrangements to Borrow (GAB) in October 1962. The GAB involved the central banks of 10 countries setting aside a $6 billion pool to maintain the stability of the Bretton Woods system.[13] The countries involved became known as the Group of Ten or G-10 and comprised a "rich countries club" of the world economy. The presence of such a club and its relationship with the IMF aroused suspicion on the part of countries not fortunate enough to be a member, especially the developing countries. The GAB was followed by a second general increase in quotas in 1965. Over time, the G-11 (including Switzerland) increased the GAB to $23 billion.

By 1965, facing the Triffin dilemma of Figure 16.1, the U.S. was in a position where it faced two unappealing options: reduce the world supply of dollars to enhance international confidence by reducing international

---

[13]The countries were Belgium, Canada, France, Italy, Japan, the Netherlands, Sweden, the United Kingdom, the United States, and West Germany.

liquidity, or expand the world supply of dollars to enhance international liquidity by reducing international confidence. Other countries (particularly France) were objecting to the central role of the United States altogether. But where was the world to turn for a reserve asset? Back to gold? Between the 1964 and 1968 annual meetings of the IMF, discussions took place in a number of fora, including the G-10. The result was the creation of an entirely new reserve asset to supplement both gold and the dollar. This reserve asset was known as a **special drawing right** or **SDR**. The SDR was "the first international currency to be created in the manner of a national paper currency—purely through a series of legal obligations to accept it on the part of members of the system" (James, 1996, p. 171) in the way envisaged by the Keynes Plan. The SDR came into being in July 1969. Ironically, given its intended use to supplement gold and the dollar, its value was set in terms of gold at a value identical to the dollar ($35 per ounce). In 1971, when the United States broke the gold–dollar link, the SDR was redefined in terms of a basket of five currencies: the dollar, the pound, the mark, the yen, and the franc.[14] SDRs were allocated in proportion to members' quotas.

SDRs never played the important role envisaged for them. They are perhaps best seen as one of many attempts to resolve the Triffin dilemma, one more event on the path from international financial system to nonsystem. Additional SDR distributions took place in 1979 and 1997, the latter to account for the fact that a number of new members had never received an allocation.

The oil price increases of 1973–1974 caused substantial balance of payments difficulties for many countries of the world. In June 1974, the IMF established an oil facility to assist these countries (see Table 16.2). The IMF acted as an intermediary, borrowing the funds from oil-producing countries and lending them to oil-importing countries. A second oil facility was established in 1975. The first oil facility had few conditions attached; the second was slightly more strict. Despite the presence of these facilities, the bulk of oil producing country revenues were "recycled" to other countries by the commercial banking system. During these years, the developing countries began to borrow under IMF conditionality. Kenya, Mexico, India, Turkey, and Jamaica were notable examples of borrowing under conditionality in the 1977 to 1981 period.

During this time, a bias towards private-sector lending helped to prevent sufficient increases in IMF quotas. As mentioned earlier, the IMF attempted to get around the quota limitation by increasing credit tranches from 25 to 37.5 percent of quota. In 1979, it also introduced the Supplementary Financing Facility (see Table 16.2). As in the oil facilities, the lenders here were the oil-producing countries.[15] In 1983, the GAB was expanded. Given the limits of the quota system, the IMF was, by necessity, becoming more of a financial intermediary and less of an international cooperative credit arrangement.

Special drawing rights (SDRs)
An international currency administered by the IMF and introduced in 1969. It is currently defined in terms of a basket of three currencies: the U.S. dollar, the euro, and the yen. Distributions of SDRs took place in 1970, 1979, and 1997, but they never played the important role envisaged for them.

---

[14] After the birth of the European Monetary Union in 1999, the deutche mark and the French franc were replaced by the euro.

[15] "The Fund became a borrower because of the difficulties in raising quotas, and the group of lenders reflected the new structure of the world economy" (James, 1996, p. 341).

Beginning in 1976, the IMF began to sound warnings about the sustainability of developing-country borrowing from the commercial banking system. The banking system reacted with hostility to these warnings, arguing that the Fund had no place interfering with private transactions. As we shall see, the Fund proved prescient on this issue.

The 1980s began with a significant increase in real interest rates and a significant decline in non-oil commodity prices. This increased the cost of borrowing and reduced export revenues. In 1982, the IMF calculated that U.S. banking system outstanding loans to Latin America represented approximately 100 percent of total bank capital: The IMF's concern in the latter half of the 1970s about the sustainability of developing-country borrowing had been justified. In August 1982, in the face of capital flight, Mexico announced that it would stop servicing its foreign currency debt.[16] At the end of the month, the Mexican government nationalized its banking system. Negotiations took place between the Mexican government, the IMF, the U.S. Federal Reserve Bank, and an advisory committee of New York banks. An agreement was established in November that involved the New York banks lending additional funds to Mexico. The New York banks complied under threat of additional regulation in response to their inability to assess country risk. A collapse in the international price of oil in 1986 brought this first adjustment program to a failed end, and a new IMF stand-by program was negotiated in September 1986.

The summer of 1982 also found debt crises beginning in Argentina and Brazil. In the case of Argentina, the crisis ensued from an overvalued exchange rate, used as a "nominal anchor" to curb inflationary expenditures. In Brazil, rates of devaluation did not keep up with rates of inflation, causing an overvalued real exchange rate.[17] The Argentinean crisis was first addressed with an IMF stand-by arrangement in January 1983. The arrangement unraveled two months later but was revived in August with a tranche release. A second stand-by arrangement was agreed upon in December 1984. This arrangement expired in June 1986. A third stand-by arrangement was not concluded until November 1979 to be followed by another in July 1991. In the case of Brazil, an IMF program was announced in November 1982 and drew on the compensatory and buffer stock facilities (see Table 16.2). As in the Mexican case, the New York banks had to be cajoled into releasing more funds. Brazil's agreement with the IMF was terminated by the Brazilian government in late 1985 but resumed again in May 1988. A new stand-by arrangement was concluded in June 1988. More systematically, the IMF introduced in March 1986 a Structural Adjustment Facility (see Table 16.2). This allowed for credits of up to 70 percent of countries' quotas. In 1987, the IMF introduced an Enhanced Structural Adjustment Facility (again see Table 16.2). This raised the total credit ceiling to 250 percent of quota.

---

[16]The lack of foresight of the financial sector with regard to this event has been noted by Krugman (1999): "(A)s late as July 1982 the yield on Mexican bonds was slightly *less* than that on those of presumably safe borrowers like the World Bank, indicating that investors regarded the risk that Mexico would fail to pay on time as negligible" (p. 41).

[17]See Chapter 4 of Franko (2003). The parallels here with the 1998 crisis in Brazil and the 2002 crisis in Argentina are striking.

Despite these efforts, international commercial banks began to withdraw credit from many of the developing countries of the world. The debt crisis became global. Within a few years of the outbreak of the crises, the phenomenon of *net capital outflows* appeared. This involved the capital account payments of debtor countries exceeding capital account receipts. The resulting capital account deficits had their counterparts in current account surpluses: The developing countries were using trade surpluses to finance debt repayment. Part of these surpluses were the result of increased exports, and part the result of reduced domestic consumption. Poverty increased substantially, and much of the developing world, particularly Latin America and Africa, entered what came to be known as *the lost decade*.[18]

By the second half of the 1980s, there developed secondary markets in which debt was trading at discounts. In 1989, U.S. Treasury Secretary Nicholas Brady proposed a plan in which IMF and World Bank lending could be used by developing countries to buy back this discounted debt. These procedures, which amounted to partial and long-needed debt forgiveness, were approved by the IMF and became known as the **Brady Plan**. The Brady Plan also allowed for extending the time periods of debt and provided for new lending.

Brady Plan
A set of procedures proposed by U.S. Treasury Secretary Nicholas Brady and approved by the IMF in 1989. The Brady Plan allowed IMF and World Bank lending to be used by developing countries to buy back discounted international debt. It was a partial but important response to the developing country debt crisis that began in the 1980s.

Starting in the 1990s, private, nonbank capital began to flow to the developing countries in the form of both direct and portfolio investment. The lost decade, however, remained lost. Furthermore, a number of highly-indebted countries began to show increasing unpaid IMF obligations. In November 1992, a Third Amendment to the Articles of Agreement allowed for suspension of voting rights in the face of large, unpaid obligations. This was hardly a sign of a well-functioning system of international adjustment.

Mexico underwent a second crisis in late 1994 and early 1995. In this instance, the IMF was unable to respond effectively to the crisis. Instead, the U.S. Treasury assembled a loan package. Beginning in July 1997, crises struck a number of Asian countries, most notably Thailand, Indonesia, South Korea, and Malaysia. In August 1998, a crisis also hit Russia. In each of these cases, sharp depreciations of the currencies resulted. In the cases of Thailand, Indonesia, and South Korea, the IMF played substantial and controversial roles in addressing the crises. Loan packages were designed with accompanying conditionality agreements. A Supplementary Reserve Facility was introduced to provide large volumes of high-interest, short-term loans to selected Asian countries (see Table 16.2). In October and November 1998, the IMF put together a package to support the Brazilian currency, the *real*. This was an attempt to prevent the Asian and Russian crises from spreading to Latin America. Despite these arrangements, Brazil was forced to devalue the real in January 1999. In late 2001, a crisis in Argentina occurred despite IMF involvement, which resulted in an economic catastrophe for this country. We take up these crises in more detail in Chapter 17.

Recent years have witnessed three important changes at the IMF. First, in 1997, the General Agreement to Borrow was supplemented by the New

---

[18]GDP per capita in Latin America was the same in 1995 as it was in 1980.

The IMF in Ethiopia

In October 1996, the IMF announced a new, 3-year loan to Ethiopia, one of the world's poorest countries, under its Enhanced Structural Adjustment Facility (ESAF). The total amount of the loan was US$127 million, with $42 million being released in the first tranche. As part of this package, objectives were set for the 1997-1999 period in the areas of real GDP growth, inflation rate, current account deficit, and gross official foreign reserves.

The second tranche of the loan was never delivered. According to the IMF, "the midterm review . . . could not be completed." Behind the scenes, however, conflicts were brewing between the Ethiopian government and the IMF. According to Wade (2001) and Nobel Laureate Stiglitz (2001), one major issue was the early repayment of a U.S. bank loan for aircraft brought to supply Ethiopian Airlines, a successful state-owned enterprise. The government lent Ethiopian Airlines the money to repay the loan. According to Stiglitz, "The transaction made perfect sense. In spite of the solid nature its collateral (an airplane), Ethiopia was paying a far higher interest rate on its loan than it was receiving on its reserves."

Both the IMF and the U.S. Treasury objected to the nature of the loan repayment. Additionally, according to Wade (2001), the IMF began to insist that Ethiopia begin to liberalize its capital account despite the fact that the IMF's Articles of Agreement do not give it jurisdiction in this area. The Ethiopian government refused, and the IMF canceled the release of the second tranche of the 1997 ESAF. In late 1997, the Ethiopian government made contact with Joseph Stiglitz, then Chief Economist at the World Bank. Stiglitz visited Ethiopia, as did the World Bank President James Wolfenson who, in turn, raised Ethiopia's case with IMF Managing Director Michel Camdessus. As a consequence of these communications, a new ESAF was concluded in October 1998, although the total amount was only $42 million.

In response to consultations with Ethiopia, the IMF expressed support of the government's economic management in July 1999. However, the ESAF was not extended in October 1999. Why? According to Wade (2001), IMF officials "saw themselves as having lost the argument the previous year due to the (illegitimate) intervention of the World Bank. They thought that the government had been let off the hook, and now they were going to bring it to heel by not agreeing to continue Ethiopia's ESAP status, even though the conditions had been fulfilled."

A new program was negotiated in October 2000 under the Poverty Reduction and Growth Facility (PRGF). This was delayed until March 2001, with the total amount set at $109 million. The first tranche made available at the time was $44 million. In March 2002, the IMF called Ethiopia's performance "commendable," and released an additional $30 million.

Sources: http://www.imf.org, Stiglitz (2001), and Wade (2001).

Arrangement to Borrow. This involves 25 IMF members agreeing to lend up to US$46 billion to the IMF in instances where quotas prove to be insufficient. Second, in 1999, a new lending facility was added. The Poverty Reduction and Growth Facility (see Table 16.2) was created to replace the 1987 Enhanced Structural Adjustment Facility. Here there was the beginning of an attempt to integrate poverty reduction consideration into the macroeconomic policy formation of the IMF. Third, in 1999, quotas were increased by 45 percent to a total of US$283 billion. Despite these changes, the inevitable controversies persist. One of these, the case of IMF lending to Ethiopia, is described in the box.

An Assessment

Aspects of the international financial system are often assessed from the point of view of their contributions to providing liquidity and adjustment. Let us briefly apply these criteria to the IMF.

When the IMF opened for business in 1947, its quotas were approximately 13 percent of world imports. As we saw in the box on "Limited Liquidity in the Early Years," even these quotas failed to address the needs of the postwar European economy. Since 1947, IMF quotas as a percent of world imports have fallen to approximately 4 percent. In the face of these facts, a number of observers (e.g., Dell, 1981; Buira, 1995; and Steeten, 1995, Second Lecture) have questioned whether the IMF has succeeded, even in part, in addressing global liquidity. In his initial Bretton Woods proposal, John Maynard Keynes envisioned a global central bank with an international currency, the *bancor*. This central bank would be responsible for regulating the expansion of international liquidity. As we mentioned earlier, this proposal was blocked during the Bretton Woods process. In light of the above concerns over liquidity, some observers have called for a return to the global central bank idea.[19]

Keynes's original Bretton Woods proposal also included adjustment requirements being distributed among deficit and surplus countries. Along with the *bancor*, this proposal was discarded, and adjustment became solely the responsibility of deficit countries. Furthermore, as Dell (1981) emphasized, deficit countries are required to adjust *no matter what the source of the deficit*. Oil shocks, commodity price declines, and rapid, unforeseen changes in interest rates, which occur through no fault of the deficit (developing) countries, become events requiring stern conditionality and massive transformations of developing country economies. Dell (1983) argued that the requisite adjustments are too severe (he uses the term "overkill") and violate the purposes of the IMF developed at Bretton Woods: to promote "the development of productive resources" and to achieve balance of payments adjustment "without resorting to measures destructive of national and international prosperity."

Reform of the existing IMF framework could involve two things: (1) reconstituting it more along the lines of a world central bank, reaffirming the role of the SDR as a reserve asset, and giving the IMF independent responsibility for regulating world liquidity through expanded quotas and SDR management, and (2) redesigning adjustment mechanisms to spread responsibility over deficit and surplus countries. These changes are radical and would require a complete redrafting of the IMF's Articles of Agreement. Because the developed countries of the world appear to be in

---

[19]See, for example, Paul Streeten (1995, Second Lecture) who states: "An extension of the powers of the IMF, in line with Keynes's proposals at Bretton Woods, in the direction of a global central bank would contribute to the stability and growth in the world economy. Whether countries are ready to coordinate their fiscal and monetary policies . . . and, to go one step further (as recommended by Keynes), by a single world currency, is, to say the least, an open question. Countries respecting democratic civil rights pride themselves on an independent judiciary. . . . Should not the same principle be applied to a global monetary authority, independent of national political control?" (p. 109).

no mood to undertake such tasks, proposals for such changes appear Utopian.[20] Eichengreen (1999) has suggested more modest reforms. These proposals address the IMF's involvement in the financial crises that began in 1997, and we take them up in the next chapter.

---

[20]Summers (1999a) notes: "it is difficult, in the near future at least, to imagine nations ceding control over their money or their banks to an international institution" (p. 13). Neither Summers (1999b) nor Fisher (2000) address the liquidity or adjustment issues.

Conclusion

During the twentieth century, the countries of the world struggled with three major transitions in financial arrangements: from a gold standard to a gold-exchange standard; from a gold-exchange standard to an adjustable gold peg (the Bretton Woods system); and from an adjustable gold peg to the current "nonsystem" where the IMF attempts to stabilize a whole host of currency arrangements. The IMF, an international financial organization, began its operations in 1946. It is based on a subscription or quota system, and members' quotas determine both their borrowing capacities and voting rights. The borrowing-repayment process takes place via a purchase-repurchase arrangement illustrated in Figure 16.2. Given the limited nature of quotas, however, a whole series of special credit facilities have been established, the most recent being the Poverty Reduction and Growth Facility in 1999. There was also an attempt to introduce special drawing rights (SDRs) into the IMF system as an international currency, but they have never played a significant role. IMF quotas themselves have also not kept pace with the growth of the world economy, restricting international liquidity. Recently, the IMF has struggled to address crises in Asia, Russia, and Latin America in the face of much criticism. A recurring problem is that international adjustment under the IMF "nonsystem" is solely the responsibility of deficit countries.

Review Exercises

1. How did the gold-exchange standard differ from the gold standard? How did the adjustable gold peg (Bretton Woods) system differ from the gold-exchange standard?

2. Why are post-Bretton Woods monetary arrangements referred to as a "nonsystem"?

3. In the IMF credit arrangements, what distinguishes the upper credit tranches from the first credit tranche?

4. What is your reaction to the different visions of the Keynes Plan and the White Plan? If you had been a participant a the Bretton Woods Conference, which would you have supported?

5. Would you be in favor of expanding the role of the SDR to make it an international currency along the lines of Keynes' *bancor*?

6. If there is an IMF member in which you have a special interest, spend a little time perusing the "Country Information" section of the IMF Web site at **http://www.imf.org**.

Further Reading and Web Resources

The reader with an interest in the material of this chapter would do well by consulting the concise and insightful book by Eichengreen (1996). A much more lengthy treatment can be found in James (1996). Solomon (1977) is also a very worthwhile insider's account of the Bretton Woods system. Skidelsky's (2000) biography of Keynes is also an important look at the period of history that gave birth to the IMF. Finally, Dighe (2002) uses the Wizard of Oz tale as an allegory of the gold standard era.

The interested reader will want to consult the IMF Web site at **http://www.imf.org**. From the site map, see the entries under "About the IMF." Nouriel Roubini's Global Macroeconomics and Financial Policy Web site is also important: **http://www.stern.nyu.edu/globalmacro**. Paul Streeten's views on the global financial system, expressed in "Global Governance for Human Development," can be read online at **http://www.undp.org/hdro/papers/ocpapers/oc4.htm**. See Section 7 on "A Global Central Bank." Barry Eichengreen maintains a very relevant home page at **http://elsa.berkeley.edu/users/eichengr/website.htm**. Eichengreen is one of the most important writers on international financial matters, including the IMF.

References

Boughton, J.M. (1998) "Harry Dexter White and the International Monetary Fund," *Finance and Development*, 35:3, 39–41.

Buira, A. (1995) *Reflections on the International Monetary System*, Essays in International Finance, No. 195, Princeton University, Princeton, New Jersey.

Dell, S. (1983) "Stabilization: The Political Economy of Overkill," in J. Williamson (ed.), *IMF Conditionality*, Institute for International Economics, Washington, D.C., 17–45.

Dell, S. (1981) *On Being Grandmotherly: The Evolution of IMF Conditionality*, Essays in International Finance, No. 144, Princeton University, Princeton, New Jersey.

Dighe, R.S. (ed.) (2002) *The Historian's Wizard of Oz: Reading L. Frank Baum's Classic as a Political and Monetary Allegory*, Praeger, Westport, Connecticut.

Eichengreen, B. (1999) *Towards a New International Financial Architecture: A Practical Post-Asia Agenda*, Institute for International Economics, Washington, DC.

Eichengreen, B. (1996) *Globalizing Capital: A History of the International Monetary System*, Princeton University Press, Princeton.

Eichengreen B. (1994) *International Monetary Arrangements for the 21st Century*, The Brookings Institution, Washington, DC.

Eichengreen, B. (1992) *Golden Fetters: The Gold Standard and the Great Depression*, 1919–1939, Oxford University Press, Oxford.

Fischer (2000) "Managing the International Monetary System," International Monetary Fund, July 26.

Franko, P. (2003) *The Puzzle of Latin American Economic Development*, Rowman and Littlefield, Lanham, Maryland.

Horsefield, J.K. (1969) *The International Monetary Fund, 1945–1965*, Vol. I: Chronicle, International Monetary Fund, Washington, DC.

Hume, D. (1924) "On the Balance of Trade," in A.E. Monroe (ed.), *Early Economic Thought*, 323–338 (originally published in 1752).

International Monetary Fund (2003) *The IMF's Poverty Reduction and Growth Facility: A Factsheet*, Washington, DC.

James, H. (1996) *International Monetary Cooperation Since Bretton Woods*, Oxford University Press, Oxford.

Keynes, J.M. (1963, orig. 1923) "Alternative Aims in Monetary Policy," in *Essays in Persuasion*, Norton, New York, 186–212.

Krugman, P. (1999) *The Return of Depression Economics*, Norton, New York.

McCloskey, D.N., and J.R. Zecher (1976) "How the Gold Standard Worked, 1880–1913," in J.A. Frenkel and H.G. Johnson (eds.), *The Monetary Approach to the Balance of Payments*, University of Toronto Press, Toronto, 357–385.

Salda, A.C.M. (1992) *International Monetary Fund*, Transaction Publishers, New Brunswick, New Jersey.

Skidelsky, R. (2000) *John Maynard Keynes: Fighting for Freedom 1937–1946*, Viking, New York.

Solomon, R. (1977) *The International Monetary System, 1945–1976*, Harper and Row, New York.

Stiglitz, J. (2001) "Thanks for Nothing," *Atlantic Monthly*, October, 36–40.

Streeten, P. (1995) *Thinking About Development*, Cambridge University Press, Cambridge.

Summers, L.H. (1999a) "Reflections on Managing Global Integration," *Journal of Economic Perspectives*, 13:2, 3–18.

Summers, L.H. (1999b) "The Right Kind of IMF for a Stable Global Financial System," *U.S. Treasury News*, December 14.

Triffin, R. (1960) *Gold and the Dollar Crisis: The Future of Convertibility*, Yale University Press, New Haven, Connecticut.

de Vries, M.G. (1976) *The International Monetary Fund, 1966–1971, Vol. I: Narrative*, International Monetary Fund, Washington, DC.

de Vries, M.G. (1985) *The International Monetary Fund, 1972–1978, Vol. I: Narrative and Analysis*, International Monetary Fund, Washington, DC.

Wade, R.H. (2001) "Capital and Revenge: The IMF and Ethiopia," *Challenge*, 44:5, 67–75.

Crises and Responses

In the summer of 1998, I was invited by a U.S. government agency to a conference on financial crises. Previous to this conference, crises had hit Mexico, Thailand, Indonesia, and Malaysia. A similar crisis was brewing in Russia. One by one, the presenters at this conference promoted sophisticated economic and statistical models for predicting the next crisis. My own presentation was much more simple. I suggested that the agency make a list of countries with fixed exchange rates, large capital account surpluses, and a significant amount of U.S. dollar-denominated debt. My short list contained Brazil and Argentina. Brazil's crisis came a year later. Argentina's crisis hit in 2002 and, at the time of this writing, is not yet fully resolved. My apparent prescience was in no way remarkable, however. Rather, there are indeed objective indicators that one can use to understand the likelihood of many (but not all) crises. Developing your understanding of such indicators is one objective of this chapter.[1]

As you will recall from both Chapters 15 and 16, we have mentioned the possibility of balance of payments crises under fixed exchange rate systems. These crises have led to policy debates regarding exchange rate management, capital flows, and the role of the International Monetary Fund (IMF). Because these issues have been so pressing and are of great deal of importance, we devote an entire chapter to them. We begin our discussion in the following two sections by using our fixed exchange rate model, developed in Chapter 15, to examine how balance of payments crises unfold. We consider both "old-fashioned" crises and "high-tech" crises. We then take up the issue of the IMF's response to crises. Finally, we discuss a number of proposals for changing the current "nonsystem" of international financial arrangements: exchange rate target zones, capital controls, the Tobin tax, and currency boards. Having studied this chapter, you should be in a position to assess much of the current debate on crises within the international financial system.

"Old-Fashioned" Balance of Payments Crises

Some observers have made a distinction between "old-fashioned" and "high-tech" crises.[2] To develop your understanding of crises, we will begin in this section with a consideration of "old-fashioned" balance of payments crises.

---

[1] Throughout the chapter, it is important for us to remember a key statement of Eichengreen (1999) in a review of economic models of crises: "Crises occur for good reasons, but this does not mean that they are predictable" (p. 141).

[2] See, for example, Chapter 1 of Eichengreen (1999).

"Old-fashioned" crises have their roots in overvalued, fixed exchange rates and large current account deficits. For example, in Chapters 15 and 16, we mentioned the possibility of a balance of payments crisis ensuing when the capital account can no longer support a current account deficit. In this section, we want to return to our fixed exchange rate model of Chapter 15 to analyze the exchange rate dynamics behind such crises. As in Chapter 15, our home country is Mexico and our foreign country is the United States. The market for Mexican pesos is depicted in Figure 17.1. This diagram depicts an initial equilibrium fixed exchange rate at e_0, plotting the value of the peso ($1/e$) on the vertical axis as in Chapters 13, 14, and 15.[3]

In Figure 17.1, let's suppose that Mexico is successful in implementing an equilibrium exchange rate at e_0. Recall from Chapter 15 that this equilibrium exchange rate requires that $e^e = e_0$. That is, the expected future exchange rate must equal the equilibrium rate. This, in turn, requires that the interest rate on the peso must equal the interest rate on the dollar or $r_M = r_{US}$. Next, suppose that we find Mexico in a position of a current account deficit. This was the actual case for Mexico in the early 1990s. For example, the current account deficit in Mexico was 8 percent of GDP in 1994. As we know from Chapter 12, such a current account deficit is always financed by a capital account surplus. In Mexico's case, in the early 1990s, the capital account surplus was primarily in the form of short-term portfolio investment, much of it denominated in dollars. When a large trade deficit is financed by an inflow of short-term capital, trouble is in the air. That it is denominated in dollars makes the trouble worse because any fall in the value of the home currency inflates the domestic currency value of the debt. Many domestic investors were aware of these problems, and began to sell pesos during 1994.

Figure 17.1 A Balance of Payments Crisis

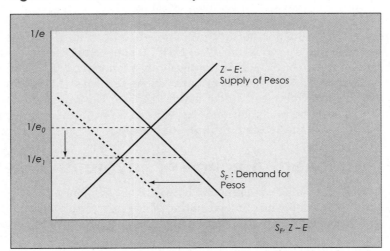

---

[3] Mexico had adopted a fixed exchange rate regime in December 1987.

Let's pretend you are a Mexican investor. If you feel that the Mexican government will have to devalue the peso in order to suppress the trade deficit, then, in your mind, $e^e > e_0$. When this occurs, the interest rate parity condition comes back into play. If $r_M = r_{US}$ and $e^e > e_0$, then the following will be true:

$$r_M < r_{US} + \frac{(e^e - e)}{e}$$

On the left-hand side of this equation is the expected total rate of return on peso-denominated assets. On the right-hand side is the expected total rate of return on dollar-denominated assets. Given that the expected total rate of return on dollar-denominated assets exceeds that of peso-denominated assets, you will adjust your portfolio, buying dollars and selling pesos. This is known as *capital flight*, and Mexican investors engaged in this type of portfolio reallocation during 1994. This situation is depicted in Figure 17.1. The change in expectations shifts the demand for pesos graph to the left. At the original exchange rate e_0, the total expected return on dollar-denominated assets exceeds the total expected return on peso-denominated assets. The equilibrium value of the peso falls to $1/e_1$. In response to such changes, in December 1994, the Mexican government devalued the peso by 15 percent. Unfortunately, this proved to be too little and simply fueled speculation of further devaluations. The demand for pesos graph in Figure 17.1 shifted further to the left, and Mexico was forced to let the peso float. Beginning in February 1995, international investors began a sudden and massive portfolio shift out of peso-denominated assets, sending the peso into a deep fall.[4]

The severity of the capital flight from Mexico has caused some observers to question the functioning of the international financial system. As Woodall (1995) put it:

> There were many good reasons behind the run on the peso—political turbulence, a widening current-account deficit, a pre-election public spending spree and a lax monetary policy. But on their own they did not justify the scale of the capital outflow or of the depreciation of the peso; the markets simply lost their heads (p. 18).

It is useful to summarize the previous discussion with a second diagram, presented in Figure 17.2. Here we see that an overvalued exchange rate causes an increase in the current account deficit (capital account surplus) and a fall in official reserve levels. As some point, expectations shift, causing capital flight. Eventually, despite strenuous denials, the government devalues the currency or shifts to floating.

The Mexican balance of payments crisis should give us an appreciation of the delicacy of managing a fixed exchange rate regime. Although at the time the crisis was contained by swift action on the part of the U.S. Treasury in supplying loans to Mexico, a similar set of crises began during the summer of 1997. This was the beginning of what now is known as the Asian crisis, which was more "high tech" than the Mexican crisis.

---

[4] A basic and well-known article on balance of payments crises is Krugman (1979). For more on the Mexican crisis, see Calvo and Mendoza (1996). An excellent and concise review of economic models of crises is presented in Appendix B of Eichengreen (1999).

Figure 17.2 An "Old-Fashioned" Balance of Payments Crisis

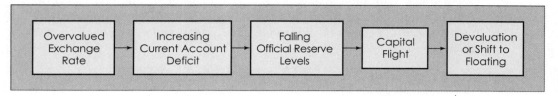

"High-Tech" Crises

Although "high-tech" crises typically include some elements of the balance of payments crises described in Figures 17.1 and 17.2, they include some less-concrete factors that are often difficult to predict. These crises combine current account deficits with weak financial sectors (especially in the banking system) and/or inappropriate capital account liberalization. For example, in the case of the Asian crisis, Stiglitz (2002) has stated that it "was, first and foremost, a crisis of the financial system" (p. 113). The "high-tech" view of crises is summarized in Figure 17.3.

The Asian crises began in Thailand, as described in the box. In some ways, the Thai crisis was similar to the Mexican crisis. It began with current account deficits amounting to nearly 8 percent of GDP under a fixed exchange rate regime. A devaluation of the baht took place on July 2, 1997. Again, the markets lost their heads. Although most analysts expected that the baht would fall by 15 to 20 percent in value against the dollar, it fell by more than 50 percent. That said, the financial sector was more at the center of the Thai crisis than the Mexican crisis. This fact has been well summarized by Reynolds et al. (2002):

> *Briefly, the (Thai) crisis occurred when banks and financial companies . . . borrowed heavily on a short-term basis from banks in other countries (mainly in Japan and the United States) and made overly risky loans to finance the construction of commercial and residential units. When the demand for such units was not forthcoming as expected, a domino effect occurred: the real estate investors who borrowed defaulted, their lenders defaulted, and the banks were left with foreign-currency-denominated loans requiring payment. A subsequent foreign exchange crisis followed the collapse of the real estate market (p. 237).*

These characteristics are what led to the loss of confidence in the financial sector depicted in Figure 17.3.

By the end of September 1999, the ensuing Asian crisis had spread to Malaysia and Indonesia. The Indonesian case was somewhat of a surprise because its current account deficit was less than 4 percent of GDP. From there, the crisis spread to the Philippines, Hong Kong, South Korea, and Taiwan. Only the Hong Kong dollar escaped devaluation.[5]

---

[5] This Asian crisis was later followed by the Russian rouble crisis of summer 1998 and the Brazilian *real* crisis of January 1999. We considered the Brazilian crisis in a box in Chapter 15.

The Baht Crisis

Until the summer of 1997, the Thai baht was pegged to the U.S. dollar. The Thai government set the rate at 25 baht per dollar. In June 1997, the baht came under pressure, and the Thai government attempted to support it through cooperative agreements with Asian central banks and controls on foreign exchange transactions. On July 2, these strategies failed, and the government attempted to devalue the baht in the face of a speculative attack. This strategy also failed, and the baht began to float. The Thai government contacted the IMF for assistance on July 27. In August 1997, the Thai government, under prime minister Chavalit Yongchaiyudh, accepted an International Monetary Fund (IMF) package of worth $17 billion.

In October 1997, the Thai finance minister resigned. In November prime minister Chavalit resigned. He was replaced by Chuan Leekpai. In December, the government closed nearly 60 financial companies that had been in very difficult financial conditions. The Thai economy, which had typically grown by over 8 percent a year, plunged into a recession. The stock market plunged. By January 1998, the baht had fallen through the crucial barrier of 50 per U.S. dollar, less than half the value of its pegged rate.

Sources: *The Economist* (1997), and Mydans (1997a,b and 1998)

What were some of the "high-tech" features of the Asian financial crisis? Here is a partial list:[6]

1. *Financial firms in the region (including banks) had significant exposures in real estate and equities, and both of these markets began to deflate prior to the crisis.*
2. *Capital accounts had been liberalized to allow firms (including banks) to take on short-term foreign debt, including debt denominated in*

Figure 17.3 A "High-Tech" Balance of Payments Crisis

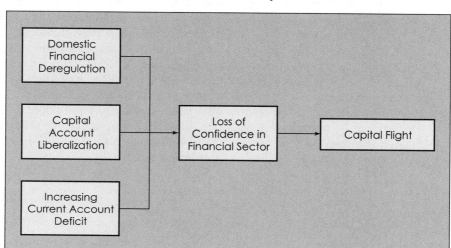

---

[6] For a fuller discussion, see Appendix C of Eichengreen (1999).

foreign currencies.[7] In two countries (Thailand and South Korea), capital account liberalization began with short-term debt, rather than long-term debt and FDI as is more prudent.[8]

3. *Banks were, in general, poorly regulated and supervised as the countries liberalized financial markets and the capital account. Indeed, banks were a crucial component of government industrial policies, which in some instances, supported systems of "crony" or "access" capitalism, rather than sound investment policies.*

4. *Due to previous confidence in fixed exchange rates, firms (including banks) were not in the practice of hedging their foreign exchange exposures in the manner we described in Chapter 13. This led them to very vulnerable positions by the eve of the crisis. When the crisis finally hit, their attempts to secure foreign exchange put extra downward pressure on the value of domestic currencies.*

These are some of the key aspects of the Asian crisis that occurred in 1997 and 1998. As depicted in Figure 17.3, loss of confidence in the financial sectors of the countries involved was a central part of the evolution of the crisis, and the banking sector was often the main culprit here. The next question we need to pursue is: How did the International Monetary Fund respond? We take a look at this controversial issue in the following section.

The IMF Response

The IMF response to the Asian and Brazilian crises has been a point of contention and debate that continues unabated. The case of Indonesia is discussed in the box. In simple form, we can characterize the IMF's policies as consisting of three elements: interest rate increases, fiscal austerity, and structural reforms. The IMF required that the afflicted economies increase their interest rates dramatically. Why? As we saw in Chapters 14 and 15 in our discussion of the interest rate parity condition, an increase in the domestic interest rate tends to increase the equilibrium value of a country's currency. The trouble with this policy is that increases in domestic interest rates also tend to suppress domestic investment and push debt-burdened firms (including banks) into default. This, in turn, can feed the sense of panic that accompanies crises. Some prominent international economists (e.g., Jeffrey Sachs, Paul Krugman, and Joseph Stiglitz) consider that the increases in interest rates were a big mistake. In the case of Brazil, the IMF insisted on interest rate increases after the *real* was allowed to float despite the fact that its value had quickly stabilized. In doing so, it may have exacerbated the crisis.[9] These economists have described the IMF interest rate policies as like shouting "Fire!" in a crowded theatre.

---

[7] "Between 1990 and 1996, roughly 50 percent of net private portfolio capital inflows into Thailand took the form of short-term borrowing. Sixty-two percent of net capital inflows in South Korea consisted of short-term borrowing in the three years 1994–97, compared with 37 percent in 1990–93" (Eichengreen, 1999, p. 156). In the case of Korea, Stiglitz (2002) alleges that "under pressure from the United States it had reluctantly allowed its firms to borrow abroad" (p. 94).

[8] We take up these sequencing issues in earnest in Chapter 23. Both Eichengreen (1999) and Stiglitz (2002) see poorly sequenced capital account liberalization as being a key cause of the Asian crisis.

[9] On the role of interest rate increases in the IMF response to crises, see especially Stiglitz (2002). The IMF (1999) defends itself as follows: "While the longer-run recessionary effects of higher interest rates are recognized, the experiences of countries whose currencies have come under attack overwhelmingly show that temporarily raising interest rates both to make the currency more attractive to hold and to avoid a depreciating-inflation spiral has been a successful strategy."

The Indonesian Crisis

One day in January 1998, the IMF's Managing Director, Michel Camdessus, met with Indonesian President Suharto to review the details of an IMF bailout package for Indonesia. Indonesia was in the throes of an exchange rate, financial, and balance of payments crisis that began in July 1997 and had resulted in the Indonesian rupiah losing 75 percent of its value. Among the conditions stipulated by the IMF was the dismantling of monopolies in cloves and palm oil owned by Suharto associates. Another condition was that the government food and energy subsidies be removed. As we discussed in Chapter 14, depreciaton of a currency increases the domestic prices of traded goods such as food and energy. This, combined with attempts to remove subsidies and a very severe drought in Indonesia, drove up food and energy prices beyond the reach of millions of the Indonesian poor. Riots were the result, and these continued for nine months afterwards. Also contributing to this unrest was a widely-distributed photograph of Camdessus hovering over Suharto with arms folded, an image with brought back bitter colonial memories.

Another component of the IMF's Indonesian program involved the closing of 16 insolvent banks. The IMF hoped that this move would restore confidence in the banking system. This seems not to have been the case. Critics alleged that the closing of these banks actually precipitated a banking panic. There was a run on remaining private banks as depositors withdrew funds and placed them in state-owned banks. IMF Chief Economist Stanley Fischer, however, denied that the closing of the banks had this effect. In his view, "the main culprits were President Suharto's illness in December, perceptions that the government would not carry out the programme, and excessive creation of liquidity by the central bank" (p. 24).

As it turned out, after receiving US$3 billion from the IMF, Indonesia reneged on its commitments. Some observers claim that Suharto never intended to abide by the agreement and that the IMF was naïve to not have recognized this. In April 1998, a new agreement was reached between the IMF and the Suharto government, and this agreement allowed for a total of US$40 billion of IMF loans to Indonesia. The funds, however, were to be delivered in billion-dollar installments based on Indonesia's progress in keeping its commitments. Food and fuel subsidies, however, were allowed to persist. In May 1998, continued rioting in Jakarta finally led to President Suharto stepping down after 32 years as president.

The Indonesian crisis was devastating to the country. The World Bank estimates that 17 million Indonesians joined the ranks of the newly poor. Real output shrank, and the country became dependent on imports of rice. World Bank president James Wolfensohn stressed these problems in his address at the annual IMF/World Bank meeting in October 1998. Wolfensohn stated: "we have learned that while the establishment of appropriate macroeconomic plans with effective fiscal and monetary policies is essential in every respect, financial plans alone are not sufficient. . . . (T)here is a need for balance. We must consider the financial, the institutional, and the social, together" (p. 5).

Sources: Fischer (1998b), Kristof (1998), Sanger (1998), and Wolfensohn (1998).

As we discussed in Chapter 12, current account deficits can result from a lack of domestic savings ($S_H + S_G$ in terms of Figure 12.2). The IMF's fiscal austerity requirements were strategies to increase S_G. Unfortunately, this strategy was probably misguided both economically and politically. The crises of Indonesia and other Asian countries were not the result of profligate governments. Rather, they generally involved excessive *private* borrowing. For example, the private sector in Indonesia carried a foreign debt of US$70 billion. For this reason, some critics have alleged that the

IMF inappropriately applied rescue packages designed for Latin America to Indonesia and Thailand.

Structural reforms refer to economic policy changes outside the fiscal and monetary realms. For example, the IMF required Indonesia to close 16 banks and dismantle. Some economists see these structural reforms as misguided. For instance, Krugman (1999) has written: "the sheer breadth of IMF demands, aside from raising suspicions that the United States was trying to use the crisis to impose its ideological vision on Asia, more or less guaranteed a prolonged period of wrangling between Asian governments and their rescuers, a period during which the crisis of confidence steadily worsened" (p. 116). In addition, the bank closures appear to have exacerbated depositor runs on other banks. Beyond these criticisms, however, a more fundamental point is at stake. In venturing into the realm of structural reforms, the IMF ventured beyond the scope of its past practices into what has traditionally been the purview of the World Bank (see Chapter 22). Nevertheless, the IMF (1999) stated that "forceful, far-reaching structural reforms are at the heart of the (recovery) programs."[10]

The IMF stood by its policies and claimed that they contributed to the recovery of the countries involved.[11] It focused on what it sees as an important role to be played by what it calls "transparency" in helping to mitigate current and future crises. In particular, it called for greater accuracy and timeliness of published data, especially in the areas of currency reserves, government finances, and banking. The notion here is that, by providing international investors with better information, exchange rates will better track the fundamentals of the economies involved. Perhaps not surprisingly given the close ties between the U.S. Treasury and the IMF, former U.S. Treasury Secretary Lawrence Summers (1999) endorsed this view. However, it is hard to see that the crises discussed in this section could have been averted simply through the greater availability of economic data. Crisis prevention must also address the sequencing and pace of financial sector liberalization, as well as the adequate regulation and supervision of the financial system, issues we take up again in Chapter 23 on structural adjustment.

Exchange Rate Target Zones

Exchange rate target zone
An exchange rate arrangement proposed by John Williamson designed to obtain the benefits of both fixed and floating exchange rate agreements. The exchange rate target zone consists of a band around the fundamental equilibrium exchange rate (FEER) on the order of ±10 percent.

The balance of payments and exchange rate crises described in the previous sections were all associated fixed exchange rate regimes. Why do countries adopt such regimes? As we mentioned in Chapter 15, it is because flexible exchange rate regimes are often volatile, and countries do not want to undergo the large changes in the home-currency prices of trade goods that come with these excessive exchange rate changes. Some international economists, notably John Williamson (1983, 1993), propose to obtain the benefits of both fixed and floating exchange rate arrangements through the use of **exchange rate target zones**.[12] In Williamson's plan,

---

[10]There is some evidence that the current Managing Director of the IMF, Horst Köhler, is simplifying the role of structural reforms in IMF conditionality packages. See *The Economist* (2001).
[11]See IMF (1999).
[12]See also *The Economist* (1993).

the center of the target zone would be what he terms a **fundamental equilibrium exchange rate (FEER)**, which could be established by the IMF. Although it is not *exactly* the case, we can consider the FEER to be the purchasing power parity (PPP) rate defined in Chapter 13.[13] As we know, the nominal exchange rate need not equal the real exchange rate and, therefore, the FEER. Williamson terms "misalignments" situations in which $e \neq re = FEER$. Such misalignments can occur as a result of countries' monetary policies.

Around the FEER, Williamson advocates the use of a broad exchange rate band, on the order of ±10 percent. Over time, the FEER changes with movements in relative price levels. Therefore, in the target zone proposal, the central rate moves slowly over time, and the exchange rate band moves with it. Finally, Williamson proposes frequent (monthly) realignments of the nominal rate in situations of misalignment. For example, Figure 17.4 depicts an exchange rate target zone with a central rate of $re = FEER$ and 10 percent bands. The nominal rate e_1 is within the band so no realignment is immediately necessary. The nominal rate e_2 is outside the upper band and calls for a nominal appreciation. As we saw in Chapter 14, this can be achieved through an increase in the domestic interest rate.

Does this proposal make sense? Holtham (1995) suggests that "to the extent that the target zones are credible, their existence provides a focus from market expectations and tends to stabilize market movements" (p. 244). The key question though is whether the zones will be credible in practice. Obstfeld and Rogoff (1995) note that even zones as large as +/–12 percent (and in one

Fundamental equilibrium exchange rate (FEER)
An exchange rate concept developed by John Williamson. The FEER can be thought of as the purchasing power exchange rate, although this is not its exact definition. In Williamson's proposal, the FEER acts as the centerpoint of an exchange rate target zone.

Figure 17.4 An Exchange Rate Target Zone

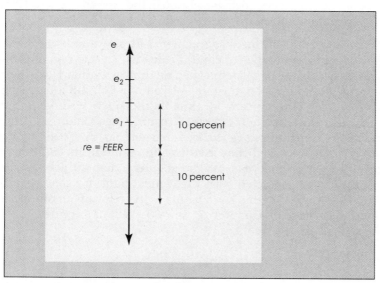

case +/–30 percent) failed to stem crises in the European Monetary System (see Chapter 18). They also suggest that a lack of credible "edges" to target zones may lead to destabilization within target zones. Nevertheless, the proposal is one that is often revisited in the wake of exchange rate crises.

Capital Controls and the Tobin Tax

In September 1997, a committee of the IMF made a recommendation to the Fund's Executive Board (see Table 16.1 in Chapter 16) that the IMF take on as an explicit policy the full convertability of the capital accounts of all its members. The IMF's Deputy Managing Director (again, see Table 16.1), Stanley Fischer, defended the proposal. Fischer (1998a) cited two arguments in support of capital account liberalization. First, he claimed, "it is an inevitable step on the path of development" (p. 2). Second, he claimed that "free capital movements facilitate an efficient allocation of savings and help channel resources into their most productive uses, thus increasing economic growth and welfare" (pp. 2–3).

Coming in the wake of the Asian crisis, the timing of this defense was more than a bit awkward. More awkwardly still, a number of prominent international economists began to argue against the proposal. Jagdish Bhagwati (1998), Dani Rodrik (1998), Paul Krugman (1999), Barry Eichengreen (1999), and Joseph Stiglitz (2002) all strongly questioned the goal of capital account liberalization and called for capital controls of one kind or another. In the view of these economists, excessive borrowing within the short-term portfolio component of the capital account was a contributing factor to the Mexican and Asian crises. Further, they allege that financial capital is too prone to panics and manias to be trusted.[14] Finally, they suggest that controls on the capital account do not appear to adversely affect the growth and development of countries with the controls.

What is one to make of this disagreement? First, we must understand that there are different types of capital controls. At one end of the continuum are strict licensing systems such as that in China. Here in order to convert the yuan into foreign currency, you must obtain a license from the government.[15] This system is akin to the quotas some countries impose on trade flows in their current accounts (see Chapter 7). At the other end of the continuum are tax systems such as that used by Chile. Chile has at times required that investments made in its country must be for a minimum of one year. It also requires that 30 percent of the investment must be deposited with the central bank for that year. This is a much more liberal regime than China's. In terms of current account restrictions discussed in Chapter 7, the 30 percent requirement acts more like a tariff than a quota.

---

[14]Rodrik (1998) wrote: "We have just gone through a lending boom-and-bust cycle in Asia that is astounding in its magnitude. In 1996, five Asian economies (Indonesia, Malaysia, the Philippines, South Korea, and Thailand) received net private-capital inflows of $93 billion. One year later, they experienced an estimated *outflow* of $12 billion, a turnaround in a single year of $105 billion" (p. 55).

[15]Krugman (1999) and Stiglitz (2002) at least partially attribute the fact that China was spared the turmoil of the Asian crisis to its capital controls.

Second, we must understand that different policies can be designed for different components of the capital account: direct investment, long-term portfolio investment, and short-term portfolio investment. Even opponents of full capital account liberalization acknowledge that controls on direct and long-term portfolio investment should be minimal. Their concern is with short-term assets used primarily for speculative purposes. For example, Chile has regulated portfolio investment based on their risk levels.

Finally, capital account liberalization is not an all-or-nothing proposition. It can (and should) be phased in gradually over time, allowing investors and domestic policy makers time to adjust to the changing regime.[16]

There is evidence that market-friendly, Chilean-style capital controls both curb the sort of market panics described in this chapter and shift the composition of capital account surpluses toward the long-term end of the asset spectrum. Consequently, countries employing them are better able to survive the panics that tend to spread from one country to another.[17] This is perhaps why even Stanley Fischer (1998b) eventually acknowledged their appropriateness and why the IMF is now in a process of studying their usefulness.[18] As summarized by Eichengreen (1999), "cautious steps in the direction of capital-account liberalization . . . should *not* extend to the removal of taxes on capital inflows" (p. 13, emphasis added).

There is another form of global control on capital accounts that has recently received a great deal of attention. In 1978, Nobel Laureate James Tobin proposed that foreign exchange transactions should be taxed to promote exchange rate stability (Tobin, 1978). At the time, Tobin notes, the proposal "did not make much of a ripple. In fact, one might say that it sank like a rock" (*The Economist*, 1996a, p. 84). Nevertheless, the **Tobin tax**, as it has come to be known, is now a topic of discussion in the international economic policy community.

> **Tobin tax**
> A small tax on foreign exchange transactions proposed by James Tobin. The purpose is to reduce the volatility of flexible exchange rates by throwing "sand in the wheels of international finance."

Tobin proposed that the tax be set at a very low level, perhaps 0.1 to 0.5 percent. For an investor moving into long-term assets, this would be negligible. For an investor moving into and out of assets on a daily basis, it would amount to a significant tax. Importantly, the tax "would have to be universal and uniform: it would have to apply to all jurisdictions, and the rate would have to be equalized across markets" (Eichengreen, Tobin, and Wyplosz, 1995, p. 165). If a single country imposed the tax, its foreign exchange markets would simply move to other countries. The IMF could handle the administration of the tax, and its proceeds might aid United Nations peacekeeping efforts.

Proponents of the Tobin tax (e.g., Eichengreen, Tobin, and Wyplosz, 1995) argue that by "throwing sand in the wheels of international finance" volatility of flexible exchange rates would be reduced. They note that, in comparison to the GATT/WTO system (see Chapter 8), the Tobin tax would be easy

---

[16]We take up the issue of phasing in Chapter 23.

[17]See the important article by Massad (1998), as well as Eichengreen (1999).

[18]Fischer (2000) stated: "That is not to say . . . that countries should open their accounts prematurely: rather they need to ensure that their economies and the financial systems are sufficiently strong; and they may particularly want to avail themselves for some time of controls on short-term capital flows."

to administer. Opponents of the Tobin tax (e.g. Garber and Taylor, 1995 and *The Economist*, 1996) question its feasibility.[19] Unlike markets for goods and services, financial markets are known for finding clever ways to avoid regulations. For example, instead of exchanging currencies, investors could exchange government bonds denominated in different currencies.

At present the Tobin tax remains a talking point, albeit one frequently visited. There appears to be no real move on the part of the world community to consider it seriously. It does, however, reflect a continued frustration with the free operation of foreign exchange markets and volatile capital flows. As was evident from both this and the previous chapters, this frustration that has been with us since the demise of the Bretton Woods system.

Currency Boards

Currency board
A type of fixed exchange rate regime where the monetary authority is required to fully back up the domestic currency with reserves of the foreign currency to which the domestic currency is pegged.

The volatility of currency values through the crises of the later 1990s led some observers to suggest the use of **currency boards** to stabilize exchange rates.[20] Currency boards are a fixed exchange rate regime in which the fixed rate has legal backing in domestic legislation. Additionally, the central bank serving as the currency board fully backs up its base money (cash and commercial bank reserves) with foreign reserves. As you saw in Chapter 15 (Table 15.2), in 1999, eight countries of the world utilized currency boards. The most well-known of these was Argentina, which introduced a currency board to help stabilize the country's economy after a period of hyperinflation.

Inflation
An increase in the overall or aggregate price level in an economy.

Currency boards are effective ways to establish sound currencies and to limit excessive money creation that can fuel **inflation**. It is not clear, however, how useful currency boards are in the long run.[21] It is also not yet clear that they can work effectively for large countries. In the case of Argentina, the currency board was introduced as part of the *Plan Convertibilidad* or Convertibility Plan in 1991, which also included a set of fiscal and structural reforms. One assessment of the currency board arrangement through 1996 used the term "miracle" and hailed it as "the most successful program in the last half-century" (Kiguel and Nogués, 1998, p. 143). Indeed, between 1991 and 1995, annual inflation fell from 170 percent to 0 percent. However, a dangerous process of **deflation** began to occur in 1998, and without an independent monetary policy, the Argentine government was helpless to address it.

Deflation
A fall in the overall or aggregate price level in an economy.

Argentina's real troubles began in July 2001 when it was required to significantly increase interest rates on its Treasury bills in order to attract investors. By December 2002, the situation had become dire. Despite ongoing talks with the IMF and limits on cash withdrawals within the country, all eyes began to focus on the country's US$135 billion public debt, and speculation grew that a devaluation was imminent, despite (typical) denials by President Fernando De la Rua. Indeed, the debt default came immediately in 2002, and the government began to prepare for a devalu-

---

[19]Despite his apparent endorsement of the Tobin tax in Eichengreen, Tobin, and Wyplosz (1995), Barry Eichengreen (1999) questions its feasibility and considers it to be second-best to Chilean-style taxes on portfolio inflows.
[20]See Enoch and Gulde (1998).
[21]See Kopcke (1999).

ation. Initially, the government attempted a 30 percent devaluation, adjusting the peg from 1.0 to 1.4 pesos per U.S. dollar. By June 2002, however, it had reached nearly 4.0 to the dollar, later appreciating back to approximately 3.5 to the dollar. At the time of this writing, the final 2002 statistics on Argentina's economy are not available. Broad indicators, however, suggest a decline in GDP of perhaps 8 percent, unemployment increasing to approximately 25 percent, and poverty expanding to perhaps 40 percent of the population. The year 2002 was the worst year for Argentina since the Great Depression.

In light of this, it is difficult to conclude that currency boards are the first-best exchange rate arrangement for large economies. Like the gold standard that it imitates, a currency board arrangement is simply too inflexible for long-term growth and stability.

Conclusion

Fixed exchange rate regimes can be very fragile. In the face of large changes in the expected future exchange rate, a government can have a very difficult time supporting the fixed rate; at some point, it simply runs out of foreign reserves. Balance of payments crises can also occur as a result of capital flight. Such changes in expectations were behind the 1994/1995 Mexican crisis, the 1997/1998 Asian crisis, the 1998 Russian crises, and the 1999 Brazilian crisis. Predicting such crises is not difficult. As stated at the beginning of the chapter, "old-fashioned" crises become likely when a country has a fixed exchange rate rate regime, large current account surpluses, and a significant amount of foreign currency-denominated debt. Weak financial (especially banking) systems add to the likelihood of "high-tech" crises where confidence in the financial system deteriorates.

The appropriateness of the IMF's responses to these crises is a subject of current debate. More generally, there are proposals for making future crises less likely, and these include exchange rate target zones, capital controls, and the Tobin tax. Unfortunately, there is little consensus on the appropriateness of these proposals. It is fair to say, however, that prudent and limited controls on capital account transactions, such as those used by Chile, are an important point of departure in the policy debate.[22]

Review Exercises

1. What is the key difference between "old-fashioned" and "high-tech" crises?

2. In Chapter 15, we addressed fixed exchange rates. Polices to maintain fixed exchange rates fell into two categories. First, there were policies to address the excess demand or supply of the

---

[22]For counterarguments to this point, see the interview with Graciela Kaminsky that follows Chapter 18.

home country (official reserve transactions). Second, there were policies to change the equilibrium exchange rate (interest rate changes). Answer the following questions with regard to the use of these policies in balance of payments crises.

  a. In a balance of payments crisis, what kind of official reserve transactions will be made?

  b. What are the limits of the official reserve transactions approach to resolving balance of payments crises?

  c. In a balance of payments crisis, what kind of interest rate policies will be used?

  d. What are the limits of the interest rate approach to resolving balance of payments crises?

3. The argument in favor of current account convertibility (free trade) is that it leads to gains from trade. Are there any reasons you can think of why we might not be able to extend this argument to the financial transactions of the capital account? Or to put it differently, are there any ways that financial markets differ from merchandise and service markets?

Further Reading and Web Resources

Readable and worthwhile reviews of crises can be found in Krugman (1999) and Stiglitz (2002). An excellent, more technical, and ultimately more important review has been written by Eichengreen (1999). The IMF position on these crises can be found in IMF (1999), and the World Bank's views can be found in Wolfensohn (1998). On exchange rate target zones, Williamson (1983) and (1993) are essential reading. The reader interested in the issue of capital account controls would do well to begin with Massad's (1998) excellent review of Chile's policies. Unlike most other polemical discussions, Massad gives a detailed and well-reasoned argument for a middle ground in the capital account convertibility controversy. A balanced view of currency boards can be found in Kopcke (1999).

International economist Kar-yiu Wong maintains a Web site at **http://faculty.washington.edu/karyiu** with information on the Asian crisis. The same is true of Nouriel Roubini at **http://www.stern.nyu.edu/ globalmacro**. The "unofficial" Paul Krugman Web site at **http://www. pkarchive.org/** is also useful. A large amount of background material on the Tobin tax, including the original article, can be found at **http:// www.globalpolicy.org/socecon/glotax/currtax/index.htm**. Also see the Windows on the World Economy Web site for *Quarterly Reports on the Argentina Crisis* at **http://reinert.swlearning.com**.

References

Bhagwati, J. (1998) "The Capital Myth," *Foreign Affairs*, May/June, 7–12.

Calvo, G.A., and E.G. Mendoza (1996) "Mexico's Balance-of-Payments Crisis: A Chronicle of a Death Foretold," *Journal of International Economics*, 41:3/4, 235–264.

The Economist (2001) "The International Monetary Fund: Köhler's New Crew," June 16, 69–70.

The Economist (1997) "Lessons for Thailand, et al," July 12, 16–17.

The Economist (1996) "Floating the Tobin Tax," July 13, 84.

The Economist (1993) "The Way We Were," May 8, 83.

Eichengreen, B. (1999) *Towards a New Financial Architecture: A Practical Post-Asia Agenda*, Institute for International Economics, Washington, DC.

Eichengreen, B., J. Tobin, and C. Wyplosz (1995) "Two Cases for Sand in the Wheels of International Finance," *Economic Journal*, 105:428, 162–172.

Enoch, C., and A.M. Gulde (1998) "Are Currency Boards a Cure for All Monetary Problems?" *Finance and Development*, 35:4, 40–43.

Fischer, S. (2000) "Managing the International Monetary System," International Monetary Fund, July 26.

Fischer, S. (1998a) "Capital-Account Liberalization and the Role of the IMF," in S. Fischer et al., *Should the IMF Pursue Capital-Account Convertibility?* Princeton Essays in International Finance, 207, May, 1–10.

Fischer, S. (1998b) "Lessons from a Crisis," *The Economist*, October 3, 23–27.

Garber, P., and M.P. Taylor (1995) "Sand in the Wheels of Foreign Exchange Markets: A Skeptical Note," *Economic Journal*, 105:428, 173–180.

Holtham, G. (1995) "Managing the Exchange Rate System," in J. Michie and J. Grieve Smith (eds.), *Managing the Global Economy*, Oxford University Press, Oxford, 232–251.

International Monetary Fund (1999) "The IMF's Response to the Asian Crisis," http://www.imf.org/external/np/exr/facts/asia.htm.

Kiguel, M., and J.J. Nogués (1998) "Restoring Growth and Price Stability in Argentina: Do Policies Make Miracles?" in H. Costin and H. Vanolli (eds.), *Economic Reform in Latin America*, Dryden, Fort Worth, 125–144.

Kopcke, R.W. (1999) "Currency Boards: Once and Future Monetary Regimes?" *Federal Reserve Bank of Boston New England Economic Review*, May–June, 21–37.

Kristof, N.D. (1998) "Has the I.M.F. Cured or Harmed Asia? Dispute Rages after Months of Crisis," *New York Times on the Web*, April 23.

Krugman, P. (1999) *The Return of Depression Economics*, Norton, New York.

Krugman, P. (1979) "A Model of Balance of Payments Crises," *Journal of Money, Credit and Banking*, 11:3, 311–325.

Massad, C. (1998) "The Liberalization of the Capital Account: Chile in the 1990s," in S. Fischer et al., *Should the IMF Pursue Capital-Account Convertibility?*, Princeton Essays in International Finance, 207, May, 34–46.

Mydans, S. (1997a) "Thai Prime Minister Falls Victim to Economic Crisis," *New York Times on the Web*, November 4.

Mydans, S. (1997b) "Economists Cheer Thailand's Tough Action on Ailing Finance Companies," *New York Times on the Web*, December 9.

Mydans, S. (1998) "Struggling Thailand Seeks Easier I.M.F. Terms," *New York Times on the Web*, January 9.

Obstfeld, M., and K. Rogoff (1995) "The Mirage of Fixed Exchange Rates," *Journal of Economic Perspectives*, 9:4, 73–96.

Reynolds, S., et al. (2002) "Forecasting the Probability of Failure of Thailand's Financial Companies in the Asian Financial Crisis," *Economic Development and Cultural Change*, 51:1, 237–246.

Rodrik, D. (1998) "Who Needs Capital-Account Convertibility?" in S. Fischer et al., *Should the IMF Pursue Capital-Account Convertibility?* Princeton Essays in International Finance, 207, May, 55–65.

Sanger, D.E. (1998) "I.M.F. Role in World Economy Is Hotly Debated," *New York Times on the Web*, October 2.

Stiglitz, J.E. (2002) *Globalization and Its Discontents*, Norton, New York.

Summers, L.H. (1999) "Reflections on Managing Global Integration," *Journal of Economic Perspectives*, 13:2, 3–18.

Tobin, J. (1978) "A Proposal for International Monetary Reform," *Eastern Economic Journal*, 4:3–4, 153–159.

Williamson, J. (1993) "Exchange Rate Management," *Economic Journal*, 103:416, 188–197.

Williamson, J. (1983) *The Exchange Rate System*, Institute for International Economics, Washington, DC.

Wolfensohn, J. (1998) The Other Crisis, World Bank, Washington, DC. (1995) "The World Economy: Who's in the Driving Seat?" *The Economist*, October 7, 1–38.

Woodall, P. (1995) "The World Economy: Who's in the Driving Seat?" *The Economist*, October 7, 1–38.

Monetary Unions

18

Imagine that you are a finance minister of a medium-sized country with extensive trade and investment relationships with fellow members of a regional trade agreement (RTA). Imagine also that you have responsibility for determining the future exchange rate regime of your country. One option you have is a flexible exchange rate regime (a "clean" or "dirty" float). If you chose this option, however, your country might be buffeted by destabilizing changes in the nominal (and hence real) exchange rate. A second option you have is a fixed exchange rate (or crawling peg). If you chose this option, however, your country might eventually stumble into a balance of payments crisis as we discussed in Chapter 17. What should you do? There is no easy answer.

There is a third option available to you, one we mentioned briefly in Chapter 8. You and the other finance ministers in the RTA could agree to do away with all the exchange rates among your countries by becoming a **monetary union** with a common currency. This is not a panacea, because you and your colleagues would still need to decide upon the exchange rate regime for the common currency. But at least you can avoid exchange rate instability with your major trade and investment partners. As it turns out, this policy was adopted as a goal by the countries of Western Europe in 1971 and has recently been implemented. Monetary union has also been a living reality for the Communauté Financière Africaine (CFA) franc zone, a group of African countries with ties to France. In this chapter, we first take up the case of the European Monetary Union (EMU), assessing both its planning and implementation. Next, we assess the EMU in light of the theory of optimum currency areas and discuss its potential adjustment problems. Finally, we briefly consider the case of the CFA franc zone.

Monetary union
A group of member countries in a common market that all use a common currency. The most notable example is the European Monetary Union or EMU.

Planning the European Monetary Union

The history of monetary integration in Europe has roots that go back to the immediate post–World War II period.[1] In Chapter 8, we discussed the evolution of the European Union in that period up through the Maastricht Treaty of 1992. For your convenience, Table 8.2 of that chapter is reproduced here as Table 18.1. The monetary union initiative began in October 1970 when a commission chaired by the then prime minister of Luxembourg, Pierre Werner, issued a report providing a detailed plan for a step-by-step movement to a European Monetary Union (EMU) by 1980.

---

[1] See Chapter 1 of Gros and Thygesen (1992) and Part I of Dinan (1999).

Table 18.1 The Evolution of the European Union

Year	Initiative	Treaty	Members Added
1951	European Coal and Steel Community	Treaty of Paris	Belgium France Germany Italy Luxembourg Netherlands
1958	European Economic Community	Treaty of Rome	
1973			Denmark Ireland United Kingdom
1981			Greece
1986			Portugal Spain
1992	European Union	Treaty on European Union (TEU) or the Maastricht Treaty	
1994			Austria Finland Sweden

The European Council of Ministers of Economics and Finance (ECOFIN) endorsed the Werner Report in March 1971. The person behind the Werner report is discussed in the box. Unfortunately, as we discussed in Chapter 16, subsequent months brought on the demise of the Bretton Woods system of global monetary arrangements. In response to this crisis, a year later, the members of the European Common Market decide to bind their exchange rates within 2.25 percent of each other. This became known as the "snake in a tunnel" or "snake." By June 1972, the British pound came under pressure and was forced out of the snake. The Danish krone also pulled out of the snake. The French franc was forced out in January 1974, reentered in 1975, and was forced out again in March 1976. Nevertheless, the "snake" continued through 1978.[2]

In October 1977, European Commission president Roy Jenkins gave a lecture at the European University in Florence. In this lecture, he called for Europe to adopt as a goal monetary union. In 1978, negotiations began in earnest over the creation of a European Monetary System or EMS. The EMS came into being as a fixed rate system in March 1979. In a very real sense, the EMS was an attempt to replicate the fixed rate Bretton Woods system among the countries of Europe.[3] A new currency was created

---

[2] See Chapter 5 of Eichengreen (1996) and especially Table 5.1 (p. 156) for a history of the snake.
[3] See Chapter 10 of James (1996).

Pierre Werner

Pierre Werner was born in Luxembourg in 1913. Importantly, he grew up in a bilingual family, speaking both German and French. His professional life spanned the fields of law and economics. He studied law at the University of Paris and economics and finance at the Paris Ecole Libre de Sciences Politiques. Unlike many leading citizens of Luxembourg who fled the country, Werner spent World War II under German occupation, witnessing many horrors firsthand. As with many Western Europeans of this generation, Werner became passionate about European integration as an antidote to war. He was elected to the Luxembourg parliament in 1945 and befriended Jean Monnet, one of the architects of the European Community (EC) formed in 1958. To Werner, Monnet, and other leading integrationists of that era, "the central aim of European unity was to prevent war. Economic gain, though useful, was a secondary consideration" (*The Economist*, 2002b, p. 85).

Werner became prime minister of Luxembourg in 1959 and remained in that post until 1974. He returned to that post in 1979, retiring from politics in 1984 to pursue a subsequent career in business. In 1993, he published his memoirs, entitled *Itinéraires Luxembourgeois et Europeens*.

Werner first floated the idea of a common European currency in a 1960 speech at Strasbourg. In 1969, the EC adopted the goal of monetary union and convened a high-level group under Werner's chairmanship to develop a plan for and EC monetary union by 1980. The plan, which became known as the Werner Report, was circulated in 1970 and endorsed by the EC in 1971. Although not mentioning the adoption of a common currency, the Werner Report called for the "total and irreversible conversion of currencies, the elimination of fluctuation in exchange rates, the irrevocable fixing of parity rates and the complete liberation of capital accounts." A continued advocate of a common currency for Europe, however, Werner had to wait until January 2002 to witness the introduction of euro notes and coins. He died six months later.

Werner had another plan as well—the introduction of a world currency to follow global economic integration. He called the world currency the "mondo." Time will tell whether this plan will ever come to fruition.

Sources: *Daily Telegraph* (2002); *The Economist* (2002b).

called the European currency unit or ECU, defined as a basket of European currencies. The ECU had a role equivalent to that initially hoped for SDR in the Bretton Woods system (see Chapter 16). Furthermore, the European Community acted in a role equivalent to the IMF, providing balance of payments credit to members.[4] The original hope was that each country would peg their currency to the ECU, but this hope did not come to pass. Instead, in the 1980s, countries began to peg their currencies to the German mark.[5] The ECU continued only as a unit of account for official European Community business. In the early years of the EMS, there was a great deal of instability. A number of parity realignments were necessary with the French franc falling against the German mark. The latter was largely due to the expansive macreconomic policies

---

[4] For example, this was the case during a March 1983 French crisis.
[5] "Structurally, Germany . . . occupied within the EMS a situation analogous to that of the United States within the classical Bretton Woods par value system, and the deutche mark constituted the European 'key currency'" (James, 1996, p. 482).

of the Socialist government of President François Mitterand. During a crisis in March 1983, Mitterand changed course in order to keep France within the EMS.[6] Thereafter, stability was restored with less frequent parity changes.

In June 1988, the European Council called upon the then president of the European Commission, Jacques Delors, to study the steps required to move towards a monetary union. The Delors report was issued in April 1989. The report called for a single currency and an integrated system of European central banks. In December 1991, a meeting of the European Community took place in the Dutch town of Maastricht. The Maastricht Treaty, agreed to at this meeting, was to serve as a constitution of the new European Union or EU, replacing the Treaty of Rome. It was signed in February 1992. The Maastricht Treaty set 1999 as a target date for a European Monetary Union or EMU. In 1994, as specified by this treaty, a European Monetary Institute (EMI) came into being. Its purpose was to plan for the future European System of Central Banks or ESCB and to plot the course towards monetary integration. The EMI was to also monitor the progress of member countries toward meeting a set of convergence criteria. These criteria concerned price stability, levels of government deficits and debt, exchange rate targets, and interest rate targets. For example, government deficits (a flow) were required to be less than 3 percent of gross domestic product (GDP), and government debts (a stock) were required to be less than 60 percent of GDP. These convergence criteria reflected the wishes of the German government.

The evolution toward the EMU proved to be more difficult than envisioned in the Delors report. In 1990, East and West Germany had reunified. This required unprecedented increases in public expenditure on the part of the German government. To prevent the German economy from expanding too quickly, the central bank pursued a tight or restrictive monetary policy. This kept the German interest rate high, caused international investors to favor mark-denominated assets over other European assets, and put downward pressure on the value of other European currencies. The EMS par-value system came under pressure. In addition, difficulties in ratification of the 1992 Maastricht Treaty ruffled investors' expectations. In particular, there were growing predictions of a "no" vote (proved to be incorrect) in the French referendum on Maastricht in September 1992. In that very same month, pressure built against the British pound and Italian lira. Despite very large interventions by European central banks to support these currencies, they were forced outside of the EMS.[7] The French franc came under a second-round attack in July 1993.[8] In response to these events, the margins around the parities were expanded from 2.25 percent to 15 percent in August.

---

[6] The adjustment came under the guidance of Minister of Economy Jacques Delors, who would later become a powerful president of the European Commisssion.

[7] The pound and lira crises were preceded by crises of the Finish markka and the Swedish krone. Later, the Irish punt, the Portuguese escudo, and the Spanish peseta were also devalued. The franc peg survived thanks to intervention by the German Bundesbank. Dinan (forthcoming) refers to this as "a move that revealed Germany's much closer relationship with France than with any other member state."

[8] Dinan (forthcoming) notes that "With international currency transactions increasing at a rapid rate and huge amounts of capital moving freely throughout the EU, the Germans felt unable any longer to support the franc."

The EMS crisis was certainly an inauspicious transition to European monetary integration. The British government, which subsequently opted out of the EMU, was particularly irritated by its forced exit from the EMS. That said, however, most EU leaders resolved to press on, and so they did. In December 1995, EU members meeting in Madrid committed themselves to introducing a common currency, called the *euro*, in January 1999. They also adopted the EMI's plan for monetary integration despite widespread misgivings. In reflecting on the Madrid meetings, Dinan (forthcoming) states: "What many dismissed at the time as a foolish act of faith looked in retrospect like a bold assertion of political will."

Implementing the European Monetary Union

In June 1997, the European Union adopted a Stability and Growth Pact, which places restrictions on EMU member countries' fiscal policies. We will discuss these measures later. In May 1998, EU leaders met again in Brussels to determine which countries were to take part in the EMU/euro as of January 1999. These were Austria, Belgium, Finland, France, Germany, Ireland, Italy, Luxembourg, the Netherlands, Portugal, and Spain. The choices reflected the extent to which the countries met the convergence criteria. Greece was the one country that wanted to join but was not allowed to do so. This decision was later reversed, and Greece joined in 2001. The United Kingdom, Denmark, and Sweden opted not to join.[9] In October 1998, *The Economist* (1998b) summed up the situation as follows: "A striking feature of the single currency arrangements is that they make no provision, legal or practical, for any participant's withdrawal or expulsion. In this adventure, Europe has left itself no choice but to succeed" (p. 82).

The centerpiece of the EMU is the ESCB. It consists of the Frankfurt-based European Central Bank (ECB) and the former national central banks in a structure modeled quite closely on that of the Federal Reserve System of the United States. The primary goal of the ESCB is the conduct of monetary policy to maintain of price stability within the EMU. The ECB is required to maintain annual increases in a harmonized index of consumer prices (HICP) at or below 2 percent. This is widely regarded as a very stringent rule, but one insisted upon by the German central bank, the Bundesbank.

The ECB is headed by a President with an 8-year, nonrenewable term. This proved difficult from the start. The European Council is the body that appoints the ECB President, and a battle ensued over who would fill this post. This inauspicious beginning of the ECB is discussed in the box. The European Council also appoints the ECB Vice President. As illustrated in Figure 18.1, the President, the Vice President, and four other individuals compose the ECB Executive Board. The Executive Board is responsible for implementing monetary policy within the EMU. The Executive Board plus the other heads of EMU member central banks, in turn, compose the ECB Governing Council. The Governing Council is responsible for formulating

---

[9] Denmark put the euro issue to a referendum in September 2000, and it was rejected, despite the fact that the Danish currency is rigidly pegged to the euro. In a similar referendum in September 2003, the citizens of Sweden also rejected the euro.

Figure 18.1 Organizational Structure of the ECB

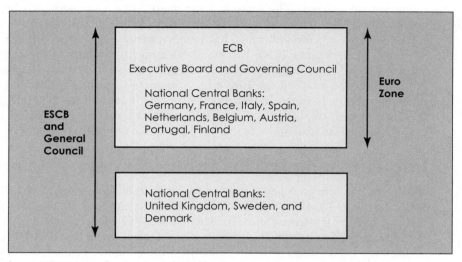

Source: European Central Bank (2003). "About the ECB." http://www.ecb.int. Note: This information may be obtained free of charge through ECB's Web site.

Figure 18.2 The Dollar Value of the Euro, 1999 to 2002

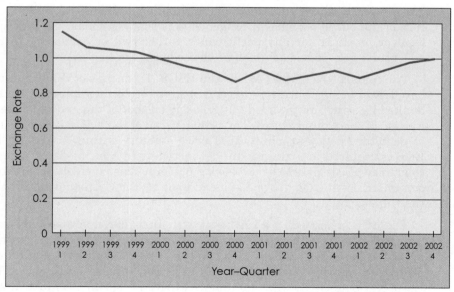

Source: Based on data in *Annual Report* for 1999, 2000, 2001, and 2002, published by the European Central Bank.

monetary policy within the EMU. There is also a General Council that adds the four heads of the EU member central banks that are not part of the EMU. However, the four members of the Executive Board other than the President and the Vice President do not have the right to vote as part

Wim Duisenberg and Jean-Claude Trichet

The European Central Bank (ECB) had a rough start in the decision over who would head that body as President. Most members of the European Council favored Wim Duisenberg, a chain-smoking Dutch economist and former Chair of the EMI. French President Jacques Chirac, however, insisted on Jean-Claude Trichet, governor of the French central bank, despite the fact that Trichet had formerly endorsed Duisenberg! Finally, Duisenberg was appointed with the understanding that he would stand down during 2003 and that Trichet would then complete a full 8-year term. As Dinan (1999) stated: "To everyone's surprise, Chirac pursued this nakedly nationalistic position to the end" (p. 476). Because this arrangement was against both the letter and the spirit of ESCB statutes, the ESC had an unglamorous start.

Wim Duisenberg was appointed as head of the European Monetary Institute in June 1997, having previously served very successfully as head of the Dutch central bank. He took over at the helm of the ECB in January 1999 and called upon the European public to consider him their "Mr. Euro." When Duisenberg took office, the value of the euro was set at $1.186 in a flexible exchange rate system. By June 1999, its value had fallen to nearly $1.00. It rallied a bit in the later half of 1999, but early in 2000, it fell below $1.00. In May 2000, the euro fell below $0.90, rallied again, but fell below $0.90 in August 2000. In September 2000, the leading central banks sold foreign exchange reserves in support of the euro. However, in October 2000, the euro reached nearly $0.80, having lost nearly 30 percent of its original value. The October slide was partly in response to Duisenberg's giving an interview to a newspaper in which he commented on the conditions under which the ECB might intervene to support the value of the euro. This comment violated a central banking taboo and resulted in calls for and rumors of his resignation. Since then, the euro has gained substantially in value.

Jean-Claude Trichet ran into his own troubles. During 2000, Trichet was caught up in the French financial scandals surrounding the bank Crédit Lyonnais. These issues related to his career at the helm of the French Treasury from 1987 to 1993 when he was responsible for the accounts of Crédit Lyonnais. Finally, in June 2003, a French court acquitted the able and ambitious Trichet. So, he can finally claim the ECB post.

Sources: Dinan (1999); Sullivan (2000).

of the General Council. The General Council is an administrative body that is responsible for the work previously undertaken by the EMI.

The euro was launched in January 1999. At this time, EMU member exchange rates became "irrevocably" locked, and monetary policy was transferred to the ECB. The ECB was capitalized at 5,000 million euros with subscriptions from the central banks of all EU countries. Since the beginning of the ECB's operations, there has been some criticism of its decision to publish its General Council minutes only after 30 years. The General Council does, however, publish abbreviated minutes and publishes quarterly reports. The value of the euro was initially set at $1.186 in a flexible exchange rate regime such as we discussed in Chapter 14. By June 1999, its value had fallen to nearly $1.00. Although some Europhiles interpreted this as a decline in the "strength of Europe," it is really a sign of the workings of a flexible exchange rate regime. Beginning in mid-2002, the euro's value against the dollar increased. By March 2003, it had reached $1.10. A time series on the dollar value of the euro is presented in Figure 18.2.

In January 2002, the ECB introduced euro notes and coins and began the process of withdrawing old notes and coins from circulation. This huge logistical task was amazingly carried out with very few problems. Europe now had its common currency. The real problems proved to be ones of effective monetary policy, and we turn to these in the following section.

Optimum Currency Areas and Adjustment in the EMU

Optimum currency area
A collection of countries characterized by (1) well-integrated factor markets; (2) well-integrated fiscal systems; and (3) economic disturbances that affect each country in a symmetrical manner.

There is an idea in international economics that is important to our discussion of the EMU. This is the notion of an **optimum currency area**.[10] An optimum currency area is a collection of countries characterized by the following:

1. *Well-integrated factor markets*
2. *Well-integrated fiscal systems*
3. *Economic disturbances that affect each country in a symmetrical manner*

Most observers, for example, agree that the United States constitutes an optimum currency area. Labor and physical capital are quite mobile among the states of the United States, and there is a great deal of integration of fiscal systems through the U.S. federal government. Finally, cycles of recession and recovery tend to affect each region of the United States in a somewhat symmetrical (albeit not equal) manner.

In the case of the EMU, there seems to be less evidence that it constitutes an optimum currency area.[11] First, despite the fact that the EMU is a subcomponent of the EU, which is, in turn, a common market (see Chapter 8), both labor and physical capital are less mobile among the countries of the EMU than in the United States. Second, the budget of the EU is relatively small in proportion to the size of the economies involved. This indicates a lack of fiscal integration of the EMU economy. Third, business cycles among the members of the EMU are somewhat asymmetrical with one country experiencing an expansion and another a contraction at the same time.

The absence of an optimum currency area in the EMU leaves some room for worry over how economic adjustment will occur within it. In the face of a recession in one country, unemployment will rise. This rise in unemployment can be addressed in four ways:

1. *An overall decline in wage rates leading to increases in quantity demanded for labor*
2. *Labor mobility out of areas of unemployment*
3. *Expansionary monetary policy (at the EU level)*
4. *Expansionary fiscal policies (at the member-country level)*

---

[10]This line of thinking in international economics was started by Mundell (1961) and McKinnon (1963).
[11]See Chapter 14 of Kenen (1994), Sheridan (1999), and Chapter 16 of Dinan (1999).

The first of these potential remedies, declining wages, can in principle address unemployment problems. However, wages in most EMU countries are notoriously "downward inflexible." The second remedy, labor mobility (migration out of the county experiencing a recession) could likewise help achieve adjustment. However, as we just mentioned, labor mobility within the EMU is not very strong. The third potential remedy is the monetary policy of the ECB. Recall, however, that the ECB is required to maintain annual increases in a harmonized index of consumer prices (HICP) at or below 2 percent.[12] The Governing Council of the ECB adopted this policy in 1998 for application to the "medium term." Most observers interpret this as being a quite restrictive monetary policy, and it is one where there is no flexibility in addressing unemployment. In the ECB's words, "It should be emphasized that the ECB's definition is intended to be a *lasting quantification* of the *primary objective* of monetary policy" (2001, p. 41, emphasis added).

The final remedy for unemployment is national fiscal policy, which, indeed, remains the responsibility of member countries. However, under the EU's Growth and Stability Pact, the convergence criteria have evolved into rules setting limits to fiscal policy of member countries. This, in the minds of some observers, might prove to be problematic. In the face of a recession and rising unemployment, member countries' fiscal policies would be bound by the 3 percent (of GDP for deficits) and 60 percent (of GDP for debt) rules except in the case of "severe" recession.[13] Thus, the last remedy for addressing unemployment is also quite limited.

These considerations leave some observers worried about the future of the EMU. Some even have gone so far as to refer to the Stability Pact as the *Instability Pact*. What is more, violation of the Stability Pact can result in fines up to as large as 0.5 percent of GDP. Some observers (e.g. Sheridan, 1999) predict political problems as a result of the absence of economic adjustment mechanisms.[14] Even more pessimistic views (e.g., Feldstein, 1997) involve scenarios of war. Although the latter scenario is quite unlikely, the former certainly is not, and managing the political conflicts will be a prerequisite for the success of the EMU experiment.

The ECB, naturally, defends the Stability Pact, stating that it "represents an important commitment to maintaining fiscal policies conducive to overall macroeconomic stability" (2001, p. 17). However, these issues surfaced in a significant way beginning in 2002 as the EU entered into recession. Even Germany, chief architect of the Stability Pact, came dangerously close to violating it, causing the European Commission to express official concern. A similar series of events unfolded in the case of France in 2003. The future of the Growth and Stability Pact and the ability of the EU to weather economic downturns remain in doubt.

---

[12]ECB monetary policy is enacted using a "two pillar strategy" of monetary targeting and inflation targeting. See Clausen and Donges (2001) and European Central Bank (2001).

[13]For further fiscal issues regarding the EMU, see Ferguson and Kotlikoff (2000).

[14]Tsoukalis (1997) recognized this problem: "EMU could divide the EU; it could destabilize it politically, if new institutions do not enjoy the legitimacy which is necessary to carry their policies through; and it could create economically depressed countries and regions. These are the main risks" (p. 186).

The CFA Franc Zone

The Communauté Financière Africaine (CFA) franc zone is a complete and functioning monetary union among 13 member countries that have adopted the CFA franc as a common currency. It has been in existence since 1945. The CFA franc zone actually consists of two subunions, the West African Monetary Union (WAMU) and the Central African Monetary Area (CAMA), associated with the Central Bank for West African States and the Bank for Central African States, respectively. This long-standing monetary union was associated, at least until the mid-1980s, with economic performance no worse than and perhaps better than neighboring countries that utilized floating or managed floating exchange rate regimes.[15] As part of the monetary union, the Central Bank for West African States and the Bank for Central African States maintain a foreign exchange reserve pool in which they keep 65 percent of their reserves with the French Treasury, an arrangement that is clearly a legacy of the colonial past.

In the case of a completed monetary union, the issue of how to manage the relationship of the common currency to the rest of the world still remains. In the case of the CFA franc zone, this was resolved in 1948 by means of a fixed peg to the French franc, the main trade partner. This management strategy proved workable up to the mid-1980s. Both controls on the capital accounts of member countries and the backing of the peg by the French Treasury helped to support the fixed rate. Beginning in the early 1980s, however, the world prices of the main CFA export goods declined significantly, and the countries involved found themselves in balance of payments difficulties. With devaluation not a possibility, adjustment was attempted by contractionary macroeconomic policies aimed at reducing import demands and maintaining high interest rates. A number of CFA members began to turn to the IMF for assistance, some of them under the structural adjustment and enhanced structural adjustment facilities mentioned in Chapter 16. Following civil unrest in Cameroon and a withdrawal of support by French Prime Minister Edouard Balladur, both in 1993, a devaluation of 50 percent against the French franc was made in January 1994.

With the launch of the euro in 1999, the franc peg became a euro peg. This makes some economic sense because the EU is the CFA franc zone's main trading partner. The key question for the future of the zone is whether the CFA franc-euro peg can be maintained.[16] If the history of fixed exchange rate regimes is any guide, a further devaluation lies in the future.

One important lesson of the CFA franc zone experience is that a monetary union, despite resolving exchange rate difficulties among its members, still can involve difficulties in the relationship of the common currency with the rest of the world. The CFA opted for a fixed exchange rate regime, and this eventually led to exactly the sort of crises we discussed in Chapter 17. The

---

[15]See Chapter 5 of Eichengreen (1996) and Chapter 14 of James (1996). Member countries of WAMU are Benin, Burkina Faso, Côte d'Ivoire, Mali, Niger, Senegal, and Togo. Member countries of CAMA are Cameroon, Central African Republic, Chad, Congo, Equatorial Guinea, and Gabon.
[16]For a fuller discussion of this issue, see *The Economist* (2002a).

history of the European Monetary Union also involved a number of crises. But as we have discussed, in the end it opted for a flexible regime between its common currency and the rest of the world. Time will tell whether this alternative arrangement works more satisfactorily than the fixed, CFA regime.

Conclusion

In his well-received book, *Globalizing Capital*, Barry Eichengreen concludes with the following statement:

> *For the majority of smaller, more open economies . . . the costs of floating are difficult to bear. While domestic political constraints preclude the successful maintenance of unilateral currency pegs except in the most exceptional circumstances, volatile exchange rate swings impose almost unbearable costs and are disruptive to the pursuit of domestic economic goals. As their economies are buffeted by exchange-market turbulence, these countries are likely to seek cooperative agreements that tie their currencies securely to that of a larger neighbor. . . . One can imagine that, with sufficient time, similar tendencies will surface in the Western Hemisphere and Asia, and that the United States and Japan will be at the center of their respective monetary blocs. But a happy conclusion to this story remains at best a distant prospect.*

Monetary unions such as those discussed in this chapter are attempts to escape the ravages of both fixed and flexible exchange rate regimes. Given the crises discussed in Chapter 17, Eichengreen's conclusion has proved prescient. A number of Latin American countries are now discussing the possibility of adopting the U.S. dollar (dollarization) as their currency in a process of unofficial and stealth monetary union that would satisfy the criteria of optimal currency areas even less satisfactorily than the EMU.[17] The fact that dollarization is a topic of discussion, and Eichengreen's statement, are both testaments to the imperfect nature of current international financial arrangements. However, as we have stated on a number of occasions, there is little political will among the powerful governments of the world to contemplate any significant changes.

Review Exercises

1. Imagine that, suddenly, the U.S. dollar was abolished and each state of the United States introduced its own currency (the Arizona, the Montana, the Wyoming, etc.). Would this alter economic life in the United States? How so? What problems would it entail?

---

[17]Panama, Ecuador, and El Salvador are countries already using the U.S. dollar as their currencies.

2. Three European Union countries (the United Kingdom, Sweden, and Denmark) chose not to be part of the EMU. Can you think of any reasons why they would do so?

3. Have you or your classmates had any experiences with the euro? What are they?

4. One region in which there is discussion of monetary union is Latin America. Would the countries of Latin America qualify as an optimum currency area?

Further Reading and Web Resources

An important and accessible source on the European Union is Dinan (1999). For a discussion of the events leading up to the formation of the EMU, see Chapter 5 of Eichengreen (1996) and Chapters 7 and 8 of Tsoukalis (1997). A very brief introduction to the EMU and the euro can be found in Solomon (1999). A slightly longer introduction is given in *The Economist* (1998a). An advanced treatment can be found in Chapter 18 of Hallwood and MacDonald (2000). An application of the optimum currency area concept to the EMU can be found in Sheridan (1999), and an assessment of the ECB through June 1999 can be found in *The Economist* (1999). For an overview of ECB monetary policy, see European Central Bank (2001).

Useful information about the euro can be found on the European Union's Web site at **http://www.europa.eu.int**. The European Central Bank's Web site is **http://www.ecb.int**. See the page "About the ECB." Giancarlo Corsetti maintains a euro home page at **http://www.econ.yale.edu/~corsetti/euro**. Also see the Windows on the World Economy Web site for *Quarterly Reports on the European Monetary Union*, including data updates at **http://reinert.swlearning. com.**

References

Clausen, J.R., and J.B. Donges (2001) "European Monetary Policy: The Ongoing Debate on Conceptual Issues," *The World Economy*, 24:10, 1309–1326.

Daily Telegraph (2002) "Pierre Werner," June 27.

Dinan, D. (forthcoming) *Europe Recast: A History of the European Union*, Lynne Rienner, Boulder, Colorado.

Dinan, D. (1999) *Ever Closer Union: An Introduction to European Integration*, Lynne Rienner, London.

The Economist (2002a) "The CFA Franc and the Euro," February 9, 63–64.

The Economist (2002b) "Pierre Werner," July 6, 85.

The Economist (1999) "Sailing in Choppy Waters," June 26, 83–84.

The Economist (1998a) "A Survey of EMU," April 11.

The Economist (1998b) "Euro Brief: Eleven into One May Go," October 17, 81–82.

Eichengreen, B. (1996) *Globalizing Capital: A History of the International Monetary System*, Princeton University Press, Princeton.

European Central Bank (2001) *The Monetary Policy of the ECB*, Frankfurt.

Feldstein, M. (1997) "The EMU and International Conflict," *Foreign Affairs*, November/December, 60–73.

Ferguson, N., and L.S. Kontlikoff (2000) "The Degeneration of the EMU," *Foreign Affairs*, March/April, 110–121.

Gros, D., and N. Thygesen (1992) *European Monetary Integration*, Longman, London.

Hallwood, C.P., and R. MacDonald (2000) *International Money and Finance*, Blackwell, Oxford.

James, H. (1996) *International Monetary Cooperation Since Bretton Woods*, Oxford University Press, Oxford.

Kenen, P.B. (1994) *The International Economy*, Cambridge University Press, Cambridge.

McKinnon, R.I. (1963) "Optimum Currency Areas," *American Economic Review*, 53:4, 717–725.

Mundell, R.A. (1961) "A Theory of Optimum Currency Areas," *American Economic Review*, 51:4, 657–665.

Sheridan, J. (1999) "The Consequences of the Euro," *Challenge*, 42:1, 43–54.

Solomon, R. (1999) "The Birth of the Euro," *Brookings Review*, Summer, 26–28.

Sullivan, R. (2000) "Duisenberg Tries to Rescue Reputation," *Financial Times*, October 20.

Tsoukalis, L. (1997) *The New European Economy Revisited*, Oxford University Press, Oxford.

Interview: Graciela Kaminsky

Graciela L. Kaminsky is currently a professor of Economics and International Affairs at George Washington University. She received her Ph.D. from MIT and was assistant professor of economics at the University of California, San Diego, and a staff economist at the Board of Governors of the Federal Reserve System before joining George Washington University. She has been a consultant and Visiting Scholar at the IMF, the World Bank, and the Inter-American Development Bank. She has also been a consultant to the Banco de España and the Korean Center for International Finance and visiting scholar to the Banco de Mexico and the Institute of International Economics, University of Stockholm. She was a visiting professor at the Department of Economics, Johns Hopkins University, Universidad de Los Andes (Bogotá, Colombia), and Universidad di Tella and Universidad San Andrés, both in Buenos Aires, Argentina. She has published extensively on issues in open economy macroeconomics. In the last few years, her areas of research have been on financial crises, contagion, herding behavior, the effects of financial liberalization, and mutual fund investment strategies.

How did your interest in international finance develop?

I was born in Argentina. In the last 30 years, Argentina has had eight major currency crises, defaulted on its debt twice, had three banking crises, and had two bouts of hyperinflation in the mid- and late 1980s. Naturally, I had to know why these dramatic events recur so often. This is why I became interested in macroeconomics and international finance.

What have been the main themes of your research on international finance?

I have been interested in evaluating credibility following the implementation of stabilization programs in Latin America. I have also studied the behavior of nominal exchange rates of industrial economies and the evolution of risk premia in foreign exchange markets. Following the Mexican crisis in 1994, I started to study the causes of currency and banking crises, as well as why currency crises are of a contagious nature. To address the latter issue, I have studied the behavior of mutual funds in emerging markets, with particular attention to their investment strategies. More recently, I have examined the effects of financial liberalization on the behavior of stock markets in developed and emerging economies, and I am currently studying the effects of international capital flows on the cyclical characteristics of macro policies.

Some of your early research focused on the debt crisis of the 1980s. Looking back at that era, what are the main policy lessons that you draw for developing countries' economic policy?

In the 1980s like in the 1990s, crises followed episodes of "excessive" borrowing, which resulted in dramatic expansions in credit and bubbles in financial markets. In the 1980s, as in the 1990s, the surge in capital inflows ended in a sudden stop—whether owing to home-grown problems or to contagion from abroad. As a consequence, prudent policy making would at a minimum ensure that policies are not procyclical (expansionary in upturns) and that the government does not overspend and overborrow when international capital markets are all too willing to lend. Ideally, bonanzas should be the time to pay down public debts, rather than adding to them. In this context, fiscal reforms aimed at designing institutional mechanisms that would discourage such procyclical behavior appear to be an essential ingredient in preventing future crises from building up.

Discouraging the private sector from borrowing abroad during boom periods may be more problematic and opens up the issue of controls or restrictions on capital inflows. Although there may be cases in which such restrictions may be desirable, such countercyclical policies are politically difficult to implement and may have many undesirable side effects. More fundamentally, their effectiveness is rather unclear. In any event, it is hard to disagree with the notion that capital controls can hardly be the solution in the medium and long run and that only prudent public policies and institutional mechanisms that give public and private agents the right incentives will hopefully some day provide a more stable financial environment for emerging countries.

Since 1997, there has been a great deal of concern with currency crises. In your view, what are the best ways to anticipate such crises? What sorts of variables should analysts focus on?

Although the earlier crises in Latin America in the 1960s and 1970s were triggered by unsustainable money-financed fiscal deficits, the debt crisis of 1982, the crises in the Nordic countries in 1992, in Mexico in 1994, and in Asia in 1997 were characterized by excessive private international borrowing in the presence of deposit insurance. In turn, the overborrowing fueled consumption and investment booms and large current account deficits, which finally led to currency crises. This suggests that possible symptoms of an upcoming crisis range from recessions to exaggerated cycles in credit markets to the deterioration of the current account. Thus, early-warning systems should track the behavior of domestic credit, money supply, stock prices, the real exchange rate, exports, imports, foreign debt, and economic activity,

Some specialists allege that financial deregulation and banking system weaknesses are a primary cause of crises. Do you agree with

this view? How do financial liberalization and banking inadequacies contribute to crises?

In my research on currency and banking crises, I have found a clear relationship between financial deregulation and banking crises. In fact, crises mostly occur within a couple of years of financial deregulation. I have also found that financial cycles in emerging economies become more pronounced in the immediate aftermath of financial deregulation. Based on this evidence, many have argued that it is very risky to open up financial systems. Before financial liberalization, banks tend to have poor balance sheets. Protected from outside competition, badly regulated and badly supervised banks do not have the pressure to run efficiently. Liberalization in this scenario unveils a new problem, as protected domestic banks suddenly get access to new sources of funding, triggering protracted financial booms. Based on these views, a standard recommendation on sequencing is to first clean up domestic financial institutions and change government institutions, then deregulate the industry and open up the capital account.

However, this discussion about sequencing may be irrelevant if the timing is such that reforms never predate liberalization, with institutional changes happening mostly as a result of financial deregulation. To shed new light on this sequencing debate, I have collected data on the quality of institutions as well as data on the laws governing the proper functioning of financial systems and have compared the timing of financial liberalization and institutional reforms. The evidence for emerging and mature economies suggests that reforms to institutions occur mostly after liberalization is implemented.

This evidence casts doubts on the notion that governments tend to implement institutional reforms before they start deregulating the financial sector. On the contrary, the evidence suggests that liberalization fuels institutional reforms. There are several reasons that can explain why financial liberalization might prompt institutional reforms. First, financial liberalization sows the seeds of destruction of the old protected and inefficient financial sector, as foreign and domestic investors (now with access to international capital markets) require better enforcement rules.

Second, the liberalization and the gradual integration of emerging markets with international financial markets by itself may help to fortify the domestic financial sector. Foreign investors have overall better skills and information and can thus monitor management in ways local investors cannot. Liberalization, moreover, allows firms to access mature capital markets. Firms listing on foreign stock markets are also in the jurisdiction of a superior legal system and have higher disclosure standards.

Third, the integration with world markets and institutions tends to speed up the reform process to achieve a resilient financial system. Capital markets can help supervise domestic financial institutions, imposing stricter market discipline, increasing transparency and the diffusion of information, and even push governments into guaranteeing that their financial systems are well supervised and regulated.

The evidence from my research on financial market cycles and financial deregulation supports the view that liberalization promotes better institutions and less volatile financial markets. I find that liberalization in the short run promotes instability in financial markets. However, if liberalization persists, excessive booms and busts disappear, and financial markets become more liquid. This evidence is also consistent with empirical evidence that suggests that financial liberalization triggers growth.

Recently, we have watched the currency board system in Argentina come undone, precipitating a severe economic crisis in that country. Was the currency board arrangement to blame or is the cause of the crisis to be found elsewhere?

The currency board collapsed under the weight of multiple vulnerabilities: Fiscal accounts were deteriorating, foreign debt was about 50 percent of GDP, the banking sector was fragile, and the domestic currency was overvalued. By 2002, Argentina had been in a recession for four years with unemployment at about 20 percent. A flexible exchange rate could have improved competitiveness and, on that account, could have avoided the recession and the ongoing deflation observed before the crisis erupted. On the other hand, a depreciating exchange rate could have triggered an adverse balance sheet effect because of the mismatch of currency of denomination of assets and liabilities of banks and nonfinancial corporations. In this environment, a devaluation could be followed by bankruptcies of firms and banks. So, there was no easy solution out of the peg. It is unclear whether having adopted a floating exchange rate regime after the Brazilian devaluation could have helped.

Part 4

Windows on the World Economy: International Economic Development

19

Development Concepts

I once spoke with a Ghanaian student who had just taken his first course in inter-national economics. He held a well-known book on globalization in his hand and gently waved it at me. "Professor," he asked, "what does all this really mean for my country? We are going nowhere!" His question was as difficult to answer as it was important. I did not answer it as well as I wished to and, to be honest, this would still be the case. However, similar questions from students over the years have pressed upon me the importance of including this final section of the book, this fourth window on the world economy—international economic development. Here you will gain some understanding of how the realms of international trade, international production, and international finance affect development processes around the world. Our consideration of the subject of international economic development will be, of necessity, too brief. For this reason, I encourage you to make use of the references at the end of each chapter to further your explorations of this important topic.

In setting out to investigate the subject of international economic develop-ment, we are confronted with a very fundamental matter, namely, to give some meaning to the word "development." From an economic standpoint, the primary goal of international economic development, as well as the trading of goods and services and the movement of capital in the world economy, is the *improvement of human well-being*. The dilemma we face, however, is the fact that it is difficult to isolate a universal conception of human well-being, and without such a universal conception, there can be no single concept and measure of economic development.[1] Many or perhaps even most international economists would claim that human well-being is best measured in terms of per capita income. Many development econo-mists, however, as well as the influential United Nations Development Program (UNDP), claim that increase in per capita income is too narrow a definition of "development." Instead, they offer a more inclusive approach, conceiving of development as human development. The purpose of this chapter is to help you sort through these competing development concepts.

We begin in the following section by considering the per capita income concept of economic development. We then turn to the more comprehensive concept known as human development. Although other concepts of econom-

---

[1] As Szirmai (1997) emphasized, "development is unavoidably a normative concept" (p. 7). The reader should be aware that these considerations also apply to "developed" economies. In this and other senses, "development is a universal goal for *all* societies and not just a 'Third World' problem" (Slim, 1995, p. 143).

ic development exist, these two are a good starting point. Finally, the appendix to this chapter discusses the Lorenz curve and the Gini coefficient ratio, two measures of the degree of income inequality in an economy.

Per Capita Income

An early and persistent conception of international economic development is economic development as increases in per capita income. This concept begins with the circular flow diagram of Chapter 12. From the circular flow diagram, it identifies national income, Y, as a crucial variable. Typically measured using gross national product or GNP, Y is divided by the total population to calculate GNP per capita. GNP per capita is an important measure of the level of economic development, and the growth rate of GNP per capita is an important measure of the pace of economic development over time.

Table 19.1 gives information on GNP per capita for twelve countries of the world.[2] As we can see, the range of per capita incomes among countries is astonishing. The average per capita income in Japan and the United States is over 300 times that in Ethiopia. From the point of view of economic development as the level of per capita income, we therefore would conclude that Japan and the United States are over 300 times "more developed" than Ethiopia. This is not necessarily a true statement of fact, but it is an implication of the per capita income perspective.

The per capita income perspective of economic development has a number of limitations that are important to recognize. These include the following:

1. *Per capita GNP only includes market activities, and many activities in developing countries take place outside the market. For example, GNP does not include farmers' production of agricultural products for consumption within his or her family, but only the amount sold on the market.*
2. *Per capita GNP does not account for certain costs associated with development such as the use of nonrenewable resources, the loss of biodiversity, and pollution. Scholars and practitioners working in the field of sustainable development address this limitation.[3]*
3. *Per capita GNP is an average measure that hides the distribution of income among the households of a country. If income distribution becomes more unequal as per capita GNP increases, the level of well-being of the poorest groups in the country might be falling. We will discuss this issue later.*
4. *Per capita GNP is not always an accurate predictor of human development. It is not always well correlated with indicators of human development such as levels of education and health. As emphasized by Sen (1989), "countries with high GNP per capita*

[2] The World Bank has recently begun using the term *gross national income* in its annual *World Development Report*. We will consider growth rates in income per capita in Chapter 20.
[3] See, for example, Barbier (1989), Elliot (1994), and Panayotou (1993).

**Table 19.1 Development Indicators for Selected Countries
(2000 except where indicated)**

Country	GNP per Capita	PPP GNP per Capita	Gini Coefficient Index	Life Expectancy	Adult Literacy	Human Development Index
	(U.S. dollars)	(U.S. dollars)	(various years)	(years)	(%)	
Ethiopia	100	660	40	44	39	0.327
India	460	2,390	38	63	57	0.577
Haiti	510	1,500	—	53	50	0.471
Indonesia	570	2,840	32	66	87	0.684
China	840	3,940	40	71	84	0.726
Turkey	3,090	7,030	42	70	85	0.742
Brazil	3,570	7,320	59	68	85	0.757
Costa Rica	3,960	8,250	46	76	96	0.820
South Korea	8,910	17,340	32	75	98	0.882
Spain	14,960	19,180	33	79	98	0.913
Japan	34,210	26,460	25	81	99	0.933
United States	34,260	34,260	41	77	99	0.939

Note: The Gini coefficient ranges from 0 to 1. The Gini coefficient index ranges from 0 to 100.

Source: Based on data in *The World Development Report*, published by the World Bank in 2002; and *The Human Development Report*, published by the United Nations Development Program in 2002.

can nevertheless have astonishing low achievements in the quality
of life" (p. 42).

5. *The nominal or currency exchange rates used to convert GNP into
U.S. dollars for comparison among countries are misleading. A
large part of economies consists of non-traded goods. Furthermore,
a large part of nontraded goods consists of services. Services tend
to be less expensive in developing countries, so a U.S. dollar buys
more in developing countries than in developed countries.*[4]

The solution to the last of these problems lies in what is now called the
purchasing power parity (PPP) methodology. This methodology is closely related to the purchasing power parity model of exchange rates that

---

[4] We mentioned nontrade goods in Chapter 13 in our assessment of the purchasing power parity
model of exchange rate determination. One of the original attempts to examine the less expensive nature of services in developing economies was Bhagwati (1984).

Surviving in Mexico City

Patrick Oster, a journalist residing in Mexico City, hired a woman by the name of Adelaida Bollo Andrade as a maid. He documented the qualities of her life in his book, *The Mexicans*. While working for the Oster family, Adelaida woke each morning at 5:00 A.M. This would allow her to catch the 6:00 A.M. bus to start her three-hour commute to work. Typically, the total daily commute of 6 hours would cost Adelaida one-half of her daily wage. Her workday of eight hours was followed by her return commute. Because she and her family could not afford even a small refrigerator, there was an additional 1-hour commute each day to the market. Adelaida was left with 9 hours for cooking, cleaning, taking care of her family, and sleep.

Adelaida's family lived in a cinderblock home 15 feet by 24 feet with a corrugated metal roof and one window. There was one bed for the four children, which left the concrete floor for Adelaida and her husband to sleep on. Light came from a single, bare bulb hanging from the ceiling. Cooking was done on a 3-burner gas stove. Aside from an old kitchen table, the only other family possession was an old, black-and-white television donated to the family by their doctor. The family latrine consisted of a hole in the back yard.

The family's water supply was contaminated, and their food consisted of tortillas, beans, and coffee. These conditions contributed to frequent illnesses among Adelaida's children, including diarrhea, vomiting, and fevers. These illnesses would require Adelaida to go into debt to pay for doctor services.

Adelaida's difficult life is not in any way unusual for Mexico City residents or for the residents of many large cities in developing countries. Lack of education, poor health, and difficult working conditions are the norm for the urban poor. The important challenge for governments, development organizations, and the private sector is to strategically improve these human lives in a broad-based way. It has proved, in many instances, to be a difficult challenge.

Source: Oster (1989).

we developed in Chapter 13. The PPP methodology uses U.S. dollar prices to value all goods in all countries. This has the effect of increasing the GNP of developing countries. Table 19.1 presents PPP GNP per capita for the 12 countries we are using as examples. Note the following in this table. First, the PPP measures are larger than the standard measures for the first 10 countries presented in the table. This reflects the cheaper nature of services and other nontraded goods in these countries relative to the United States. This helps us to understand how it is possible for individuals to survive in these countries with such low levels of GNP per capita. Some of these survival challenges are presented in the box. Second, the PPP GNP per capita for the United States is identical to its GNP per capita because the same prices are used in both calculations. Third, the PPP GNP per capita is lower for Japan than its GNP per capita. This reflects the fact that its services and other nontraded goods are more expensive than in the United States. Incomes do not go as far in Japan as in the other countries of the table.

Related to, but not always emphasized in, the per capita income measure is the question of the distribution of total income among the households of the economy. This is typically measured using the **Lorenz curve**

Lorenz curve
A graph relating the cumulative percentage of income to the cumulative percentage of households, the latter ranked from low- to high-income. It is a visual measure of income inequality.

Gini coefficient
A summary measure of the Lorenz curve that gives an overall value to the degree of income inequality. It varies between zero (perfect equality) and one (perfect inequality).

and the **Gini coefficient**. Calculation of these measures is discussed in the appendix to this chapter. The Gini coefficient ranges from the extreme of zero (perfect equality) to unity (perfect inequality). In practice, the coefficient ranges from approximately 0.25 (relatively low inequality) to 0.60 (relatively high inequality). The Gini coefficient *index* multiplies the Gini coefficient by 100 and therefore ranges from 0 to 100. Gini coefficient indices for the countries in our sample are presented in Table 19.1. The important point evident here is that income distribution is, to some extent, independent of the level of per capita income. A middle-income country such as Brazil can have a worse income distibution than a low-income country such as India. There is some evidence that equality of income can lead to a higher growth rate of total output. One such study will be mentioned in Chapter 20.

Human Development

A conception of international economic development more recent than the per capita income approach is what we can call economic development as **human development**. The United Nations Development Program (UNDP) has been a leading advocate of this perspective. In 1990, the UNDP published the first of what was to be an annual *Human Development Report (HDR)*.[5] This report began with the following statement:

> *People are the real wealth of a nation. The basic objective of development is to create an enabling environment for people to enjoy long, healthy and creative lives (p. 9).*

Human development index (HDI)
A conception of economic development introduced by the United Nations Development Program that stresses health and education levels along with per capita income. The human development index is reported in the annual Human Development Report.

The human development perspective sees the growth of income per capita as an important but limited measure of the rate of economic development. For example, the 1995 HDR stated the following:

> *The human development concept consistently asserts that growth is not the end of development—but the absence of growth often is. Economic growth is essential for human development. But to fully exploit the opportunities for improved well-being that growth offers, it must be properly managed, for there is no automatic link between economic growth and human progress (pp. 122–123).*

The most fundamental contribution of the HDR was the introduction of the human development index (HDI). A brief description of its originator, Pakistani economist Mahbub ul Haq, is presented in the box. The HDI measures development as reflecting three important components: per capita income, health, and education. The construction of the HDI can be represented as in Figure 19.1. The HDI consists of equal, one-third components of per capita income, life expectancy, and education. The per capita income is calculated in such as way that higher levels receive declining weights. Therefore, increases in per capita incomes are more important from low levels than from high levels.[6] Life expectancy is

---

[5] The human development perspective and the *Human Development Report* have their roots in the work of Sen (1989) on the role of capabilities in economic development.
[6] The way in which PPP per capita incomes were discounted at higher levels in the *Human Development Reports* changed in 1999, so that higher income levels were not discounted as severely as before. See UNDP (1999), "Technical Note," pp. 159-163.

Mahbub ul Haq and the HDI

The *Human Development Report* and its HDI were originally developed by the Pakistani development economist Mahbub ul Haq. ul Haq was educated at Cambridge, Yale, and Harvard universities and worked at the World Bank. From 1982 to 1988, he was finance minister of Pakistan. He then moved to the United Nations Development Program and began to work on the human development paradigm. At his invitation, this work was done in collaboration with the Indian development economist Amartya Sen.

Sen recalled that "I did not, I must admit, initially see much merit in the HDI itself, which, as it happens, I was privileged to help him devise. I had expressed to Mahbub considerable skepticism about trying to focus on a crude index of this kind, attempting to catch in one simple number a complex reality about human development and deprivation. . . . In fact, the crudeness had not escaped Mahbub at all. He did not resist the argument that the HDI could not but be a very limited indicator of development. But after some initial hesitation, Mahbub persuaded himself that the dominance of GNP could not be broken by any set of tables. 'We need a measure,' Mahbub explained to me, 'of the same level of vulgarity as the GNP—just one number—but a measure that is not as blind to social aspects of human lives as the GNP is.' Mahbub hoped that not only would the HDI be something of an improvement on, or at least a helpful supplement to, the GNP, but also that it would serve to broaden public interest in the other variables that are plentifully analyzed in the *Human Development Reports*. Mahbub got this exactly right, I have to admit, and I am very glad that we did not manage to deflect him from seeking a crude measure. By skilful use of the attracting power of the HDI, Mahbub got readers to take an involved interest in the large class of systematic tables and detailed critical analyses presented in the *Human Development Reports*."

ul Haq was a long-time opponent of military spending in South Asia, seeing it as being at odds with human development in the region. However, when he died in July 1998, he had just witnessed the revival of nuclear testing in India and Pakistan. And he missed the awarding of the Nobel Prize in Economics to his old friend, Amartya Sen, in October of that year.

Sources: *The Economist* (1998); and Sen (1999).

Figure 19.1 The Human Development Index

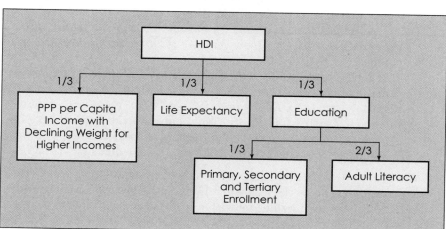

taken as an overall measure of health. Education is measured with one-third weight being given to primary, secondary, and tertiary enrollment and two-thirds weight being given to adult literacy. Thus, there is more of an emphasis placed on educational outcomes than enrollment. HDI measures for our sample of countries, along with information on life expectancy and adult literacy, are presented in Table 19.1.

The first important point to note in the last three columns of Table 19.1 is that, although there appears to be a general positive correlation between GNP per capita and both life expectancy and adult literacy, some important variation from this norm is possible. For example, Costa Rica has an average life expectancy and an adult literacy rate equivalent to that of the United States despite its GNP per capita being only slightly over one-tenth of the U.S. value. Consequently, Costa Rica's HDI is above that of many other countries in its income group. It is these kinds of variations that are captured by the human development concept but not by the per capita income concept.

The HDI has been criticized in many instances for at least three reasons. Some observers claim that its weighting scheme among per capita income, health, and education is arbitrary. This is certainly the case, but to be fair, the same could be said of the per capita income perspective, which assigns a weight of unity to per capita income alone. The HDI has also been criticized for being "too political" in its assigning declining weights to higher per capita incomes. For example, Gillis et al. (1996) stated that the declining weights imply that "raising per capita income from the level of Colombia or Lithuania to that of Switzerland contributes nothing to human development" and that this "may reflect the political opinions of its compilers" (p. 76). Finally, the HDI has been criticized for relying on measures for which data are unreliable.

In defense of the HDI, development economist Paul Streeten (1995, Lecture 1) has usefully pointed out the following:

1. *When there is an upward movement in the HDI, it almost always reflects an improvement in human well-being, something that is not always true of per capita income measures.*
2. *Closing gaps in HDIs among the countries of the world "is both more important and more feasible than reducing international income gaps" (p. 24).*
3. *The HDI registers (negatively) the potential impact of overdevelopment in capturing the "diseases of affluence" such as heart disease that reduce the HDI through its health component.*
4. *The HDI, according to Streeten, is appropriately political: "it focuses attention on important social sectors, policies, and achievements, which are not caught by the income measure" (p. 25).*

Whatever our interpretation of the disagreements surrounding the HDI, we can at least state the following. Having the last three columns of Table 19.1 in front of us provides us with a little more information than the per capita income measures alone do. Because these columns of information are readily available and impact people's lives so directly, it is very useful to glance at them, along with the income measures, when assessing development levels among sets of countries. Additionally, as we will see in Chapter 20, there are important feedbacks among the three components of the HDI that can be crucial mechanisms in development successes and failures.

In more recent years, the UNDP has introduced additional indices to supplement the HDI. These are summarized in Table 19.2. In 1996, it introduced the gender-related development index (GDI) and the gender-empowerment measure (GEM). The GDI adjusts the HDI downward to account for levels of gender inequality. For some countries, this makes a significant difference. In 1997, the UNDP introduced the human poverty indices 1 and 2 (HPI-1 and HPI-2), focusing on poverty in developing and developed countries, respectively. The former is especially relevant in capturing basic deprivations in education and health.

The UNDP and its wide array of development measures are part of a set of Millennium Development Goals set by the United Nations in 2000. These are discussed in the box.

Table 19.2 Additional Human Development Indices and Their Components

Index	Health	Education	Standard of Living	Social Exclusion
HDI	Life expectancy	Adult literacy rate and enrollment ratio	PPP income per capita	
GDI	Female and male life expectancy	Female and male adult literacy rate and female and male enrollment ratio	Female and male PPP income per capita	
HPI-1	Probability of not surviving to age 40	Adult illiteracy rate	Deprivation as measured by lack of access to safe water, lack of access to health services, and underweight children	
HPI-2	Probability of not surviving to age 60	Adult functional illiteracy rate	Percentage of population below poverty line, defined as 50 percent of median income	Long-term unemployment rate

Source: Adapted from United Nations Development Program (2000). *Human Development Report 2000*. New York: United Nations Development Program.

Millennium Development Goals

In September 2000, members of the United Nations (UN) met in New York City for a Millennium Summit. At the summit, the UN General Assembly adopted a resolution entitled the United Nations Millennium Declaration. The declaration stated that: "the central challenge we face today is to ensure that globalization becomes a positive force for all the world's people." More specifically, UN members pledged to "spare no effort to free our fellow men, women and children from the abject and dehumanizing conditions of extreme poverty, to which more than a billion of them are currently subjected." In addition to endorsing a number of "fundamental values," UN members established a set of goals, which are now known as the Millennium Development Goals.

The first millennium development goal is to eradicate extreme poverty and hunger. It has two targets: to halve by 2015 the proportion of people whose income is less than a dollar a day (in PPP values) and to halve by 2015 the proportion of people who suffer from hunger. The second millennium goal is to achieve universal primary education for boys *and* girls with a target of 2015. The third development goal, related to the second, is to promote gender equality and empower women. We will discuss why this goal is important in Chapter 20 on growth, trade and development. The fourth development goal is to reduce the under-five mortality rate with a target of two-thirds by 2015.

The fifth development goal is to improve maternal health with a target of reducing the maternal mortality rate by three-fourths by 2015. The sixth development goal is to combat HIV/AIDS, malaria, and tuberculosis, and the seventh development goal is to ensure environmental sustainability. The last goal is a "global partnership for development," a subject taken up at the 2002 Summit on Sustainable Development in Johannesburg, South Africa.

The UNDP's own Web site on the Millennium Development Goals already acknowledges that "progress towards the goals has been mixed." More pointedly, it states that "none of the goals are likely to be reached at the current rate of global progress." The UN General Secretary will issue a report on this progress in 2005. It will make for interesting reading.

Source: Based on United Nations Development Programme (2003). *Millennium Development Goals.* http://www.undp.org/mdg.

Conclusion

From an economic standpoint, the primary goal of international economic development, as well as the trading of goods and services and the movement of capital in the world economy, is the improvement of human well-being. However, it is hard to isolate a universally accepted conception of human well-being. Keeping in mind this limitation, this chapter investigates two complementary concepts of economic development: income per capita and human development. The latter, measured by the human development index, is more comprehensive but is still subject to some controversy. It combines income per capita with measures of health and education.

Whatever our measure of development, as we stressed in Chapter 1, levels of development differ in profound ways among the countries of the world. Our hope is that increased integration of countries via trade, production, and financial linkages would promote some convergence in levels of development, but this is not always the case. We will spend the remainder of this book assessing these divergent outcomes. In doing so, you will perhaps develop you own partial answers to the question posed to me by the Ghanaian student mentioned at the beginning of this chapter.

Review Exercises

1. In your opinion, is income per capita a sufficient measure of economic development? Why or why not?

2. How can the PPP adjustment to income per capita change the ranking of countries' levels of economic development? Is this an important adjustment to make?

3. A controversial aspect to the human development index is its use of declining weights for per capita income. Do you agree with this adjustment? Why or why not?

4. The human development index takes into account health and education as well as per capita income. Why might health and education be important considerations in the process of economic development?

5. Take some time to explore the UNDP's Web site at **http://www. undp.org**. Try to locate the human development indicators that are a part of the most recent *Human Development Report* (**http://www.hdr.undp.org**). Look up the indicators for a country in which you have an interest.

Further Reading and Web Resources

Comprehensive texts in economic development include Cypher and Dietz (1997), Gillis et al. (1996), Szirmai (1997), and Weaver et al. (1997). A collection of readings discussing various point of view of human well-being can be found in Ackerman et al. (1997). An excellent overview of the issues discussed in this chapter can be found in the First Lecture of Streeten (1995). Readers with an interest in the human development concept would benefit from a close reading of Sen (1989). This essay provides a philosophical foundation for the human development alternative to income per capita. These readers with an interest in the HDI itself should turn to the United Nations Development Program's annual *Human Development Report*. A more traditional annual review is the World Bank's *World Development Report*. Both of these reports are essential sources of data on developing countries.

Those readers with an interest in the issues discussed in this chapter can consult the *Journal of Human Development*, which began publication in 2000.

The UNDP's Web site can be found at **http://www.undp.org**. Its *Human Development Report* series can be found at **http://www.hdr.undp.org**. The World Bank's *World Development Report* series can be found at **http://www.worldbank.org/wdr**.

References

Ackerman, F., D. Kiron, N.R. Goodwin, J.M. Harris, and K. Gallagher (eds.) (1997) *Human Well-Being and Economic Goals*, Island Press, Washington, DC.

Barbier, E.B. (1989) *Economics, Natural Resource Scarcity and Development*, Earthscan Publications, London.

Bhagwati, J. (1984) "Why Are Services Cheaper in the Poor Countries?" *Economic Journal*, 94:374, 279–286.

Cypher, J.M., and J.L. Dietz (1997) *The Process of Economic Development*, Routledge, London.

The Economist (1998) "Obituary: Mahbub ul Haq," July 25, 84.

Elliott, J.A. (1994) *An Introduction to Sustainable Development*, Routledge, London.

Gillis, M., D. Perkins, M. Roemer, and D. Snodgrras (1996) *Economics of Development*, Norton, New York.

Oster, P. (1989) *The Mexicans: A Personal Portrait of a People*, Harper and Row, New York.

Panayotou, T. (1993) *Green Markets: The Economics of Sustainable Development*, ICS Press, San Francisco.

Sen, A. (1999) "Mahbub ul Haq: The Courage and Creativity of His Ideas," *Journal of Asian Economics*, 10:1, 1–6.

Sen, A. (1989) "Development as Capability Expansion," *Journal of Development Planning*, 19, 41–58.

Slim, H. (1995) "What Is Development," *Development in Practice*, 5:2, May 1995, 143–148.

Streeten, P.P. (1995) *Thinking About Development*, Cambridge University Press, Cambridge.

Szirmai, A. (1997) *Economic and Social Development*, Prentice Hall, London.

United Nations Development Program (1999) *Human Development Report 1999*, Oxford University Press, Oxford.

United Nations Development Program (1995) *Human Development Report 1995*, Oxford University Press, Oxford.

United Nations Development Program (1990) *Human Development Report 1990*, Oxford University Press, Oxford.

Weaver, J.H., M.T. Rock, and K. Kusterer (1997) *Achieving Broad-Based Sustainable Development*, Kumarian Press, West Hartford, Connecticut.

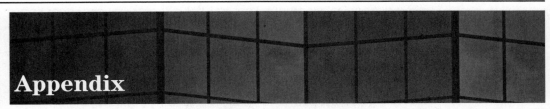

Appendix

The Lorenz Curve and Gini Coefficient

The standard means of measuring income inequality based on the personal distribution of income is using the Lorenz curve and the associated Gini coefficient. The Lorenz curve is depicted in Figure 19.A1. It relates cumulative percentage of income received (measured on the vertical axis) to the cumulative percentage of population (measured on the horizontal axis). The diagonal line in the figure is therefore the line of perfect equality, where each person receives the same income. Actual Lorenz curves, however, lie below the diagonal line, and the farther they are to the southeast corner of the box, the greater the level of inequality. The Gini coefficient is measured using the area between the diagonal and the actual Lorenz curve, area A, and the area under the diagonal, area $A+B$. It is measured as:

$$\text{Gini Coefficient} = \frac{A}{A + B}$$ **Gini coefficient**

Figure 19.A1 The Lorenz Curve

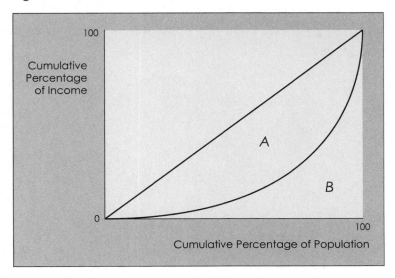

Cumulative Percentage of Income

A

B

0

100

Cumulative Percentage of Population

The greater the area of A, the higher the value of the Gini coefficint, and the greater the degree of inequality. In theory, Gini coefficients range from the extremes of zero (perfect equality) to unity (perfect inequality). In practice, the coefficient ranges from approximately 0.25 (relatively low inequality) to 0.60 (relatively high inequality).

Growth, Trade, and Development

In the last chapter, I mentioned a question posed to me by a Ghanaian student concerning the role of his country in the world economy. He said: "Professor, what does all this really mean for my country? We are going nowhere!" Indeed, although in the 1960s, per capita income in Ghana exceeded those of Malaysia and Thailand, by the 1990s, it had fallen significantly below the latter values. In 2000, per capita GNP in Ghana was only US$350, while those in Malaysia and Thailand were $3,400 and $2,000, respectively. Ghana, it seems, has slipped behind. Furthermore, Ghana's 1998 human development index was only 0.548, ranking 129th in the world. This reflects a relatively low life expectancy and unsatisfactory educational attainment. How can Ghana "get somewhere" rather than "go nowhere?" What roles might trade, education, and health play in this process? This chapter will help you to answer these questions.

Economists are increasingly concerned with explanations of per capita income levels and their rates of growth. For such explanations, economists turn to what is known as **growth theory**. In this chapter, we will consider two variants of growth theory: "old" growth theory and "new" growth theory.[1] In the case of new growth theory, we will make an explicit link to the human development framework we discussed in Chapter 19. Next, we will consider the interrelationships among trade, education, and growth. Finally, we will consider the interrelationships among education, health, and population. For the interested reader, an appendix to the chapter presents some of the algebraic details of growth theory.

Old Growth Theory

Why was Ghana's 2000 per capita income $350 rather than $1,350 or $10,350? A first attempt to answer such questions was provided by Nobel Laureate Robert Solow (1956) in what is now known as "old" growth theory. Growth theory begins with what economists call a **production function**.[2] In particular, it utilizes the **intensive production function** illustrated in Figure 20.1. The intensive production function relates two economic variables. The first is per capita income or per capita output and is denoted by y. The second is the capital-labor ratio and is denoted by k. Figure 20.1 indicates that there is a positive relationship between the capital-labor ratio and

Growth theory
In its "old" and "new" variants, growth theory is the explanation of economics of the sustained increase in per capita incomes over the long run. It is based on the intensive production function.

Production function
A mathematical relationship between the output of a firm, sector, or economy and inputs such as labor and physical capital.

Intensive production function
A production function expressed on a per capita basis.

---

[1] We can only touch the surface of this important area of research. Interested readers can pursue this subject further in Jones (1998). Also, Cypher and Dietz (1997, Chapter 8) provide an interesting discussion of the applicability of "new" growth theory to international economic development.
[2] See Chapter 13 of Mankiw (2004) for a description of the production function.

Figure 20.1 The Intensive Production Function and Capital Deepening

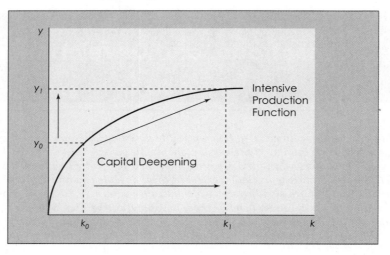

per capita income. For example, as the capital-labor ratio increases from k_0 to k_1 and each worker has more physical capital to work with, per capita income increases from y_0 to y_1. This is a process known as **capital deepening**. Figure 20.1 also indicates that the relationship between the capital-labor ratio and per capita income is decreasingly positive (the graph becomes flatter as k increases). This is the result of diminishing returns to labor and capital.[3] Consequently, increases in k at lower levels add more to per capita income than increases in k at higher levels.

Capital deepening
An increase in the overall capital-labor ratio in a country.

Figure 20.1 indicates that increases in per capita income in Ghana can occur through capital deepening. There is, however, a second possible source of increases in per capita income that is also important. This is *technological change* and is depicted in Figure 20.2. Technological change, being a variable that does not appear on either axis of the intensive production function diagram, shifts the graph. Improvements in technology, in particular, shift the graph upward as depicted in Figure 20.2. For example, at a given capital-labor ratio, k_0, per capita income increases from y_0 to y_1.[4]

Figures 20.1 and 20.2 tell us some important things about increasing per capita incomes in Ghana or in any other county. Let's summarize them:

> **Increases in per capita incomes can come about through increases in the capital-labor ratio (capital deepening) or through improvements in technological efficiency.**

---

[3] Diminishing returns to labor and capital appear as diminishing marginal products. Again, see Chapter 13 of Mankiw (2004).
[4] The contrast between Figure 20.1 and 20.2 is one of many cases of the important difference in economics between a *movement along* a graph and a *shift of* a graph, respectively. When a variable on one of the two axes changes, there is a movement along a graph. When a variable *not* on one of the two axes changes, there is a shift of a graph.

Figure 20.2 Technological Change in the Intensive Production Function

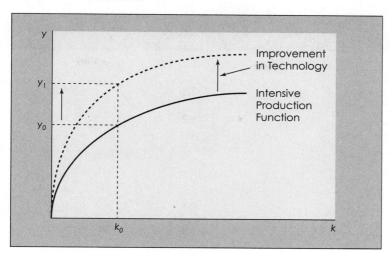

How fast can increases in capital-labor ratios or improvements in technology make economies grow? Table 20.1 presents some examples. In this table, Ghana has been added to the countries reported on in Chapter 19, and is highlighted in bold. As you see in Table 20.1, most economies grow only a few percentage points each year. China, however, grew by over 10 percent in both the decade of the 1980s and the decade of the 1990s. Some economies, such as Haiti, actually shrink over time, despite rising populations, condemning their citizenries to increasing poverty.

We can use Figure 20.1 to understand some additional requirements for **economic growth** in Ghana based on capital deepening. To do this, however, we need to supplement it with some important relationships concerning Ghana's capital-labor ratio, k. Increases in k require increases in the capital stock that more than offset any increases in population. Increases in the capital stock, in turn, require investment. Finally, investment requires saving. The relationship between saving and investment was depicted in the circular flow diagram of Chapter 12. We reproduce that diagram here in Figure 20.3. Focus your attention on the capital account in Figure 20.3. As we showed in Chapter 12, "things add up" for the capital account. That is, expenditures equal receipts. In the language of Chapter 12, this implies that:

Domestic Investment = Domestic Savings + Foreign Savings

How does this equation relate to our discussion in this chapter? Increases in per capita incomes through capital deepening require investment. Investment has two sources: domestic savings (household and government) and foreign savings. In the absence of technological improvements, increases in domestic and foreign savings are the only sources of growth in per capita incomes. As mentioned earlier, these increases in savings must be large enough to increase the capital stock sufficiently so that it more

Economic growth
A sustained increase in per capita income over time.

Table 20.1 How Fast Do Economies Grow?

Country	Gross National Product per Capita (U.S. dollars, 2000)	Average Annual Growth Rate 1980 to 1990	Average Annual Growth Rate 1990 to 2000
Ethiopia	100	1.1	4.6
Ghana	**350**	**3.0**	**4.3**
India	460	5.8	6.0
Haiti	510	−0.2	−0.6
Indonesia	570	6.1	4.2
China	840	10.2 .	10.3
Turkey	3,090	5.4	3.7
Brazil	3,570	2.7	2.9
Costa Rica	3,960	3.0	5.4
South Korea	8,910	9.4	5.7
Spain	14,960	3.0	2.4
Japan	34,210	4.0	1.3
United States	34,260	3.0	3.4

Source: Adapted from Tables 1 and 3 in World Bank Group (2002). *World Development Report*. Washington, DC: World Bank Group Publications. 232–237.

than offsets any increase in population. If they are not large enough, k and y will fall even though the capital stock increases through investment.[5]

Let us return to the sources of savings in Ghana. Increasing domestic savings is often a matter of making institutions available to the households of the economy to facilitate savings. Importantly, these institutions should be as broad-based as possible, being accessible to rich and poor, rural and urban. Increasing government savings is a matter of decreasing government expenditures and increasing government tax revenues, moving the government budget toward surplus. An important caveat here is that some types of government expenditures (e.g., education) can positively affect the level of technology. Also, some government investments are complementary to private investments (see Chapter 23). Finally, increasing foreign savings, as we saw in Chapter 12, is a matter of increasing the capital account

---

[5] It is useful here to think of k as the ratio $k = K/L$, where K is the capital stock and L is the population assumed also to be equal to the labor force. The algebraic condition for investment to increase k is given in the appendix to this chapter.

Figure 20.3 An Open Economy with Government, Savings, and Investment

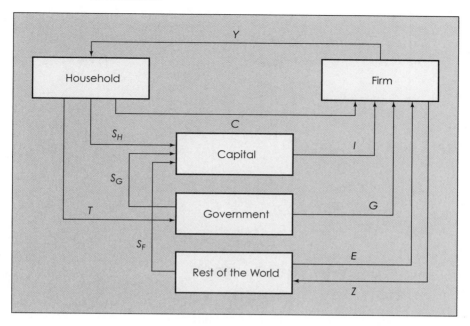

surplus on the balance of payments. Here, it is important to pay attention to the form and magnitude of the capital account surplus. As we discussed in Chapter 17 on crises, large capital account surpluses based on short-term investments are risky and could be damaging to Ghana in the long run.

"Old" growth theory contributes greatly to our understanding of how per capita incomes are determined. It draws our attention to savings and technology as central variables that can be affected by various institutional and policy regimes among the countries of the world. It turns out, however, that this theory leaves a lot to be explained. This is represented in Figure 20.4. Here, in an initial year, we observe Ghana with a capital-labor ratio of k_0 and a per capita income of y_0. In a subsequent year, we observe a capital-labor ratio of k_1 and a per capita income of y_1. The double-headed arrow in this diagram indicates the amount of the unexplained growth in per capita incomes, which is known as the *Solow residual*. In practice, these Solow residuals can be quite large. How can we begin to account for this unexplained growth? One explanation we have discussed already. As we showed in Figure 20.2, a change in our technology parameter shifts the intensive production function graph upward. But technology is simply an *exogenous* parameter in our model. How is it determined in the real world? This is the question that "new" growth theory attempts to answer.[6]

---

[6] *The Economist* (1992) assessed the "old" growth theory and concluded that it is "patently inadequate—so much so that its teachings have had virtually no influence on policy makers" (p. 15). The theory "supposes . . . that new technologies rain down from heaven as random scientific breakthroughs" (p. 16).

Figure 20.4 Unexplained Growth in per Capita Incomes

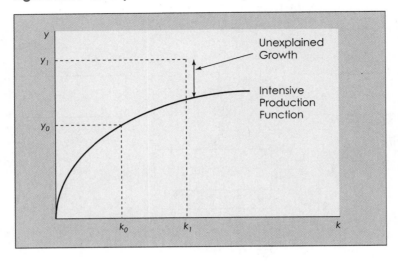

New Growth Theory and Human Development

It is easy to say that Ghana needs to improve its technical efficiency to help improve per capita income, but what does this entail? "Old" growth theory has little to say about this. "New" growth theory, however, provides us with some insights.[7] The models of the new growth theory are varied, and we cannot attempt a serious review of them here. Instead, we will consider a single approach that is closely linked to our discussion in the previous section and will lead us into the material of the remainder of the chapter. A number of new growth theory models emphasize the role of a third factor of production in addition to labor and physical capital. This is **human capital**. Including this factor acknowledges that labor is more than just hours worked. It reflects skills, abilities, and education. Further, because productive knowledge can be embodied in workers, there appears to be a direct link between human capital and technological efficiency. These considerations lead some economists to modify the intensive production function so that increases in human capital shift it upward (as in Figure 20.2) through a positive impact on technological efficiency. Greater levels of education and training allow an economy to operate in a state of greater technical efficiency.

In this new intensive production function, technology is now an *endogenous* variable that can be influenced by education and training policies. The implication of this can be seen in Figure 20.5. The increase in human capital from period 0 to period 1 shifts the intensive production function upwards. The amount of unexplained growth from Figure 20.4 (the Solow residual) declines, and changes in human capital are an important component in this decline. This result has been empirically verified. As shown by

Human capital
Investments made in the education, training, and capabilities of a labor force.

---

[7] The "new" growth theory traces its roots back to a 1983 University of Chicago doctoral dissertation written by Paul Romer. This dissertation, in turn, spawned two important articles (Romer 1986, 1990) and, subsequently, an entire literature. See also Lucas (1988) and Romer (1993).

Mankiw, Romer, and Weil (1992) and Rodrik (1994), including human capital in growth models can contribute to their ability to explain the variation of per capita incomes among the countries of the world.[8]

The inclusion of human capital in a growth model, along with contributing to empirical validity, suggests that there might be some important relationships among the three components of the human development index (HDI) presented in Chapter 19. This is illustrated in Figure 20.6. As is shown here (and in Figure 19.1), education has a direct impact on the

Figure 20.5 Human Capital and Unexplained Growth in Per Capita Incomes

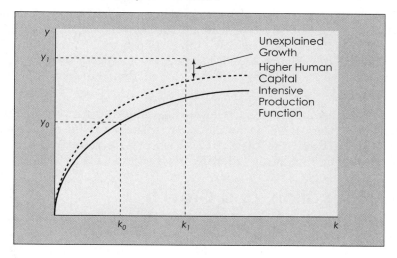

Figure 20.6 Education, Health, Growth, and Human Development

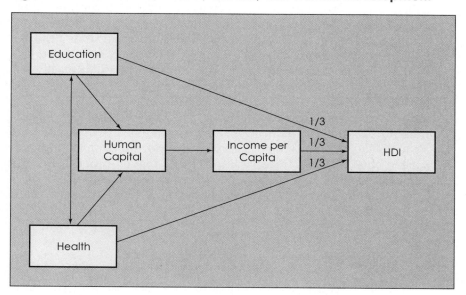

---

[8] Szirmai (1997) states that: "The inclusion of human capital in growth accounting studies substantially reduces the unexplained residual in growth" (p. 147).

HDI through its one-third weight. However, it also can have an indirect impact on the HDI via its impact on human capital and, thereby, on per capita income through the intensive production function. Health also has a direct impact on the HDI through its one-third weight. However, health might also contribute to human capital and therefore have an indirect impact on the HDI via per capita income. These indirect impacts have been stressed by Pio (1994) who advocated devoting "particular attention . . . to the role of human capital with an emphasis on the adjective human; that is to say, on the levels of health, education, and nutrition of the population and the implications of changes in such levels for long-term growth" (p. 278). He concluded that "the inclusion of a broader definition of human capital (encompassing health and nutrition as well as education) seems useful both in the construction of models and in their empirical verification" (p. 297). These indirect effects can be all the more powerful because, in addition, there is a two-way, positive interaction between education and health, illustrated in Figure 20.6. Educated persons (particularly women) contribute to healthy children, and healthy children are more likely to become educated.[9]

Given the direct and indirect relationships illustrated in Figure 20.6, it would seem that there is ample room to explore the connections between the HDI and the "new" growth theory for countries such as Ghana. We will do this in the following two sections of the chapter.

Trade, Education, and Growth

Many development economists and international trade economists suggest that countries' openness to international trade has a positive impact on growth in per capita incomes and, therefore, on human development. They suggest that this might be a way forward for countries such as Ghana. The notion here is that technological efficiency responds to two impulses. The first impulse is domestic innovation, and the accumulation of human capital through education positively affects domestic innovation. The second impulse is the absorption of new technology from the rest of the world.[10] It is thought that openness to trade, and exports in particular, facilitates this absorption of technology from abroad.[11] For this reason, exports are seen as having a positive externality for the country in question. That is, exports generate additional technology gains on the supply side of the economy. This thinking has caused a number of international economic institutions (especially the World Bank) to call for **export promotion** as an important development strategy. This strategy contrasts with that of **import substitution** in which domestic industrialization occurs in response to tariff and quota protection of the kind we discussed in Chapter 6.[12] Some time ago, the World

Export promotion
An economic development strategy promoted by the World Bank in which development occurs by encouraging export sectors.

Import substitution
A development strategy that attempts to replace previously-imported goods with domestic production.

---

[9] For one empirical verification of the link between education and health, see Kassouf and Senauer (1996).

[10] See, for example, Romer (1993).

[11] For example, in the 1998/99 *World Development Report*, the World Bank claimed: "Trade can bring greater awareness of new and better ways of producing goods and services: exports contribute to this awareness through the information obtained from buyers and suppliers" (p. 27).

[12] Bruton (1998) offers an excellent overview of import substitution and export promotion strategies. Chapters 9 and 10 of Cypher and Dietz (1997) offer a sympathetic review of import substitution.

Bank (1994) put it this way: "Because exports are so beneficial to growth, countries should consider the needs of exporters carefully and apply an 'exporters first' rule" (p. 11). The World Bank explicitly recommended this policy to Ghana and other African countries.

The logic of export promotion is illustrated in Figure 20.7. P^G is Ghana's autarky price, and P^W is the world price. In the absence of a positive export externality, as the price increases from P^G to P^W in the movement from autarky to trade, quantity supplied increases from point A to point B, and exports of E_0^G appear. In the presence of export externalities, however, the process continues one step further. The initial export level, E_0^G, facilitates the absorption of technological knowledge from abroad, and the subsequent improvement in production technology makes possible an increase in supply or a shift in Ghana's supply curve from S_0^G to S_1^G.[13] Given P^W, Ghanaian firms move from point B to point C, and exports expand to E_1^G. In simplified form, this is how some international and development economists view the role of exports in the development process.

What is the evidence for the process depicted in Figure 20.7? In an important article, Edwards (1998) used statistical techniques to show that the more open countries are to international trade, the faster their growth in per capita incomes. You should not be too quick, however, to claim that exports of *all kinds* generate positive technological externalities. In another article, Levin and Raut (1997) showed that these externalities are notably absent in the case of primary product exports, which characterize many developing countries, including Ghana. Furthermore, some prominent international economists remain unconvinced by the process depicted in Figure 20.7. For example, Dani Rodrik (1999) categorically states that "there is little reason to believe that one dollar of exports will contribute to

Figure 20.7 Export Externalities for Ghana

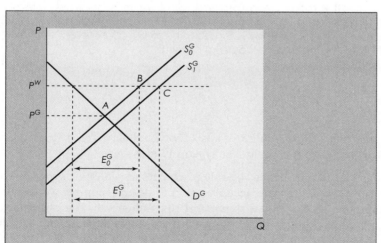

---

[13]Recall from Chapter 2 that reductions in input prices and improvements in technology shift the supply curve to the right, while increases in input prices and technology setbacks shift the supply curve to the left.

Trade and Growth in East Asia

The large increases in per capita incomes in the countries of East Asia was one of the most notable successes of the world economy in the post–World War II era. One observation made about the East Asian economies is that the growth of per capita incomes was accompanied by a significant expansion of exports, especially in Japan, South Korea, and Taiwan. Some observers, especially those affiliated with the World Bank, have concluded that export promotion policies pursued by these economies explains a great deal of their success in increasing per capita incomes. For example, this was the point of view expressed in a major World Bank report entitled *The East Asian Miracle: Economic Growth and Public Policy*, issued in 1993.

According to the World Bank, export promotion positively affects per capita incomes via *technology effects*. These can arise in a few ways. First, exports help firms to earn the foreign exchange necessary to purchase new equipment from abroad. This new equipment can embody a more sophisticated technology than the older equipment of the firm. Second, the presence of exports signals foreign firms that the country in question would be a good place in which to engage in export-oriented direct foreign investment. This direct foreign investment can bring with it new technology. Third, exports signal that the exporting firms are competitive and are therefore taken seriously in technology cross-licensing schemes. Thus, the World Bank claims that "the relationship between exports and productivity growth (arises) from exports' role in helping economies adopt and master international best-practice technologies" (p. 317).

Not all international economists agree with this interpretation. For example, Rodrik (1994) finds this export-technology link to be unconvincing. His interpretation of the East Asian development experience is that exports are largely a *result*, not a cause, of successful development. He attributes the increases in per capita incomes to levels of education and the equal distributions of income and land. He stresses the role of these initial conditions in the subsequent economic development of East Asia. With regard to the role of exports in improving countries' technological capabilities, Rodrik (1994) states that "whether export orientation generates spillovers and productivity benefits . . . is still unclear" (p. 48).

More generally, Rodrik (1999, Chapter 2) demonstrates that there are many instances where high export-to-GDP ratios are associated with low rates of growth. He goes further (1999, Chapter 3) to demonstrate for a sample of 47 countries that increases in export-to-GDP ratios follow increases in investment-to-GDP ratios. The implication here is that exports are a *consequence* of growth rather than a cause of growth.

Sources: World Bank (1993); Rodrik (1994, 1999).

an economy more than a dollar of any other kind of activity" (p. 24). These issues are discussed further in the box on East Asia.

There is another caveat to the role of exports in economic growth. There is some agreement that the accumulation of human capital we discussed in the previous section is an important prerequisite to the absorption of technology from abroad. For example, in its study of economic development of East Asia, the World Bank (1993) acknowledged:

Access to international best-practice technology and rapid formation of human capital supplement and reinforce one another. . . . The externalities generated by manufactured *exports in the high-performing Asian economies in the form of cheaper and more effective knowledge transfers would have undoubtedly been less productive had there been fewer skilled workers to facilitate their absorption (pp. 320–321, emphasis added).*

There is some empirical evidence to support the conclusion that human capital and manufactured exports interact positively in supporting the growth of per capita incomes. The statistical analyses of both the World Bank (1993) and Levin and Raut (1997) indicate that such interactions are significant. Levin and Raut's evidence shows that the contribution of human capital depends on the level of manufactured exports, and the contribution of manufactured exports depends on the level of human capital. In this way, trade and education can contribute to increases in per capita incomes and, thereby, to the HDI both directly and indirectly. This interaction, however, is restricted to manufactured exports. Primary product exports do not necessarily generate the same effects. Ghana, as a primary product exporter, needs to take note of this limitation. Increasing exports of gold and cocoa, for example, may do little for technical gains and the utilization of human capital.

Education, Health, and Population

In the previous two sections, we have discussed the role of human capital or education in relationship to exports and growth. In Figure 20.6, we also hinted at a possible role of health. In this section, we will focus on the relationships among education, health, and population. We will consider these three areas in turn.

Education

Our discussions in the previous two sections focused on education or human capital accumulation as a single entity. However, given the obviously limited nature of educational resources, it is often important to distinguish among primary, secondary, and tertiary (higher) education. There is now a body of evidence suggesting that primary education plays a particularly important role in the development process. To quote Weaver, Rock, and Kusterer (1997), "studies suggest that no country since 1850 has achieved self-sustaining growth without first achieving universal primary education" (p. 166). More formally, the work of Psacharopoulos (1985 and 1994) has shown that the social returns on investments in primary education *exceed* the social returns on investments in secondary or tertiary education. This suggests that primary education should be a first priority in development strategies. Government subsidies to tertiary education should be very low until universal primary and secondary education has been achieved.

Table 20.2 gives us some sense of the patterns of educational levels and expenditures in the world. In this table, Ghana has been added to the countries reported on in Chapter 19 and is highlighted in bold. Per capita GNP, used to rank the countries in the table, is also included. You will note that primary school enrollment ratios can be very low. Haiti stands out here with a primary school enrollment ratio of less than 20 percent. Ghana also stands out as having a relatively low primary school enrollment ratio.

Both Haiti and Ghana are distinctive in having primary school enrollment rates below adult literacy rates. These gaps do not bode well for the future of these two countries.

As is evident in Table 20.2, there is a significant gender aspect to educational levels. It is often the case that educational levels (and therefore literacy rates) are lower for girls and women than for boys and men. Take the case of India. In this country, there is a spread of over 20 percentage points between male and female literacy rates. As we will see, increased educational levels for women have important implications in the realms of health and population. Also, Psacharopoulos (1994) and Schultz (2002) have shown that social returns to education for women are higher than those for men. This gives added significance to the disadvantage of girls and women evident in the table.

Table 20.2 Education Indicators

Country	GNP per Capita (U.S. dollars, 2000)	Primary School Enrollment (1997, percent of relevant age group)	Adult Literacy (2000, percent of age 15 and above)		Educational Expenditures (1995–1997, percent of GNP)	Tertiary Educational Expenditures (1994–1997, percent of all levels)
			Female	Male		
Ethiopia	100	35	31	47	4	16
Ghana	**350**	**43**	**63**	**81**	**4**	**—**
India	460	77	45	69	3	14
Haiti	510	19	48	52	2 (1987)	11 (1987)
Indonesia	570	99	82	92	1	24
China	840	100	76	92	2	16
Turkey	3,090	100	77	93	2	35
Brazil	3,570	97	85	85	5	27
Costa Rica	3,960	92	96	96	5	28
South Korea	8,910	100	96	99	4	8
Spain	14,960	100	97	99	5	17
United States	34,210	100	99	99	5	25
Japan	34,260	100	99	99	4	12

Sources: Based on data in the *World Development Report*, published by the World Bank in 2002, and in the *Human Development Report*, published by the United Nations Development Program in 2002.

Education expenditure levels range from 1 percent of GNP in the case of Indonesia to 5 percent of GNP in the cases of Costa Rica, Spain, and the United States. Lower levels of education have greater social returns than higher levels of education. It is therefore important to examine the percent of total educational expenditures on tertiary education. In some countries, such as Turkey and Brazil, this is very high. In other countries, such as South Korea and Japan, it is very low. It is typical of successful East Asian countries to have a large portion of total expenditures on primary and secondary education rather than on tertiary education. These countries consciously recognized the social returns of lower educational levels and adjusted their educational policies accordingly.[14] This enlightened approach to educational policy has contributed greatly to the development of East Asia. Ghana, with a primary school enrollment of only 43 percent of the relevant population group, should take note.

Health and Development

From a per capita income perspective on development, health is important because it contributes to the effectiveness of labor in both its hours-worked and human capital dimensions. The per capita income perspective, then, views health as well as education as a *means* to economic development. In contrast, the human development perspective described in Chapter 19 views health as an *end*. Improved health contributes directly to human development via the life expectancy component of the HDI. Both of these views are represented in Figure 20.6.

Quantitative indicators of the health of a country's population include demographic indicators such as the life expectancy and infant and child mortality, morbidity indicators, and health service indicators.[15] Each of these measures has significant limitations. Demographic indicators may not fully reflect the health of the surviving population. Morbidity indicators are difficult to collect, and health service indicators ignore quality measures. Despite the weaknesses of these measures, they are all that is available to gain some sense of health levels in countries and to gauge the effects of health policies.

Table 20.3 presents four health indicators. In this table, Ghana has been added to the countries reported on in Chapter 19 and is highlighted in bold. Per capita GNP, used to rank the countries in the table, is also included. Life expectancy and under-5 mortality are demographic indicators. The prevalence of malnutrition is a morbidity indicator, and doctors per 100,000 population is a health service indicator. For each of these indicators, we can see that there is a broad range of values among the low-income, middle-income, and high-income countries. Ethiopia stands out as a country with a very low life expectancy, very high under-5 mortality, a high level of malnutrition, and a low level of medical services. Costa Rica stands out as a country with very good health indicators despite its status as a middle-income country. This, of course, is what contributes to its relatively high HDI.

---

[14]See Chapter 9 of Weaver, Rock, and Kusterer (1997).
[15]See Chapter 5 of Szirmai (1997).

Table 20.3 Health Indicators

Country	GNP per Capita (U.S. dollars, 2000)	Life Expectancy (1999, years)	Under-5 Mortality Rate (1999, per 1,000)	Prevalence of Malnutrition (percent 1997–1999)	Doctors per 100,000 Population (1990–1999)
Ethiopia	100	42	166	49	—
Ghana	**350**	**58**	**109**	**15**	**6**
India	460	63	90	23	48
Haiti	510	53	118	56	8
Indonesia	570	66	52	6	16
China	840	70	37	9	162
Turkey	3,090	69	45	—	121
Brazil	3,570	67	40	10	127
Costa Rica	3,960	77	14	5	141
South Korea	8,910	73	9	—	136
Spain	14,960	78	6	—	424
United States	34,210	77	8	—	279
Japan	34,260	81	4	—	193

Sources: Based on data in the *World Development Report*, published by the World Bank in 2002, and in the *Human Development Report*, published by the United Nations Development Program in 2002.

The field of health and development is an interdisciplinary one in which we find economists, sociologists, anthropologists, health professionals, and public policy professionals all involved. Within this field, there is a general agreement that child morbidity and mortality are important indicators of the general state of health in a country. For this reason, much of the focus on health in developing countries rightly focuses on children. What we find here is that the leading contributors to child morbidity and mortality are diarrhea, respiratory infections (e.g., pneumonia), undernourishment, vaccination-preventable diseases (e.g., measles), and violence in certain countries. Because of women's traditionally close relationship to children, it also turns out that the educational levels of women contribute positively and significantly to child health. The mediating factors here are hygiene, nutrition, and child-care factors.

This is a reason, beyond those discussed here, for focusing attention on women's education in developing countries.[16]

Population Issues

Population and development is field of study in itself. Like health and development, it is an interdisciplinary field in which economists, sociologists, anthropologists, health professionals, and public policy professionals are all involved. We will provide only the briefest introduction to this field, relating our previous discussion in this chapter to the population issue.[17]

Two important variables in the study of population and development are the *crude birth rate* (r_b) and the *crude death rate* (r_d). These measures are respectively defined as the number of live births and deaths per 1,000 population. Behind the crude birth rate is the *total fertility rate*, defined as the average number of children a woman will give birth to during her lifetime. The crude birth rate and crude death rate together determine the **natural rate of population growth** (a percentage measure) as follows:[18]

$$n = \frac{(r_b - r_d)}{10} \quad \textbf{Natural rate of population growth}$$

Natural rate of population growth
An exogenous measure of the rate of population growth used in growth theory.

The natural rate of population growth is important because, along with the rate of growth of physical capital, it determines the level of the capital-labor ratio, k. This, in turn, determines the level of per capita income, y, as we discussed earlier in this chapter. The higher the natural rate of population growth, the less likely will increases in investment translate into increases in per capita income.

A survey of the population and development field reveals a causal chain determining the natural rate of population growth something like what is presented in Figure 20.8. Let us begin with the total fertility rate. A primary factor here is socio-cultural factors such as the availability of birth control and the role of women. Generally, the more favorable a society to the full participation of women, the lower the total fertility rate. The level of per capita income is also important: the higher the level, the lower the total fertility rate. Finally, the higher the level of women's education, the lower the total fertility rate. Here, our discussion of education, including the work of Psacharopoulos (1985, 1994), comes again to the fore. The total fertility rate contributes positively and directly to the crude birth rate and, in turn, positively to the natural rate of population growth.

---

[16]For example, in their study of parental education and health in Brazil, Kassouf and Senauer (1996) concluded: "Some 25% of preschool children with mothers who had less than 4 years of schooling suffered from severe or moderate stunting (of growth). This figure would fall to only 15 percent if these mothers had a primary education of at least 4 but less than 8 years, and only 3 percent if these mothers had a secondary education of at least 11 years of schooling. Although not as strong as the effect of maternal education . . . improved paternal education would also lead to substantial reductions in child malnutrition" (p. 832). See also Schultz (2002).

[17]For a good introduction, see Chapter 4 of Szirmai (1997) and the references therein. See also Demeny and McNicoll (1998).

[18]The natural rate of population growth combines with the net migration rate to determine the *actual* rate of population growth.

Figure 20.8 Explaining the Natural Rate of Population Growth

```
┌─────────────────┐   ┌─────────────────┐   ┌─────────────────┐
│ Socio–Cultural  │   │   Per Capita    │   │     Health      │
│ Factors         │   │  Income Level   │   │    Policies     │
│ (role of women) │   │                 │   │                 │
└─────────────────┘   └─────────────────┘   └─────────────────┘
        │                                            │
        ▼                                            ▼
┌─────────────────┐   ┌─────────────────┐   ┌─────────────────┐
│  Total Fertility│◄──│ Level of Women's│──►│      Child      │
│      Rate       │   │    Education    │   │    Mortality    │
└─────────────────┘   └─────────────────┘   └─────────────────┘
        │                                            │
        ▼                                            ▼
┌─────────────────┐   ┌─────────────────┐   ┌─────────────────┐
│   Crude Birth   │──►│  Natural Rate of│◄──│   Crude Death   │
│   Rate $(r_b)$  │   │ Population Growth│   │   Rate $(r_d)$  │
│                 │   │       $(n)$     │   │                 │
└─────────────────┘   └─────────────────┘   └─────────────────┘
```

Let us continue with child mortality. Obviously, health policies can contribute to the level of child mortality. As suggested in our discussion of health, the level of women's education plays an important role. The higher the level of women's education, the lower the child mortality. Child mortality contributes positively and directly to the crude death rate and, in turn, negatively to the natural rate of population growth.[19]

A main conclusion drawn from Figure 20.8 is that the role and education of women are crucial for population issues in particular and for human development in general. Given the role that this insight plays in contemporary development policy, it deserves special mention:

> **The role and education of women are crucial for health and population issues in particular and for human development in general.**

[19]On the role of women in development generally, see Chapter 8 of Sen (1999). The *Human Development Report* of the United Nations Development Program has recently focused a great deal of attention on the role of women, going so far as to develop a gender-related development index (GDI), mentioned in Chapter 19.

Conclusion

So what should Ghana do? We need to be careful in answering this question, because there is some controversy regarding the role of exports in economic growth and, therefore, in human development. One thing has become clear, however. Whereas, in Chapter 19, we treated the HDI as having three *independent* elements of per capita income, health, and education, our discussion in the current chapter has shown that these three elements are *interdependent*, with education playing a central role. It is possible for education, health, and international trade to interact in positive ways to promote the growth in per capita incomes. If this has not happened in Ghana, positive interactions are missing.

Ghana's education picture, detailed in Table 20.2, is poor. Its health picture, detailed in Table 20.3, is not much better. It is overreliant on primary product exports. Improved education and health levels need to interact positively with manufactured (and service) exports before Ghana will "get somewhere" rather than "go nowhere." As it turns out, Ghana was, for a long time, a test case of World Bank structural adjustment policies that were to generate sustainable long-term growth. We turn to this aspect of the Ghanaian economy in Chapter 23.

Another way to view the discussion of this chapter is by returning to Figure 1.3 in Chapter 1. This figure illustrated the presence of linkages among the realms of international trade, international production, international finance, and international economic development. We have shown that it is possible for two of these four realms to interact in a positive manner. The trade relationships of a country can result in the absorption of new technology, and this absorption can be facilitated by the accumulation of the appropriate types of human capital. It is important to recognize, however, that this scenario is not the only possible outcome, as Ghana and a large number of other developing countries show.

Review Exercises

1. Given the discussion of this chapter with regard to trade, education, and health, what policies do you think countries ought to pursue to ensure that international trade supports increases in per capita incomes?

2. Are there any connections you can find between the discussion of this chapter and the Porter diamond covered in Chapter 12? In particular, are there links between our discussion of education and Porter's thinking about factor conditions?

3. The World Bank suggests that there are important externalities associated with exports. In general, such positive externalities call for subsidies on the part of governments. Given our discussion of the GATT/WTO system in Chapter 8, do you detect any problems with the use of export subsidies?

4. This is the first chapter in which we have raised gender issues in our discussion. Are there any other aspects of the world economy in which gender issues are important? How might these issues arise in the realms of international trade, international production, and international finance?

Further Reading and Web Resources

Jones (1998) is a basic reference on the theory of economic growth, and Rodrigo (2001) addresses the case of East Asian growth and development. (See also *The Economist* (1996).) For the role of trade policies in economic development, a useful starting point is Bruton (1998) and the references therein. Szirmai (1997) and Cypher and Dietz (1997) present the roles of education, health, and population in economic development in an accessible manner. On population and development, see also Demeny and McNicoll (1998).

Jonathan Temple maintains a Web site on the subject of economic growth at **http://bris.ac.uk/Depts/Economics/Growth**. The Groningen Growth and Development Centre Web site is at **http://www.eco.rug.nl/ggdc/homeggdc.html**. The World Bank's Web site on economic growth research can be found at **http://www.worldbank.org/research/growth**.

References

Bruton, H.J. (1998) "A Reconsideration of Import Substitution," *Journal of Economic Literature*, 36:2, 903–936.

Cypher, J.M., and J.L. Dietz (1997) *The Process of Economic Development*, Routledge, London.

Demeny, P., and G. McNicoll (eds.) (1998) *The Reader in Population and Development*, St. Martin's Press, New York.

The Economist (1996) "Economic Growth: The Poor and the Rich," May 25, 23–25.

The Economist (1992) "Economic Growth: Explaining the Mystery," January 4, 15–18.

Edwards, S. (1998) "Openness, Productivity and Growth: What Do We Really Know?" *Economic Journal*, 108:447, 383–398.

Jones, C.I. (1998) *Introduction to Economic Growth*, Norton, New York.

Kassouf, A.L., and B. Senauer (1996) "Direct and Indirect Effects of Parental Education on Malnutrition Among Children in Brazil: A Full Income Approach," *Economic Development and Cultural Change*, 44:4, 817–838.

Levin, A., and L. Raut (1997) "Complementarities Between Exports and Human Capital in Economic Growth: Evidence from Semi-industrialized Countries," *Economic Development and Cultural Change*, 46:1, 155–174.

Lucas, R.E. (1988) "On the Mechanics of Economic Development," *Journal of Monetary Economics*, 22:1, 3–42.

Mankiw, N.G. (2004) *Principles of Economics*, South-Western/Thomson Learning, Mason, Ohio.

Mankiw, N.G., D. Romer, and D. Weil (1992) "A Contribution to the Empirics of Economic Growth," *Quarterly Journal of Economics*, 107:2, 407–438.

Pio, A. (1994) "New Growth Theory and Old Development Problems," *Development Policy Review*, 12:3, 277–300.

Psacharopoulos, G. (1994) "Returns to Investment in Education: A Global Update," *World Development*, 22:9, 1325–1343.

Psacharopoulos, G. (1985) "Returns to Education: A Further International Update and Implications," *Journal of Human Resources*, 20:4, 583–597.

Rodrigo, G.C. (2001) *Technology, Economic Growth and Crises in East Asia*, Edward Elgar, Aldershot.

Rodrik, D. (1999) *The New Global Economy and Developing Countries: Making Opennes Work*, Overseas Development Council, Washington, DC.

Rodrik, D. (1994) "King Kong Meets Godzilla: The World Bank and *The East Asian Miracle*," in A. Fishlow et al., *Miracle or Design: Lessons from the East Asian Experience*, Overseas Development Council, Washington, DC.

Romer, P. (1993) "Two Strategies for Economic Development: Using Ideas and Producing Ideas," in L.H. Summers and S. Shah (eds.), *Proceedings of the World Bank Annual Conference on Development Economics 1992*, The World Bank, Washington, DC, 63–91.

Romer, P. (1990) "Endogenous Technological Change," *Journal of Political Economy*, 98:5, S71–S102.

Romer, P. (1986) "Increasing Returns and Long-Run Growth," *Journal of Political Economy*, 94:5, 1002–1037.

Schultz, T.P. (2002) "Why Governments Should Invest More to Educate Girls," *World Development*, 30:2, 207–225.

Sen A. (1999) *Development as Freedom*, Knopf, New York, 1999.

Solow, R. (1956) "A Contribution to the Theory of Economic Growth," *Quarterly Journal of Economics*, 70:1, 65–94.

Szirmai, A. (1997) *Economic and Social Development*, Prentice Hall, London.

Weaver, J.H, M.T. Rock, and K. Kusterer (1997) *Achieving Broad-Based Sustainable Development*, Kumarian Press, West Hartford, Connecticut.

World Bank (1993) *East Asian Miracle*, Oxford University Press, Oxford.

World Bank (1994) *Adjustment in Africa*, Oxford University Press, Oxford.

World Bank (1999) *World Development Report 1998/99*, Oxford University Press, Oxford.

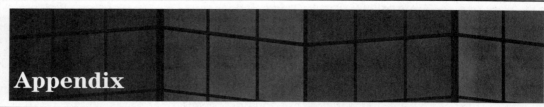

Appendix

Growth Theory Algebra

This appendix presents some of the algebra behind the growth theory presented in this chapter.

Growth theory begins with what economists call a production function:

$$Y = A \times F(L, K) \tag{20.A1}$$

This equation presents what is known as the *aggregate* production function. In this equation, Y is total output and total income. L is the aggregate labor force, and K is the aggregate stock of physical capital. A refers to an *exogenous* measure of technology.

"Old" growth theory assumes that production takes place according to **constant returns to scale**. Constant returns to scale means that a doubling of both L and K will lead to a doubling of Y. More generally, multiplying both L and K by some factor θ will increase Y by that same factor. In other words,

$$\theta Y = A \times F(\theta L, \theta K) \tag{20.A2}$$

Solow's growth model uses Equation 20.A2 and introduces a little trick. The trick is to set θ equal to $1/L$. This gives us the following equation:

$$\frac{1}{L} Y = A \times F\left(\frac{1}{L} L, \frac{1}{L} K\right) \tag{20.A3}$$

Equation 20.A3 is a little confusing. To make sense of it, we are going to consider each of its terms in turn. Let's begin with the term on the left-hand side of the equation, Y/L. This we can interpret as *per capita income*. We are going to denote per capita income with a lowercase y: $y = y/L$. The second term, A, we have already seen. It is just our technology term. Inside the parentheses, we next encounter L/L. This term is equal to 1, a constant, and we can therefore ignore it. Finally, we have K/L. This is known at the *capital-labor ratio*. We are going to denote the capital-labor ratio with a lowercase k: $k = K/L$. Given all of this, we can rewrite Equation 20.A3 as follows:

Constant returns to scale
A condition of production in which a doubling of all inputs leads to a doubling of output.

$$y = A \times F(1, k) = A \times f(k) \qquad \text{(20.A4)}$$

This equation is the intensive production function used in this chapter.

New growth theory often works with a modified intensive production function of the form:

$$y = A(h) \times f(k) \qquad \text{(20.A5)}$$

where h is a measure of per capita human capital, H/L. Trade issues in new growth theory involve adding an additional variable to this equation as follows:

$$y = A(h \times e_m) \times f(k) \qquad \text{(20.A6)}$$

where e_m is manufacturing exports' share in gross national product. Note in Equation 20.A6 that A is a function of the *product* of h and e_M.* Therefore, the contribution of human capital depends on the level of manufactured exports, and the contribution of manufactured exports depends on the level of human capital.

The natural rate of population growth discussed in this chapter is important because, along with the rate of growth of physical capital, $\Delta K/K$, it determines the level of the capital-labor ratio, k. This, in turn, determines the level of per capita income, y. More specifically, an increase in y will require that:

$$\frac{\Delta K}{K} \times 100 > n \qquad \text{(20.A7)}$$

The higher the natural rate of population growth, the less likely this will be.

---

*See, for example, Levin and Raut (1997).

Hosting Multinational Enterprises

21

Years ago, I attended a conference on the economies of Latin America that took place just outside the city of San José, Costa Rica. Before the conference began, I took a long walk through the neighborhoods surrounding the conference hotel. As I walked, I passed the factory gates of many foreign corporations who were operating in the area. During the conference, I spoke to a representative of the Costa Rican government. With some passion, she said, "Foreign firms are buying our companies! We are losing ownership of our economy!" This statement made an impact on me, and upon my return to the United States, I pulled an old book written in 1987 by John Sheahan off my shelf. Entitled Patterns of Development in Latin America, *the book includes a chapter on multinationals. I glanced through the chapter, reading only what I had underlined years ago, and I came across this statement: "A particularly important concern is that foreign investment may foreclose opportunities for domestic investment and learning by . . . taking over existing domestic firms and eliminating independent national management" (p. 165). If she could have read this passage, I imagined the Costa Rican official would have said, "Exactly!"*

As the years have passed since this conference, Costa Rica has continued to rely on foreign investment as a central part of its development strategy. This was highlighted in the late 1990s when the computer-chip maker Intel decided to build a plant on the outskirts of San José, near where I had taken my walk some years earlier. The plant began operations in 1998. As a result of this and other computer-related foreign investment, computer products accounted for 35 percent of Costa Rica's exports in 1999. This FDI-based development strategy was not an accident. The Costa Rica Investment Board (CINDE) actively pursued this approach. CINDE has been strongly influenced by the thinking of Michael Porter, which we discussed in Chapter 11, especially by the notion of spatial clusters. Indeed, CINDE officials have consciously attempted to promote a computer cluster in Costa Rica, even going so far as to visit Porter at Harvard University before their first presentation to Intel. They succeeded in convincing Intel to locate in Costa Rica, and this represented a *new* investment rather than a U.S. takeover of a Costa Rican firm.

What role does foreign direct investment (FDI) play in international economic development? Is it a positive force or a negative force? What would your posture be if you were an economic official in the Costa Rican government? This chapter will help you to answer these questions. We begin in the following section by characterizing the benefits and costs of hosting MNEs from a development perspective. We then describe the various policy stances that a host country can adopt toward inward FDI. Next, we consider the especially important issue of linkages between MNEs and host-country firms. Finally, we consider the issue of transfer pricing and the global institutional framework governing FDI practices and polices. Throughout the chapter, we will be exploring the link between international production and international economic development illustrated in Figure 1.3 of Chapter 1.

Benefits and Costs

If you were an economic official in the Costa Rican government, trying to decide upon your posture toward FDI in the development of your country, it might be a good idea to have some sense of both the benefits and costs that FDI might entail.[1] We are going to discuss the benefits and costs with the help of Table 21.1. The items we will consider are employment, competition, education and training, technology, balance of payments, health and the environment, and culture.

Employment

If a foreign firm engages in FDI in a home-country sector in which there is unemployment, it is possible for the FDI to increase the total number of jobs in the sector. This is a positive employment effect and constitutes a benefit of FDI. Such direct employment benefits can be supplemented by indirect employment benefits when local firms supply the foreign MNE with intermediate products, something we will discuss later. It is also possible, however, for a simple transfer of jobs from local to foreign firms to occur with no net increase in employment. Depending on one's point of view, this might be interpreted as a cost of FDI.

Competition

If a foreign firm engages in FDI in a home-country sector characterized by imperfect competition, it is possible for the FDI to increase competition in the sector. As you learned in introductory microeconomics, an increase in competition tends to lower prices and increase quantities supplied. Because this benefits consumers, this positive competition effect constitutes a benefit of FDI. On the other hand, in cases where the foreign MNE possesses a large amount of market power compared to the host country firms, FDI could worsen competition. This would be a cost of FDI.

Education and Training

As we saw in Chapter 20, the accumulation of human capital via education and training is a crucial component of economic development. It is possible for foreign MNEs to provide education and training to host-country workers that were not available from domestic firms. This provides benefits to the host-country economy as a whole. It is equally possible, however, for the foreign MNE to restrict education and training to its own transplanted

---

[1] Allowing for both benefits and costs of FDI is a point of view that Hill (2000, Chapter 7) describes as "pragmatic nationalism." It also recognizes a degree of ambiguity over the net benefits of FDI in the literature on the subject.

Table 21.1 The Benefits and Costs of Inward FDI

Item	Benefits	Costs
Employment	Generate direct and indirect increases in employment.	Transfer jobs from home to foreign firms.
Competition	Promote competition by increasing the number of firms in an industry.	Retard competition in cases where the foreign firm has a large amount of market power.
Education and training	Improve the education and training of host-country workers.	Restrict education and training to expatriate employees. Discriminate against host-country workers.
Technology	Transfer technology from developed to developing countries.	Technology employed might not be appropriate for the host-country economy.
Balance of payments	Improve the import and export components of the current account. Improve the direct investment component of the capital account.	Worsen the import component of the current account. Worsen the net factor receipt component of the capital account.
Health and the environment	Employ new technology that is more environmentally sound. Increase incomes and thereby make more resources available for the enforcement of existing environmental regulations.	Increase the amount of pollution and subject workers to unsafe workplaces.
Culture	Introduce progressive aspect of business culture in the areas of organizational development and human resource management.	Increase dominance of urban and Western culture over rural and non-Western culture.

Source: Adapted from Hill (2000).

employees and to even discriminate against host-country workers. Such discrimination would constitute a cost of FDI to the host country.

Technology

Many developing countries lack access to the technologies available in developed countries.[2] Recall from Chapter 1 that MNEs account for

---

[2] "It is widely accepted that the ability to create, acquire, learn how to use and effectively deploy technological capacity is one of the key ingredients of economic success in virtually all societies" (Dunning, 1993, p. 287).

approximately three-fourths of worldwide civilian research and development. Consequently, hosting MNEs from developed countries is one way to gain access to that technology. There are two problems, however. First, MNEs will employ the technology that most suits their strategic needs, and these strategic considerations of an MNE can differ from the development needs of the host country. For example, foreign MNEs might employ processes that are much more capital intensive than would be desired on the basis of host-country employment considerations. Second, it is a strong empirical fact that most MNEs conduct their research and development in their home bases rather than in host countries.[3] Consequently, there are limits to the transfer of new technologies to host countries.[4]

Balance of Payments

We presented the balance of payments accounts for Mexico in Chapter 12 as consisting of the current account and the capital account. For your convenience, these are reproduced here as Table 21.2.[5] The process of FDI can affect a few of the components of both the current and capital accounts. The setting up of a production facility in the host country causes an inflow (positive balance) in the direct investment component of the capital account and thus tends to improve the balance of payments. Unless further expansion of the production facility occurs, this initial impact is a one-time-only impact. If the subsidiary experiences positive earnings, some of these earnings will be eventually repatriated to the MNE's home-base country. This causes an outflow (negative balance) on the net factor receipts component of the current account.

If the good produced by the MNE is sold domestically and replaces previously-imported goods, the FDI will have the effect of making the trade balance component of the current account more positive (less negative). However, the MNE might import a significant amount of intermediate products, and this would tend to make the trade balance component of the current account less positive (more negative). Finally, if the MNE exports the good it produces, this would tend to make the trade balance component of the current account more positive (less negative). Clearly, the net effect of all these balance-of-payments influences would need to be evaluated on a case-by-case basis.

Health and the Environment

Recently, a great deal attention has been focused on the impacts of MNEs on health and the environment. It is clear that, in resource extractive

---

[3] "With the exception of some European-based companies, the proportion of R&D activity by MNEs undertaken outside their home countries is generally quite small and, in the case of Japanese firms, negligible" (Dunning, 1993, p. 301).

[4] There is a presumption in much of the literature on FDI that MNEs provide positive "spillovers" in the form of technology upgrading to domestic firms in the host country. This line of thinking goes back to Caves (1974), who tested this possibility for Canada and Australia. The evidence of *generalized* technology spillovers, however, is mixed. For example, Haddad and Harrison (1993) and Kokko, Tansini, and Zejan (1996) failed to find such effects for Morocco and Uruguay, respectively.

[5] Recall that the year 1993 was chosen in Chapter 12 to illustrate certain interesting and problematic features of the Mexican economy in that year.

Table 21.2 Mexican Balance of Payments, 1993 (billions of U.S. dollars)

Item	Gross	Net	Major Balance
Current Account			
1. Exports	61		
2. Imports	77		
3. Trade balance		−16	
4. Net factor receipts		−11	
5. Transfers		4	
6. Current account balance			−23
Capital Account			
7. Direct investment		4	
8. Portfolio investment		29	
9. Official reserves balance		−7	
10. Errors and omissions		−3	
11. Capital account balance			23
12. Overall balance			0

Source: Based on data in *International Financial Statistics Yearbook*, published by the International Monetary Fund in 1994

industries, certain MNEs have been grossly negligent. For example, the box presents a brief discussion of the petroleum industry in the Ecuadorian Amazon region. A similar story applies to the petroleum industry in Nigeria.[6] More generally, Dunning (1993, Chapter 19) points out that MNEs are heavily involved in pollution-generating sectors. They affect the location of pollution-intensive production processes, establish health and safety environments of their workforces, and are involved in the international trade of many hazardous products. Sometimes, MNEs have utilized production technologies in host countries that were banned in their home countries. For example, Standard Fruit, Dole Fruit, and Chiquita used the worm-killing chemical DBCP on their banana plantations even after its severe health impacts were well known. As a result, they subsequently had to cope with legal actions.[7] All of these cases involve significant costs to the host countries. Despite attention to such costs, it is possible for FDI to have environmental benefits for host countries. For example, MNEs

---

[6] See Hill (2000), pp. 113–116.
[7] See *The Economist* (1995).

The Petroleum Industry in the Ecuadorian Amazon

U.S. petroleum MNEs began to involve themselves in petroleum development in the Ecuadorian Amazon in 1967. The most important petroleum MNE was Texaco, which began to pump oil in 1972. Other U.S.-based MNEs operating in this region during the 1970s and 1980s included Occidental Petroleum, ARCO, Unocal, Conoco, and Mobil. It is estimated that, while it was in operation, Texaco's oil pipeline dumped into the region the equivalent of one and a half times the petroleum as the famous *Exxon Valdez* oil spill. It has also been estimated that, during the 1980s, the petroleum sector was dumping millions of gallons of toxic waste into the Ecuadorian Amazon *per day*. Consequently, health disorders increased substantially.

There is evidence that petroleum MNEs also had detrimental impacts on the indigenous cultures of the region. Some have claimed that the activities of these MNEs significantly contributed to the destruction of the culture of the Cofan Indians. In his book *Savages*, Joe Kane documents the struggles of the Huaorani Indians against petroleum development in their traditional lands. He documents in great detail how the petroleum MNEs (and North American environmental organizations) routinely failed to take Huaorani interests and well-being into account. However, it is important to note, the Ecuadorian national petroleum company, Petroecuador, seems not a bit more concerned than the MNEs Ecuador hosts. Kane reports:

"While I was in Toñampare a valve in an oil well near the Napo (River) broke, or was left open, and for two days and a night raw crude streamed into the river—at least 21,000 gallons and perhaps as many as 80,000, creating a slick that stretched from bank to bank for 40 miles. Ecuador's downstream neighbors, Peru and Brazil, declared states of emergency, but Petroecuador shrugged off the problem. 'It looks much worse than it is,' an official said. 'The water underneath is perfectly fine.' Three weeks later the pipeline itself burst, in the Andean foothills that rise beyond the west bank of the Napo, and spilled another 32,000 gallons into the watershed" (p. 157).

The wrath of Ecuadorian environmentalists and the affected native people of Ecuador has been directed against Texaco, which they see as the worst offender. The resulting lawsuits are still in progress. The case of petroleum MNEs in the Ecuadorian Amazon, though, offers a sad, cautionary tale of the potential environmental impacts of some MNEs.

Source: Kane (1996).

can be involved in the development of new, environmentally-friendly production processes and clean-up technologies.

Culture

MNEs serve as conduits of their home countries' national and business cultures. They also sometimes introduce new goods with cultural content into host countries. These activities can further the dominance of urban and Western culture over rural and non-Western culture and, in some developing host countries, exacerbate already existing tensions between these cultural/regional poles. In the case of extensive, resource extraction activities, FDI can and has resulted in the elimination of local indigenous peoples. In these ways, FDI can impose significant cultural costs on host countries. More positively, however, MNEs can introduce progressive elements of business culture into their host countries. These might include new practices in the areas of organizational development and human resource management.[8]

In the case of Intel's new investment in Costa Rica, most of the previously mentioned items were benefits rather than costs. Intel was generating new employment and bringing new technology. It went so far as to assist the Costa Rican government in the education and training of future Intel workers. Its exports would generate foreign exchange. One significant potential cost, however, was in the environmental category in the form of toxic industrial waste. The solution to this problem was to re-export this waste back to the United States to be processed by U.S. companies.

One would hope that, by assessing each of the items in Table 21.1, we could make a general statement about the degree to which FDI supports the process of international economic development. It appears, however, that this is not the case. Even some of the best minds that have focused on the issue do not agree on the matter. Consider the following. Dani Rodrik (1999) is relatively pessimistic about the role of FDI in development, stating: "Absent hard evidence to the contrary, one dollar's worth of FDI is worth no more (and no less) than a dollar of any other kind of investment" (p. 37). UNCTAD (1999) offers a somewhat less pessimistic view: "The role of FDI in countries' processes and efforts to meet development objectives can differ greatly across countries, depending on the nature of the economy and the government. . . . In a globalizing world economy, governments increasingly need to address the challenge of development in an open environment. FDI can play a role in meeting this challenge" (pp. 29 and 49). A somewhat more enthusiastic view has been offered by Moran (1998): "The direct and indirect benefits from well-constructed FDI projects are substantially greater than commonly assumed, but they do not come easily" (p. 153).

Can FDI generate net benefits for host countries? Yes. Does it always do so? No. The role that FDI plays in international economic development needs to be assessed on a case-by-case basis, with close attention being paid to the country characteristics, firm characteristic and strategy, and the national policy environment. Once these features have been carefully accounted for, we can begin to assess the benefits and costs of the FDI project under consideration.

Policy Stances

As a Costa Rican economic official helping your country to host a foreign MNE, you want to minimize the costs and maximize the benefits of the FDI. Attempts to achieve this are usually made through policy stances towards the MNE. These policies can be grouped into **ownership requirements** and **performance requirements**. Ownership requirements may be absolute as in the case of foreign firms being excluded from certain sectors on national security grounds. Mexico has done this in its

Ownership requirements
A limit placed on the degree of foreign ownership of firms by a country's government.

Performance requirements
A large host of measures placed on the performance of multinational enterprises by a government. A subset of these is known as trade-related investment measures.

---

[8] For an introduction to some of these cultural issues, see Adler (2002) and Lewis (2002).

petroleum sector, for example. Alternatively, they may simply limit foreign ownership to a maximum specified amount. For example, China once limited foreign enterprises to joint ventures with Chinese firms in which the foreign firm could own a maximum of fifty percent of the venture.[9]

Performance requirements place controls on the behavior of the foreign firm in a number of areas. For example, a host country might require that the MNE maintain a minimum level of locally-sourced intermediate inputs. This is known as a local content requirement. Other performance requirements can include requirements in the areas of training, technology transfer, exports, local research and development, and the hiring of local managers. These matters are usually settled in negotiations between the host-country government and the foreign MNE. Most East Asian countries have used performance requirements focused on local content and export performance. However, some Latin American countries (e.g., Argentina, Chile, Colombia, Mexico, and Venezuela) have significantly relaxed their performance requirements over time.

Trade-related investment measures
A subset of performance requirements, including export requirements and domestic content requirements, some of which are now prohibited by the World Trade Organization.

Many of these requirements are also known as **trade-related investment measures (TRIMs)** and are listed in Table 21.3. The Marrakesh Agreement on Trade in Goods (see Chapter 7) included an Agreement on TRIMs. This agreement prohibits some types of TRIMs in the case of goods. These include domestic content, trade balancing, foreign exchange balancing, and domestic sales requirements. Export performance requirements were *not* prohibited. Investment-related policies in services are covered under the General Agreement on Trade in Services (GATS) (again see Chapter 7). Many international economic policy experts are now calling for policies that would go beyond TRIMs to require the abandonment of all policies that discriminate between domestic and foreign firms. We take up this issue in a discussion of institutional considerations.

Export processing zone (EPZ)
An area of a host country in which multinational enterprises can locate and in which they enjoy, in return for exporting the whole of their output, favorable treatment in the areas of infrastructure, taxation, tariffs on imported intermediate goods, and labor costs.

Another policy stance toward hosting MNEs is to set up an **export processing zone (EPZ)**. An EPZ is an area of the host country in which MNEs can locate and in which they enjoy, in return for exporting the whole of their output, favorable treatment in the areas of infrastructure, taxation, tariffs on imported intermediate goods, and labor costs. EPZs have been a popular policy and used in many countries around the world. Indeed, some estimates suggest that there are over 500 EPZs in over 70 host countries.[10] In most cases, EPZs involve relatively labor-intensive, "light" manufacturing such as textiles, clothing, footwear, and electronics. A number of studies have tried to assess EPZs from the benefit and cost framework of Table 21.1.[11] These studies show that in many (but not all) cases, the benefits do outweigh the costs. For example, Jayanthakumaran (2003) assessed EPZs in China, Indonesia, Malaysia, the Philippines, South Korea, and Sri Lanka. He concluded that the EPZs were an important source of employment in all six of these countries. Also, in all but the Philippines, the benefits outweighed the costs. In the case of the Philippines, the infrastructure cost in setting up the EPZ was too high for a net positive benefit.

---

[9] Recall the example of Beijing Jeep in Chapter 9.
[10] See Schrank (2001) and references therein.
[11] See, for example, Johansson and Nilsson (1997), Schrank (2001), and Jayanthakumaran (2003).

Table 21.3 Types of Trade-Related Investment Measures

Measure	Explanation	WTO Legal?
Local content requirement	Requires that a certain amount of local input be used in production.	No
Trade balancing requirement	Requires that import be a certain proportion of exports.	No
Foreign exchange balancing requirement	Requires that use of foreign exchange for importing be a certain proportion of exports and the foreign exchange brought into the host country by the firm.	No
Domestic sales requirement	Requires that a proportion of output be sold locally.	No
Manufacturing requirement	Requires that certain products be manufactured locally.	
Manufacturing restriction	Prohibits the manufacturing of certain products in the host country.	
Export performance requirement	Requires that a certain share of output be exported.	
Exchange restriction	Limits a firm's access to foreign exchange.	
Technology transfer requirement	Requires that certain technologies be transferred or that certain R&D functions be performed locally.	
Licensing requirement	Requires that the foreign firm license certain technologies to local firms.	
Remittance restriction	Limits the right of the foreign firm to repatriate profits.	
Local equity requirement	Restricts the amount of a firm's equity that can be held by local investors.	

Note: A blank in the final column indicates that the measure was not specifically mentioned in the Annex of the TRIMs Agreement.

Source: Low, P. and Subramanian, A. (1996). "Beyond TRIMs: A Case for Multilateral Action on Investment Rules and Competition Policy?" in W. Martin and L.A. Winters, eds., *The Uruguay Round and the Developing Countries*, Cambridge: Cambridge University Press. 380-408.

It is not clear that the policies measures presented in Table 21.3 can always be counted on to shift the effects of hosting MNEs away from costs and towards benefits.[12] There is, however, accumulating evidence that net

---

[12]Balasubramanyam (1991), however, made a case for local content and local equity requirement, and Moran (1998) makes a case for export performance requirements.

benefits can be gained by promoting *linkages* between foreign MNEs and host-country firms. These linkages are also important to securing the success of EPZs. It is therefore worth our while to examine linkage promotion in some detail.

Promoting Linkages

Backward linkages
The purchase of goods from local suppliers by foreign multinational enterprises.

One way of maximizing the benefits of FDI in the areas of employment and technology is through facilitating the use of local suppliers on the part of the foreign MNE. Particularly in developing countries, these **backward linkages** have historically been weak. For example, Battat, Frank, and Shen (1996) report that U.S. MNEs operating for export assembly in Northern Mexico (known as *maquiladoras*) source only 2 percent of their inputs from Mexican firms. This is of concern from the Mexican point of view because the increased use of local firms as sources of intermediate products would increase their levels of employment and support their technological development. The increased role of MNEs in an economy without significant backward linkages results in what are termed "enclaves" with little connection to the rest of the economy and little contribution beyond direct employment effects. Traditionally, the means to avoid enclave FDI was via the local content requirements discussed in the previous section.

Some new thinking in the area of facilitating backward linkages suggests that local content requirements should be replaced by efforts to support local suppliers in their efforts to secure contracts with foreign MNEs. If a foreign MNE can be induced to source inputs locally rather than by importing them, the host country can gain a number of important benefits:

1. *Employment can increase because the sourced inputs are new production.*
2. *The balance of payments can improve because the inputs will no longer be imported.*
3. *Production technologies can be better adapted to local conditions.*
4. *The tangible and intangible assets we discussed in Chapter 10 can be, to some degree at least, passed from the foreign MNE to the local, host-country suppliers. Such a transfer can have significant benefits for both the foreign MNE and the local suppliers because, as we discussed in Chapter 11, local suppliers can coalesce into a spatial cluster that supports innovation and upgrading.*

This last potential benefit has been emphasized by Battat, Frank, and Shen (1996):[13]

Rapid changes in design and technology have made it necessary to make more frequent modifications of inputs at all stages of production. In such cases, subcontracting based on a long-term consultative or networked

---

[13]See also Lim and Fong (1982) on the case of Singapore.

relationship becomes more desirable. . . . While price competitiveness is still important, the ability of the supplier to react quickly to the manufacturer's changing design and production needs has often become an even more crucial factor than price. This form of backward linkage is of particular interest to developing countries because it makes the relationship between suppliers of inputs and the company purchasing the inputs more stable than the relationship between suppliers of off-the-shelf goods and the purchasers of such goods. This stability, in turn, helps suppliers to make better planning and technological decisions. The relationship typically requires intensive interchange between buyers and suppliers, and encourages technology transfer, managerial training, and the sharing of market information between suppliers and buyers (p. 5).

The key policy question for developing countries is how to foster backward linkages between foreign MNEs and potential local suppliers. The linkage promotion process involves many players, including the government, the foreign MNEs, the local suppliers, professional organizations, commercial organizations, and academic institutions. The key role of the government is one of coordination, attempting to bridge the "information gaps" among the players. The government can do this in a number of different ways:[14]

1. *In the realm of information, attempts can be made to provide a matching service between MNEs and local suppliers. This can be done by inviting the relevant players to linkage promotion forums.*
2. *In the realm of technology, efforts can be made to provide support in standards formation, materials testing, and patent registration. For example, these have been some of the functions of the Singapore Institute of Standards and Industrial Research. In addition, foreign MNEs can be invited to be involved in programs designed to upgrade local suppliers' technological capabilities.*
3. *In the realm of human resource development, efforts can be made to provide technical training and managerial training. For example, these have been some of the functions of the Taiwanese China Productivity Center.*
4. *In the area of finance, obstacles to access on the part of small firms can be removed. For example, this has been one of the functions of the Korean Technology Banking Corporation.*

Efforts in these and other areas typically must be coordinated by a lead agency. In the case of Singapore, the Singapore Economic Development Board has played this role. As mentioned in the introduction, in the case of Costa Rica, the Costa Rican Investment Board has played this role. In the case of Ireland, a National Linkage Program under the direction of the Industrial Development Agency has played this role. A case study of the Irish success in this endeavor is given in the box.

---

[14]See Battat, Frank, and Shen (1996) and United Nations Development Program (2001).

Foreign Direct Investment in Ireland[15]

A friend of mine, who grew up in Ireland in the 1970s, told me that, as a child and teenager, he had one major ambition: to emigrate. Even as of the mid-1980s, Ireland was recognized as a fairly poor country and was plagued with a number of serious difficulties: declining employment, high levels of emigration, and rapidly-rising levels of debt. At that time, a number of government agencies and business incentive programs were created in an attempt to curb the country's economic stagnation. Particular attention was placed on FDI, and by 1996, some 1,200 foreign-based companies had established manufacturing facilities in the country.

Included in these efforts was the world's oldest free trade zone (FTZ), the Shannon Free Trade Zone, which met with great success. The positive outcome of the Shannon FTZ inspired the creation of the International Financial Services Center (IFSC) in the capital city of Dublin in 1987. The establishment of the IFSC was an attempt at urban renewal in which a 75-acre dockside site in the heart of Dublin was converted into an attractive business center. Today, more than 700 financial services companies have located in the IFSC, operating in the following five areas: funds management, insurance, reinsurance, and captive insurance; treasury operations and general banking services; corporate lending; asset finance; and securities trading.

In coordinating efforts to support the IFSC, the Industrial Development Authority of Ireland (IDA Ireland) has played a key role. The government also supported the IFSC with a state-of-the-art telecommunications network and an educated workforce. World Bank data show that Ireland spends a larger portion of its GNP on education (over 6 percent) than other EU countries except Denmark, Norway, and Sweden.

Ireland's economic growth rates during the decade of the 1990s were often on par with those of East Asia, and in May 1998 Ireland was one of the 11 countries of the European Union selected for inclusion in the European Monetary Union (EMU). Success in hosting MNEs contributed significantly to these positive changes in the Irish economy. Emigration is no longer the prime goal of talented, young Irish citizens.

Sources: McCann FitzGerald (1995, 1997); World Bank (1999).

Transfer Pricing

Transfer pricing
The manipulation of the prices of intra-firm trade by multinational enterprises to reduce their global tax payments.

There is a common practice among MNEs that can, in some circumstances, be detrimental to the countries hosting them. This practice is known as **transfer pricing**. Transfer pricing problems arise from the fact that MNEs are global corporations, whereas tax systems are locally defined. MNEs can therefore adjust the *internal* pricing of their intra-firm trade to shift declared profits of subsidiaries to low-tax countries. The goal is to maximize the post-tax profits of the firm. Consider, for example, a vertically integrated MNE producing copper. Perhaps this MNE mines the copper in an African country and engages in some elementary processing of the ore in that country. The ore is then exported and is further processed in the MNE's home country. This is an example of intra-firm trade, discussed in Chapter 10. The price of the partially-processed ore exported out of the African country is therefore an intra-firm price. Consequently, the firm

---

[15]M.G. Evans contributed to the material in this box.

can pay an artificially low price for the copper ore in the country, reducing its profits and tax obligations there. Given the administrative and enforcement resources, the African country could require the firm to pay world prices for the ore, but resources in most African countries are very scarce. MNEs also have the option of artificially inflating its costs in the African country. As explained by one author: "One simple way to transfer money out of a country is to send a management team on a visit (holiday) and then charge a large amount for their services" (Baker, 1995, p. 466n). In this situation, the gains from trade described in Chapters 2 and 3 may not appear for the African country.[16]

The solution to the transfer pricing problem is multifaceted. Dunning (1993, Chapter 18) provides a good review. Although unilateral policy options exist, "because there is competition for MNE activity between home and host countries, and between different host countries, the opportunities for MNEs to play one nation against another are enhanced without the establishment of supranational institutions and harmonized intergovernmental action towards (transfer pricing)" (p. 523). Options include international guidelines and codes of conduct, international standardization of invoicing and customs procedures, global tax harmonization, negotiating and concluding international conventions, and the establishment of international arbitration procedures. For many developing countries, however, resources may need to be provided for them to effectively combat transfer pricing abuses.

Institutional Considerations

As we have seen in Chapters 7 and 16, institutions governing international trade and international finance exist in the form of the GATT/WTO and the IMF. No such counterpart exists in the realm of international production. Indeed, as stated by Serra et al. (1997), "The existing legal framework for foreign direct investment is exceedingly complex and difficult to understand" (p. 37). For example, there are over 1,600 bilateral investment treaties (BITs) among the countries of the world.[17] These numerous agreement, plus many agreements that comprise parts the regional trade agreements (RTAs) discussed in Chapter 8, result in a confusing institutional framework for international production.

One organization promoting multinational approaches to FDI has been the Paris-based Organization for Economic Cooperation and Development (OECD). OECD-sponsored agreements include the 1961 Code of Liberalization of Capital Movements and the 1976 Declaration of International Investment and Multinational Enterprises. In 1991, the OECD tried to develop a comprehensive set of investment rules but failed. In the annual meeting of June 1995, OECD ministers announced the beginning of a second effort, this time to develop a Multilateral Agreement on Investment or MAI. Discussions among OECD ministers began in September 1995. The

---

[16]The problems caused by transfer pricing for African countries are discussed in Barratt Brown and Tiffen (1992).
[17]See *The Economist* (1998).

purpose of the agreement was to liberalize the cross-border flows of foreign direct investment. It would have required host countries to apply "national treatment" to all foreign firms. This would prevent host countries from implementing the ownership and performance requirements discussed earlier in this chapter. However, the OECD consists of fewer than 30, mostly high-income countries, and is hardly representative of WTO and IMF membership.[18] Consequently, despite a 140-page draft text, the hoped-for signing of the MAI in 1998 did not occur.

Despite the efforts by India and Malaysia to oppose the MAI, it would be a mistake to blame its failure on the reluctance of developing countries alone. France, Canada, the European Union, and the United States all advanced exceptions to the MAI draft text. Indeed, these exceptions exceeded the MAI draft text in page length. In addition, labor and environmental groups protested against the absence of standards in the draft MAI.

It is now clear that any further progress in this area should take place under the auspices of the World Trade Organization (WTO) in future multilateral trade negotiations. The WTO possesses a number of advantages over the OECD. First, it has a much more representative membership in comparison to the OECD. Second, it is very experienced in developing and managing complicated negotiations and rules. Third, as discussed in Chapter 7, it has a dispute settlement mechanism already in place. Fourth, some argue that given the close links between trade and investment, the WTO is a natural venue.[19] Fifth, because WTO negotiations include large numbers of issues simultaneously, there is more scope for compromises and trade-offs between issues. Finally, if WTO members are unable to agree on a new investment framework, the option exists of developing a plurilateral agreement, which only a subset of members would sign.[20]

All of these considerations lead to the conclusion that the institutional environment for FDI needs to be addressed by the WTO and its members in future negotiations. Whether this will indeed be the case remains to be seen, however. Although a working group on the issue was established at the 1996 WTO ministerial meeting in Singapore, it was not possible to establish a negotiating group at the 1999 ministerial in Seattle. Work on this issue then, has been confined to the working group. In a detailed review of this issue, Hoekman and and Saggi (2000) see no compelling reason for further negotiations in this area.[21]

---

[18]*The Economist* (1998) reported: "Few developing countries seemed prepared to sign something they did not help to shape. Instead, the governments of developing countries increasingly see MAI as an exercise in neo-colonialism, designed to give rich-world investors the upper hand" (p. 81).

[19]For an alternative, developing country view of this matter, see Khor (1996).

[20]The Marrakesh Agreement establishing the WTO contains an Annex 4 of plurilateral agreements to which members are not required to adhere. Graham (1996) writes: "All of the nations that would sign an OECD agreement would presumably also sign such a plurilateral agreement, and some nations not party to the OECD agreement might sign on as well. In such a case, a plurilateral WTO agreement would definitely be preferable to an OECD-only agreement" (p. 104).

[21]Because Hoekman is a previous WTO official and currently heads the international trade research group at the World Bank, this conclusion holds some weight.

Conclusion

What do you, imagining yourself as a Costa Rican government official, take from this chapter? Most importantly, you understand that inward FDI into your country can both provide benefits and impose costs on a host country. These benefits and costs occur in the areas of employment, competition, education and training, technology, balance of payments, health and the environment, and culture. You can potentially manage the investment process through ownership and performance requirements. However, a more effective means of maximizing the benefits of inward FDI might be through the support of domestic suppliers linked to foreign MNEs in long-term relationships. The institutional structure governing the FDI process in the world economy is not well developed. Despite efforts on the part of the OECD to resolve this issue, it is really the WTO that would provide the best location for a multilateral or plurilateral agreement on investment. Such an agreement remains a possible future task for WTO members.

Review Exercises

1. Table 21.1 lists a set of benefits and costs of hosting foreign MNEs in the areas of employment, competition, education and training, technology, balance of payments, health and the environment, and culture. Are there any additional benefits and costs that you think are important? Are there additional considerations that a host government should address before hosting foreign MNEs?

2. In this chapter, we discussed the problem of transfer pricing. Relate this discussion to the benefits and costs of hosting foreign MNEs, as well as to the Chapter 10 discussion of intra-industry trade and multinational value networks.

3. The Agreement on Trade-Related Investment Measures (TRIMs) of the Marrakesh Agreement requires WTO members to phase out local content requirements. Do you think this is a good idea? Why or why not?

4. The final section of this chapter states that the WTO, rather than the OECD, should be the organization overseeing a multilateral agreement on investment. Do you agree? Why or why not?

Further Reading and Web Resources

A concise summary of some of the issues discussed in this chapter can be found in Chapter 7 of Hill (2000). A more expanded discussion can be found in Graham (1996) and Moran (1998). Dunning (1993) is also an excellent reference for the material of this chapter. In particular, see his Chapter 11 on technology transfer, Chapter 13 on human capital, Chapter 14 on the balance of payments, Chapter 15 on competition issues, Chapter 16 on linkages, and Chapter 19 on environmental and cultural issues. Discussions of linkage issues can be found in Battat, Frank, and Shen (1996), Reinert (1998), and United Nations Conference on Trade and Development (2001).

The OECD maintains a Web site at **http://www.oecd.org**. It provides materials on its activities in the area of international investment. The United Nations Conference on Trade and Development (UNCTAD) publishes an annual *World Investment Report*. This is a good place to turn for data on and discussion of FDI from a developing country point of view. Their Web site is **http://www.unctad.org**. The *World Investment Report* is at **http://www.unctad.org/wir**.

References

Adler, N.J. (2002) *International Dimensions of Organizational Behavior*, South-Western Thomson Learning, Cincinnati.

Baker, S.A. (1995) *International Economics*, Blackwell, Oxford.

Balasubramanyam, V.N. (1991) "Putting TRIMs to Good Use," *World Development*, 19:9, 1215–1224.

Barratt Brown, M., and P. Tiffen (1992) *Short Changed: Africa and World Trade*, Pluto Press, London.

Battat, J., I. Frank, and X. Shen (1996) *Suppliers to Multinationals: Linkage Programs to Strengthen Local Companies in Developing Countries*, Foreign Investment Advisory Service, The World Bank, Washington, DC.

Caves, R.E. (1974) "Multinational Firms, Competition, and Productivity in Host-Country Markets," *Economica*, 41:162, 176–193.

Dunning, J.H. (1993) *Multinational Enterprises and the Global Economy*, Addison-Wesley, Workingham.

The Economist (1998) "The Sinking of the MAI," March 14, 81–82.

The Economist (1995) "The Cost of Bananas," September 16, 54.

Graham, E.M. (1996) *Global Corporations and National Governments*, Institute for International Economics, Washington, DC.

Haddad, M., and A. Harrison (1993) "Are There Positive Spillovers from Direct Foreign Investment? Evidence from Panel Data for Morocco," *Journal of Development Economics*, 42: 1, 51–74.

Hill, C.W.L. (2000) *International Business: Competing in the Global Marketplace*, Irwin McGraw-Hill, Boston.

Hoekman, B., and K. Saggi (2000) "Assessing the Case for Extending WTO Disciplines on Investment-Related Policies," *Journal of Economic Integration*, 15:4, 629–653.

Jayanthakumaran, K. (2003) "Benefit-Cost Appraisals of Export Processing Zones: A Survey of the Literature," *Development Policy Review*, 21:1, 51–65.

Johansson, H., and L. Nilsson (1997) "Export Processing Zones as Catalysts," *World Development*, 25:12, 2115–2128.

Kane, J. (1996) *Savages*, Vintage, New York.

Khor, M. (1996) "The WTO and Foreign Investment: Implications and Alternatives for Developing Countries," *Development in Practice*, 6:4, 304–314.

Kokko, A., R. Tansini, and M.C. Zehan (1996) "Local Technological Capability and Productivity Spillovers from FDI in the Uruguayan Manufacturing Sector," *Journal of Development Studies*, 32:4, 602–611.

Lewis, R.D. (2002) *The Cultural Imperative: Global Trends in the 21st Century*, Intercultural Press, Yarmouth, Maine.

Lim, L.Y.C., and P.E. Fong (1982) "Vertical Linkages and Multinational Enterprises in Developing Countries," *World Development*, 10:7, 585–595.

Low, P., and A. Subramanian (1996) "Beyond TRIMs: A Case for Multilateral Action on Investment Rules and Competition Policy?" in W. Martin and L.A. Winters (eds.), *The Uruguay Round and the Developing Countries*, Cambridge University Press, Cambridge, 1996, 380–408.

McCann FitzGerald (1997) *Dublin's International Financial Services Centre: A Guide to the Legal, Regulatory and Taxation Issues Affecting Companies*, Dublin.

McCann FitzGerald (1995) *Dublin's International Financial Services Centre: A Guide to Funds Management Operations*, Dublin.

Meier, G.M. (1995) *Leading Issues in Economic Development*, Oxford University Press, Oxford.

Moran, T.H. (1998) *Foreign Direct Investment and Development, Institute for International Economics*, Washington, DC.

Reinert, K.A. (1998) "Whither the Linkage Concept? External Economies and Firm Networks," *Science, Technology and Development*, 16:3, 77–91.

Rodrik, D. (1999) *The New Global Economy and Developing Countries: Making Openness Work*, Overseas Development Council, Washington, DC.

Schrank, A. (2001) "Export Processing Zones: Free Market Islands or Bridges to Structural Transformation?" *Development Policy Review*, 19:2, 223–242.

Serra, J., et al. (1997) *Reflections on Regionalism*, Carnegie Endowment for International Peace, New York.

Sheahan, J. (1987) *Patterns of Development in Latin America*, Princeton University Press, Princeton.

United Nations Conference on Trade and Development (2001) *World Investment Report*, Geneva.

United Nations Conference on Trade and Development (1999) *World Investment Report*, Geneva.

World Bank (1999) *World Development Report 1998/99*, Washington, DC.

The World Bank

22

The late 1970s was a calamitous time for the Ghanaian economy: Agricultural and industrial output stagnated, budget deficits and inflation rates increased substantially, a fixed exchange rate regime began to generate foreign exchange shortages, and Nigeria expelled one million Ghanaian citizens, sending them back to Ghana. The political situation deteriorated as well. Flight lieutenant Jerry Rawlings brought the Armed Forces Revolutionary Council to power in a coup in June 1979. This government gave way to a democratically elected president in September, but Rawlings overthrew this government in December 1981. He assumed chairmanship of the Provisional National Defense Council (PNDC) and became head of state. Despite the brutal and undemocratic nature of the Rawlings regime, the International Monetary Fund and the World Bank, herein referred to as the Bank, began negotiations with it in September 1982. These negotiations led to an official recovery and adjustment program that began in 1983. This was the start of a long relationship between Ghana and both the IMF and World Bank, which lasts to this day. In the 1980s, Ghana became known as the World Bank's "star pupil," and Rawlings the father of Ghana's "economic miracle." Today, the star's shine is somewhat diminished.[1]

You have a good understanding of the IMF from reading Chapter 16, but what about the World Bank? This institution sits across 19th Street in Washington, DC, from the IMF, and is equally important. As we mentioned in Chapters 7 and 16, both institutions grew out of the Bretton Woods conference held in July 1944 in the wake of World War II. In the current chapter, we take up the **World Bank**, or more precisely, the **World Bank Group**, in earnest. We begin in the following section by considering the early history of the World Bank in its infrastructure project lending and poverty reduction lending phases. We then discuss the shift of the Bank to a policy-based lending phase and the application of this approach to Ghana. Finally, we consider recent modifications to policy-based lending within the Bank.

Along with the IMF, the World Bank is a controversial institution. Both of these organizations are targets of increasingly disruptive protests during their annual joint meetings by a host of groups dedicated to their "radical reform." I hope that this chapter provides you with a balanced, historical assessment of the Bank that is critical but informed, and that it helps you to form your own opinions about this important institution.

World Bank
An international organization founded in 1944 by the Bretton Woods conference. It was originally designed to assist in the reconstruction of postwar Europe but quickly became a lender to developing countries in support of development projects and structural adjustment. The World Bank actually consists of the International Bank for Reconstruction and Development and the International Development Association.

World Bank Group
A collection of five organizations: the International Bank for Reconstruction and Development; the International Development Association; the International Finance Corporation; the International Center for Settlement of Investment Disputes; and the Multilateral Investment Guarantee Agency.

---

[1] See *The Economist* (2002).

Early History and Administrative Structure

In November 1943, U.S. Treasury Secretary Henry Morgenthau proposed via memorandum a "United Nations Bank for Reconstruction and Development." As in the case of the U.S. proposal for the International Monetary Fund discussed in Chapter 16, U.S. Treasury official Harry Dexter White was the main author of the Bank proposal. Some months later, in April 1944, the British briefly responded to this proposal, and the two countries entered into the Bretton Woods conference in July of that year, ready to discuss the creation of such a bank. The Bretton Woods conference initially focused on the IMF, but in response to the concerns of countries damaged by the war, as well as of less developed countries, a group was finally constituted to work on the Bank under the supervision of John Maynard Keynes.[2]

The discussion at Bretton Woods focused on the relative roles of postwar reconstruction (emphasized by the European countries) and economic development (emphasized by the developing countries). The ensuing Articles of Agreement of the International Bank for Reconstruction and Development (IBRD) left room for both activities, although, as we shall see, attention was first given to reconstruction. The IBRD was the first of five components of what was later to be called the World Bank Group (see Figure 22.1). We will introduce the other components as we continue through this section of the chapter.

The IBRD's Articles of Agreement set out the purposes of the institution:

1. *To promote loans to assist in the reconstruction and development of countries*
2. *To promote private foreign investment*
3. *To promote long-term "balanced growth of international trade and the maintenance of equilibrium in balances of payments"*
4. *To operate "with due regard to the effects of international investment on business conditions in the territories of members"*

IBRD membership is confined to countries that are already members of the IMF. Therefore, *IMF membership is a prerequisite for IBRD membership.* The capital stock of the Bank is based on members' subscription shares, which, in turn, are based on the members' quotas in the IMF. Upon joining it, a member pays 10 percent of its subscription, and the remaining 90 percent is "callable". The funds from which the Bank makes loans come from a number of sources: members' subscription shares, retained earnings on investments, bond issues, and loan repayments.[3] The main source of funds, however, is bond issues. IBRD bonds achieved a "triple A" rating in the mid-1950s and have held this rating since then.

---

[2] We mentioned Keynes' role in negotiating the IMF agreement in Chapter 16. We also utilized his theory of money demand in the appendices to Chapters 14 and 15. Keynes chaired the Bretton Woods commission that established the World Bank; Harry Dexter White chaired the commission that established the IMF. Skidelsky (2000) notes: "White's aim in making Keynes chairman of the Bank Commission was to neutralize him. . . . If he could keep him occupied on Bank business, he would have no energy or time left for Fund business. The strategy worked" (p. 349).

[3] The fact that the IBRD borrows on world capital markets is one major characteristic distinguishing it from the IMF.

Figure 22.1 The Components of the World Bank Group

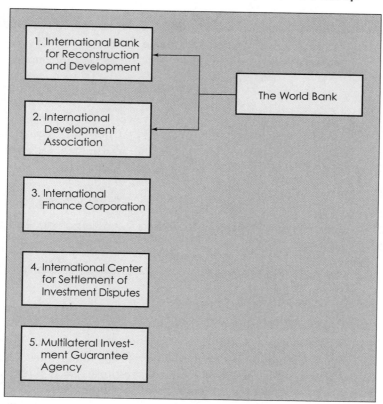

The World Bank's organization and management are summarized in Table 22.1. As with the IMF, its major decision-making body is its Board of Governors to which each member appoints a Governor and an Alternate Governor. An Executive Board, comprised of 24 Executive Directors and the Bank President, conducts the day-to-day business of the Bank. Five Bank members with the largest capital shares appoint five of the Directors. Governors representing various groups of other countries elect the remaining Directors. The President chairs the Executive Board and is ultimately subject to its control. Traditionally, the President is a U.S. citizen appointed by the executive branch of the U.S. government.[4] Recall from Chapter 16 that the Executive Director of the IMF has traditionally been a European. In staffing these two positions, then, the major Bretton Woods actors ensured their subsequent control of the Bretton Woods institutions (BWIs).

The IBRD opened in June 1946 with an initial subscription capitalization of $10 billion.[5] The balance between reconstruction and development

---

[4] "Once it was conceded that the president should be a U.S. national, the task of finding a candidate acceptable at the highest levels of U.S. government and in the U.S. financial community inevitably devolved upon the executive branch of the U.S. government" (Mason and Asher, 1973, p. 89).
[5] Keynes had died two months earlier.

Table 22.1 Administrative Structure of the World Bank

Body	Composition	Function
Board of Governors	One Governor and one Alternate Governor for each member	Meets annually; highest decision-making body
Executive Board	24 Executive Directors plus President	Day-to-day operations; approve loans and bond issues
President	Traditionally U.S. citizen	Chair of Executive Board; responsible for staffing and general business
Vice President		Assists President
Advisor Council	Appointed by Board of Governors	Advises on general policy matters
Staff	Citizens of members	Run departments of Bank

Sources: Adapted from Mason and Asher (1973) and Salda (1995).

tilted quickly toward reconstruction. The first set of loans went to France, the Netherlands, Denmark, and Luxembourg. These loans were funded by the United States and were used primarily to purchase U.S. exports. The tilt towards reconstruction was soon offset by the introduction of the U.S. Marshall Plan and European Recovery Program, which surpassed the resources of the World Bank and IMF.[6] Subsequent to these programs, the IBRD made loans to Chile, Mexico, and Brazil. The Bank's first bond issue in July 1947 quickly traded at a premium over the offer price. The IBRD was on its way to a respectable position in U.S. and world capital markets. In September 1959, the Bank's subscription capital more than doubled to $21 billion.

In 1956, the IBRD Executive Directors created the International Finance Corporation (IFC) and followed in 1960 with the International Development Association (IDA). These two organizations became the second and third components of the World Bank Group (see Figure 22.1). Importantly (and unfortunately from the standpoint of countries with small Bank shares), these institutions were not created via a process of international consultation as in the case of the IMF and IBRD.[7]

The IFC is very different from the IBRD. IBRD loans require guarantee of repayment by borrowing-country governments. This is not the case for the IFC, whose purpose is to encourage productive *private* enterprise in less developed countries, supplementing the activities of the IBRD. The IFC has its own staff, although some of these individuals also hold posi-

---

[6] Recall our discussion of this in Chapter 16.
[7] See Mason and Asher (1973), p. 79.

tions in the Bank. Membership in the IFC is contingent upon membership in the Bank and, therefore, upon membership in the IMF. Initially, the IFC encountered difficulties because, despite being limited to private projects, it was excluded from equity investments. This stipulation was later relaxed with an equity ceiling of 25 percent.

The IDA is very different from the IFC. It can be seen as a "soft loan" version of the IBRD. The IDA and IBRD share staff and officers and together comprise what has come to be known as the World Bank (see Figure 22.1). Indeed, the IDA is often called a "fiction" because it is really a special fund or "window" of the World Bank. The official purpose of the IDA is to promote economic development and raise living standards by providing loans on terms that are significantly more flexible than the IBRD. More specifically, the IDA provides no-interest loans for long time periods (35–40 years) with significant grace periods (10 years).[8] Unlike the IBRD, the IDA is primarily dependent on contributions from high-income member countries. Occasionally, this causes problems when appropriated funds are not delivered when promised.

In 1966, the fourth member of the World Bank Group was added (see Figure 22.1). The International Center for Settlement of Investment Disputes (ICSID) provides arbitration between foreign investors and host-country governments. In previous years, the Bank had been called upon to mediate in such disputes, and Bank officials thought that the presence and operation of the ICSID would support the flow of FDI into developing countries. The Administrative Council of the ICSID is chaired by the President of the World Bank and meets annually. Recall from Chapter 21 that many developing countries have concluded bilateral investment treaties (BITs) with other countries. Many of these BITs explicitly include advance consents to utilize the ICSID in the case of disputes. So do some regional trade agreements (RTAs) such as NAFTA and Mercosur.

In 1988, the final member of the World Bank Group was introduced. This was the Multilateral Investment Guarantee Agency (MIGA) (see Figure 22.1). The purpose of MIGA is to encourage the flow of FDI to developing countries, a process we analyzed in Chapter 21. To support this aim, MIGA engages in three kinds of activities. First, it issues guarantees against noncommercial risks in recipient member countries. Specifically, MIGA insures against transfer restriction, expropriation, breach of contract, and war and civil disturbance. Second, it engages in investment marketing through capacity building, information dissemination, and investment facilitation. Third, it provides a host of legal services to World Bank member countries to support FDI. In this last function, MIGA engages in activities somewhat similar to that of the ICSID.[9]

With a current subscription capitalization of approximately $180 billion and a staff of approximately 10,000, the World Bank Group has become a

---

[8] As has been stated by Mason and Asher (1973): "Prior to the establishment of the IDA a number of poor countries to which the Bank had loaned extensively were considered to have about reached the limits of their ability to absorb and service foreign loans on Bank terms" (p. 117).
[9] See Shihata (1986) for an early comparison of the MIGA and the ICSID.

powerful institution in the world economy. Its main purpose is to productively transfer resources to its developing country members to enhance economic and human development. Given its role in development finance and its promotion of FDI and trade liberalization, it is fair to say that the World Bank is involved in all four of our windows on the world economy (see Figure 1.3 in Chapter 1), trying to promote positive linkages among them. The rest of this chapter is dedicated to your understanding of the history of the Bank's policies and the way it has attempted to influence development processes around the globe.

Infrastructure Project Lending and Poverty Alleviation Phases

In its early years, the IBRD directed its efforts toward large-scale infrastructure projects. This could be called its *infrastructure project lending phase*. The projects funded by the Bank included ports, railways, flood control, power plants, roads, telecommunications facilities, and dams. Additionally, project lending was often accompanied by "program lending" (or "nonproject lending"), which helped to finance the importation of intermediate products necessary for infrastructure projects. Missing, however, was any lending in the social realm such as for education, health, agricultural development, or urban planning, although the IDA focused more on agriculture than did the IBRD. Some observers attributed this lack of attention to the social realm to a belief that large-scale infrastructure was a prerequisite for development; others attributed it to a reluctance to disturb the capital markets with social-realm lending and, thereby, compromise the Bank's triple-A rating. There was also the observation on the part of the Bank that the large capital investments would be unlikely to be made by private capital, so the Bank should fill in the gap.

The project lending phase of the Bank's operations was tempered to some extent in the 1960s. Subsequent to severe droughts in South Asia, the Bank began to pay more attention to agriculture in cooperation with the United Nations Food and Agriculture Organization (FAO). It even began to venture into education in cooperation with the United Nations Educational, Scientific and Cultural Organization (UNESCO). Nevertheless, "between fiscal years 1961 and 1965, 76.8 percent of all Bank lending was for electric power or transportation. Only 6 percent was for agricultural development, and a paltry 1 percent for social service investment" (Ayres, 1983, pp. 2–3).

In 1968, Robert McNamara took over as World Bank president, a position he held until 1981. The McNamara presidency coincided with a second phase for the World Bank, one we can call the *poverty alleviation phase*. This phase was characterized by a focus on the eradication of absolute poverty (defined in terms of minimum incomes) through rural and urban development.[10] Within the Bank, these new ideas were operationalized via the concept of *redistribution with growth*. This idea called for the harnessing of *new* sources of income to help the poor. It avoided any

---

[10]For a recent assessment of the Bank's efforts to measure poverty levels, see Deaton (2001).

redistribution of existing incomes and assets. For example, World Bank projects did not address inequitable patterns of land ownership. In this sense, it was quite conservative and, in instances where asset redistribution was crucial to development, ineffectual.

In an important way, the redistribution with growth concept has persisted at the Bank to the present, although now it is called *shared growth*, a more accurate term. For example, the World Bank used the concept of shared growth to analyze East Asian economies (World Bank, 1993). In this case, too, it ignored the important role of asset distribution in the form of land and human capital in explaining East Asian success.[11] Nevertheless, at the time, the redistribution with growth concept did significantly affect patterns of Bank lending.

During the poverty alleviation phase, lending increased dramatically. World Bank staff increased, as did the proportion of the staff from developing countries. Subscription capital increased to $27 billion in June 1971. Perhaps most importantly, especially after 1973, lending was channeled in new directions. Agriculture and rural development, education, health, and urban development all took on increasing importance, and none of these changes appeared to hurt the financial position of the Bank *vis-à-vis* the capital markets. In the case of rural development, the notion of "projects" changed, moving towards what was called *integrated rural development*.[12] Integrated rural development involved constellations of activities focused on targeted regions of member countries. These activities included agricultural credit, roads, agricultural support services, irrigation, rural education, agricultural research and extension, and social services such as health clinics. The goal was to increase the productivity of the rural poor, but the targeted population was the small-scale, owner-operator farmer. Lending for integrated rural development had beneficial effects on these small-scale farmers, but ignored those that became known as "the poorest of the poor," namely, the rural landless agricultural workers.

Despite some limitations to alleviating absolute poverty among the landless, the integrated rural development strategy was a significant change from Bank agricultural lending under the infrastructure project lending phase, which had primarily benefited the owners of large farms. To some development policy analysts (e.g., Paarlberg and Lipton, 1991), it is a strategy unfortunately absent from subsequent Bank lending. That said, the Bank has recently taken some interest in land redistribution issues, as discussed in the box.[13]

Under its poverty alleviation phase, the Bank also began to recognize the growing importance of urban areas in developing countries and, consequently, began to focus on urban poverty. The important areas of lending were affordable housing for the poor, small-scale enterprises, water supply, sewerage, transportation, and community services (e.g., health clinics and schools). As in the case of rural development, the Bank avoided land ownership issues in urban areas. The Bank has maintained an active

---

[11]See Rodrick (1994).
[12]See Chapter 5 of Ayres (1983).
[13]For more on this issue, see the interview with Michael Lipton that follows Chapter 23.

Land Redistribution in Brazil

In 1997, the World Bank made an interesting announcement. For the first time in a half-century of operations in Brazil, it had approved a US$90 million loan to support land reform. The project, *Cédula da Terra*, was aimed at 15,000 poor and landless farmers in the northeastern states of the country. In announcing the loan, the Bank stated, "The problems associated with Brazil's land tenure are one of the most important issues affecting rural poverty in the country." Most important, indeed. Brazil has one of the most highly skewed land distributions in the world. It has been estimated that the top 5 percent of farms by size account for 70 percent of arable land, while the bottom 50 percent account for only 2 percent of arable land. The country has approximately 5 million landless peasants.

Embracing land reform was a serious break from World Bank traditions. This break was made possible by the fact that the *Cédula* project was "market-based." This term refers to a process in which landless peasants take out a loan, begin a negotiating process with landowners, and then purchase the land on the "open market." According to the World Bank, these transactions are facilitated by freely-organized, local associations of landless peasants. There is evidence, however, that these associations are actually strongly influenced by state governments, local politicians, and even the landowners themselves and that, given how underdeveloped land markets are in Brazil, prices paid by landless peasants reflect to a great degree the peasants' weak bargaining position. An independent assessment of the program commissioned by the Brazilian government found that almost one-third of the participating peasants were unaware that they had taken out a loan. One critic, Schwartzman (2000), claims: "This is in reality not a 'market-based' land reform project at all, but a land reform project that devolves responsibility for land reform from the federal government to state governments—precisely those more susceptible to pressure and manipulation of local and regional elites."

Despite such criticisms, the World Bank is pressing on with its market-based approach to land reform. It its own assessment, "First experiences confirm the expectation that beneficiaries are well capable of participating proactively in the project. Initial indications of impact in terms of family income and productivity are also highly encouraging." In late 2000, the Bank announced a continuation of the *Cédula* project in a second phase, supported by a US$200 million loan. The long-term effects of this market-based approach to land reform remain to be seen, and this will be a closely-watched area of Bank activity.

Sources: Deininger and Binswanger (1999), Franko (2003), Lindsay (2000), Schwartzman (2000).

loan portfolio in urban development up to the present, with poverty alleviation being one of many thematic areas within this lending category.

Policy-Based Lending

During the late 1970s, at the same time that flight lieutenant Jerry J. Rawlings was establishing his control over Ghana, an important change was taking place at the World Bank. As we mentioned earlier, the World Bank president is traditionally a U.S. citizen appointed by the executive branch of the U.S. government. In 1981, the Reagan administration entered into office in the United States and replaced McNamara with A.W. Clausen, a banking executive. The Reagan administration took a dim view of the poverty alleviation phase of World Bank lending and, as the largest

Bank donor, began to demand a change. With Clausen at the helm, the World Bank undertook a significant adjustment in its lending. In 1982, the year negotiations began with Ghana, Clausen stated:[14]

> *The World Bank . . . will remain a bank. And a very sound and prudent bank. It is not in the business of redistributing wealth from one set of countries to another set of countries. It is not the Robin Hood of the international financial set, nor the United Way of the development community. The World Bank is a hard headed, unsentimental institution that takes a very pragmatic . . . view of what it is trying to do.*

This statement is inaccurate in its allegation that the goal of the Bank during its poverty alleviation phase was to redistribute wealth, but it captures well the sentiment of the change in Bank lending that took place.[15] Clausen introduced what has been called the *policy-based lending phase* of the Bank, which more or less persists up the current time. This third phase of Bank lending has a number of characteristics: cofinancing, an expansion of the role of the IFC, macroconditionality, and structural adjustment lending. Let's examine each of these areas in turn.

Cofinancing

Cofinancing involves the World Bank joining with private commercial banks in making loans. The World Bank provides information to the commercial banks and encourages them to make loans that they might not have made without World Bank participation. In practice, because commercial banks have little interest in the poorest countries of the world, co-financing has often been restricted to middle-income countries.

Expanded Role of the IFC

As we mentioned earlier, the IFC's purpose is to make debt and equity investments in private enterprises in developing countries. Clausen, with the support of the Reagan administration, began to emphasize the role of the IFC relative to the other members of the World Bank Group. However, many observers have questioned whether the IFC has been able to make effective antipoverty loans to the poorest countries. For example, the IFC's investments in Africa have primarily been in the traditional extractive industries such as oil, gas, and mining, which appear to have little positive impact on poverty levels (*The Economist*, 1996).

Conditionality

Conditionality or "macroconditionality" ties Bank lending to prescribed policy changes on the part of the recipient government. In actuality, World Bank loans always carried limited conditions. The change that occurred in the 1980s was that these conditions were broadened from the sectoral or subsectoral level to the national, macroeconomic level. As we discussed in

Conditionality
Policies pursued by the World Bank and International Monetary Fund in which loans are made only to countries that promise to institute a set of prescribed policy changes.

---

[14]Address to the Yomiuri International Economic Society, Tokyo. Quoted in Ayres (1983), p. 236.
[15]"During the Clausen Presidency . . ., the McNamara interpretation of the world was largely swept aside" (Mosley, Harrigan, and Toye, 1995, pp. 23–24).

The Washington Consensus

In 1990, John Williamson of the Institute for International Economics introduced a new term into the international economic policy lexicon. The new term was "Washington consensus." At the time, the term meant to convey the "lowest common denominator" of policy advice being offered by the World Bank and the IMF. According to Williamson, this common denominator consisted of 10 policy components:

1. Fiscal discipline
2. A redirection of government expenditures to primary health care, primary education, and infrastructure
3. Tax reform
4. Financial and interest rate liberalization
5. Competitive exchange rate
6. Trade liberalization
7. Liberalization of foreign direct investment
8. Privatization
9. Deregulation
10. Secure property rights

Since 1990, the term "Washington consensus" has taken on a slightly different meaning. It has come to stand for "market fundamentalism," "neoliberal obsession," or "global laissez-faire." It has also become the target of many participants in the antiglobalization movement demonstrating at the annual Bank–Fund meetings, as well as of many in the global, nongovernmental organization community. Interestingly, Williamson himself is in disagreement

Chapter 16, the IMF also imposes conditionality on its loans. In contrast to IMF conditionality, Bank conditionality tends to be more numerous, detailed, and involve longer time horizons. There is evidence that the World Bank has shown an inability to set priorities in its conditionality, with some loan agreements involving a hundred or more conditions. Meeting this number of conditions has often been beyond the capacity of borrowing countries. Bank conditionality also tends to be more difficult to monitor than Fund conditionality. This can lead to greater amounts of negotiation in the release of additional loans from the Bank than from the Fund.

During the 1980s, the policy thinking of the Bank and Fund began to converge on a common set of conditions. As described in the box, these policy components became known in economic and international policy communities as the "Washington consensus." Consequently, the Washington consensus became intimately associated with the policy-based lending phase of the Bank.

Structural adjustment lending (SAL)
Nonproject lending of the World Bank to support adjustment in the face of balance of payments difficulties. Based on policy conditionality.

Structural Adjustment Lending

Structural adjustment lending (SAL) began in 1980 under McNamara's leadership at the Bank and currently accounts for approximately one-fourth of Bank lending despite an initial plan to limit it to 10

with "market fundamentalism," stating, "I would not subscribe to the view that such policies offer an effective agenda for reducing poverty." What, then, is Williamson's position?

First, Williamson now repudiates the financial and interest rate liberalization component included in the previous list, recognizing that such liberalization can contribute to financial instability (see Chapter 23). Second, Williamson is opposed to the across-the-board liberalization of capital accounts supported, at least until recently, by the IMF. Third, as we discussed in Chapter 17, Williamson is opposed to both the purely flexible exchange rate regimes and to currency boards, both (intriguingly) often advocated by supporters of "market fundamentalism." Instead, he supports exchange rate target zones. Fourth, with regard to the components of privatization and deregulation, his policy proposals are rather nuanced. He only favors privatization if it is carried out in a manner that prevents the transfer of formerly state-owned enterprises to a narrow group of elites, and he is indeed in favor of many types of government regulation. He only calls for the deregulation of entry and exit barriers, not the "rollback of the state" called for by many market fundamentalists.

Despite these qualifications, doubts about the Washington consensus still exist (e.g., Naím, 2000). It would be fair to say that many development economists (as opposed to international economists) would find it lacking as a development strategy. Even among international economists, there is disagreement about its appropriateness as a guide to effective policy. The idea, however, persists in many debates in the development policy arena.

Sources: Naím (2000), Williamson (1990, 2000).

percent.[16] It involves *nonproject* lending to support adjustment in the face of balance of payments difficulties and includes the conditionality component described earlier.[17] In the words of an early SAL advocate:

> *Structural adjustment lending is intended to assist governments to adopt necessary, though often politically difficult, policy and institutional reforms designed to improve the efficiency of resource use. By focusing on the policy and institutional reforms required to correct distortions in the pattern of incentives and to adapt each economy to the changed international price structure and trading opportunities, structural adjustment lending also helps create a more appropriate environment for the Bank's project lending. In this way, the two forms of assistance are complementary, not alternatives (Stern, 1983, p. 89).*

The Bank's SAL has been controversial for a number of reasons. First, SAL begins to encroach upon the work of the IMF. Some have argued that, in contrast to the IMF's fundamentally short-term and macroeconomic focus, the Bank's SAL has a medium-term and microeconomic focus.

---

[16]The SAL proposal was introduced at the Bank's annual meeting in September 1979. It had been called for by McNamara himself at an UNCTAD meeting in Manila in April of that year. See Chapter 2 of Mosley, Harrigan, and Toye (1995).

[17]We will consider the economics of structural adjustment in some detail in Chapter 23.

Others have argued that this is too simplistic, and that the real issue lies in the different capabilities of the two institutions.[18] The potential for conflict between the two Bretton Woods institutions came to a head in 1988. The Bank approved a large SAL package to Argentina in the absence of an agreement between this country and the IMF. This conflict led to a concordat or joint memorandum in 1989 delineating World Bank and IMF roles.[19] In the *condordat*, the Fund's responsibilities were defined as "surveillance, exchange rate matters, balance of payments, growth-oriented stabilization policies and their related instruments" (Polak, 1994, p. 42). The Bank's responsibilities were defined as "development strategies, sector and project investments; structural adjustment programs; policies which deal with the efficient allocation of resources in both public and private sectors; priorities in government expenditures; reforms of administrative systems, production, trade and financial sectors; (and) the restructuring of state enterprises and sector policies" (Polak, 1994, p. 41). The difference in the lengths of these two lists speaks volumes about the contrasting natures of the Bank and Fund.

The second controversy over SAL relates to bargaining over conditionality. Some observers have alleged that those countries in greatest need of SAL support are in the weakest bargaining position *vis-à-vis* the Bank and, therefore, accept the greatest amount of requisite policy changes. However, the countries in greatest need of SAL are not necessarily those with the greatest need of policy reform because the need for support can be set off by changes in global economic conditions (e.g., export price declines) rather than by bad policies. Consequently, policy reform can be concentrated where it is not really needed.[20]

A third concern is that the growth of SAL has come at the expense of rural development (e.g., Paarlberg and Lipton, 1991). An often-quoted fact is that four of every five poor individuals in developing counties reside in rural areas. However, during the SAL era, there has been a *decline* in the real (inflation adjusted) World Bank lending for rural development. Furthermore, the Bank plays a large role in defining the world's development agenda, and, until recently at least, the role of rural areas in this agenda was disappearing. Finally, the Bank's expertise and staffing in the areas of agriculture and rural development have diminished.[21]

A final criticism of the Bank's SAL program is that it tends to hurt the poor. Much of this argument is related to the rural development issue just mentioned. However, starting in the 1980s, UNICEF sponsored a series of studies that criticized the Bank's SAL and called for what it termed "adjustment with a human face" or an attempt to offset adjustment's effects on the

---

[18]"(A)lthough the Fund is effectively overseeing the management of the principal macroeconomic aggregates, it lacks the functional and sectoral specialists able to analyze in depth the long-term development implications of alternative macroeconomic strategies. Nor does the Fund have the frequent staff-government contacts afforded the Bank through its economic and sector missions and its extensive project work" (Stern, 1983, p. 106).

[19]One can also argue that the structural adjustment and enhanced structural adjustment facilities of the IMF encroached upon the Bank's IDA. This point is made by Polak (1994), p. 9. Polak offers a detailed analysis of the Bank–Fund conflict over Argentina, as well as a similar incident over Turkey.

[20]See Mosley, Harrigan, and Toye, 1995, p. 41.

[21]A crucial force in pushing the rural sector back into the policy limelight has been the annual *Rural Poverty Report* of the International Fund for Agricultural Development. See http://www.ifad.org.

poor.[22] As a result of these and other critiques, the Bank began to pay attention to the role of SAL and conditionality on the poor. Nevertheless, a number of Bank representatives (e.g., Ribe et al., 1990 and Summers and Pritchett, 1993) argued that SAL actually helps the poor in most cases. It would be an understatement to say that the two sides of this debate tend not to listen to one another. For example, the Summers and Pritchett article does not reference a single piece of work other than the World Bank's. A commendable effort to bridge the gap between the two sides of this debate is the work of Stewart (1995).

Engaging with Ghana

As stated earlier, the advent of the policy-based lending phase of the World Bank coincided with the coming to power of the Rawlings regime in Ghana in the early 1980s. Initially, Rawlings and his PNDC were anticapitalist and antimarket. Between January 1982 and March 1983, the PNDC pursued a more populist and socialist policy. However, economic conditions continued to worsen, and there were two coup attempts in 1982. The PNDC was losing credibility, even from the political left in Ghana. From an economic standpoint, the fixed value of the currency (the cedi) was at such an overvalued rate that most currency transactions were undertaken at black-market rates. The official rate was all but ignored. A debate over economic policy emerged within the PNDC itself. As summarized by Kwesi Botchwey, the secretary for finance and economic planning at the time:[23]

> *There were two options: We had to maneuver our way around the naiveties of leftism, which has a sort of disdain for any talk of financial discipline. . . . Moreover, we had to find a way between this naiveté and the crudities and rigidities and dogma of monetarism, which behaves as if once you set the monetary incentives everybody will do the right thing and the market will be perfect.*

For better or worse, the PNDC was ready to take the plunge. We will take up the analysis of the ensuing structural adjustment program in the next chapter. Here, we will just mention some of its components. An economic recovery program was negotiated with the World Bank in 1983. In April of that year, a large *de facto* nominal devaluation was effected through import taxes and export subsidies.[24] In October, the nominal rate itself was adjusted from 2.75 cedi per U.S. dollar to 30 cedi per dollar. Further devaluations were to follow in 1984 (to 50 cedi per dollar), 1985 (to 60 cedi per dollar), and 1986 (90 cedi per dollar). Subsequently, the value of the cedi was market-determined. Import restrictions were reduced, especially after 1986 when the first official structural adjustment program (SAP) began.

Importantly, the Ghanaian government began to place an emphasis on revenue generation to address central government deficits. In 1985, the government formed a new National Revenue Secretariat. The purpose of this new unit was to broaden the tax base away from a previous

---

[22]See Jolly and Cornia (1984) and Cornia, Jolly, and Stewart (1987).
[23]Quoted in Jebuni (1995), p. 20.
[24]Years later, in 2001, Argentina was to use this same policy to offset an overvalued, fixed exchange rate in the form of a currency board. Some things never change!

emphasis on cocoa export taxes and to improve collection efficiency. Revenues as a percent of GDP responded significantly. Additionally, however, there were substantial layoffs of public-sector workers, particularly in state-owned enterprises, although retained public-sector workers were rewarded with raises.

The initial results of the SAP were startling. As shown in Figure 22.2, both GDP growth and manufacturing value-added (MVA) growth rebounded very quickly. Inflation slowed and exports expanded. Subsequently, economic conditions began to take a turn for the worse. Inflows of FDI never appeared. MVA growth became very unsteady after 1987. Inflation returned, and unemployment remained stuck at approximately 25 percent of the labor force. Worse still, both internal and external debt increased substantially to over US$5 billion by 1995. In that year, a Ghanaian government budget statement lamented that "We have hovered on the edge of recovery for too long, now threatening to relapse into the bleak decade that preceded the recovery programme." In 1997, Finance Minister Kwame Peprah admitted that "The same issues are still with us as they were in 1983 when we had to explain them to the people."[25]

Figure 22.2 Growth Rates in GDP and Manufacturing Value Added in Ghana

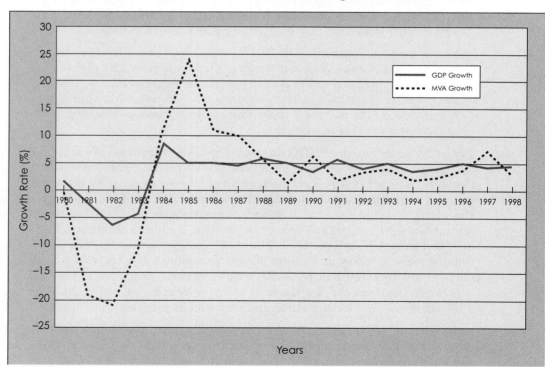

Source: Based on data in World Bank Group (2002). *World Development Indicators 2002 on CD-ROM*, Washington, DC: World Bank Group Publications.

---

[25]These two quotes are due to Ben Kwame Fred-Mensah and Asare Koti, respectively.

In 1997, World Bank president James Wolfensohn visited Ghana to talk about progress in adjustment. His hosts complained about a lack of results, despite nearly 15 years of hardship. Wolfensohn advised Jerry Rawlings and the Ghanaian government to cut government spending and fight corruption. This limited advice was a disappointment to all Ghanaians.

What were the missing ingredients holding Ghana back? In a country study published in 1984, the World Bank itself emphasized that:

> *The constraints facing Ghana's long-term growth are population growth, the inadequate supply of skilled and educated personnel, . . . and lack of diversification of the economic base. The need for a systematic approach to come to grips with these issues should not be overlooked even in the face of the present short-term economic crisis (p. xxiii).*

It seems that, to some extent, the World Bank forgot its own advice. A lack of focus on health and education failed to lower fertility rates that compare unfavorably to those of South Asia. As emphasized by Lall (1995), a lack of attention to skill development is one main cause of the poor MVA performance illustrated in Figure 22.2. Also, despite some increase in nontraditional exports of tuna, roses, and pineapples, the economy remains very dependent on exports of gold and cocoa with the associated booms and busts. Structural adjustment has not been a substitute for an integrated development policy.

Recent Shifts in Direction

In 1973, Mason and Asher stated that "(t)he IBRD has not . . . paid enough attention to the ecological or environmental effects of the projects it has financed" (p. 259). In retrospect, this was a prophetic statement. The environmental issue rose to the surface 10 years later. Bruce Rich, then an attorney with the Natural Resources Defense Council (later with the Environmental Defense Fund), launched an attack on the World Bank–supported Polonoroeste project in Brazil. The term "Polonoroeste" stands for North-West Regional Development Pole. Rich criticized the project on environmental grounds in articles and appearances before committees of the U.S. Congress. As a result of Rich's efforts, the project was canceled in 1986. This decision, and the new Bank presidency of Barber Conable in 1986, launched a change in the Bank's policy toward the environment.[26] Conable began to speak publicly on the Bank's role with regard to the environment in 1987. In Conable's (1989) words, "The Bank is now convinced that the pervasive nature of environmental issues dictates a new approach: integrating environmental management into economic policymaking at all levels of government, supplementing the traditional project-by-project approach" (p. 6).

Conable committed the Bank to increasing its environmental staff, beginning a series of environmental issue papers, financing environmental programs, and involving grass-roots environmental organizations in

---

[26]See Chapter 4 of Stone (1992) as well as Rich (1990) and (1994).

Wolfensohn's New Development Framework

Wolfensohn's proposed development framework for the World Bank returns to some of the themes from the poverty alleviation phase described here, and it tries to avoid some of the pitfalls of the project lending phase. Wolfensohn argues that the development framework should be composed of:

1. Good governance, including the free flow of information and commitments to fight corruption.
2. Institutional elements such as the enforcement of contracts and the sound regulation of financial systems.
3. Social inclusion policies directed toward girls and women, indigenous peoples, and the unemployed.
4. Attention to the provision of public goods and infrastructure—not just a focus on projects, however, but a renewed focus on rural and urban development.
5. Environmental and human sustainability, which respect both biological and cultural conditions.
6. Ownership and participation to develop strategies that countries can buy into and commit themselves to.

Wolfensohn has suggested that the World Bank will test this new framework in two countries from each region of the world through inclusive policy fora. He promises to report on the outcome in a few years time. Many people will certainly be interested to see whether the World Bank will be committed to and successful in this new endeavor.

Source: Wolfensohn (1998).

the Bank's decision making. Whether these changes have actually amounted to anything is currently under debate. Andrew Steer, the director of the Bank's Environmental Department espoused what he called a "new environmentalism" and estimated the Bank's environmental loans at US$11 billion (Steer, 1996). The original protagonist in the debate, Bruce Rich, was less sanguine, stating that "(t)he Bank continues to stress its commitment to the environment, but deep institutional and political contradictions prevent it from implementing reform in any meaningful way" (1990, p. 307). What is certain is that the environmental issue will continue to grow in importance for the Bank.

One change introduced at the World Bank under the McNamara presidency was the use of loan volumes as a measure of success. In retrospect, this proved unfortunate. There is evidence that the quality of Bank lending suffered as a result of this change, and this might explain some of the lack of attention to environmental matters that called Bruce Rich into action.[27] More fundamentally, there has been a lack of attention to *process* and *results* that appears to have plagued the Bank. Kamarck (1996) quotes a bank managing director who summed up the changes currently impinging upon this Bretton Woods institution: "(F)our broad themes . . . are coming through very strongly from the outside and increasingly from the inside.

---

[27]Lewis Preston, Bank president from 1991 to 1995 stated: "Every guy in this bank thought he was going to get promoted based just on the number of loans he could get approved. It was a crazy way to run a railroad" (Kamarck, 1996, p. 121). Preston was succeeded by James Wofensohn.

First, the need to focus on people (. . . education and health lending, private sector entrepreneurship, how the environment affects the poor); second on participation . . . ; third on partnerships (. . . with other agencies); and finally, on results" (p. 125). These kinds of changes will be necessary if the World Bank is to fulfill its mission with regard to development and escape the intense criticisms that have been directed towards its SAL program and neglect of the environment. Recently, World Bank president James Wolfensohn appears to have taken these matters on board. His proposals are discussed in the box.

One practical outcome of the criticisms levelled at both the World Bank and the IMF is a new poverty reduction strategy (PRS) initiative launched in 1999. From the World Bank's perspective, the PRS is closely related to Wofensohn's development framework. The Bank has adopted six principles to guide the PRS. These are that the strategies should be country driven, results oriented, comprehensive, prioritized, partnership oriented, and long term. The IMF, in turn, has supported the PRS with a Poverty Reduction and Growth Facility (see Chapter 16). The PRS has become a prerequisite for debt relief.

Perhaps inevitably, the PRS has itself become controversial. Although the country-driven nature of the PRS is supposed to involve "broad-based participation by civil society and the private sector in all operational steps," in the case of Ghana, key elements of the PRS were kept secret by the government. It has also been the case that SAP agreements have forced the PRS process in certain directions, leaving some Ghanaian observers to wonder what the purpose of the PRS really is. At the current time, these operational issues remain unresolved and are under review by the Bank.

Conclusion

Originally focused on the reconstruction of Europe after World War II, the World Bank Group quickly turned to the realm of economic development. In its early history, the Bank concentrated on infrastructure project lending. Then, under the McNamara presidency, it focused on poverty alleviation, including integrated rural development. In the 1980s, its direction shifted substantially to policy-based lending. This phase included cofinancing, an expanded role of the International Finance Corporation, conditionality, and structural adjustment lending. More recently, the Bank has recognized the importance of environmental sustainability, social inclusion, and participation, although implementation of these concerns remains a real issue.

A central structural adjustment program in which the World Bank has been involved is that of Ghana. Despite early positive signs, this program has not solved some fundamental growth and development problems in that country. Because the structural adjustment policies of both the IMF and the World Bank have proved to be such a contentious issue in development debates, we dedicate the final chapter of this book to the formal analysis of these programs.

Review Exercises

1. The World Bank and the IMF are the two major institutions of international finance in the world economy. How do their missions and operations differ? Are there any areas in which these missions and operations overlap?

2. How does the poverty alleviation phase of the World Bank differ from its previous infrastructure project lending phase? In what ways does the latter policy-based lending phase represent a break with the poverty alleviation phase?

3. Should environmental considerations be used in Bank lending decisions? Why or why not?

4. To some extent, the World Bank has returned to poverty considerations in its poverty reduction strategy (PRS) program. If you were to design such a program, what would your own core principles be?

5. If there is a World Bank member in which you have a special interest, spend a little time perusing the "Countries and Regions" section of the Bank's Web site at **http://www.worldbank.org**.

Further Reading and Web Resources

For a discussion of the early history of the World Bank, there is no better source than Mason and Asher (1973). For the poverty alleviation phase, the reader should consult Ayres (1983). For the structural adjustment phase, see Mosley, Harrigan, and Toye (1995). A balanced view of the structural adjustment debate can also be found in Stewart (1995). The relationship between the World Bank and the IMF is concisely discussed in Polak (1994). For a recent assessment of the Bank's operations by economists associated with it, see Gilbert and Vines (2000). The World Bank disseminates its own research through its journal, the *World Bank Research Observer*. You can view recent issues of this journal at **http://www.wbro.oupjournals.org**.

The World Bank's its main Web site is **http://www.worldbank.org**. It also maintains the Development Gateway Web site at **http://www.developmentgateway.org**. The latter is particularly important in tracking development projects around the world. The International Center for Settlement of Investment Disputes Web site is at **http://www.worldbank.org/icsid**. The Multilateral Investment Guarantee Agency's Web site can be found at **http://www.miga.org**. The Bretton Woods Project monitors World Bank (and IMF) activities, and provides a great deal of information on the World Bank from a critical perspective. You can access their Web site at **http://www.brettonwoodsproject.org**.

References

Ayres, R.L. (1983) *Banking on the Poor: The World Bank and World Poverty*, MIT Press, Cambridge, Massachusetts.

Conable, B. (1989) "Development and the Environment: A Global Balance," *Finance and Development*, 26:4, 2–4.

Cornia, G.A., R. Jolly, and F. Stewart (1987) *Adjustment with a Human Face*, Oxford University Press, Oxford.

Deaton, A. (2001) "Counting the World's Poor: Problems and Possible Solutions," *World Bank Research Observer*, 16:2, 125–147.

Deininger, K. and H. Binswanger (1999) "The Evolution of the World Bank's Land Policy: Principles, Experience, and Future Challenges," *World Bank Research Observer*, 14:2, 247–276.

The Economist (2002) "Ghana as an Economic Model," April 27, 46.

The Economist (1996) "Investment in Africa: Primary Problems," November 9, 95.

Franko, P. (2003) *The Puzzle of Latin American Economic Development*, Rowman and Littlefield, Lanham, Maryland.

Gilbert, C.L., and D. Vines (eds.) (2000) *The World Bank: Structure and Policies*, Cambridge University Press, Cambridge.

Jebuni, C.D. (1995) *Governance and Structural Adjustment in Ghana*, World Bank Private Sector Development Department, Occasional Paper No. 16, Washington, DC.

Jolly, R., and G.A. Cornia (1984) *The Impact of World Recession on Children*, Pergamon Press, Oxford.

Kamarck, A.M. (1996) "The World Bank: Challenges and Creative Responses," in O. Krishner (ed.), *The Bretton Woods-GATT System*, M.E. Sharpe, London.

Lall, S. (1995) "Structural Adjustment and African Industry," *World Development*, 23:12, 2019–2031.

Lindsay, R. (2000) "Land Reform Returns to Center Stage in Brazil," *Washington Report on the Hemisphere*, 20:12.

Mason, E.S., and R.E. Asher (1973) *The World Bank Since Bretton Woods*, Brookings, Washington, DC.

Mosley, P., J. Harrigan, and J.F. Toye (1995) *Aid and Power: The World Bank and Policy-Based Lending*, Routledge, London.

Naím, M. (2000) "Washington Consensus or Washington Confusion?" *Foreign Policy*, Spring, 86–103.

Paarlberg, R. and M. Lipton (1991) "Changing Missions at the World Bank," *World Policy Journal*, 8:3, 475–498.

Polak, J.J. (1994) *The World Bank and the International Monetary Fund: A Changing Relationship*, Brookings, Washington, DC.

Ribe, H., et al. (1990) *How Adjustment Programs Can Help the Poor: The World Bank's Experience*, World Bank, Washington, DC.

Rich, B. (1994) *Mortgaging the Earth: The World Bank, Environmental Impoverishment, and the Crisis of Development*, Beacon Press, Boston.

Rich, B. (1990) "The Emperor's New Clothes: The World Bank and Environmental Reform," *World Policy Journal*, 7:2, 305–329.

Rodrik, D. (1994) "King Kong Meets Godzilla: The World Bank and *The East Asian Miracle*," in A. Fishlow et al., *Miracle or Design: Lessons from the East Asian Experience*, Overseas Development Council, Washington, DC.

Salda, A.C.M. (1995) *World Bank*, Transaction Publishers, New Brunswick, New Jersey.

Shihata, I.F.I. (1986) "The Role of ICSID and the Projected Multilateral Investment Guarantee Agency (MIGA)," *Aussenwirtschaft*, 41:1, 105–122.

Schwartzman, S. (2000) "The World Bank and Land Reform in Brazil," *Environmental Defense*, Washington, DC.

Skidelsky, R. (2000) *John Maynard Keynes: Fighting for Freedom 1937–1946*, Viking, New York.

Steer, A. (1996) "Ten Principles of the New Environmentalism," *Finance and Development*, 33:4, 4–7.

Stern, E. (1983) "World Bank Financing of Structural Adjustment," in J. Williamson (ed.), *IMF Conditionality*, Institute for International Economics, Washington, DC., 87–107.

Stewart, F. (1995) *Adjustment and Poverty: Options and Choices*, Routledge, London.

Stone, R.D. (1992) *The Nature of Development*, Knopf, New York.

Summers, L.H., and L.H. Pritchett (1993) "The Structural Adjustment Debate," *American Economic Review*, 83:2, 383–389.

Williamson, J. (2000) "What Should the World Bank Think About the Washington Consensus?" *World Bank Research Observer*, 15:2, 251–64.

Williamson, J. (1990) "What Washington Means by Policy Reform," in J. Williamson (ed.), *Latin American Adjustment: How Much Has Happened?* Institute for International Economics, Washington, DC, 5–38.

Wolfensohn, J. (1998) *The Other Crisis*, World Bank, Washington, DC.

World Bank (1993) *East Asian Miracle*, Oxford University Press, Oxford.

World Bank (1984) *Ghana: Policies and Program for Adjustment*, Washington, DC.

Structural Adjustment

In Chapter 15, you learned that, in a fixed exchange rate regime, an overvalued domestic currency (Mexican peso or Ghanaian cedi) is associated with an excess demand for foreign currency (U.S. dollar or euro). This excess demand for foreign currency is often met by the central bank drawing down its foreign reserves. The drawing down process is not sustainable, however, and can result in a balance of payments crisis. In Chapter 16, you learned that, in most circumstances, the International Monetary Fund (IMF) stands ready to assist member countries in dealing with such balance of payments crises. If this assistance involves the member country's moving into its upper credit trances (which it almost always does), the IMF imposes policy conditionality on its loans. You learned about some recent cases of this in Chapter 17 on crises and responses. In Chapter 22, you learned that, beginning in the 1980s, the World Bank began structural adjustment lending to countries facing balance of payments difficulties, also imposing policy conditionality in the process. You were introduced to the case of Ghana in that chapter.

As you have seen, then, for developing countries with balance of payments crises caused by fixed exchange rates or changes in global economic conditions, structural adjustment under the supervision of the IMF and World Bank is, for better or worse, an inescapable reality. The effectiveness of these structural adjustment programs has been the source of a significant amount of disagreement among international economists. It is now time to tie the discussion of Chapters 15, 16, 17, and 22 together in a close examination of the structural adjustment process.

We will develop your understanding of **structural adjustment** in five steps. First, we will distinguish between traded and nontraded goods. Second, we will utilize the traded/nontraded dichotomy to introduce the concepts of internal and external balance. Third, we will analyze the process of structural adjustment via both demand reduction and demand switching. Fourth, we will address the structuralist critique to the standard internal and external balance arguments. Finally, we consider the related matter of the order of economic liberalization.

Traded and Nontraded Goods

For the purposes of this chapter, imagine that you are an international economist advising the Ghanaian government on their approach to structural adjustment. You need to somehow simplify the complexities of the adjustment processes to clarify your own thinking and to communicate with government representatives. One useful first step is to distinguish

Structural adjustment

The process of change in an economy that takes place in response to internal and/or external imbalances. It typically requires demand reduction and currency devaluation.

Traded goods
Goods and services
that can be imported
or exported.

**Nontraded
goods**
Goods such as local
services that are not
imported or exported.

between **traded goods** and **nontraded goods**. Recall that in Chapter 13 in our assessment of the PPP model of exchange rate determination, we said, "Many goods are *nontraded*. For example, a large part of most economies consists of locally-supplied services such as many kinds of cleaning, repairs, and food preparation. These services are not typically traded." In the Ghanaian context, you might imagine the following:

Traded Goods	**Nontraded Goods**
Petroleum	*Tailoring*
Gold	*Auto repair*
Cocoa	*Education*
Food	*Health services*

There are two crucial things that you must understand about the difference between traded and nontraded goods. These are described in Table 23.1. First, the prices of traded goods are determined in world markets; the prices of nontraded goods are determined in domestic markets. So, for Ghana, the price of petroleum is a world price denominated in U.S. dollars. The price of tailoring, on the other hand, is a domestic price, denominated in cedis. Second, for traded goods, domestic consumption and domestic production can differ in value, causing a trade surplus or deficit. However, domestic consumption and domestic production of nontraded goods must be exactly the same in value.

Having divided the Ghanaian economy into traded and nontraded goods, we can represent the supply side of this economy with a production possibilities frontier (PPF) as we did in Chapter 3 to discuss comparative advantage.[1] This is done in Figure 23.1. The production of traded goods as an aggregate entity (petroleum, gold, cocoa, food) is measured along the vertical axis, and the production of nontraded goods as an aggregate entity (tailoring, auto repair, education, health services) is measured along the horizontal axis. The PPF depicts the combinations of output of traded goods and nontraded goods that the economy can produce given its available resources and technology. The PPF is depicted as the concave line in this figure. Given the available resources and technology, Ghana can produce anywhere on or inside the PPF.

Table 23.1 Traded Goods Versus Nontraded Goods

Good	Price Determination	Consumption and Production
Traded	Prices of traded goods are determined in world markets.	Domestic consumption and domestic production of traded goods can differ, causing a trade surplus or deficit.
Nontraded	Prices of nontraded goods are determined in domestic markets.	Domestic consumption and domestic production must be equal.

[1] The PPF was introduced in the appendix to Chapter 3. If you need to, please review this appendix.

Figure 23.1 Ghana's PPF

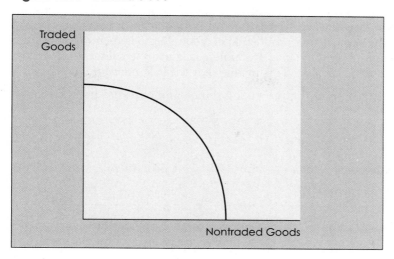

With these characteristics of traded and nontraded goods in mind, you are ready to be introduced to the concepts of internal and external balance. We do this in the following section.

Internal and External Balance

The concepts of **internal balance** and **external balance** relate directly to the PPF diagram we introduced in Figure 23.1, and we are going to use this PPF to help you understand them. We do this in Figure 23.2. In this figure, Ghana's production point is given by point B. Because the production point B is on the PPF rather than inside it, all of Ghana's resources are efficiently employed. This is what we mean by internal balance. In Figure 23.2,

Internal balance
A situation in an economy in which all resources are fully employed.

External balance
A situation in an economy in which trade (the current account) is balanced.

Figure 23.2 Internal and External Balance

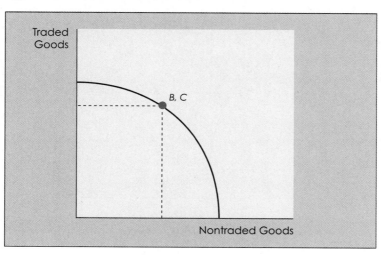

Ghana's consumption point is given by point C and is exactly the same point as point B. A dotted line proceeds to the left from points B and C to the vertical axis. This tells us that the consumption of tradable goods (point C) is exactly the same as the production of tradable goods (point B). Because consumption and production of tradable goods are the same, there is no trade deficit or trade surplus. This means that there is *external balance*.[2]

Let's summarize the internal balance and external balance concepts:

> **Internal balance:** All resources are efficiently employed.
>
> **External balance:** Consumption and production of tradable goods are equal.

Next consider Figure 23.3. As in Figure 23.2, the production point B is on the PPF. For this reason, there is internal balance. This figure also shows two consumption points, C_{TS} and C_{TD}. If consumption is at C_{TD}, the consumption of traded goods exceeds the production of traded goods along the vertical axis. This implies that Ghana has a trade deficit (TD). To simplify a bit, we will interpret this trade deficit as a current account deficit.[3] If there is a current account deficit, we know that there must be a capital account surplus. This capital account surplus can come from positive direct or portfolio investment balances or from drawing down foreign reserves.

If consumption in Figure 23.3 is at C_{TS}, the production of traded goods exceeds the consumption of traded goods along the vertical axis. This implies that Ghana has a trade surplus (TS). Again to simplify matters,

Figure 23.3 External Imbalances

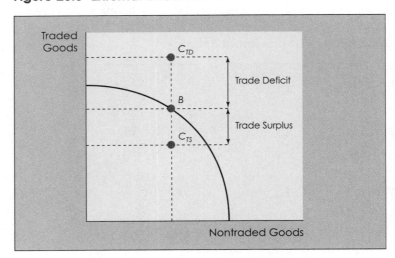

[2] The concepts of internal and external balance were first presented by Salter (1959). A more recent discussion is contained in Chapter 1 of Corden (1986).
[3] That is, we ignore net factor receipts and transfers, items 4 and 5 in Table 12.2.

we will interpret this trade surplus as a current account surplus. If there is a current account surplus, we know that there must be a capital account deficit. This capital account deficit can come from negative direct or portfolio investment balances or from building up foreign reserves. In contrast to Figure 23.2, in both the trade deficit and trade surplus cases in Figure 23.3, there is *external imbalance*. As always, consumption and production of nontraded goods are the same, as we stated in Table 23.1. Therefore, point C is either directly above or directly below point B.

To understand some issues behind balance of payments adjustment, we are going to consider Ghana in an initial position of a trade (current account) deficit. This situation is depicted in Figure 23.4. Included in this figure are price ratio lines. As we discussed in Chapter 3, the price ratio line is tangent to the PPF at the point of production B. We use P_T to denote the price of traded goods and P_N to denote the price of nontraded goods. A price ratio line with the same slope passes through the consumption point C_{TD}. This is to indicate that consumers as well as firms face the price ratio P_N/P_T. You can call this price ratio the "relative price of nontraded goods." The vertical distance between B and C_{TD} is sustained by a capital account surplus. Ghana has internal balance but external imbalance at points B and C_{TD}.

Difficulties in Figure 23.4 emerge if the inflows on the capital account begin to disappear. Suppose, for example, that direct and portfolio investment decline (foreign savings falls).[4] It is still possible for Ghana to maintain its current account deficit by drawing down its foreign reserves. This situation clearly is not sustainable, however. It can last only as long as the central bank has foreign reserves to sell. Eventually, the foreign reserves will be exhausted, and the country will face a balance of payments crisis. It

Figure 23.4 A Current Account Deficit

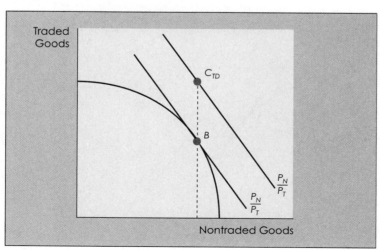

_____

[4] This could occur despite increases in Ghana's interest rate if foreign investors are changing their expectations or preferences with regard to portfolio allocations among countries.

is your job to advise the Ghanaian government on how to adjust from the unsustainable situation depicted in Figure 23.4.

What could you advise Ghana to do? One possibility comes from recognizing that the external imbalance problem comes from the demand for tradable goods being too high. Recognizing this, you could suggest that Ghana engage in **demand reduction** to reduce the demand for tradable goods. This policy is one usually suggested by the IMF. A significant limitation here is that *demand reductions typically cannot be confined to traded goods alone*. In most instances, demand falls for both traded and nontraded goods. An example of adjustment via demand reduction is depicted in Figure 23.5. We begin with consumption at C_{TD0} and production at B_0. The (unsustainable) current account deficit is at TD_0. Demand reduction consists of reducing the income households have for consumption. Under the reasonable assumption that both traded and nontraded goods are normal goods, as income falls, demands for both goods fall.[5]

Suppose Ghana succeeds in reducing household incomes to the value of production at point B. Consumption would fall from C_{TD0} to C_{TD1}. The difficulty here is that there is *still a current account deficit* equal to TD_1, even though there is unemployment at the new production point B_1. Eliminating the trade deficit therefore requires reducing incomes below the value of production at point B_0, and this requires further unemployment. One scenario would involve maintaining the employment of resources in the traded goods sector and moving production and consumption to point B_2, C_2. Here, finally, the trade deficit has been eliminated. However, production is now far inside the PPF; the demand reduction has caused a significant amount of unemployment. To put it another way, external balance adjustment via demand reduction has been achieved *at the expense of internal balance*.

Demand reduction
The decrease in domestic demand made in an attempt to move an economy toward external balance.

Figure 23.5 Adjustment via Demand Reduction

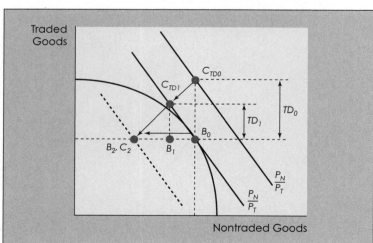

---

[5] Recall that a *normal good* is one where there is a positive relationship between income and demand. This contrasts with an *inferior good*, where there is a negative relationship between income and demand, a rare case.

This result is important to you in your advising of the Ghanaian government, so let's summarize:

> **Adjustment via demand reduction alone occurs at the expense of internal balance.**

The development economist Francis Stewart (1995) studied the ways in which demand reduction policies have been implemented in many countries of the world and their impacts on the poor in those countries. Her conclusions were as follows:[6]

> *Demand restraint has unambiguously negative effects on the poor. . . . Demand-reducing policies include cuts in government expenditure, rises in taxation, reductions in real wages and credit restraint. The policies cut into real incomes by reducing employment and real wages of those in employment. . . . Public sector employees are usually most immediately affected by reduced employment, but this has knock-on effects for the rest of the economy. . . . (T)he poor . . . (are) especially hurt by reduced food subsidies (p. 23).*

This would not be a positive outcome for Ghana, and if you could avoid it, you certainly should. What else could you suggest to the Ghanaian government? Fortunately, it turns out that, in principle at least, a country can achieve external balance and maintain internal balance. The key here, as stated by the international economist Max Corden (1986): "If it is desired to attain two targets—external balance and internal balance—it is necessary to have *two* instruments. The (demand reduction) instrument is not enough. . . . The second instrument required is a **switching** policy" (pp. 9–10). In the typical case, the switching policy is implemented by a change in the nominal exchange rate defined in Chapter 13.

Switching
The use of a devaluation of a country's currency to move the economy towards external balance.

Remember from Chapter 13 that a devaluation or depreciation of the domestic currency ($e\uparrow$) causes an increase in the domestic (cedi) prices of both imports and exports. Therefore, if Ghana were to devalue the cedi, there would be an increase in the relative price of tradable goods or a decrease in the relative price of nontradable goods. The price lines in our PPF diagrams indicate the relative price of nontradable goods, so these would become flatter when the cedi is devalued. This has two effects. First, it increases the incentive to produce traded goods. Second, it decreases the incentive to consume traded goods. Both of these effects tend to reduce the trade deficit. This is the process of moving down the $Z - E$ curve in Figure 14.2 in Chapter 14. The usefulness of a devaluation switching process can be seen in Figure 23.6.

As in Figure 23.5, Ghana begins in a position of a current account deficit measured by the vertical distance between C_{TD0} and B_0. The adjustment,

---

[6] Stewart, F. (1995). *Adjustment and Poverty: Options and Choices*. London: Routledge, 23. The terms "real wages" and "real incomes" in the following excerpt refer to wages and incomes, respectively, which have been adjusted for changes in the overall price level. This is done by dividing the wages and incomes by price indices such as those discussed in the appendix to Chapter 13.

Figure 23.6 Adjustment via Demand Reduction and Switching

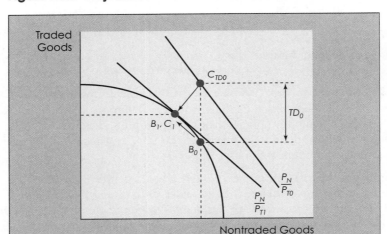

however, is different. There is demand reduction, but it is combined with the switching policy of devaluation. The devaluation increases the cedi price of traded goods, and this lowers the relative price of nontraded goods and makes the price line in the figure less steep. Ghanaian firms switch their production toward traded goods, and Ghanaian consumers switch their consumption away from traded goods. Production and consumption move to point B_1, C_1, where there is both external balance (no current account deficit) and internal balance (full employment). The lesson here is that a successful adjustment program must combine both demand reduction and switching elements:

> **In order to avoid internal imbalance (unemployment), successful adjustment program must combine *both* demand reduction and switching elements.**

This discussion helps you to visualize certain processes that accompany countries' struggles to come to terms with a balance of payments crisis. It is important to understand that the correspondence of our graphical analysis to the actual experience of adjusting countries probably will not be complete. It is also important to note that we have said nothing about the composition of demand reduction. Is the country in question reducing military expenditures and industrial subsidies or is it reducing health and education expenditures? The answer to this question will have important economic and social consequences.[7] Finally, our model assumes that all things happen at once. In reality, policy changes occur over time, and the order in which they occur can be important. We will take up the order of economic liberalization later in this chapter.

---

[7] See Stewart (1995) for a discussion of some of these issues.

The Structuralist Critique

In the preceding section, we addressed a simple model of internal and external balance, relating this model to the structural adjustment processes. In this section, we address the **structuralist critique** of the standard internal and external balance view of adjustment. It is not possible to describe a single structuralist model that would counterpose the one developed in the previous section. A single model would be anathema to the structuralists. Rather, these economists argue that we must account for the structural diversity of developing economies undergoing balance of payments crises and adjustment programs. For example, Lance Taylor, a leading structuralist, stated: "The real question is whether economic reform, or reconfiguration of the system to meet challenges posed by changes in both internal and external circumstances, is feasible in a given country's historical and institutional context" (1993, pp. 43–44). Given this point of view, our purpose here will be to elucidate some common elements in the structuralist critique.[8] Some of these might be relevant to you as an advisor to the Ghanaian government.

First, productive resources may not be mobile between sectors. In terms of the diagrams of the previous section, certain barriers can prevent productive resources in Ghana from moving freely to the traded sector from the nontraded sector. For example, urban workers in the nontraded sector might face a number of barriers (e.g., culture and family ties) to relocating to rural areas to increase the supply of agricultural products. Gold production might simply be constrained by the capital stocks of mines. An extreme case of this is presented in Figure 23.7. In this diagram, the immobility of resources is depicted as a rectangular PPF. Consequently, an increase in the nominal exchange rate will not shift production toward

Structuralist critique
A school of thought in development economics that argues in favor of accounting for the historical and institutional structures of an economy in the design of adjustment programs in coping with external imbalances and balance of payments crises.

Figure 23.7 Adjustment Under Resource Immobility

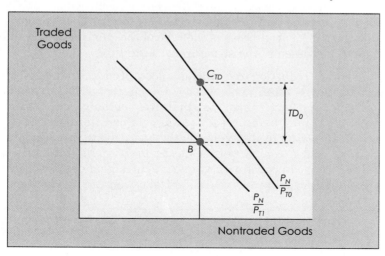

---

[8] For a more complete discussion, see Taylor (1983, 1987, 1993), Bacha (1987), and Chapter 20 of Hallwood and MacDonald (2000).

African Economists Speak

In 1999, the Council for Development of Social Science Research in Africa published its report on structural adjustment entitled *Our Continent, Our Future*. Its subtitle was *African Perspectives on Structural Adjustment*. In this book, African economists Thandika Mkandawire and Charles Soludo addressed the problem of a lack of productive investments in human capital as part of structural adjustment programs. Here is what they have to say:

"Only recently, the dire shortage of critical skills and personnel in Africa has been recognized as an impediment to policy implementation and industrialization. We must not lose sight of the fact that much of the so-called lack of capacity in Africa is donor imposed. How can capacity develop when much of the financial aid is tied to technical assistance, which ensures that much of the money goes to pay foreign advisers who have turned Africa into laboratories for testing their pet theories about development? It is becoming a joke that there will soon be more foreign experts in Africa than there are Africans for them to advise. Some analysts estimate that nearly 40 percent of the multilateral aid and financial assistance is spent on foreign experts, and about 4 billion (U.S. dollars) goes annually to fund foreign technical assistance in Africa. If such an amount were used for training programs, R&D, technological upgrading, and diversification of production structures, Africa's human-capital situation would certainly be different" (p. 111).

Source: Mkandawire and Soludo (1999).

traded goods as in Figure 23.6 even as the relative price of nontraded goods falls. The only available adjustment mechanism is via a reduction in demand as in Figure 23.5.

Second, domestic production may be highly dependent on imported intermediate and capital goods. The devaluation of the cedi raises the domestic prices of these traded goods. If the increase in the price of imported intermediate and capital goods puts them out of reach of domestic firms, production may decline and unemployment may occur. The economy will move inside the PPF. This process is one type of the "contractionary effects of devaluation" discussed in the structuralist literature.

Third, demand reduction can include lost productive investments. Demand reduction is often achieved by reducing government expenditures. However, some government expenditures, notably certain kinds of public investment, may be necessary to support private investment and production. In the structuralist view, public and private investments are complementary, and a contraction of public investment (infrastructure, public utilities, etc.) can cause a subsequent contraction of private investment and, thereby, future productive potential as represented by the PPF.[9]

---

[9] "There is . . . mounting evidence that growth prospects have become increasingly impared by fiscal constraint" (Tarp, 1993, p. 138). See also Taylor (1993). In this respect, there seems to be agreement between the structuralists and some World Bank economists. In a World Bank study, Thomas and Nash (1991) write: "In the 1980s, reductions in the fiscal deficit came primarily from cuts in public expenditure rather than from increases in revenue, and the largest percentage of reductions came in capital spending. . . . There is systematic evidence . . . to confirm that investment in infrastructure has a positive effect on the profitability of the private sector. Thus, reducing public investment in infrastructure which is complementary to private investment would undermine the supply response" (pp. 107–109).

A similar story can be told with regard to productive investments in human capital, as the box attests.

Fourth, adjustment often takes place under negative foreign savings (capital outflows or capital flight) as we discussed in Chapter 17. In terms of our diagrams of this chapter, it is *not* simply a matter of regaining external balance but of generating a trade or current account surplus to accommodate a capital account deficit. Therefore, adjustments have proceeded farther that we assumed in our analysis, and the potential structuralist syndromes discussed in this section appear even stronger. Demand reduction is sharper, price increases of imported intermediate and capital goods are greater, and cuts in productive public investments are even more severe. Countries become caught in trade-surplus/low-growth traps with little future hope for poverty reduction. Such an outcome may apply to sub-Saharan African countries, almost all of which are undergoing IMF/World Bank sponsored adjustment.[10]

What, then, do the structuralists recommend? This, of course, would depend on the country in question. However, in general, structuralists would call for:

1. *Measures to ensure that key productive investments are not sacrificed in demand reduction*
2. *Import quotas and* **export subsidies** *to reduce trade deficits in order to require lower nominal exchange rates and, thereby, preventing inflation and poverty problems*[11]
3. *Government involvement in allocating scarce foreign exchange*
4. *Foreign debt forgiveness to prevent the necessity of generating large trade surpluses*

Export subsidy
A subsidy to exports provided by the government of a country.

We will not pass judgment on the relative merit of the structuralist policy recommendations *vis-à-vis* the standard IMF/World Bank recommendations. Our purpose in raising the structuralist point of view is to alert us to potential pitfalls in the adjustment process and to prevent a false satisfaction with our simple PPF diagram. It is important for us to keep in mind that the realities of actual economies are always more complex than simple economic models.

The Order of Economic Liberalization

Typically, the adjustment programs designed by the IMF and World Bank to address balance of payments crises include more components than demand reduction and switching. Inspired by the Washington consensus discussed in Chapter 22, these programs also include a number of kinds of market liberalization. These two Bretton Woods institutions have an abiding concern with reducing the losses in welfare associated with import tariffs, import

---

[10]On sub-Saharan African countries, Lipumba (1994) wrote: "(A)s World Bank staff would readily acknowledge, the performance of all these countries remains inadequate: the growth rate of even the best performing country, Ghana, is still too low to reduce mass poverty in the medium term" (p. 17).

[11]Rodrik (1990), not a structuralist, also sees a role for export subsidies before the removal of import tariffs and quotas.

quotas, and export taxes. They also call for privatization of all state-owned enterprises. For these reasons, structural adjustment programs often include the following components:

1. *Exchange rate depreciation or devaluation*
2. *Reductions in government expenditures, including reduction in public-sector workforces, elimination of agricultural and industrial subsidies, and elimination of food and medical subsidies*
3. *Wage controls to reduce demand and to prevent inflation*
4. *Elimination of import quotas and export taxes*
5. *Reduction of ad valorem tariffs to "moderate" levels of 10 to 15 percent*
6. *The privatization of state-owned enterprises*
7. *The liberalization of domestic financial markets*

Historically, there has been a tendency for the IMF and World Bank to call for the implementation of the above components *all at once*. For example, this was the advice given the "Southern Cone" countries of Chile, Argentina, and Uruguay in the late 1970s and early 1980s. In this instance, the results were not positive.[12] Subsequently, international economists have stressed that it is very important to pay attention to the order of economic liberalization.[13] However, it has sometimes appeared that the World Bank does not recognize the importance of these new ideas. For example, in a report on adjustment in Africa (World Bank, 1994), the issue was more or less ignored, and in the accompanying case studies, Husain and Faruqee (1994) state: "Given the close relationship between import liberalization, public enterprise reform, government finance, and financial sector reforms, this whole set of reforms should be attempted simultaneously and consistently" (p. 435).[14] Because there is evidence that failure to heed the warnings of the order of economic liberalization literature can significantly compromise the sustainability of adjustment policies, we will present in a simple fashion the arguments of this literature.

Suppose that Ghana faces a balance of payments crisis such as that described in the previous sections. It is financing the current account deficit by selling foreign exchange reserves. The central government is running a deficit. Additionally, suppose that the government owns some enterprises on which it depends for some revenue, the government restricts imports using a set of quotas, and the exchange rate is fixed. The question this country faces is how to order the steps it will take in alleviating the balance of payments crisis and securing sustainable adjustment. In what follows, we present one possible sequence and provide an accompanying rationale.

First, *seek a means of securing central government revenue through a broad-based tax*. The government accounts are in deficit, and the government may be called upon to lower trade taxes and sell its enterprises, both of which will involve a loss of revenue sources. Alternative revenue sources

---

[12]In 1984, Edwards wrote: "A decade after these reforms were first implemented, the evidence indicates that they were to a large extent a failure" (1984, p. 1).
[13]See, for example, Edwards (1984), McKinnon (1993), and Part III of Lipumba (1994).
[14]A more subtle analysis of these issues on the part of the World Bank is presented in Chapter 5 of Thomas and Nash (1991). However, these authors still generally approved of simultaneity of reform measures except in certain extenuating circumstances.

must be found.[15] Possible sources are sales taxes, producer taxes, or value-added taxes. These should be broad-based and set at low rates. The increase in tax revenues will lower the government deficit, which will tend to narrow the gap between domestic investment and domestic savings that underlies the current account deficit. It will also position the government for further reforms without precipitating a fiscal crisis.

Second, *depreciate or devalue the exchange rate.* As we have stated a number of times, reducing the value of the domestic currency begins a switching process. Imports are reduced and exports can expand, the latter usually taking longer than the former. Both of these effects tend to reduce the current account deficit. Lipumba (1994) was adamant that this switching policy take place before trade liberalization. He was critical of cases in which the World Bank and the IMF suggested trade liberalization to African countries that had not adjusted their exchange rates, stating the following:

> *(R)eal exchange rate depreciation should be undertaken before liberalization of international trade. . . . Free trade without real depreciation will increase imports, which will out-compete domestic production and lead to a rapid exhaustion of foreign exchange reserves. Exports take longer to respond to . . . a depreciation of the real exchange rate than imports. If countries are not willing to depreciate their currencies, it is irresponsible for them to liberalize imports (p. 57).*

This point also has relevance for Latin America. The effects of trade liberalization with an overvalued currency in Colombia in the early 1980s was reviewed by Urrutia (1998):

> *The liberalization policy of the early 1980s contained many mistakes common in the frustrated liberalization episodes in other countries. The currency was overvalued, and tariffs and nontariff barriers were decreased where they were highest: in consumer goods. The result was a rapid increase in the import of consumer durables, especially automobiles, and this makes it difficult to sustain liberalization, both due to the rapid drawing down of international reserves and to the difficulty of justifying a policy that diminishes investment in machinery and equipment and that seems to benefit primarily wealth consumers. Add to this the Latin American debt crisis, and the return to controls was inevitable (p. 221).*

Avoiding such problems requires that an appropriate exchange rate be established before trade liberalization occurs.

Third, *tariffy quotas on imports of consumer goods and remove quotas on imports of intermediate and capital goods.* In Chapter 6, we saw that a quota on imports of a good causes a quota premium equal to the amount by which the domestic price of the good increases above the world price as

---

[15]"(T)he liberalizing government must quickly develop a regularized tax system for retrieving the revenue lost from giving up ownership of the means of production. . . . Until a full-fledged internal revenue service for collecting taxes from the private sector can be put in place, many industrial assets and most natural resources best remain government-owned as revenue sources for the public treasury" (McKinnon, 1993, pp. 4–5).

a result of the quota. It is possible for the government to set an ad valorem or specific tariff that maintains an excess of the domestic price over the world price equal to the previous quota premium. This is known as an *equivalent tariff.* The advantage of this tariffication process is that it converts quota rents into government revenue. This helps to alleviate the government's budget deficit. The removal of quotas on intermediate and capital goods will ensure that these goods are available to domestic producers. This will tend to lower the domestic prices of the goods, offsetting the effect of exchange rate depreciation and addressing structuralist concerns about declining production. Any tariffs on these goods should be set very low. Care should be taken to maintain existing government revenues from trade taxes despite the measures discussed here.[16]

Fourth, *selectively begin to privatize government-owned enterprises.* The privatization process in developing and formerly-socialist economies deserves a book in itself, and there are many competing views. McKinnon (1993) suggested that privatization be attempted early in the adjustment/liberalization process, whereas Lipumba (1994) questioned whether it is necessary at all. Here we take an intermediate position. We do not suggest that the government deal with the intricacies of privatization early on. Rather, we suggest that it first turn its attention to revenue raising, the exchange rate, and tariffication. Those tasks accomplished, it might be in a better position to evaluate what and how to privatize. Issues of fair value, broad-based ownership, and competition will be paramount. For example, creating unregulated private monopolies owned by a few domestic or international agents will not increase welfare and promote development. As emphasized by Harberger (2001), an advocate of the Washington consensus, countries must avoid the "excess of zeal" involved in privatization "right now, no matter to whom, no matter under what conditions" (p. 550). Unfortunately, such advice has not always been heeded.

Fifth, *liberalize the foreign direct investment component of the capital account.* Much of the early discussion on the order of economic liberalization concerns whether to first liberalize the current or capital accounts of the balance of payments. Edwards (1984) reviewed this literature and concluded that the capital account should be liberalized only *after* the current account is liberalized. He stated:

> (B)oth the historical evidence and . . . theoretical considerations . . . suggest that the more *prudent strategy is to liberalize the current account first. . . . Only after the initial steps towards stabilization and external adjustment have been taken and the trade account has been opened should capital restrictions be* slowly *relaxed" (p. 19, emphasis added).*

---

[16]"In general, a reduction in revenues from trade taxes must be avoided, *even* when it looks like alternative revenue sources may be available. In view of the fiscal crisis, it is probably better to *increase* overall revenues by implementing these alternatives than to have them substitute for reduced import duties" (Rodrik, 1990, p. 941). Urrutia (1998) noted that trade taxes in Colombia composed one-fourth of total central government revenue in the late 1980s when trade policy reform began for a second time.

As we discussed in Chapter 12, the capital account can be divided into direct investment and portfolio investment. As we stated in that chapter, direct investment involves ownership and control of physical capital, whereas portfolio investment reflects ownership alone of government bonds, corporate equities, corporate bonds, and bank deposits. Portfolio investment can be further broken down into long-term and short-term components. In general, portfolio investment (especially short-term portfolio investment) tends to be highly volatile, as the recent experiences of Mexico and Asia have shown. Therefore, it makes sense for a country to begin liberalization of the capital account with direct foreign investment.[17] As we discussed in Chapters 9 and 10, FDI is conducted as part of firms' strategic decisions as to the construction of international value-added networks. In general, these decisions will not be taken lightly and are not as easily reversed as portfolio investment. For this reason, it is with FDI that capital account liberalization should begin. Beyond that, countries should engage in what Eichengreen (1999) calls "cautious steps in the direction of capital account liberalization," which as we discussed in Chapter 17, "should not extend to the removal of taxes on capital inflows" (p 13).

Sixth, in preparation for an eventual liberalization of the domestic financial industry and the capital account, *develop an effective system of bank regulation*. As emphasized by Eichengreen (1999) and others, banks in developing countries both predominate the provision of financial services and pose the most serious threat to financial stability due to their inherent instability.[18] Eichengreen states that "banking crises have typically occurred in the wake of financial liberalization that ignited a credit boom in which the banks significantly expand their lending activities" (p. 41), often triggered by a rise in global interest rates. The prevention of financial crises requires a well-developed system of banking supervision. This involves giving attention to capital adequacy requirements, auditing, loan policies, and degree of foreign borrowing. Until these systems are in place, financial sector liberalization is irresponsible.

As we mentioned earlier, the whole question of the order of economic liberalization was raised after the unsatisfactory experience with the adjustment/liberalization process in the Southern Cone of Latin America during the late 1970s and early 1980s. Since that time, there have been many more examples of troubled adjustment/liberalization experiences. One possible explanation for this unimpressive history is that failures to design order of economic liberalization strategies to the particularities of the countries involved has led to a lack of sustainability of the adjustment policies. This point was made by Rodrik (1990) who argued that, where a conflict between idealized adjustment policies and the economic and political sustainability of these policies exists, the idealized policies must be compromised. In particular, Rodrik argued that the welfare benefits of liberalization policies such

---

[17]In the case of Africa, Lipumba (1994) concluded that "the most important capital account liberalization measure is promotion of foreign direct investment to complement local investment" (p. 60).
[18]See also Bird and Rajan (2001) and Stiglitz (2000).

as privatization and the removal of trade restrictions must be weighed against potential costs in terms of sustainability.

Rodrik introduced a distinction between the *range* and the *magnitude* of policy reform programs. The notion of range relates to the number of areas in which reforms are to take place, whereas the notion of magnitude refers to the degree of change in any particular policy. Figure 23.8 indicates four possible combinations of range and magnitude in policy reform programs. Many of the programs developed by the World Bank and IMF are to be found in box 4 of this diagram. They call for large changes in many different policy areas, often at the same time.[19] These strategies often prove unpalatable to the countries involved for economic or political reasons and are reversed to some degree. With an eye to sustainability, Rodrik suggested box 2. Here, the country focuses on a *limited* number of policy areas and tries to make some significant changes in those areas. This will lead to sustainable programs that will not be reversed. The six areas presented in this section of the chapter, properly sequenced, are candidates for inclusion in box 2.

Adjustment and Development

As we discussed in Chapter 22, Ghana has been participating in a structural adjustment process since 1983. However, as we discussed in Chapter 20, Ghana's health and education statistics, and hence human development overall, are still quite disappointing. What do you, as an advisor to the Ghanaian government make of this? One thing that you might notice from all the PPF diagrams in this chapter is that adjustment involves restruc-

Figure 23.8 Range and Magnitude in Adjustment/Liberalization

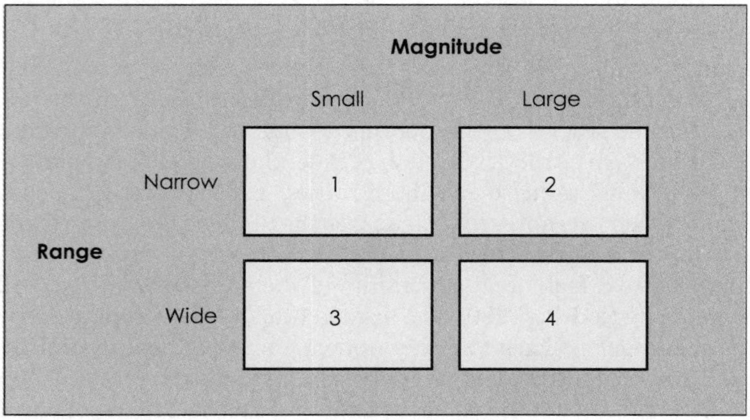

Source: Rodrik, D. (1990). "How Should Structural Adjustment Programs be Designed?" *World Development* 18(7): 933-947.

[19]"The World Bank . . . has hundreds of good ideas but no priorities. Standard bank programs call on weak, debt-ridden governments to introduce value-added taxes, new customs administration, civil-service reform, privatisation of infrastructure, decentralized public administration and many other wonderful things—often within months" (Sachs, 1996, p. 19).

turing domestic production away from nontraded goods and toward traded goods. For nontraded goods such as tailoring and auto repair, this is perhaps no great loss. For nontraded goods such as education and health services, however, the future human capital of the country is compromised. Compromising human capital, in turn, compromises long-run growth, as the new growth theory discussed in Chapter 20 indicates. The challenge to you as an advisor is to help the government achieve adjustment without sacrificing productive human investments that are essential for long-run growth and development. Additionally, productive government investments that are complementary to private investment must also be maintained where possible. If these productive investments are not maintained, adjustment will be achieved at the expense of development.

Conclusion

An overvalued exchange rate is not always sustainable. A home-country central bank, in Ghana or elsewhere, can run out of foreign reserves to sell. External balance then needs to be restored. Achieving external balance by demand reduction alone will sacrifice internal balance (cause unemployment) and exacerbate poverty. Therefore, adjustment must also include demand switching achieved by a devaluation of the domestic currency. Structuralists question whether the standard demand reduction/demand switching policies of the World Bank and International Monetary Fund will work effectively in all cases, and their policy prescriptions call for measures to ensure that key productive investments are not sacrificed in demand reduction. Another group of international economists stresses the order of economic liberalization in structural adjustment programs. Proper sequencing of reforms is necessary to maintain the sustainability of the adjustment process.

Whatever the specifics of structural adjustment programs, caution must be exercised not to sacrifice long-run growth and development on the altar of short-run adjustment. Productive human and physical capital must somehow be maintained for development to occur. Too often over the years, the World Bank and the IMF have forgotten this.

Review Exercises

1. In our discussion of internal and external balance, we saw that a devaluation of a fixed exchange rate moves production in an economy toward traded goods. A revaluation of a fixed exchange rate, in contrast, would move production in an economy towards nontraded goods. Carefully explain the intuition of these results.

2. Structuralist economists maintain that resources are often not mobile among sectors of an economy. Consequently, PPFs tend

to be nearly square, and switching effects small. Can you think of any reasons why resources might not be mobile among sectors?

3. In Chapter 17, we discussed the controversy over capital controls. We mentioned that China currently has firm controls on its capital account. In this chapter, we have talked about how, in the view of Edwards and McKinnon, the liberalization of the capital account should come after the liberalization of the current account. Suppose that you were advising China on the liberalization of its capital account. What would you advise? How should the steps towards liberalization be sequenced?

4. In the antiglobalization movement, structural adjustment is often portrayed as inherently undesirable. In your opinion, are there elements of structural adjustment programs that do in fact appear necessary? If so, what are they?

Further Reading and Web Resources

Chapter 1 of Corden (1986) provides a classic account of adjustment via demand reduction and switching policies. Another account is available in Chapter 3 of Hossain and Chowdhury (1998). Stewart (1995) is also well worth consulting on adjustment issues. On the role of structural adjustment in economic development, important sources are Atta Mills and Nallari (1992), Rodrik (1990), Stewart (1995), and Tarp (1993). The order of economic liberalization is effectively discussed by Lipumba (1994) and McKinnon (1993). Readers interested in obtaining an African perspective on the issues discussed in this chapter should consult Lipumba (1994) and Mkandawire and Soludo (1999).

The World Bank's Structural Adjustment Participatory Review Initiative (SAPRI) maintains a Web site at **http://www.worldbank.org/ research/sapri**. The Structural Adjustment Participatory Review International Network has launched a "Citizen's Challenge to Structural Adjustment" and maintains a Web site at **http://www. saprin.org**. The IMF defends its enhanced structural adjustment facility (ESAF) at **http://www.imf.org/external/pubs/ft/esaf/exr**.

Chocolate lovers can contribute to Ghana's export earnings by consuming chocolate bars manufactured by Jamieson's in Ghana. Visit their Web site at **http://www.chocolatebyjamieson.com**.

References

Atta Mills, C., and R. Nallari (1992) *Analytical Approaches to Stabilization and Adjustment Programs*, Economic Development Institute Seminar Paper Number 44, The World Bank, Washington, DC.

Bacha, E.L (1987) "IMF Conditionality: Conceptual Problems and Policy Alternatives," *World Development*, 15:12, 1457–1467.

Bird, G., and R.S. Rajan (2001) "Banks, Financial Liberalisation and Financial Crises in Emerging Markets," *World Economy*, 24:7, 889–910.

Corden, W.M. (1986) *Inflation, Exchange Rates, and the World Economy*, University of Chicago Press, Chicago.

Edwards, S. (1984) *The Order of Liberalization of the External Sector of Developing Countries*, Essays in International Finance 156, Princeton University Press, Princeton, New Jersey.

Eichengreen, B. (1999) *Towards a New International Financial Architecture: A Practical Post–Asia Agenda*, Institute for International Economics, Washington, DC.

Hallwood, C.P., and R. MacDonald (2000) *International Money and Finance*, Blackwell, Oxford.

Harberger, A.C. (2001) "The View from the Trenches: Development Processes and Policies as Seen by a Working Professional," in G.M. Meier and J.E. Stiglitz (eds.), *Frontiers of Development Economics*, Oxford University Press, New York, 541–561.

Hossain, A., and A. Chowdhury (1998) *Open-Economy Macroeconomics for Developing Countries*, Edward Elgar, Cheltenham.

Husain, I., and R. Faruqee (eds.) (1994) *Adjustment in Africa: Lessons from Country Case Studies*, World Bank, Washington, DC.

Lipumba, N.H.I. (1994) *Africa Beyond Adjustment*, Overseas Development Council, Washington, DC.

McKinnon, R.I. (1993) *The Order of Economic Liberalization*, Johns Hopkins University Press, Baltimore.

Mkandawire, T., and C.C. Soludo (1999) *Our Continent, Our Future: African Perspectives on Structural Adjustment*, Council for the Development of Social Science Research in Africa, Dakar, Senegal.

Rodrik, D. (1990) "How Should Structural Adjustment Programs Be Designed?" *World Development*, 18:7, 933–947.

Sachs, J. (1996) "Growth in Africa," *The Economist*, 29 June, 19–21.

Salter, W.E.G. (1959) "Internal and External Balance: The Role of Price and Expenditure Effects," *Economic Record*, 35:71, 226–238.

Stewart, F. (1995) *Adjustment and Poverty: Options and Choices*, Routledge, London.

Stiglitz, J. (2000) "Two Principles for the Next Round or, How to Bring Developing Countries in from the Cold," *World Economy*, 23:4, 437–454.

Tarp, F. (1993) *Stabilization and Structural Adjustment*, Routledge, London.

Taylor, L. (1993) "Stabilization, Adjustment, and Reform," in L. Taylor (ed.), *The Rocky Road to Reform*, MIT Press, Cambridge, Massachusetts, 39–94.

Taylor, L. (1987) "IMF Conditionality: Incomplete Theory, Policy Malpractice," in R.J. Myers (ed.), *The Political Morality of the International Monetary Fund*, Transaction Books, Oxford, 33–45.

Taylor, L. (1983) *Structuralist Macroeconomics*, Basic Books, New York.

Thomas, V., and J. Nash (1991) *Best Practices in Trade Policy Reform*, Oxford University Press, Oxford.

Urrutia, M. (1998) "Economic Reform in Colombia," in H. Costin and H. Vanolli (eds.), *Economic Reform in Latin America*, Dryden, Fort Worth, Texas, 217-241.

World Bank (1994) *Adjustment in Africa*, Oxford University Press, Oxford.

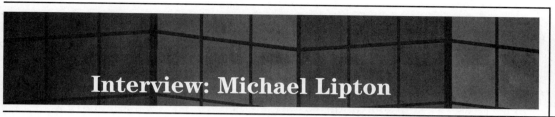

Interview: Michael Lipton

Michael Lipton holds the positions of Research Professor and Director of the Poverty Research Institute at the University of Sussex, as well as Professor of Development Economics at the Poverty Research Institute. He earned an MA degree from Oxford University and a D.Litt. degree from the University of Sussex. In the past, he has held positions at the Institute of Development Studies, All Souls College, Oxford, the International Food Policy Research Institute, and the World Bank. His extensive research record has focused on agriculture and rural development, land distribution, poverty, demographics, and nutrition. Most recently, he has contributed to the International Fund for Agricultural Development's 2001 Report on Rural Poverty.

How did your interest in development economics begin?

As a student at Oxford University, I was asked to comment on Gunnar Myrdal's book, then in draft, *Beyond the Welfare State.* This led to an invitation to work on his huge review of Asian achievements and frustrations in the search for development, *Asian Drama.* My work in 1960–1962 for this book—mainly on levels of living, economics of climate, demography, and "economic planning"—convinced me that development economics was, at that time, what had been previously known as "economics." That is, the analysis of poverty and its reduction and of the "natural progress of opulence," seen both as an issue of resource allocation by individuals and firms and as an issue of public policy choice.

Your involvement in development economics has been very much focused on the rural sector. How did this particular interest develop?

Again, this had its roots in my work with Gunnar Myrdal on *Asian Drama.* Extensive literature reviews, required for this work, convinced me that then (even more than now) the economic analysis of development issues was both absurdly neglectful of the 60 to 70 percent of economic agents in developing countries who live and work in rural areas and, through this neglect, involuntarily supportive of policy biases against rural people and the agricultural sector, and hence against the efficient poor. Also, it was clear that rural farm households presented a great chance to deepen our understanding of economics at the general level—as the last four decades of economics of risk and uncertainty, and of technical progress, confirm. In 1966, my eight months in an Indian village, learning about and from smallholders' decisions and responses, deepened my involvement in rural issues as the core of early development and poverty reduction.

Why is rural development so important for poverty alleviation?

Of the world's "dollar-poor" (those consuming below $1 a day at 1993 international purchasing power parity), 70 percent now live in rural areas, and the best projection is that half will still do so in 2035. Antipoverty policies in most cases need to address the poor where they are. The technical and economic feasibility, and great developmental and growth benefits, of rural-based poverty strategies were demonstrated by huge poverty reductions during the "green revolution"—in India (1975–1989), South East Asia (1970–1995) and, in the context of egalitarian land privatization, China (1977–1985). The efficiency and labor intensity of small-scale farming, and its crucial role in creating subsequent demand for labor-intensive rural industrialization, further demonstrate the concordance of efficiency, equity, and rural development.

In your view, are multilateral development institutions, such as the World Bank and the United Nations Development Program (UNDP), appropriately focused on rural poverty issues?

No. Agriculture, which provides the main income source for about two-thirds of the world's dollar-poor, now receives barely 12 percent of sectorally allocable aid. The absolute real value of aid to agriculture fell by over 60 percent between the late 1980s and the late 1990s. The World Bank led the way in recognizing the role of agriculture and supporting it with appropriate aid in the 1970s—and still leads in rural and agricultural sector analysis—but, tragically, also led this catastrophic retreat in support for agricultural infrastructure, which, especially in Africa, has in no way been compensated by private or governmental flows.

The UN specialized agencies, such as the UNDP, lack the resources to provide major support to the rural sector, though the Food and Agricultural Organization, the World Health Organization, and the International Labor Organization make important local contributions. The International Fund for Agricultural Development, with an almost ideal mandate and goals (to focus on agriculture, especially with nutritional benefits, for the poorest people in the poorest countries), has some excellent micro-activities and analyses, but is hamstrung by lack of cash and of clear strategy and priorities.

What are the most pressing policy changes required to successfully address rural poverty?

One pressing need, the reduction of the price squeeze on agriculture, has been largely met since the mid-1980s. However, urban elite groups are no less powerful in most developing countries. So better farm prices—apart from being undermined by EU, U.S. and other actions to artificially glut world farm markets (see next reply)—are offset by other public policy changes, even further cutting rural people's shares of key public goods, merit goods, and infrastructure provision. The fiscal crisis of African governments precludes such provision, and policies of fee assessment for health and education, although often justified in general, impinge especially severely on rural people. They are poorer and consequently receive worse services. Large rises in the share of public energies and expenditures going to provide rural roads, properly staffed and stocked clinics and schools, and perhaps above all means of water control and management (not subsidies), would in a large majority of developing countries be both poverty-reducing and growth-enhancing. In the medium term, however, the most pressing single policy change that is needed in many developing countries is to raise substantially the priority of agricultural research directed at raising yield and lowering risk for labor-intensive, smallholder farmers.

Trade economists often mention continuing agricultural protection in the United States, the European Union, and Japan as significant inhibitors of rural development in the poorer countries of the world. Are they correct in this assessment?

Yes. Returns to farming in poor countries are pushed right down by huge, artificial oversupply of farm products in the United States, European Union, and Japan. There are also more subtly harmful indirect effects: increased instability, because the European Union and many other farm suppliers are partly insulated from the need to respond to market signals through output shifts; encouragement of developing-country governments to think that rural and farm development is hopeless (because it will be undermined from EU and other rich producing countries) and needless (because farmers of those countries will force them to give food aid); and, most insidious of all, the massive and increasing biasing of research (notably into genetically modified seeds) toward the priorities of artificially stimulated, big and capital-intensive farms in the West, to the neglect of research that meets the central needs of tiny farmers in poor countries for higher yields and greater robustness under moisture stress.

Much of the current research on the trade and development process is focused on growth as an objective of development. In your view, what role does growth play in the development process?

There are few, if any, examples of sustained poverty reduction without growth. Much recent work suggests that more growth is normally better for the poor than less growth, across a large sample of countries. However, this misses the important point that the responsiveness of poverty to faster growth varies enormously across countries, and within the same country across time periods. Hence there is great scope for "events" or policies to alter the effectiveness of a given (politically and economically) attainable growth rate in reducing poverty.

Policies, not just events, can increase the poverty-reducing effects of growth—without damaging, indeed sometimes while benefiting, the rate of growth itself. First, a very unequal initial distribution of income and assets greatly reduces the impact of *subsequent* growth on poverty reduction. For example, there is evidence that more equal distribution of either operated farmland (e.g., achieved by land reform) or education raises the rate of growth. Second, countries that are more successful at reducing fertility rates substantially accelerate poverty reduction. This implies huge advantages, both for growth and for poverty reduction, from policies increasing incentives and options for fertility reduction. Such policies include attacks on child mortality, better options and lower opportunity costs for education, and better employment prospects for parents, especially women. But it is imperative for such policies to focus, far more than they now do, on groups left behind by demographic transition, and still with high fertility and few incentives to cut it: the poor and the rural.

Epilogue: Connecting the Windows

When we introduced our four windows on the world economy in Chapter 1, we made it clear that each window offers an important view, but that each also has a frame, that is, a limitation to a *complete* view of central processes and problems of the global economy. We recognized that the realms of international trade, international production, international finance, and international economic development each offer some insight into the world economy that needs to be supplemented by one or more of the other windows. In Chapter 1, we mentioned a couple of examples of these connections among the windows on the world economy, but before we conclude the introduction to international economics offered in this book, we should return to these connections and integrate what you have learned in previous chapters in a more formal manner. This is the purpose of this brief epilogue; to connect the windows on the world economy.

We will talk about six connections, namely those we represented by the six double-headed arrows in Figure 1.3 of Chapter 1. We will then conclude the epilogue by briefly addressing a set of challenges facing international economic policy. This epilogue is not meant to be authoritative, but suggestive of some themes you might take with you as you depart from this text.

International Trade ⇔ International Production

As you will recall from Chapter 9, trade and production are two alternative means for firms to supply foreign markets. From this perspective, international trade and foreign direct investment (FDI) are *substitutes* for each other. For example, either Honda produces motorcycles in Japan and exports them to Vietnam or it produces the motorcycles in Vietnam through FDI as we discussed in Chapter 9. Indeed, this substitute nature of trade and production often comes to the fore when we consider a single element of a value chain in isolation. Alternatively though, when we consider multiple elements of a value chain, international trade and international production can be *complements* rather than substitutes. For example, the Swedish firm Svenska Cellulosa Anktiebolaget (SCA) produces liner and corrugated boxes in France through FDI, as we discussed in Chapter 10. However, to do this, it exports wood pulp from Sweden to France in a process of intra-firm trade. From the point of view of liner and corrugated boxes, trade and investment are substitutes. But from the point of view of wood pulp, however, FDI (in liner and boxes) and trade (in pulp) are complements. To state it another way, although trade and investment are horizontal substitutes, they can be vertical complements. It is important for you to be open to both possibilities if you are to have a full understanding of the linkages between these two key processes of global integration.

As we discussed in Chapter 7, trade issues at the global level are the WTO's realm of responsibility. As we discussed in Chapter 21, some observers, citing the potential complementary nature of trade and investment, call for a new Multilateral Agreement on Investment (MAI) to bring investment activities under the auspices of the WTO. Others, with a closer focus on the substitutive nature of trade and investment, would demur, calling instead for a World Investment Organization (WIO) or no multilateral agreement at all.[1] If either of these proposals moves forward, however, it will need to be with broader support of the nations of the world than in the past.

International Trade ⇔ International Finance

In a very simple world, the processes of international trade and international finance would be mutually supportive in entirety. In such a world, currency transactions would be primarily for the support of trade transactions. As we noted in Chapter 1, however, foreign currency transactions are many multiples of international trade transactions, because currency transactions are conducted primarily for portfolio reasons. Given this more complex world, and the difficulties of designing effective exchange rate regimes and financial systems, crises and near-crises are not uncommon. Such crises, discussed in Chapter 17, often have the result of suppressing international trade, at least to some extent. When the seas of international finance are calm, finance can support trade. When they are rough, however, finance can suppress trade. Supporting the welfare benefits that ensue from most types of trade, then, requires effective exchange rate and financial system management. Unfortunately, as we discussed both in Chapters 17 and 23, the latter do not come easily. They must be consciously built, step by step.

If the realm of international finance is to support the realm of international trade, steps must be taken to ensure the smooth functioning of financial systems. The prudential regulation of domestic financial systems and the application of care to the liberalization of capital accounts are therefore necessary elements for the support of world trade.[2]

International Trade ⇔ International Economic Development

Extravagant claims are often made for the way international trade can support international economic development. The most extravagant claims are probably exaggerated, especially when they are generalized to all and every type of trade.[3] For example, there is evidence that among the

---

[1] See, for example, Hoekman and Saggi (2002).
[2] See Eichengreen (1999). For an application to the case of China, see Chan-Lee, Liu and Yoshitomi (2002).
[3] See Rodrik (1999) and United Nations Development Program (2003) for a thorough discussion.

least-developed countries increased primary product exports contribute to increased poverty levels relative to other kinds of exports.[4] That said, it is clear from many cases that trade *can* substantially contribute to economic development. From the increased manufactured exports of East Asia after World War II to the more recent expansion of exports from China and Chile, trade has clear benefits. Even from the point of view of environmentally sustainable development, trade is key. The first issue that arises in any scheme to increase production of environmentally-friendly products (e.g., tree crops such shade-grown coffee and *yerba maté*) is that of potential export markets.

What conditions must be present for the benefits of trade to arise? Two conditions appear to be crucial. First, the revenues from exports must be utilized for broadly-distributed, productive use. Enriching a historically-entrenched, narrow elite through primary-product exports typically does little for development, for example. Utilizing export revenues for broadly-distributed, productive use can occur both through private and government channels and might involve special tax schemes. Second, the exports must support, and in turn draw upon, the skill development of the labor force. This will entwine trade and the human capital accumulation of the economy. It is fair to say that in cases where the expansion of international trade has clearly supported the development process, both of these conditions were present. Where the expansion of international trade has not supported the development process, one or both of these conditions were absent.[5]

The health crises in some parts of the world have revealed the potentially stark limitations of the "trade and development" paradigm. As some African government ministers have recently suggested, "free trade is of no use when you are dead." The long-term success of the World Health Organization's Global Fund to Fight AIDS, Tuberculosis, and Malaria might well now be a *precondition* for positive interactions between trade and development. To be successful, international economic policy must recognize this.

International Production ⇔ International Finance

Many developing countries face the need to finance current account deficits by generating a capital account surplus. As we discussed at a number of junctures in this book (e.g., Chapters 17 and 23), portfolio investment, particularly when it is short term, is a fickle means of finance. If liberalization of capital accounts takes place first with FDI, these positive entries on the capital account can provide the necessary finance for a current account deficit that is of a relatively stable nature. In this way, international production can support international finance. International finance can also support international production in the same way that it supports international trade by providing the financing needed for FDI. Similarly, though,

---

[4] See United Nations Conference on Trade and Development (2002).
[5] See, for example, Chapter 1 of Bulmer-Thomas (1994).

financial crises can impede international production. To some extent, then, international production requires the difficult-to-obtain, calm financial seas mentioned earlier.

There is another, more local, relationship between production and finance. We mentioned in both Chapters 11 and 21 that there are gains to an economy when it hosts a spatial cluster of related firms involved in buyer–supplier relationships. If this is indeed the case, and evidence suggests that it is, an important policy issue is how such clusters can be effectively financed. A number of countries have experimented with new equity markets to effectively direct capital to emergent clusters. This will no doubt be an area for continued policy concern and experimentation.

International Production ⇔ International Economic Development

As we discussed in Chapter 21, hosting multinational enterprises (MNEs) has the potential to further the development context under certain conditions. In keeping with the understanding of international business scholars (if not all international economists), Chapter 21 took a cost–benefit approach to hosting foreign MNEs. A key policy realm, therefore, would address the means to maximize the benefits and minimize the costs of inward FDI. One important condition to maximize benefits is to promote backward linkages from the MNEs to domestic suppliers. Potential benefits here include employment increases, improvement in the balance of payments, better adaptation of technologies to local conditions, and the absorption of the MNE's tangible and intangible assets into the local environment. In addition, there is the possibility of developing local clusters. With regard to minimizing costs, there is the need to prevent exploitative FDI relationships, particularly in extractive industries such as petroleum, where little or no benefits accrue to the host country.

As we mentioned in Chapter 21, the Agreement on Trade-Related Investment Measures (TRIMs) has limited the potential realm of countries to engage in investment policies. Nevertheless, there is still ample room for creative *coordinative* policies to strengthen the link between international production and international economic development. As we outlined in that chapter, this involves bridging information gaps among the government, the foreign MNEs, the local suppliers, professional organizations, commercial organizations, and academic institutions.

International Finance ⇔ International Economic Development

The term "finance and development" is a title of a joint publication of the International Monetary Fund and the World Bank. In the view of these international financial institutions, finance supports development, and this indeed should be the goal of international financial policy. It is clear, however, after the string of crises from Mexico in 1994 to Argentina in 2002, that we have a distance to go before reaching this goal. If we can believe the analysis of most experts in this area, the key element in moving toward the goal is to ensure that emerging countries maintain confidence in their financial sectors, especially banking systems. This, in turn, appears to require financial and capital account liberalization that is approached gradually and wisely. Unfortunately, consensus on this is not complete, with some global players clinging to overly rapid liberalization as a policy goal. The question here is not whether to liberalize, but how, and room needs to be made for gradual liberalization that includes market-friendly taxation of short-term capital flows. Again, calm financial seas are crucial.

Last Words: Global Challenges

The challenges of managing global integration in the world economy are many. Any inquiry into these challenges suggests a daunting agenda for international policy makers. Some of the agenda items are the following:

1. *Building commitment to multilateral approaches to policy development that put global welfare ahead of narrow commercial interests.* This includes truly development-oriented rounds of multilateral trade negotiations (including increased market access in agriculture, textiles, and clothing) and further promotion of development-friendly FDI. The recent failure of the WTO's Cancún Ministerial does not bode well for success in this area.

2. *Generating global commitment to addressing the millions of annual deaths due to AIDS, tuberculosis, and malaria in order to prevent dramatic worsening in levels of human development, especially in Africa and Asia where most of the world's poor already reside.* If this commitment is not generated, efforts in other realms may well be for naught. WTO members must quickly carry forward efforts to ensure affordable access to medicines through the TRIPs council in Geneva. Countries must also show increased commitment to World Health Organization's Global Fund to Fight AIDS, Tuberculosis, and Malaria.

3. *Developing some degree of consensus with regard to international financial arrangements that does not force countries into premature financial and capital account liberalization.* Forging this consensus will probably require an acceptance of market-friendly, capital account taxation as a legitimate policy posture.

4. *Ensuring economic inclusion of large parts of the global citizenry more or less left behind in globalization processes through global trade and production networks.* This includes generating new opportunities for participation in the world economy through trade and FDI in ways that would ensure that benefits are widely shared and poverty alleviating. "Globalists" and "antiglobalists" must compromise on their entrenched positions to acknowledge the actual (as oppose to the supposed) links between trade and development.

5. *Developing models of international management that resolves the paradox between global efficiency and innovation, on the one hand, and local responsiveness and responsibility on the other.*[6] As we

---

[6] See, for example, Bartlett and Ghoshal (2002).

mentioned in Chapter 11, a key issue here is the management of knowledge. Any understanding of the role of MNEs in the modern world economy must include an understanding of the development, transmission, and application of knowledge that effectively spans both countries and cultures.

Responsibility for meeting challenges such as these is not distributed evenly among the nations composing the global community. It is a political reality that the tone of policy is largely determined by a relatively small group of countries. These include the United States, the European Union, Japan, China, India, Canada, Brazil, and a few others. In a smaller way, Bangladesh and Tanzania represent the interests of the least-developed countries. Success will depend on cooperative engagement among these key players.

What role will you play? Whether as a student or a professional, you are part of the global systems. In one small way or another, you will have an influence. I hope this book has helped your understanding of the world economic system in which you operate and that it directs your influence in positive directions.

References

Bartlett, C.A., and S. Ghoshal (2002) *Managing Across Borders: The Transnational Solution*, Harvard Business School Press, Boston, Massachusetts.

Bulmer-Thomas, V. (1994) *The Economic History of Latin America Since Independence*, Cambridge University Press, Cambridge.

Chan-Lee, J., L.-G. Liu, and M. Yoshitomi (2002) *Policy Proposals for Sequencing the PRC's Domestic and External Financial Liberalization*, Asian Policy Forum and Asian Development Bank Institute, Tokyo.

Eichengreen, B. (1999) *Towards a New Financial Architecture: A Practical Post–Asia Agenda*, Institute for International Economics, Washington, DC.

Hoekman, B., and K. Saggi (2000) "Assessing the Case for Extending WTO Disciplines on Investment-Related Policies," *Journal of Economic Integration*, 15:4, 629–653.

Rodrik, D. (1999) *The New Global Economy and Developing Countries: Making Openness Work*, Overseas Development Council, Washington, DC.

United Nations Conference on Trade and Development (2002) *The Least-Developed Countries Report 2002: Overview*, United Nations, Geneva.

United Nations Development Program (2003) *Making Global Trade Work for People*, Earthscan, London.

Glossary

A

Absolute advantage: The possibility that, due to differences in supply conditions, one country can produce a product at a lower price than another country.

Adjustable gold peg: An international financial arrangement that was part of the Bretton Woods system. It involved pegging the U.S. dollar to gold at US$35 per ounce and allowing all other countries to either peg to the U.S. dollar or directly to gold. The currency pegs (other than the U.S. dollar) were to remain fixed except under conditions that were termed "fundamental disequilibrium."

Appreciation: An increase in the value of a currency under a flexible or floating exchange rate regime.

Assets: Financial objects characterized by a monetary value that can change over time and make up individuals' and firms' wealth portfolios.

Assets-based approach: A model of exchange rate determination that views foreign exchange deposits as assets held as part of an overall wealth portfolio.

Autarky: A situation of national self-sufficiency in which a country does not import or export.

B

Backward linkages: The purchase of goods from local suppliers by foreign multinational enterprises.

Balance of payments: A detailed set of economic accounts focusing on the transactions between a country and the rest of the world. Two important subaccounts are the current account and the capital account.

Binding: A major GATT/WTO principle. As negotiations proceed through the rounds of trade talks, tariffs are bound at the agreed-upon level. They may not in general be increased in the future.

Brady Plan: A set of procedures proposed by U.S. Treasury Secretary Nicholas Brady and approved by the IMF in 1989. The Brady Plan allowed IMF and World Bank lending to be used by developing countries to buy back discounted international debt. It was a partial but important response to the developing country debt crisis that began in the 1980s.

Bretton Woods system: An international financial system introduced at the Bretton Woods conference in 1944 involving an exchange rate arrangement known as the adjustable gold peg.

C

Capital account: A subsection of the balance of payments recording transactions between a country and the world economy that involve the exchange of assets.

Capital deepening: An increase in the overall capital-labor ratio in a country.

Capital flight: A situation in which investors sell a country's assets and reallocate their portfolios towards other countries' assets. It tends to cause a capital account deficit for the country in question.

Capital gain (loss): An increase (decrease) in the price of an asset.

Change in demand: A shift of a demand curve due to a change in income, wealth, preferences, expectations, and prices of related goods.

Change in quantity demanded: A movement along a demand curve due to a change in the price of a good.

Change in quantity supplied: A movement along a supply curve due to a change in the price of the good.

Change in supply: A shift of the supply curve due to a change in technology or input prices.

Circular flow diagram: A graphical representation of the flow of incomes and expenditures in an economy. It involves Firm, Household, Government, Capital, and Rest of the World accounts.

Common market: An agreement on the part of a set of countries to eliminate trade restrictions among themselves, to adopt a common external tariff, and to allow the free movement of labor and physical capital among member countries.

Comparative advantage: A situation where a country's relative autarkic price ratio of one good in terms of another is lower than that of other countries in the world economy.

Competitive advantage: A situation where a firm can sustain global, market competitiveness in a particular product niche.

Conditionality: Policies pursued by the World Bank and International Monetary Fund in which loans are made only to countries that promise to institute a set of prescribed policy changes.

Constant returns to scale: A condition of production in which a doubling of all inputs leads to a doubling of output.

Consumer surplus: The benefit accruing to consumers from the fact that, in equilibrium, the consumers receive a price lower than their willingness to pay for lesser quantities.

Contracting: A mode of foreign market entry where a home-country firm contracts a foreign-country firm to engage in production in the foreign country. Includes both licensing and franchising.

Crawling band: An exchange rate regime in which monetary authorities intervene to maintain the nominal exchange rate in a band of prescribed width around a central rate.

Crawling peg: An exchange rate regime in which a country fixes its nominal exchange rate in terms of another currency but changes this fixed rate gradually over time in small increments.

Cultural synergy: The possibility of workers within a multinational enterprise developing means to turn cultural differences into assets by identifying complementarities among cultures.

Currency board: A type of fixed exchange rate regime where the monetary authority is required to fully back up the domestic currency with reserves of the foreign currency to which the domestic currency is pegged.

Current account: A subsection of the balance of payments recording nonofficial transactions between a country and the world economy that do not involve the exchange of assets.

Customs union (CU): An agreement on the part of a set of countries to eliminate trade restrictions among themselves and adopt a common external tariff.

D

Deflation: A fall in the overall or aggregate price level in an economy.

Demand reduction: The decrease in domestic demand made in an attempt to move an economy toward external balance.

Depreciation: A decrease in the value of a currency under a flexible or floating exchange rate regime.

Devaluation: A decrease in the value of a currency under a fixed exchange rate regime.

Direct investment: An entry in the balance of payments that records the net inflows of foreign direct investment.

Dissemination risk: The possibility of a foreign-country partner firm obtaining technology or other know-how from a home-country firm and exploiting it for its own commercial advantage.

E

Economic growth: A sustained increase in per capita income over time.

Efficiency seeking: One motivation for foreign direct investment that involves the pursuit of firm-level economies in which intangible assets are spread over a greater number of international productive activities.

Exchange rate exposure: The loss of revenues in a home country currency by an exporting or multinational enterprise due to an increase in the nominal value of the home currency.

Exchange rate target zone: An exchange rate arrangement proposed by John Williamson designed to obtain the benefits of both fixed and floating exchange rate agreements. The exchange rate target zone consists of a band around the fundamental equilibrium exchange rate (FEER) on the order of ±10 percent.

Export promotion: An economic development strategy promoted by the World Bank in which development occurs by encouraging export sectors.

Export processing zone (EPZ): An area of a host country in which multina-tional enterprises can locate and in which they enjoy, in return for exporting the whole of their output, favorable treatment in the areas of infrastructure, taxation, tariffs on imported intermediate goods, and labor costs.

Export subsidy: A subsidy to exports provided by the government of a country.

External balance: A situation in an economy in which trade (the current account) is balanced.

F

Financial intermediary: Financial institutions such as banks, mutual funds, and brokers that receive funds from savers and use these funds to make loans or buy assets, thereby placing the funds in the hands of investors.

Firm-level economies: Economies accruing to a firm from spreading the cost of intangible assets over larger numbers of production facilities, including production facilities in more than one country.

Firm-specific assets: Capabilities and resources possessed by a firm that contribute to its sustained competitiveness. They can be tangible or intangible.

Fixed exchange rate: An exchange rate policy in which a country sets its nominal or currency exchange rate fixed in terms of another currency.

Flexible or floating exchange rate regime: An exchange rate policy in which a country allows the value of its currency to be determined by world currency markets.

Flexible manufacturing: A recent phase of manufacturing history in which information technology combines with machinery in a way to promote rapid switching among products and processes. Also known as "Toyotism."

Fordism: See Managerial capitalism.

Foreign direct investment (FDI):
Occurs when a firm acquires shares in a foreign-based enterprise that exceed a threshold of between 10 to 20 percent, implying managerial control over the foreign enterprise. Contrasts with portfolio investment. FDI may be horizontal, backward vertical, or forward vertical.

Foreign market entry: Sales on the part of a firm in a foreign country via trade, contractual, or foreign direct investment modes.

Foreign savings: An inflow of funds into an economy from the rest of the world. It occurs when foreign investors buy the assets of the economy in question.

Forward rate: The rates of current contracts for transactions in currencies that usually take place one, three, or six months in the future.

Free trade area (FTA): An agreement on the part of a set of countries to eliminate trade restrictions among themselves. In contrast to a customs union, it does not involve a common external tariff.

Fundamental accounting equations: Derived from the circular flow diagram, it appears in two forms. The first is Domestic Investment – Domestic Savings = Foreign Savings = Trade Deficit. The second is Domestic Savings – Domestic Investment = Foreign Investment = Trade Balance.

Fundamental equilibrium exchange rate (FEER): An exchange rate concept developed by John Williamson. The FEER can be thought of as the purchasing power exchange rate, although this is not its exact definition. In Williamson's proposal, the FEER acts as the centerpoint of an exchange rate target zone.

G

Gains from trade: Advantages that accrue to a country from engaging in importing and exporting relationships. In an absolute advantage framework, gains from trade are identified as a net gain between consumer and producer surplus effects. In a comparative advantage framework, gains from trade are identified as an increase in consumption of all goods.

General Agreement on Tariffs and Trade (GATT): Established in 1946, the GATT was to be part of an International Trade Organization (ITO). The ITO was never ratified, but the GATT and its articles served as an international vehicle for trade relationships until 1995, when it became embodied in the Marrakesh Agreement establishing the World Trade Organization. As part of the Marrakesh Agreement, it is now known as GATT 1994.

General Agreement on Trade in Services (GATS): Part of the Marrakesh Agreement of 1994. Applies the GATT/WTO principle of nondiscrimination to a restricted number of services.

Gini coefficient: A summary measure of the Lorenz curve that gives an overall value to the degree of income inequality. It varies between zero (perfect equality) and one (perfect inequality).

Gold standard: An international financial arrangement in existence from approximately 1870 to 1914. Under the gold standard, countries defined the value of their currencies in terms of gold and held gold as official reserves.

Gold-exchange standard: An international financial arrangement introduced in the 1920s to replace the gold standard. It consisted of a set of center countries tied to gold and a set of periphery countries tied to the center country currencies.

Gross domestic product (GDP): The value of all final goods and services produced within a country's borders during a year.

Gross national product (GNP): The value of all final goods and services produced by a country's factors of production during a year.

Growth theory: In its "old" and "new" variants, growth theory is the explanation of economics of the sustained increase in per capita incomes over the long run. It is based on the intensive production function.

Grubel-Lloyd index: An index of the degree of intra-industry trade that varies between 0 and 100.

H

Heckscher-Ohlin model: A model of international trade based on differences in factor endowments among the countries of the world.

Home base: The country in which a multinational enterprise is incorporated and holds its central administrative capabilities.

Human capital: Investments made in the education, training, and capabilities of a labor force.

Human development index (HDI): A conception of economic development introduced by the United Nations Development Program that stresses health and education levels along with per capita income. The human development index is reported in the annual Human Development Report.

I

Import licenses: A right to import under a quota given either to domestic importers or foreign exporters.

Import substitution: A development strategy that attempts to replace previously-imported goods with domestic production.

Industrial capitalism: An early phase in the history of manufacturing in which the focus was on the procurement of industrial inputs on the part of colonial powers from their colonies in order to promote the manufactured exports of the colonial powers.

Inflation: An increase in the overall or aggregate price level in an economy.

Intensive production function: A production function expressed on a per capita basis.

Interest rate parity condition: The equilibrium condition in the assets approach to the exchange rate determination model. It relates a country's interest rate to the expected rate of depreciation of its currency and the interest rate of another country.

Inter-industry trade: A pattern of trade in which a country either imports or exports in a given sector.

Internal balance: A situation in an economy in which all resources are fully employed.

Internalization: The process of taking a transaction along a value chain and bringing it within a firm.

International development: A concept with many meanings, including increases in per capita incomes, improvements in health and education, structural change toward manufacturing and services production, and institutional "modernization."

International finance: The exchange of assets among the countries of the world economy.

International production: A production of a good or service with processes located in more than one country.

International trade: The exchange of merchandise and services among the countries of the world economy.

Intra-firm trade: Trade that takes place within a multinational enterprise.

Intra-industry trade: A pattern of trade in which a country both imports and exports in a given sector.

J

Jamaica Agreement: A 1976 amendment to the IMF's Articles of Agreement that allowed for floating exchange rates.

L

Local-global paradox: A term referring to the fact the global production also involves increased localization in the countries hosting foreign direct investment.

Lorenz curve: A graph relating the cumulative percentage of income to the cumulative percentage of households, the latter ranked from low- to high-income. It is a visual measure of income inequality.

M

Managed floating regime: An exchange rate regime in which a country allows its currency to float but intervenes in currency markets to affect its value when it determines that such intervention would be desirable.

Managerial capitalism: A middle stage in the history of manufacturing where the focus is on achieving economies of scale. Also known as "Fordism."

Market entry: The process of a home-country firm supplying a foreign market through exports, contracting, or foreign direct investment.

Market seeking: A motivation for foreign direct investment in which the multinational enterprise engages in FDI to better serve a foreign market.

Marrakesh Agreement: Signed in 1994, the Marrakesh Agreement concluded the Uruguay Round of trade talks, begun in 1986, and established the World Trade Organization. Among others, it includes a multilateral agreement on trade in goods, an agreement on trade in services, and an agreement on trade-related aspects of intellectual property rights.

Merchant capitalism: Part of the colonization efforts of the European powers during the sixteenth and seventeenth centuries that included state-supported trading companies such as the British East India Company, the Dutch East India Company, and the Royal African Company.

Milieu: The firms, knowledge, institutions and government supporting a spatial cluster with rules, norms, and business culture.

Monetary union: A group of member countries in a common market that all use a common currency. The most notable example is the European Monetary Union or EMU.

Money demand: The amount of money households want to hold at any particular time.

Money supply: The amount of money set in an economy by a central monetary authority such as a central bank or treasury.

Most-favored nation (MFN): A principle of the GATT/WTO system in which each member must treat each other member as generously as its most-favored trading partner.

Multinational enterprise (MNE): Also known as the multinational corporation or the transnational corporation. A firm operating production, sales, and service operations in more than one country.

Multinational value network: A collection of value chains in a number of countries.

N

National treatment (NT): A principle of the GATT/WTO system under which foreign goods within a country should be treated no less favorably than domestic goods with regard to tax policies.

Natural rate of population growth: An exogenous measure of the rate of population growth used in growth theory.

Net factor receipts: An item in the current account of the balance of payments. It records the difference between factor income and factor payments, both of which reflect income earned on physical capital.

Nominal exchange rate: The number of units of a country's currency that trade against a world currency such as the U.S. dollar or euro.

Nondiscrimination: A major GATT/WTO principle achieved via the subprinciples of most favored nation (MFN) and national treatment.

Nontariff barrier (NTB): An import restraint other than a tariff. A quota is one example.

Nontariff measure (NTM): An import restraint or export policy other than a tariff. An import quota is one example.

Nontraded goods: Goods such as local services that are not imported or exported.

North American Free Trade Agreement (NAFTA): A free trade area among Canada, the United States, and Mexico.

O

Official reserves balance: The element of the capital account of the balance of payments that reflects the actions of the world's central banks.

OLI framework: A theory of the multinational enterprise based on ownership, location, and internalization advantages.

Open-economy accounts: The accounting identities derived from the firm, household, government, capital, and rest of the world accounts of the circular flow diagram.

Opportunity cost: What has to be given up to gain something. Along a production possibilities frontier, there is an opportunity cost of increasing the output of one good in the form of less production of another good.

Optimum currency area: A collection of countries characterized by (1) well-integrated factor markets; (2) well-integrated fiscal systems; and (3) economic disturbances that affect each country in a symmetrical manner.

Overvaluation: Under a fixed exchange rate regime, a value of a home currency above its equilibrium value, which causes an excess supply of the home currency.

Ownership requirements: A limit placed on the degree of foreign ownership of firms by a country's government.

P

Performance requirements: A large host of measures placed on the performance of multinational enterprises by a government. A subset of these is known as trade-related investment measures.

Policy trilemma: A necessary policy choice facing all countries of only two of the following three desired objectives: monetary independence, exchange rate stability, and capital mobility.

Porter diamond: A diagrammatic and conceptual device introduced by Michael Porter to explain the sources of competitive advantage in a firm's home base.

Preferential trade area (PTA): An agreement on the part of a set of countries to reduce but not eliminate trade restrictions among themselves.

Price level: A measure of the average or overall level of prices in a country.

Includes the GDP price deflator and the consumer price index.

Producer surplus: The benefit accruing to producers from the fact that, in equilibrium, the producers receive a price higher than their willingness to accept for lesser quantities.

Product life cycle theory: An early theory of the multinational enterprise that viewed production as being confined to the home base of an MNE during the early phases of a product life cycle due to the need for technologically sophisticated production techniques. During later phases of the production cycle, as the production of the good becomes more routine and established, production can move to subsidiaries in foreign countries in order to take advantage of lower labor costs.

Production function: A mathematical relationship between the output of a firm, sector, or economy and inputs such as labor and physical capital.

Production possibilities frontier (PPF): A diagram that illustrates the constraints on production in general equilibrium imposed by scare resources and technology. It shows all the combinations of two goods that a country can produce given its resources and technology.

Purchasing power parity model (PPP model): A long-run model of exchange rate determination based on the notion that the nominal exchanges rate will adjust so that the purchasing power of currencies will be the same in every country.

Q

Quota: Usually applied to imports. A maximum amount of imports allowed by a government.

Quota premium: The increase in the domestic price of a good as a result of an import quota.

Quota rents: The income accruing to the holder of a right to import a good into a country.

R

Real exchange rate: The rate at which two countries' goods (not currencies) trade against each other. The real exchange rate adjusts the nominal exchange rate using the price levels in the two countries under consideration.

Regional trade agreement (RTA): An agreement by a number of countries to grant preferential access to their markets to other members of the agreement. Examples include free trade areas and customs unions.

Resource seeking: One of the motivations for foreign direct investment in which a multinational enterprise backward integrates into resource supply in a foreign country.

Revaluation: An increase in the value of a currency under a fixed exchange rate regime.

Rules of origin: A means to determine whether a product is from a partner country in a regional trade agreement (RTA). These can be defined in a number of ways, including by amount of value added in an RTA partner country or by degree of product transformation, often measured by a change in tariff classification.

S

Smithsonian Conference: A conference that took place in Washington, DC, in December 1971 to attempt to repair the damaged adjustable gold peg system of the Bretton Woods system.

Spatial cluster: A collection of interrelated firms in a geographic area that engage in cooperative information sharing and, thereby, contribute to their collective efficiency and competitiveness.

Special drawing rights (SDRs): An international currency administered by the IMF and introduced in 1969. It is currently defined in terms of a basket of three currencies: the U.S. dollar, the euro, and the yen. Distributions of SDRs took place in 1970, 1979, and 1997, but they never played the important role envisaged for them.

Specific factors: Factors of production that cannot move easily from one sector to another.

Spot rate: The current, nominal exchange rate between two currencies.

Stolper-Samuelson theorem: A result of international trade theory concerning the politics of trade. It states that an increase in the relative price of a commodity (e.g., as a result of trade) raises the return to the factor used intensively in the production of that good and lowers the return to the other factor.

Strategic asset seeking: A motivation for foreign direct investment in which the multinational enterprise wants to acquire productive assets as part of the strategic game among competitors in an industry.

Structural adjustment: The process of change in an economy that takes place in response to internal and/or external imbalances. It typically requires demand reduction and currency devaluation.

Structural adjustment lending (SAL): Nonproject lending of the World Bank to support adjustment in the face of balance of payments difficulties. Based on policy conditionality.

Structuralist critique: A school of thought in development economics that argues in favor of accounting for the historical and institutional structures of an economy in the design of adjustment programs in coping with external imbalances and balance of payments crises.

Switching: The use of a devaluation of a country's currency to move the economy towards external balance.

T

Tariff: A tax on imports, which could be either in ad valorem or specific form.

Tariffication: The process of replacing quotas by equivalent tariffs.

Tariff rate quota: An import restraint involving two tariff levels: a lower tariff for levels of imports within the quota and a higher tariff for levels of imports above the quota.

Terms-of-trade effects: The effects of a country having an impact on the world prices of the merchandise and services it trades.

Tobin tax: A small tax on foreign exchange transactions proposed by James Tobin. The purpose is to reduce the volatility of flexible exchange rates by throwing "sand in the wheels of international finance."

Toyotism: See Flexible manufacturing.

Trade creation: A potential outcome of a free trade area or a customs union in which imports switch from a high-cost source to a low-cost source.

Trade diversion: A potential outcome of a free trade area or a customs union in which imports switch from a low-cost source to a high-cost source.

Trade-related investment measures: A subset of performance requirements, including export requirements and domestic content requirements, some of which are now prohibited by the World Trade Organization.

Traded goods: Goods and services that can be imported or exported.

Transfer pricing: The manipulation of the prices of intra-firm trade by multinational enterprises to reduce their global tax payments.

Triffin dilemma: A critique of the gold-exchange standard developed by

Robert Triffin. It involved a contradiction between the requirements of international liquidity and international confidence.

U

Undervaluation: Under a fixed exchange rate regime, a value of a home-country currency below its equilibrium value causing an excess demand for the currency.

V

Value chain: A series of value-added processes involved in the production of a good or service.

W

World Bank: An international organization founded in 1944 by the Bretton Woods conference. It was originally designed to assist in the reconstruction of postwar Europe but quickly became a lender to developing countries in support of development projects and structural adjustment. The World Bank actually consists of the International Bank for Reconstruction and Development and the International Development Association.

World Bank Group: A collection of five organizations: the International Bank for Reconstruction and Development; the International Development Association; the International Finance Corporation; the International Center for Settlement of Investment Disputes; and the Multilateral Investment Guarantee Agency.

World Trade Organization (WTO): The WTO was established in 1995 as part of the Marrakesh Agreement ending the Uruguay Round of trade talks. It is an international organization with a legal foundation for managing world trading relationships.

Index

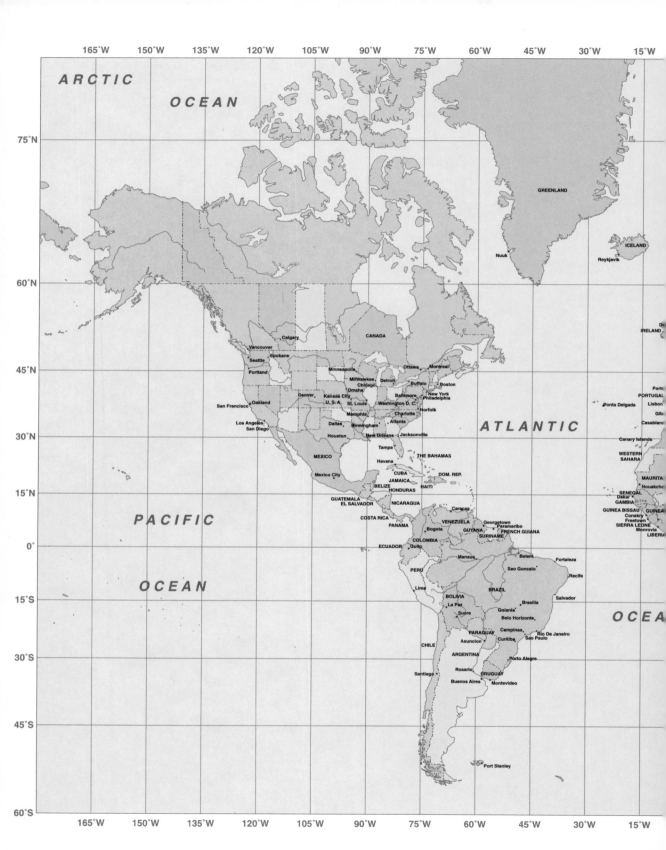